AIDA Europe Research Series on Insurance Law and Regulation

Volume 14

The AIDA Europe Research Series on Insurance Law and Regulation is the first book series of its kind and area of specialization. It comprises volumes on topics researched and written with an international, comparative or European perspective.

The regulatory response to the financial crisis in 2008 has pushed towards the adoption of transnational principles and rules also in the field of insurance by encouraging the convergence of national regulations to common regulatory framework. The need for a common legal language emerges to fully understand the process of transnational convergence in place and its impact on national legislation. On the other hand, persisting national peculiarities must be examined in the light of the transnational convergence of rules and concepts. Moreover, new risks, business practices and customers' issues are emerging worldwide, so requiring increasingly global responses.

The scope of the series is to bring together academics, practitioners and policy makers in order to exchange views and approaches to the topics concerned, which are based on the new transnational dimension of insurance law, business and regulation. All contributions are peer reviewed.

Cristina Poncibò • Piotr Tereszkiewicz
Editors

European Insurance Law within the Digital Age

Springer

Editors
Cristina Poncibò
Department of Law
University of Turin
Torino, Italy

Piotr Tereszkiewicz
Private Law Department
Jagiellonian University
Kraków, Poland

ISSN 2662-1770 ISSN 2662-1789 (electronic)
AIDA Europe Research Series on Insurance Law and Regulation
ISBN 978-3-031-96495-4 ISBN 978-3-031-96496-1 (eBook)
https://doi.org/10.1007/978-3-031-96496-1

This Springer imprint is published by the registered company Springer Nature Switzerland AG
The registered company address is: Gewerbestrasse 11, 6330 Cham, Switzerland

Foreword

The transformation of insurance law in Europe has been remarkable. The insurance industry stands at a crossroads between tradition and innovation resulting from rapid technological advancements, shifting consumer expectations, and evolving regulatory landscapes. The rise of digital insurance models, extensive use of artificial intelligence (AI) in underwriting and claims processing, and the increasing reliance on data-driven personalization of insurance contracts are fundamentally reshaping the industry. This book, "The Evolution of European Insurance Law in the Digital Age", provides a comprehensive analysis of these ongoing transformations, offering invaluable insights into the challenges and opportunities that characterize the current legal landscape of insurance. It is a timely resource that addresses the industry's pressing issues.

The contributions in this volume, authored by leading academics and experts, tackle some of the most significant legal and regulatory challenges that the insurance sector encounters today. The book begins by outlining the broader legal, regulatory, and theoretical challenges posed by digitalization. It then examines specific technological applications in insurance law. The editors, Professors Cristina Poncibò and Piotr Tereszkiewicz, have gathered this wealth of expertise to explore how digitalization is reshaping insurance regulation, the role of AI and big data in contract formation and compliance, and the implications of automation for consumer protection.

The first section examines the broader impact of digitalization on the insurance industry. Professors Cristina Poncibò and Piotr Tereszkiewicz open with a comparative legal perspective on the digital insurance landscape within the European Union, setting the stage for the discussions that follow. Their analysis is crucial for understanding how different jurisdictions adapt their legal frameworks for insurance to accommodate digital developments.

Professor Phillip Hellwege provides a historical perspective on innovation and insurance law, offering a vital context for the discussion of digitalization. By tracing the evolution of insurance regulation, Hellwege highlights the cyclical nature of legal adaptation in response to technological change. This historical grounding serves as a reminder that, while the current wave of digital disruption is unprecedented in scope, insurance law has always been a dynamic field that has adapted to new economic and societal realities.

Several chapters here focus on the personalization of insurance contracts and the regulatory concerns that arise from data-driven approaches. Dr. Przemysław Pałka and Katarzyna Wiśniewska explore the normative considerations involved in data-driven personalization, while Professor Marta Infantino discusses the prospects and challenges of automated personalization in European law. Their analyses raise fundamental questions about fairness, discrimination, and transparency in an industry increasingly relying on algorithms and big data.

Dr. Katarzyna Południak-Gierz builds on these discussions by examining the implications of personalized advertising in the insurance sector. Targeted advertising and data-driven marketing raise ethical and legal questions regarding consumer autonomy and informed decision-making. Additionally, Dr. Marta Ostrowska's chapter on information asymmetry in insurance law delves into the implications of technological advancements on pre-contractual disclosure requirements, which are crucial for consumer protection in the digital age.

A group of scholars, Dr. Agnieszka Jabłonowska, Dr. Francesca Lagioia, Dr. Rūta Liepiņa, Professor Hans-W. Micklitz, and Professor Giovanni Sartor explore AI's use in insurance compliance assessment. Within the framework of the Claudette and Scudo projects, the authors examine AI's potential to detect unfair clauses in insurance contracts, highlighting both the opportunities and challenges associated with automating legal assessments.

The section also features a timely discussion by Professor Jonas Knetsch on data protection rights and automated decision-making in insurance, a topic of increasing relevance given the European Union's General Data Protection Regulation (GDPR). Dr. Ewa Cichowicz and Professor Piotr Tereszkiewicz address the role of digital literacy among consumers, analysing how consumers inform themselves about insurance products in the digital age. Their empirical study provides valuable insights into the effectiveness of digital disclosures and the challenges consumers face when navigating the complexities of digital insurance.

Finally, Dr. Antti Talonen's chapter examines the role of supervisors as value creators within the digital insurance ecosystem. He discusses how digitalization is reshaping the role of insurance supervisors in fostering innovation and consumer protection, using real-world examples to illustrate the industry's evolving dynamics at the intersection of the public and private sectors.

The book's second section moves from theoretical discussions to examine specific applications of digitalization in insurance law. The contributions focus on the legal challenges posed by smart contracts, blockchain technology, automated decision-making, and the integration of artificial intelligence (AI) in various aspects of insurance regulation and distribution.

Andrea Durovic's chapter on smart contracts in insurance law analyses their potential for automation, efficiency, and consumer protection. While promising, smart contracts face legal challenges in enforceability, dispute resolution, and regulation. The chapter examines global regulatory efforts and questions whether current frameworks can fully support blockchain-powered insurance products.

Professor Eliza Mik's chapter addresses the "oracle problem" in blockchain-based insurance, emphasizing the dependence of smart contracts on external data sources that are neither entirely reliable nor secure. Oracles introduce risks of incorrect or manipulated data, which can limit the reliability of smart contracts. This chapter critiques their inability to verify off-chain information and the necessity for straightforward, binary payout conditions, ultimately questioning their practical role in consumer insurance.

Dr. Victorine Tournaire explores how French insurance law adapts to accommodate smart vehicles, focusing on liability, risk assessment, and consumer rights. While existing motor liability rules broadly cover accidents involving automated vehicles, adjustments to contract law may be necessary regarding risk statements and claims. This chapter also examines product liability for manufacturers and the potential need for compulsory insurance, highlighting areas that require further legal clarification.

Finally, Professor Adolfo Paolini discusses the impact of AI-driven decision-making on corporate governance and the Directors and Officers (D&O) insurance market. As companies integrate robotic directors, challenges arise in applying traditional liability standards and adapting insurance coverage. This chapter looks into the "black box" problem in AI decision-making. It suggests modifications to directorial duties and insurance frameworks, considering whether corporate liability models need to evolve to address risks associated with AI.

Together, the contributions in this volume provide a critical and timely exploration of the evolving legal landscape of European insurance in the digital age. This book offers insights into how AI, big data, and blockchain reshape insurance law. The analyses presented will contribute to ongoing discussions on navigating this rapidly changing landscape, making it a crucial read for academics, legal practitioners, regulators, and industry stakeholders.

Insurance scholars should thank the contributors for their insightful and thought-provoking chapters and the editors, Professors Cristina Poncibò and Piotr Tereszkiewicz, for their dedication in assembling this comprehensive and timely work. As the insurance sector evolves in response to digital transformation, this book is a valuable roadmap for understanding and addressing the legal challenges ahead.

Malta–Milan
12 March 2025

Pierpaolo Marano

Preface

The regulation of insurance in the EU is undergoing a profound transformation, driven by the accelerating pace of technological innovation and its disruptive impact on legal, economic, and social arrangements. This volume, *European Insurance Law within the Digital Age*, brings together leading scholars from across EU jurisdictions to critically examine the interplay between digital innovation and the legal architecture governing insurance in the European Union.

Our goal as editors has been to frame the discussion within the broader field of comparative and EU insurance law, while highlighting the unique pressures that InsurTech, datafication, and algorithmic decision-making exert on traditional regulatory paradigms. By focusing on both structural and doctrinal developments, our volume aims to contribute to the growing body of academic research that analyses digital transformation not simply as a technical or sectoral development, but as a legal phenomenon that invites a rethinking of the core principles of insurance contract law, consumer protection, and market supervision.

InsurTech and the Challenge to Legal Orthodoxy

The term *InsurTech* is often used to describe the application of technology—ranging from artificial intelligence and big data analytics to blockchain and the Internet of Things (IoT)— to streamline and improve the insurance value chain. At first glance, many of these innovations appear to be neutral tools for enhancing efficiency. Yet, as this volume demonstrates, the implications of InsurTech for legal systems are far from straightforward. Technological solutions challenge the foundations of existing legal frameworks that were developed in and for a very different world—one in which underwriting was manual, risk pools were relatively homogenous, and regulatory oversight assumed a degree of transparency and comprehensibility that is now called into question.

This disruption is particularly pronounced in the EU, where the insurance sector is shaped not only by domestic legal traditions, but by the multilayered and evolving body of EU insurance legislation and jurisprudence. At the heart of this shift lies a paradox: while technology promises greater precision and personalisation, it also introduces new asymmetries of information, opacity in decision-making, and challenges to fundamental rights such as privacy and non-discrimination. These tensions form the backdrop to many of the chapters in this book, which address the legal and regulatory implications of technologies that are rapidly becoming embedded in the business models of insurance providers.

A Comparative and Interdisciplinary Perspective

Insurance law has always been a fertile ground for comparative analysis. The core principles that govern the formation, interpretation, and performance of insurance contracts are often shaped by divergent legal cultures and national regulatory choices. In the digital age, these differences become even more significant. As insurers adopt digital tools, jurisdictions diverge in their responses—some embrace innovation through regulatory sandboxes and adaptive supervision, while others emphasize caution and consumer protection. The comparative method enables scholars to examine these differences, drawing lessons from how various legal systems accommodate or resist technological change.

At the same time, digital insurance is inherently transnational. Cross-border data flows, the use of globally developed AI systems, and the emergence of EU-level initiatives, such as the Artificial Intelligence Act, the Data Act, the Digital Markets Act (DMA), and the Digital Services Act (DSA), highlight the need for an integrated approach to regulation. The chapters in this volume adopt a variety of methodological approaches, doctrinal, empirical, and theoretical, to explore these issues, reflecting the interdisciplinary nature of InsurTech research. The law is situated here not only as a system of rules, but as a mode of governance and a normative framework for shaping technological development.

Key Themes in the Volume

This book is divided into two main sections. The first explores *theoretical and structural perspectives* on digitalisation within EU insurance law. Here, the contributions set out the broader legal, ethical, and historical context for understanding the current transformation. Several chapters in this section, notably those by Hellwege and Jabłonowska et al., demonstrate that today's regulatory dilemmas have historical analogues—reminding us that insurance law has always evolved in response to socio-technological change. Others, such as those by Infantino and Pałka and Wiśniewska, grapple with the emerging challenges of data-driven personalization, algorithmic opacity, and fairness in consumer-facing insurance practices.

The second section focuses on *applied perspectives*, addressing concrete technological applications such as blockchain-based insurance, AI-driven compliance, and the regulation of automated vehicles. These chapters examine the friction between innovation and legal certainty, questioning whether traditional doctrines (e.g., causality, consent, good faith) can adequately respond to systems that are probabilistic, dynamic, and often non-deterministic. The contributions highlight that innovation does not obviate the need for law—rather, it intensifies the importance of clear, adaptive, and just regulatory frameworks.

Particularly noteworthy is the attention paid to supervisory and institutional responses. As Dr. Talonen argues, regulators are no longer mere enforcers of compliance, but increasingly act as *value creators* in shaping digital insurance ecosystems. This insight resonates with broader debates in law and governance about the government's proactive role in guiding innovation in the public interest.

The European Legal Framework: Fragmentation and Integration

The EU's regulatory framework for insurance is currently at a critical juncture. On the one hand, the Solvency II Directive, the Insurance Distribution Directive (IDD), and a host of horizontal instruments, including GDPR and the AI and data regulations, create a dense legal environment. On the other hand, the emergence of new business models and digital tools exposes the gaps, inconsistencies, and rigidities of this framework. One recurring theme in this volume is the difficulty of reconciling sectoral regulation with horizontal, technology-neutral rules. For instance, while GDPR provides a strong foundation for data protection, it offers limited guidance on the specific risks associated with AI-based underwriting or automated claims processing.

In this context, the volume provides a platform for forward-looking academic inquiry into how European Insurance Law should evolve. It considers whether the EU ought to develop a dedicated InsurTech regulation or whether adaptation of existing instruments may prove sufficient. It reflects on the means by which enforcement can be improved in a landscape where digital complexity often outpaces legal capacity. It also examines the potential role of soft law, co-regulation, and technical standards in addressing the compliance challenges presented by an increasingly digital insurance market.

These are not merely technical questions. They touch on fundamental issues of justice, accountability, and the role of law in mediating technological change. This book does not offer simple answers, but it does provide a structured and critical framework for engaging with these urgent questions.

Looking Ahead: Research Agenda and Policy Dialogue

This volume is in no way intended to be the final word, but merely a springboard for further research. Much remains to be studied in the field of digital insurance law. Future research might include deeper empirical studies on consumer understanding and digital literacy, longitudinal analyses of regulatory effectiveness, and further exploration of the intersection between insurance and other digital markets such as health, mobility, and energy.

We also believe that legal scholarship has a vital role to play in shaping policy dialogues. As the EU continues to chart its digital future, it is crucial that legislators and regulators engage with the nuanced analyses provided by legal scholars, particularly those with a comparative and interdisciplinary lens. Academic research should not only diagnose regulatory gaps but also contribute proactively to designing future-proof legal frameworks that uphold public values while enabling innovation.

Torino, Italy Cristina Poncibò
Krakow, Poland Piotr Tereszkiewicz

Acknowledgements

We are deeply grateful to all the contributors for their rigour, creativity, and collegiality. Early versions of several chapters contained in this book were presented and discussed during workshops at the Jagiellonian University in Krakow, in May 2022 and January 2023, supported by the National Research Centre (NCN) in Poland, grant no. 2018/29/B/HS5/01281. The NCN grant supported also the publication of several chapters.

We are indebted to Professor Pierpaolo Marano (University of Malta/Università Cattolica del Sacro Cuore in Milan/University of Latvia) for the support he has extended to our project, including the publication of the book in the AIDA Research Series on European Insurance Law and Regulation. We gratefully acknowledge the assistance of Tatjana Mikoni, a doctoral student at the University of Turin. Finally, we thank the institutions and networks that have supported the research behind this book, including the Jagiellonian University in Krakow, the University of Turin, the Polish National Science Centre, and the Collegio Carlo Alberto in Turin.

Above all, we hope that this volume will serve as a meaningful contribution to the evolving field of digital insurance law and stimulate further dialogue across disciplines, jurisdictions, and professional communities. The questions raised by InsurTech and the digital transformation of insurance are not only technical or regulatory—they are deeply human. EU Law must rise to the challenge.

We dedicate this book to the lasting memory of Professor Bogusław Gawlik, the esteemed mentor of one of us, whose wisdom was only matched by his generosity.
Torino and Kraków, April 2025

Cristina PonciboPiotr Tereszkiewicz

Contents

Challenges and Opportunities: New Business Models, AI and Data in the Insurance Sector

EU Digital Insurance: Comparative Legal Perspectives

Cristina Poncibò and Piotr Tereszkiewicz

1 Introduction

The traditional insurance landscape is undergoing a paradigmatic transformation precipitated by the rapid integration of digital technologies. No longer confined to the actuarial tables and cumbersome paper trails of the past, modern insurance has become a dynamic, data-driven ecosystem.[1]

At the epicentre of this revolution is digital insurance, an emerging field that leverages state-of-the-art technologies, such as machine learning (ML), artificial intelligence (AI), and advanced data analytics to reimagine the possibilities of risk assessment, underwriting, insurance customer engagement, and claims processing. Through open, connected software platforms and customer-centric digital interfaces like mobile apps and websites, digital insurance is not merely streamlining existing

[1] See Hellwege (this volume).

Acknowledgment: This chapter has been written within the framework of a research project supported by the National Science Centre (NCN) in Poland, grant number 2018/29/B/HS5/01281. The Open Access fee for this publication has been supported by a grant from the Priority Research Area (DigiWorld) under the Strategic Programme Excellence Initiative at Jagiellonian University in Kraków.

C. Poncibò
Department of Law, University of Turin, Turin, Italy
e-mail: cristina.poncibo@unito.it

P. Tereszkiewicz (✉)
Private Law Department, Jagiellonian University, Krakow, Poland
e-mail: piotr.tereszkiewicz@uj.edu.pl

C. Poncibò, P. Tereszkiewicz (eds.), *European Insurance Law within the Digital Age*, AIDA Europe Research Series on Insurance Law and Regulation 14,
https://doi.org/10.1007/978-3-031-96496-1_1

processes; it enables entirely new ways of doing business that are more efficient, adaptive, and user-focused.[2]

Digital insurance draws upon various data technologies, including cloud computing and marketing analytics, to create many benefits for insurers and consumers. The strategic implementation of these technologies has been shown to boost profitability, enhance employee productivity, speed up claim settlement cycles, and radically improve insurance customer experience. In addition, advances in predictive analytics are helping insurers combat fraudulent activities more effectively than ever, providing a more secure and trustworthy environment for consumers.[3] In terms of product development, insurers can now harness large-scale data to devise innovative insurance products that are attuned to the behaviour and preferences of digitally savvy consumers.[4]

Our edited book, for which this chapter sets the scene, offers a deep dive into the fast-evolving landscape of digital insurance, mapping out its revolutionary impact across multiple facets of the insurance ecosystem. The book discusses real-world examples and cases from different EU member states to demonstrate how digital technologies modernise traditional insurance practices, including smart contracts,[5] smart vehicles,[6] and robo-directors.[7] By capturing these diverse elements, the book offers a comprehensive understanding—based on an interdisciplinary and comparative approach to research—of how digital insurance is shaping the future of risk management, providing insights valuable for industry stakeholders, policymakers, and academics alike in the European Union and other legal systems.

At its core, the book delves into the complex legal regimes governing digital insurance, explicitly examining the sectorial provisions of EU Insurance Contract Law,[8] the EU Digital Acquis (specifically the DSA[9] and AI Act[10]), and, lastly, EU

---

[2] See Pisoni (2021).

[3] See Ceylan (2022); see Cichowicz and Tereszkiewicz (this volume).

[4] Different aspects of digitally enabled personalisation, individualisation, or mass-customisation in insurance are discussed in Pałka and Wiśniewska (this volume), Infantino (this volume), and Południak-Gierz (this volume).

[5] See Durovic (this volume) and Mik (this volume).

[6] See Tournaire (this volume).

[7] See Paolini (this volume).

[8] Directive 2009/138/EC of the European Parliament and of the Council of 25 November 2009 on the taking-up and pursuit of the business of Insurance and Reinsurance (Solvency II) (recast), OJ L 335, 17.12.2009, pp. 1–155; Directive (EU) 2016/97 of the European Parliament and of the Council of 20 January 2016 on insurance distribution, OJ L 26, 2.2.2016, pp. 19–59.

[9] Regulation (EU) 2022/2065 of the European Parliament and of the Council of 19 October 2022 on a Single Market For Digital Services OJ L 277, 27.10.2022, pp. 1–102, http://data.europa.eu/eli/reg/2022/2065/oj.

[10] Regulation (EU) 2024/1689 of the European Parliament and of the Council of 13 June 2024 laying down harmonised rules on artificial intelligence, OJ L, 2024/1689, 12.7.2024, http://data.europa.eu/eli/reg/2024/1689/oj. For a visual overview of the EU Digital Acquis, see the table by Zenner et al. (2023).

Consumer Law applicable to insurance contracts.[11] While not discussed in this chapter, the EU legal framework on data and personal data protection, specifically the Data Act[12] and the General Data Protection Regulation (GDPR),[13] remain relevant for the digitalisation of the insurance sector and the protection of policyholders' rights.[14] Indeed, these three overlapping legal regimes may create inconsistencies and gaps in achieving the goal of protecting the rights of consumers in insurance. They may also result in uncertainty for insurance platforms while making it challenging for platform operators to navigate and comply with the regulatory landscape effectively. Indeed, scholars have yet to discuss the resulting complex legal framework, its shortcomings, and possible ways to coordinate it.[15] Thus, the effectiveness of consumer protection within digital insurance is at substantial risk of being undermined. The risk stems from the prevailing high uncertainty surrounding the applicable rules, their interpretation, and the enforcement mechanisms in place.

Our introductory chapter and the book aim to offer an integrated perspective that bridges technological innovation with European Union and comparative law, ultimately fostering responsible and sustainable digital transformation in insurance. The following is an overview of the regulatory architecture of digital insurance markets in the EU. The book's other chapters will pursue detailed analyses of numerous specific questions.

2 Digital Insurance Platforms

Before we analyse the applicable legal framework, it is important to define two fundamental notions of this chapter: 'digital insurance' and 'insurance platforms'. As shown below, they have been elaborated on in economics scholarship. Under a broad definition, digital insurance is a disruptive and systemic innovation.[16] It blurs the distinction between insurance companies, telecommunication organisations, traders, and intermediaries. Under a narrow technical meaning, digital insurance refers to providing and operating insurance and connected financial services using

---

[11] Directive (EU) 2019/2161 of the European Parliament and of the Council of 27 November 2019 as regards the better enforcement and modernisation of Union consumer protection rules, 2019 OJ L 328; Directive 2002/65/EC of the European Parliament and of the Council of 23 September 2002 concerning the distance marketing of consumer financial services and amending Council Directive 90/619/EEC and Directives 97/7/EC and 98/27/EC, OJ L 271, 9.10.2002, pp. 16–24.

[12] Regulation (EU) 2023/2854 of the European Parliament and of the Council of 13 December 2023 on harmonised rules on fair access to and use of data and amending Regulation (EU) 2017/2394 and Directive (EU) 2020/1828 (Data Act), OJ L, 2023/2854, 22.12.2023.

[13] Regulation (EU) 2016/679 on the protection of natural persons with regard to the processing of personal data and on the free movement of such data, OJ L 119, 4.5.2016, pp. 1–88.

[14] See Knetsch (this volume).

[15] See Bogucki et al. (2021).

[16] See Nicoletti (2016), p. 4.

digital solutions.[17] The scope of the services may include transactions to buy insurance or personal investments, administer policies and claims, and access customised information.

In the context of innovation in insurance, it is suggested digital insurance should have the following elements:

- it should deliver a customised but consistent customer experience across all channels and points of interaction.
- it should be underpinned by analytics and digitisation.
- it should reflect a change in the branding and the operating model, namely products and services, processes, organisation, culture, skills, ICT platforms, and possibly even business models.
- it should deliver demonstrable and sustainable value to customers and insurance company stakeholders.[18]

While 'digital insurance' is not a legal notion, this chapter provides an overview of the legal regime applicable to the digital distribution of insurance products under EU law.

The second crucial concept is that of a digital (online) 'insurance platform'. An insurance platform is a broad notion that may include entities acting as risk carriers, intermediaries, or service providers.[19] Insurers develop their own digital platforms as risk carriers (underwriters) to channel interactions with clients at different stages of the insurance value chain.[20] Further, insurers and intermediaries develop digital platforms to advertise, market, and sell insurance products.[21] Finally, as service providers, platform operators offer various financial and non-financial services, such as payments, process automation, or data analytics.[22] While the concept of 'a digital platform' refers primarily to new business models in the digital economy, under EU law and policy, there are instances in which the concept has been defined.

First, at a general level, a definition of an 'online platform' has been provided in Article 3(i) DSA. It reads as follows:

> 'online platform' means a hosting service that, at the request of a recipient of the service, stores and disseminates information to the public, unless that activity is a minor and purely ancillary feature of another service or a minor functionality of the principal service and, for objective and technical reasons, cannot be used without that other service, and the integration of the feature or functionality into the other service is not a means to circumvent the applicability of this Regulation;

[17] See Nicoletti (2016), p. 17.

[18] See Nicoletti (2016), p. 21.

[19] See, e.g., the classification in Ocampo et al. (2023), p. 3; see also Joint European Supervisory Authorities response to the European Commission's February 2021 Call for Advice on Digital Finance, ESA 2022 01, 31.01.2022.

[20] See the websites and smartphone apps of different insurers.

[21] See Marano (2019), p. 301: 'digital intermediaries'.

[22] See Nicoletti (2016), p. 39.

Importantly, an 'online platform' is distinguished from an 'online search engine' in Article 3 (j) DSA.

Second, in a discussion paper by the European Insurance and Occupational Pensions Authority (EIOPA), the concept of the 'platform' is distinguished from that of an ecosystem and defined as follows:

> a platform is the technical infrastructure necessary for multiple participants to connect and interact with each other and create and exchange value. On the other hand, an ecosystem is an interconnected set of services that allow participants to address a wide variety of client needs in one integrated experience. Hence, it could be stated that an ecosystem approach goes beyond pure platforms (e.g., it could be cross-industry/cross-sectorial with the aim of providing a full consumer experience rather than isolated products or services).[23]

The concept of the 'platform' adopted in the EIOPA discussion paper is fairly broad and reflects our view that a 'digital platform' is primarily a business model to which different legal provisions apply, and a universal legal definition will not have significant explanatory value.

The emergence of digital platforms as a business model in the insurance sector justifies the question about the involvement of Big Tech firms there. Currently, there are two typical forms of such involvement. First, Big Tech entities often act as insurance intermediaries and are registered or licensed. Integrating insurance products or services into the customer journey of big tech businesses is considered a form of embedded insurance.[24] 'Embedded insurance' offered by Big Tech generally involves products that are closely linked to their non-insurance products or services; it is designed to provide a seamless and convenient experience for customers by offering insurance at the point of sale or as a part of the overall user experience. This includes e-commerce platforms, fintech apps, ride-sharing platforms, or travel booking websites.[25] A different business model is an 'insurance marketplace'. The latter involves Big Tech companies partnering with several insurers to offer a wide range of insurance products that are not directly linked to their other digital services through their one-stop online insurance shopping platform.[26] Significantly, the presence of Big Tech companies in the European Union insurance markets is still limited compared to the US and China.[27] Nonetheless, legal questions arising in this

[23] See "Discussion paper on insurance value chain and new business models arising from digitalisation", 14 April 2020. 13. https://www.eiopa.europa.eu/consultations/discussion-paper-reinsurance-value-chain-and-new-business-models-arising-digitalisation_en. On the concept of an ecosystem in the insurance sector, see Talonen (this volume).

[24] See Ocampo et al. (2023), p. 14.

[25] For instance, consumers are offered device insurance when buying a smartphone and travel insurance when booking a flight or train connection. In the EU, examples include AppleCare+ or Amazon Protect.

[26] E.g., Amazon Insurance Store in the UK.

[27] Most insurance marketplaces are in Asia, see Ocampo et al. (2023), p. 7. According to the European Supervisory Authority, reasons for their limited presence in Europe include regulation, low profit margin, consumer preferences (more trust in incumbents), and lack of know-how about the insurance business (see the Joint European Supervisory Authority response (ESA 2022 01), at 30).

context have begun attracting attention, specifically concerning novel forms of insurance intermediaries. It must be emphasised that running insurance intermediaries is a much lower risk and cost model than operating an insurance undertaking itself. Often, Big Tech companies operating as insurance intermediaries appear to have more substantial market power when partnering with insurers than traditional insurance intermediaries. In 2021, the EIOPA noted the market power imbalance between Big Tech intermediaries and insurers, calling it 'reverse-outsourcing' from intermediaries to insurers.[28]

From the perspective of insurance consumers, interactions with digital platforms typically occur in the following stages of the insurance value chain: sales and distribution, claims management, and post-sale and policy management.[29]

3 Digital Insurance and EU Insurance Law

The operation of the insurance sector in the EU is subject to the supervisory framework of the Solvency II Directive.[30] Under Recital 16 to Solvency II, 'The main objective of insurance and reinsurance regulation and supervisions is the adequate protection of policyholders and beneficiaries'.[31] Solvency II addresses the pursuit of insurance business and the protection of policyholders in general and requires insurance and reinsurance undertakings to have in place an effective system of governance which provides for sound and prudent management of the business (Article 41(1)). While there is also no specific EU legal act dealing with digital insurance operations, EU bodies have long followed and subsequently also begun to regulate digital insurance markets. First, in 2014, the EIOPA issued a Report on Good Practices on Comparison Websites.[32] The Report emphasised that insurance comparison websites may not be suitable for certain insurance products, such as some life insurance products, i.e., unit-linked policies.

---

[28] EIOPA (2021): (Re)insurance value chain and new business models arising from digitalisation: feedback statement to the discussion paper, EIOPA-BoS-21-219 4 May 2021, p. 7.

[29] We define the insurance value chain as (1) product design and development, (2) pricing and underwriting, (3) marketing, (4) sales and distribution, (5) claims management, and (6) post-sale and policy management, see Ocampo et al. (2023), p. 3; Eling and Lehmann (2018), p. 362; Cappiello (2018), pp. 12–13; Nicoletti (2021), p. 43.

[30] Directive 2009/138/EC of the European Parliament and of the Council of 25 November 2009 on the taking-up and pursuit of the business of Insurance and Reinsurance (Solvency II) (recast), OJ L 335, 17.12.2009, pp. 1–155.

[31] See Heiss (2023), pp. 305–313, on the Solvency II Directive's relevance for the understanding of the complex legal character of EU insurance law as regulatory law.

[32] EIOPA (2014), Report on Good Practices on Comparison Websites, https://eiopa.europa.eu/Publications/Reports/Report_on_Good_Practices_on_Comparison_Websites.pdf.

Second, the EIOPA Opinion on sales via the Internet of insurance and pension products was issued in 2015.[33] The EIOPA recommended that national authorities take the necessary and proportionate supervisory actions to ensure that online distributors comply with a duty of advice towards their clients if such a duty exists in national law or when sales are so promoted.[34] Moreover, the EIOPA opined that national authorities should also ensure that customers are provided with appropriate information on the selling process of the online distributor to avoid unsolicited or mistakenly concluded contracts.

Third, Directive 2016/97 on Insurance Distribution (IDD),[35] which harmonises national provisions concerning insurance and reinsurance distribution in the EU, applies to all modes of distribution, including online distribution. It aims to achieve the same level of protection for insurance customers, irrespective of the distribution channel through which insurance products are marketed and sold.[36] IDD provisions consider the growing importance of digitalisation in the insurance business. According to the approach towards client protection underlying the IDD, consumers should benefit from the same level of security despite the differences between distribution channels.[37] This assumption is reflected in the basic concept of the IDD, that of 'insurance distribution'. The notion of 'insurance distribution' in Article 2.1 (1) IDD is expansive and comprises digital insurance platforms:

> 'insurance distribution' means the activities of advising on, proposing, or carrying out other work preparatory to the conclusion of contracts of insurance, of concluding such contracts, or of assisting in the administration and performance of such contracts, in particular in the event of a claim, including the provision of information concerning one or more insurance contracts in accordance with criteria selected by customers through a website or other media and the compilation of an insurance product ranking list, including price and product comparison, or a discount on the price of an insurance contract, when the customer is able to directly or indirectly conclude an insurance contract using a website or other media.

Recital 12 of the IDD, which refers to comparison shopping websites, clarifies this:

> This Directive should apply to persons whose activity consists of the provision of information on one or more contracts of insurance in response to criteria selected by the customer, whether via a website or other media, or the provision of a ranking of insurance products or a discount on the price of an insurance contract when the customer is able to directly or indirectly conclude an insurance contract at the end of the process. This Directive should not apply to websites managed by public authorities or consumers' associations which do not aim to conclude any contract but merely compare insurance products available on the market.

---

[33] EIOPA (2015), Opinion on sales via the Internet of insurance and pension products, EIOPA-BoS-14/198, available at https://www.eiopa.europa.eu/publications/sales-internet-insurance-and-pension-products_en.

[34] See Tereszkiewicz (2020).

[35] Directive (EU) 2016/97 of the European Parliament and of the Council of 20 January 2016 on insurance distribution, OJ L 26, 2.2.2016, pp. 19–59.

[36] See Kohne and Brommelmeyer (2018), p. 723; Marano (2019), p. 298.

[37] See Recital 6 IDD.

This means that comparison shopping websites (i.e., insurance platforms) that directly or indirectly enable consumers to conclude insurance contracts are subject to the IDD and, most importantly, its provisions regulating the insurance platform-insurance consumer relationship. Furthermore, the IDD applies to ancillary insurance intermediaries, i.e. distributors of goods and services who distribute insurance products complementary to the goods and services they sell.[38] This is particularly important within the digital platform economy.

At a more general level, digital insurance distributors are subject to the same rules as other categories of insurance distributors.[39] Operators of digital insurance platforms or insurance mobile apps are required to register as intermediaries in the meaning of the IDD and its implementing legislation within the Member States legal orders. As a result, the sale of insurance products through digital platforms and applications falls within the scope of the respective insurance distribution regulatory framework.

Further, in their response to the European Commission's Call for Advice on Digital Finance issued in 2021,[40] European Supervisory Authorities recommended updating the existing rules on insurance distribution to make them fit for the digital age. The ESA also recommended enhancing consumer protection and the conduct of business rules to address risks of mis-selling, in particular concerning tied and bundled financial products, and overcome potential weaknesses in complaints handling processes.[41] Moreover, the European Supervisory Authorities highlighted the need for a holistic approach to regulating and supervising the financial services value chain and ensuring the effective regulation and supervision of so-called mixed activity groups.[42]

Finally, the EIOPA addressed the growing relevance of AI in the insurance sector in its 2021 report.[43] To promote an ethical and trustworthy AI in the European insurance sector, the EIOPA's expert group developed six AI governance principles. These principles, which take into account the specific character of the insurance sector, include: proportionality; fairness and non-discrimination; transparency and explainability; Human Oversight; data governance of record keeping; Robustness and Performance.[44] These high-level principles are accompanied by additional

[38] See De Maesschalck (2017), p. 63.

[39] See Article 2(1)(4) IDD; De Maesschalck (2017), p. 63.

[40] European Commission (2021a), *Request to EBA, EIOPA and ESMA for technical advice on digital finance and related issues*, Ref. Ares(2021)898555, 2 February 2021.

[41] See Joint European Supervisory Authorities response to the European Commission's February 2021 Call for Advice on Digital Finance, ESA 2022 01, 31.01.2022.

[42] Idem.

[43] See Artificial Intelligence Governance Principles: Towards Ethical and Trustworthy Artificial Intelligence in the European Insurance Sector, A report from EIOPA's Consultative Expert Group on Digital Ethics in insurance, available at https://www.eiopa.europa.eu/eiopa-publishes-report-artificial-intelligence-governance-principles-2021-06-17_en.

[44] Idem, p. 8.

guidance for insurance firms on how to implement them in practice throughout the AI system's lifecycle.[45]

4 Digital Insurance and the EU Digital Acquis

For several years now, the EU has been developing various legislative measures to regulate digital platforms, artificial intelligence (AI), and other emerging technologies.[46] As a result, the current EU Digital Acquis is broad, fragmented, and articulated.[47] In our chapter, we will examine two main legal regimes relevant to digital insurance markets.

First, insurance platforms are subject to the DSA.[48] The DSA focuses on updating and modernising the legal framework governing digital services, including online platforms. It aims to ensure user safety, address content moderation issues, and promote the accountability and transparency of online platforms (Article 28 DSA). While the scope of the DSA extends beyond AI platforms, it applies to platforms that facilitate online commerce, including those leveraging AI technology. The DSA includes provisions relevant to consumer protection, such as ensuring transparency in terms and conditions, countering unfair commercial practices, and establishing effective mechanisms to handle user complaints and disputes.[49] Compliance with the DSA requires insurance platforms to meet the Act's obligations concerning transparency, user protection, and fair practices.[50]

Second, when driven by an AI system, digital insurance is also potentially subject to rules governing AI. Specifically, the AI Act aims to establish a new comprehensive regulatory framework for AI systems, focusing on risk-based approaches, transparency, and accountability. While the primary focus of the AI Act is not consumer protection, it indirectly addresses consumer-related risks associated with AI technologies. The Act includes provisions promoting transparency and accountability and mitigating high-risk AI practices that could harm consumers. The AI Act protects consumers from risks by imposing obligations on AI system developers and operators. It also highlights the importance of addressing issues such as transparency, fairness, and the explainability of AI systems, which are relevant to consumer protection. However, it applies only to high-risk AI systems and, consequently, does not cover insurance platforms that do not involve high-risk AI (according to the list

[45] On different applications of AI in the insurance sector see: Ostrowska (this volume), Jabłonowska et al. (this volume), and Paolini (this volume).

[46] See Ebers (2022); Schulze and Staudenmayer (2020), pp. 2–3.

[47] See Zenner et al. (2023).

[48] Regulation (EU) 2022/2065 of the European Parliament and of the Council of 19 October 2022 on a Single Market for Digital Services and amending Directive 2000/31/EC (Digital Services Act), OJ L 277, 27.10.2022, 1–102.

[49] See Chapter III DSA: Due Diligence Obligations for a Transparent and Safe Online Environment.

[50] See Mak and Busch (2021), p. 10; Mischau (2022), p. 11.

provided in the annex to the proposal).[51] The relevance of the abovementioned provisions appears limited as of this writing; this may yet change soon. The following sections will examine these two issues in detail.

4.1 Digital Insurance Platforms Under the DSA

The DSA plays a fundamental and general role in regulating platforms in online commerce, even when platform operators extensively deploy AI systems for tasks such as running chatbots, personalising services, and conducting extensive consumer profiling.[52] The question is whether the recently established DSA will effectively address consumer protection concerns in the growing landscape of AI. The DSA is not only a 'consumer protection measure' but a more general regulatory instrument with several different goals.[53]

The duties and obligations outlined in the Digital Services Act (DSA) generally apply to online platforms, including those that employ AI technologies.[54] While the DSA does not explicitly target AI platforms, it encompasses a broad range of online services as its notions of 'online platform' and 'online search engine' are broadly defined.[55] Typically, insurance platforms fall within its scope.

The DSA regulates online services to ensure accountability, transparency, and user safety. As such, if an AI platform fits the DSA's definition of a very large online platform, it is subject to the specific duties and obligations applicable to such platforms, which include obligations related to content moderation, risk assessment, transparency, complaint handling, and cooperation with authorities.

The DSA introduces a classification system for online platforms.[56] Platforms are categorised as either hosting services, which primarily store user-generated content, or intermediary services, which go beyond mere storage and have a more active role in content moderation and recommendation. In insurance, digital platforms acting as intermediaries provide rankings of products in respective categories.

---

[51] See Das et al. (2021); Dequen and Birot (2020); Kumar and Grover (2020).

[52] The legal basis for the DSA is Article 114 of the Treaty on the Functioning of the European Union (TFEU), which allows for harmonising national laws to establish and facilitate the functioning of the internal market. Under this legal basis, the EU can adopt measures to regulate specific aspects of a matter, while the Member States can continue exercising their own competence as long as a particular aspect is not regulated by the Union (pre-emption). However, it should be noted that in the realm of technological development, the shared competence of the Union allows Member States to retain their own competence in the matter, as outlined in Article 4(3) of the TFEU.

[53] See in particular recital 10 DSA, stipulating that 'for reasons of clarity, this Regulation should be without prejudice to Union law on consumer protection (…), and on the protection of personal data (…)'; see also Cauffman and Goanta (2021), p. 1.

[54] See Article 1.1 DSA.

[55] See Article 3(i) and Article 3(j) DSA for both definitions.

[56] See Articles 4, 5 and 6 DSA.

Online platforms, including those employing AI technologies, are subject to due diligence obligations to address illegal content, activities, or goods on their platforms. These obligations include implementing measures to prevent and swiftly remove illegal content, and taking appropriate actions to mitigate risks associated with AI systems (Article 23 DSA).

The DSA emphasises transparency for online platforms. Platforms must provide clear and easily accessible information about their terms and conditions, content moderation policies, and advertising practices (Article 25–27 DSA).[57] Users should have a clear understanding of how AI algorithms shape their experiences and should be provided with mechanisms for redress and dispute resolution.

The DSA introduces stronger mechanisms to ensure the oversight and accountability of online platforms. These platforms must establish internal complaint-handling procedures and conduct regular risk assessments. If they are located outside the EU, they must also appoint a legal representative within the EU.

Online platforms are expected to cooperate with competent authorities and provide the information necessary to certify compliance with the DSA. They may be required to provide data, cooperate in investigations, and respond to requests related to enforcement actions.[58]

The DSA introduces provisions important for safeguarding user interests in insurance consumer protection. Platforms are required to establish effective procedures for handling user complaints and disputes, ensuring that users can access adequate redress.[59] This includes establishing internal complaint-handling systems and offering alternative dispute resolution mechanisms to resolve disputes between users and platforms.[60] To comply with the DSA, insurance platforms engaged in online commerce must meet the obligations set forth by the Act. These include ensuring transparency in their operations, protecting user data and privacy, implementing fair practices concerning pricing and advertising, and establishing effective systems for handling user complaints. By adhering to the requirements of the DSA, insurance platforms can contribute to a safer, more accountable, and transparent digital environment for consumers.

Overall, the DSA's provisions relevant to consumer protection aim to foster trust and confidence in online platforms, including those leveraging AI technology. Compliance with the DSA is essential for insurance platforms to meet the obligations set forth concerning transparency, user protection, and fair practices, ultimately enhancing consumer trust and ensuring a positive online experience for users.

---

[57] BEUC (2022).

[58] Ebers (2021), p. 1.

[59] See Article 20 DSA (internal complaint-handling systems) and Article 21 DSA (out-of-court dispute settlement).

[60] Cauffman and Goanta (2021), p. 758.

4.2 Digital Insurance Platforms and Very Large Online Platforms

Very large online platforms (VLOPs) often utilise AI technologies in various aspects of their operations. AI algorithms analyse vast user data, including browsing history, purchase behaviour, and preferences, to provide personalised recommendations. These platforms use AI to understand user interests and tailor content, products, and services to each individual, enhancing user engagement and driving conversions. Very large platforms deal with massive volumes of user-generated content. AI automates content moderation tasks, including identifying and filtering out inappropriate or violating content such as hate speech, spam, or fake accounts. AI-powered moderation helps platforms maintain a safer and more secure user environment.

Additionally, AI is crucial in search engines and large-scale platforms with vast content. AI algorithms are used to improve search results and enhance the ranking of relevant content, ensuring that users find the most accurate and valuable information quickly and efficiently. Very large platforms often employ NLP techniques to understand and analyse textual data. AI-powered chatbots and virtual assistants leverage NLP to provide automated insurance customer support, answer user inquiries, and handle routine tasks, offering round-the-clock assistance to users. AI algorithms are extensively used for ad targeting and optimisation on large advertising platforms. AI analyses user behaviour, demographic data, and browsing history to deliver targeted advertisements, improve ad relevance, and maximise the effectiveness of advertising campaigns.

The Digital Services Act recognises the pivotal role played by very large platforms in shaping the digital landscape, and it seeks to establish a framework that ensures accountability, transparency, and user protection within this context. The DSA goes beyond general regulations to introduce specific rules and obligations tailored to these influential platforms, reflecting the unique challenges they pose and their potential impact on society.

The DSA has laid down transparency as a fundamental principle for very large platforms. These platforms are required to provide clear and easily accessible terms and conditions, including content moderation policies. By doing so, platforms enable users to understand the rules governing their content, the criteria used for moderation decisions, and the avenues available for redress. Transparency empowers users to make informed choices and promotes a sense of trust and fairness in platform operations.

The DSA mandates the implementation of risk assessments to address risks associated with very large platforms.[61] Platforms are tasked with identifying potential risks related to their services, mainly systemic risks that could impact public health, safety, or fundamental rights. These risk assessments drive the development and implementation of appropriate measures to mitigate identified risks effectively. By

---

[61] See Section 5 DSA.

undertaking these assessments and taking proactive steps to minimise potential harms, platforms demonstrate their commitment to user protection and responsible digital service provision.

Accountability for algorithmic systems is another significant aspect covered by the DSA. Very large platforms are required to provide users with clear and comprehensive information about how algorithms and AI-driven systems influence the information they receive. This includes disclosing the key parameters determining content ranking and presentation, including advertising. By fostering transparency in algorithmic processes, the DSA aims to empower users, reduce information asymmetry, and encourage platforms to develop fair and unbiased algorithms.

To ensure independent scrutiny and accountability, the DSA introduces the concept of independent audits for very large platforms. These audits, conducted by third-party entities, assess platforms' compliance with the DSA's obligations and requirements. By subjecting platforms to external evaluation, independent audits provide an additional layer of assurance and reinforce the transparency and accountability expectations placed on very large platforms.

Finally, the DSA emphasises the importance of cooperation between very large platforms and public authorities. Platforms must collaborate with authorities, providing relevant information and assistance in addressing illegal activities or content. This cooperation facilitates effective enforcement, enabling authorities to take necessary action against violations, protect users, and maintain the integrity of the digital environment.

Including specific rules and obligations for very large platforms in the DSA acknowledges their influential role. The aim is to ensure they adhere to high transparency, accountability, and user protection standards. By setting these requirements, the DSA fosters a digital ecosystem that is more accountable, user-centric, and conducive to trust and confidence among all the stakeholders involved, i.e., insurers, intermediaries, and insurance customers.

4.3 Insurance and AI Systems

The AI Act governs artificial intelligence systems within the European Union. It aims to establish a harmonised regulatory framework to ensure the ethical and trustworthy development and deployment of AI while safeguarding fundamental rights and addressing potential risks. The Act applies to AI systems deployed or used within the EU and AI systems developed outside the EU but intended for use within it.[62]

Certain practices are prohibited outright due to their high-risk nature, such as AI systems that manipulate human behaviour in a deceptive or harmful manner or AI systems used for social scoring by governments without appropriate safeguards.

[62] Bogucki et al. (2021).

Additionally, AI systems deemed high-risk (such as those used in critical infrastructure, health care, transportation, or law enforcement) must comply with specific obligations. These include data quality and documentation requirements, transparency,[63] human oversight, robustness, and accuracy. High-risk AI systems must also undergo a conformity assessment before being placed on the market or in service. This assessment involves examining technical documentation, conducting tests, and ensuring compliance with the requirements set out in the Act. National supervisory authorities will be established or designated to enforce the provisions of the AI Act, oversee conformity assessments, and impose administrative penalties for non-compliance.

Consequently, insurance platforms will only residually fall within the scope of the AI Act: the pre-identification of a limited number of high-risk AI applications.[64] The AI Act excludes most solutions developed by large digital platforms for their consumer-facing AI deployment, including content moderation, search engines, and recommendation systems.[65]

One of the primary challenges is the rapid speed of technological advancements in AI, which often outpaces the regulatory response. The EU legal framework dealing with digital platforms and AI is continuously subject to adaptation. Still, it may need help to keep up with the dynamic nature of AI technologies and their associated risks to consumers. The rapid advancement and evolution of AI technologies indubitably necessitate a proactive and adaptable approach to regulation. Therefore, it is imperative to establish clear and robust guidelines that address critical aspects of AI deployment, including algorithmic transparency, bias mitigation, accountability mechanisms, and privacy protection. These guidelines should safeguard

[63] The AI Act emphasises the importance of transparency, requiring that users be informed when interacting with an AI system. Users must be provided with information about AI systems' capabilities, limitations, and intended purposes to ensure they can make informed decisions.

[64] The AI Act classifies as high-risk AI systems intended to be used as safety components of products, for example, as well as systems that pose a high risk of harm to health and safety and that are used in specific areas. The Act lists examples of high-risk AI systems, including systems used as safety components in managing and operating the supply of water, gas, heating and electricity, and systems used to evaluate the creditworthiness of natural persons in relation to essential private and public services. With respect to insurance, Recital 58 in the AI Act states what follows: 'However, AI systems provided for by Union law for the purpose of detecting fraud in the offering of financial services and for prudential purposes to calculate credit institutions' and insurance undertakings' capital requirements should not be considered to be high-risk under this Regulation. Moreover, AI systems intended to be used for risk assessment and pricing in relation to natural persons for health and life insurance can also have a significant impact on persons' livelihood and if not duly designed, developed and used, can infringe their fundamental rights and can lead to serious consequences for people's life and health, including financial exclusion and discrimination.'

[65] For example, recommender systems fall within the scope of both the DSA and AI Act. However, they approach recommender systems in two distinct ways. The DSA looks at recommender systems implemented by VLOPs and very large online search engines, while the AI Act focuses mainly on a narrow subset of high-risk systems. As only some recommender systems used by VLOPs also qualify as high-risk AI systems, most will be subject to either the rules of the AI Act or the DSA, but not both.

consumer rights and interests, ensuring that insurance platforms operate fairly, responsibly, and are trustworthy.

Furthermore, the complexity and opacity of AI algorithms present challenges regarding transparency and accountability. Consumers may need more insight into and knowledge about how AI systems make decisions that affect them, which raises concerns about potential biases, discrimination, or lack of explainability. The current legal framework may not provide sufficient mechanisms to address these issues adequately.

Another crucial aspect to consider in the context of consumer protection and AI-powered platforms is their cross-border nature. These platforms often operate globally, serving users and conducting business activities across multiple jurisdictions. While the EU legal framework, including regulations like the AI Act and the Digital Services Act, primarily applies to entities operating within the EU, enforcing these regulations on platforms outside the EU presents significant challenges.

Moreover, a key challenge is the jurisdictional complexity of regulating cross-border platforms. Consumer protection laws and regulations vary from jurisdiction to jurisdiction, and platforms must navigate a patchwork of legal frameworks. This can result in inconsistencies and gaps in consumer protection because platforms may be subject to varying regulatory oversights depending on their jurisdictions.

Moreover, the legal mechanisms and cooperation frameworks necessary for effective cross-border enforcement often must be developed more. Cooperation among regulatory authorities across different jurisdictions can be complex and hindered by differences among legal systems, cultural norms, and enforcement priorities. This can hamper coordinated efforts to ensure consistent consumer protection across borders and address non-compliant platforms operating outside the EU.

The cross-border nature of digital insurance also raises questions about the effectiveness of the remedies and forms of recourse available to consumers. When issues arise, consumers may encounter difficulties in seeking redress, primarily if the platform operates in a jurisdiction with limited legal avenues for dispute resolution or if the costs of pursuing legal action outweigh the potential benefits.

Enhanced international cooperation and collaboration are needed to address these challenges and ensure robust consumer protection in the cross-border context. This includes strengthening regulatory cooperation frameworks, promoting information sharing between jurisdictions, and encouraging the development of international standards for consumer protection in AI-powered platforms. Additionally, designing mechanisms for cross-jurisdictional enforcement and promoting dialogue among regulators can foster a more consistent and practical approach to consumer protection in the rapidly evolving landscape of cross-border insurance platforms.

In addition, the rapid advent of generative AI[66] is again changing the landscape by rapidly putting the new regulatory framework at risk of becoming outdated. One of the primary concerns is the potential for misinformation and fake content. Generative AI can produce highly realistic and convincing content, such as text,

[66] Haluza and Jungwirth (2023).

images, and videos. This poses a significant risk because malicious actors can exploit this technology to create and disseminate false information. Consumers may unknowingly encounter fabricated news articles, counterfeit products, or manipulated reviews, leading to confusion, financial loss, or reputational harm.

Generative AI also enables manipulation and social engineering. Deepfake videos and audio recordings generated by AI models can deceive consumers by presenting false or misleading information. This manipulation can be used for fraud, such as identity theft or disinformation. The challenge lies in enabling consumers to discern between genuine and manipulated content that erodes trust in digital media and exposes individuals to potential harm.

Privacy and data protection are further concerns associated with generative AI. These models require extensive datasets for training, and these may involve personal data. If not handled with appropriate consent and safeguards, this data usage can lead to unauthorised access or misuse of personal information, potentially resulting in privacy breaches. Moreover, the content generated by AI models may also violate individuals' privacy rights by including sensitive or private information.

Bias and discrimination are also concerns associated with generative AI. Like other AI systems, generative AI models can reflect and amplify existing biases in the training data.[67] This can result in the generation of biased or discriminatory content that perpetuates stereotypes, marginalises certain groups, or reinforces inequalities. Consumers may be exposed to content that discriminates against individuals or exacerbates societal divisions. The rapidly evolving nature of AI technology often outpaces the development of comprehensive legal frameworks.

5 Digital Insurance and the EU Consumer Law

The European Union Consumer Law[68] emerges in particular from three main directives: the Unfair Contractual Terms Directive ('UCTD'),[69] the Unfair Commercial Practice Directives ('UCPD'),[70] and the Consumer Rights Directive ('CRD'),[71] all

[67] See Knetsch (this volume).

[68] On the concept of EU Consumer Law see Howells (2018), p. 1.

[69] Council Directive 93/13/EEC of 5 April 1993 on unfair terms in consumer contracts, OJ L 95, 21.4.1993, pp. 29–34.

[70] Directive 2005/29/EC of the European Parliament and of the Council of 11 May 2005 concerning unfair business-to-consumer commercial practices in the internal market and amending Council Directive 84/450/EEC, Directives 97/7/EC, 98/27/EC and 2002/65/EC of the European Parliament and of the Council and Regulation (EC) No 2006/2004 of the European Parliament and of the Council, OJ L 149, 11.6.2005, pp. 22–39; see Duivenvoorde (2022), p. 11.

[71] Directive 2011/83/EU of the European Parliament and of the Council of 25 October 2011 on consumer rights, amending Council Directive 93/13/EEC and Directive 1999/44/EC of the European Parliament and of the Council and repealing Council Directive 85/577/EEC and Directive 97/7/EC of the European Parliament and of the Council Text, OJ L 304, 22.11.2011, pp. 64–88 (referred to as the Consumer Rights Directive).

as amended in 2019 by the Modernisation Directive ('MD'),[72] which introduced penalties and additional rules for transparency in online marketplaces. Importantly, the Consumer Rights Directive does not apply to 'contracts for financial services' unless a Member State elected to extend its scope of application beyond the minimum harmonisation standard.[73] With respect to subject matters covered by the Consumer Rights Directive, contracts for financial services, including insurance contracts, are subject to Directive 2002/65/EC on the Distance Marketing of Consumer Financial Services ('DMFSD').[74] Under a recent EU proposal, it is intended to end the overall exclusion of financial services from Directive 2011/83/EU by broadening its scope to include financial services concluded at a distance.[75] Despite the exclusion of insurance contracts from the scope of the Consumer Rights Directive, this Directive remains relevant for the operation of insurance platforms as it may apply to products and services to which insurance is an ancillary product.[76]

Existing EU consumer protection acts, such as the Consumer Rights Directive and the Unfair Commercial Practices Directive, provide a comprehensive framework for consumer protection across various sectors, including digital insurance. These provisions aim to ensure fair trade practices, protect consumers from misleading or aggressive commercial practices, and provide redress and dispute resolution mechanisms. They apply to insurance platforms and e-commerce businesses subject to the exemptions laid down in those acts.[77]

However, the interpretation of existing consumer protection laws in the context of insurance platforms raises a significant challenge. In addition, the application of traditional consumer protection principles to emerging AI technologies requires their careful reinterpretation and adaptation if the specific issues and risks involved are to be adequately addressed. However, the absence of standardised interpretations and guidelines gives rise to inconsistency and ambiguity in determining the appropriate rules and obligations to safeguard consumers effectively. Enforcement of consumer protection laws in the context of digital insurance also exhibits notable gaps. The dynamic and global nature of digitisation and the jurisdictional

[72] Directive (EU) 2019/2161 of the European Parliament and of the Council of 27 November 2019 as regards the better enforcement and modernisation of Union consumer protection rules, OJ L 328, 8.12.2019, pp. 7–28.

[73] Directive 2011/83/EU of the European Parliament and of the Council of 25 October 2011 on consumer rights, amending Council Directive 93/13/EEC and Directive 1999/44/EC of the European Parliament and of the Council and repealing Council Directive 85/577/EEC and Directive 97/7/EC of the European Parliament and of the Council, OJ L 304, 22.11.2011, pp. 64–88.

[74] Directive 2002/65/EC of the European Parliament and of the Council of 23 September 2002 concerning the distance marketing of consumer financial services and amending Council Directive 90/619/EEC and Directives 97/7/EC and 98/27/EC, OJ L 271, 9.10.2002, pp. 16–24.

[75] Proposal for a Directive of the European Parliament and of the Council amending Directive 2011/83/EU concerning financial services contracts concluded at a distance and repealing Directive 2002/65/EC, COM(2022) 204 final.

[76] As to when platform users qualify as consumers under EU law, see the CJEU judgment of 25 January 2018, C-498/16, Maximilian Schrems v Facebook Ireland Limited ECLI:EU:C:2018:37.

[77] See Durovic and Kaprou (2024).

complexities of cross-border operations raise challenges against enforcing consistent consumer protection measures. The diversity of enforcement capabilities and priorities among regulatory authorities further compounds these challenges, generating potential inconsistencies in the application and enforcement of consumer protection rules.

Thus, insurance platforms are subject to duties and obligations under EU consumer law, which generally aims to create a transparent and fair environment for users engaging with online platforms. Specifically, insurance platforms must comply with EU provisions that prohibit unfair commercial practices and misleading advertising that also apply to online platforms.[78] This means they are prohibited from engaging in deceptive or misleading commercial practices that characterise the digital environment, such as targeting, dark patterns, hidden costs, or providing too limited and/or inaccurate pre-contractual information about the products or services offered online.[79]

A direct and robust connection between the use of unfair commercial practices, such as hiding, omitting information or providing erroneous information, and the unfairness of contractual terms caused by the non-transparency was recognised in the CJEU *Pereničová* judgment.[80] There, the Court was confronted with the question of whether a finding that a commercial practice of using contractual terms that could mislead consumers as to the scope of their rights and obligations was unfair, influences (or possibly even determines) the outcome of the assessment of whether these terms are to be considered unfair under Article 4(1) of the Unfair Contract Terms Directive. The Court thus took the view that finding that a commercial practice in using a specific contract term meets the test of unfairness under the UCPD is merely one of the factors to be taken into account in the assessment as to whether contract terms are at the same time unfair under the Unfair Contract Terms Directive.[81] While the requirements provided under both the Directives in question

---

[78] See Twigg-Flesner (2018a), p. 53.

[79] See EP IMCO Committee Study, *New aspects and challenges in consumer protection: Digital services and artificial intelligence* (2020), at https://www.europarl.europa.eu/RegData/etudes/STUD/2020/648790/IPOL_STU(2020)648790_EN.pdf. See also BEUC (2022), p. 12.

[80] Judgment of the Court of 15 March 2012, Jana Pereničová and Vladislav Perenič v SOS financ spol. s r. o., Case C-453/10, ECLI:EU:C:2012:144.

[81] 'A commercial practice such as that at issue in the main proceedings which consists in indicating in a credit agreement an annual percentage rate of charge lower than the real rate must be regarded as "misleading" within the meaning of Article 6(1) of Directive 2005/29/EC […] in so far as it causes or is likely to cause the average consumer to take a transactional decision that he would not have taken otherwise. […] A finding that such a commercial practice is unfair is one element among others on which the competent court may, pursuant to Article 4(1) of Directive 93/13, base its assessment of the unfairness of the contractual terms relating to the cost of the loan granted to the consumer. Such a finding, however, has no direct effect on the assessment, from the point of view of Article 6(1) of Directive 93/13, of the validity of the credit agreement concluded.' Judgment of the Court of 15 March 2012, Jana Pereničová and Vladislav Perenič v SOS financ spol. s r. o., Case C-453/10, ECLI:EU:C:2012:144, para. 47.

should thus be examined independently of each other, the outcome of the assessment under the Unfair Contract Practices Directive retains relevance for the assessment under the Unfair Commercial Terms Directive. The CJUE's position in *Pereničová* justifies the view that UCPD's and UCTD's open-texted standards may be a robust consumer protection measure in the digital economy.[82]

The Modernisation Directive and the Distance Marketing of the Consumer Financial Services Directive play a significant role in safeguarding consumers in digital environments.[83] While these Directives do not explicitly address AI technology, their provisions apply to platform operators utilising AI systems and algorithms to deliver products and services. They lay down provisions on pre-contractual information, delivery and performance of goods and services, right of withdrawal, and remedies for non-conformity or breach of contract. One crucial aspect the Directives cover is the provision to consumers of accurate and transparent product descriptions and pre-contractual information on product and services. This is particularly important and complex in the context of AI platforms, where algorithms analyse data to generate product recommendations. The Directives aim to ensure that consumers receive clear and reliable information about the products they are purchasing, helping them make informed decisions.

Furthermore, similar to the IDD in the context of insurance products distribution, the MD and DMFSD emphasise pricing transparency. This, too, is of absolute importance with insurance platforms that often utilise AI algorithms to optimise pricing strategies based on various factors.[84] These Directives require that pricing practices be transparent and that consumers can access clear and accurate information regarding product prices, discounts, and additional charges.

Another critical aspect of insurance consumer protection addressed by the MD and DMFSD is the right to withdraw. Under EU law, insurance consumers have the right to withdraw from distance contracts within 14 calendar days without penalty and without giving any reasons.[85] Remarkably, the DMFSD is the first Directive to provide for a right of withdrawal on a maximum harmonisation basis.[86] This right of withdrawal extends to purchases made through AI-powered platforms as well.

---

[82] See EP JURI committee study, *Update the Unfair Contract Terms directive for digital services* (2021), at https://www.europarl.europa.eu/RegData/etudes/STUD/2021/676006/IPOL_STU(2021)676006_EN.pdf.

[83] See Loos (2020), pp. 407–424; Maultzsch (2022), p. 158.

[84] On personalised pricing in insurance see Thouvenin et al. (2019), pp. 210–211; Soyer (2022), pp. 169–170; Tereszkiewicz et al. (2024).

[85] See Article 9 CRD and Article 6 DMFSD with respect to insurance contracts except for contracts falling within the life insurance directive (Directive 2002/83/EC, 2002 O.J. L345/1) and personal pension operations, for which the withdrawal period is 30 calendar days. See also the judgment of CJUE of 19 December 20213, C-209/12 Walter Endress v Allianz Lebensversicherung AG, ECLI:EU:C:2013:864.

[86] See Twigg-Flesner (2018b), p. 117.

Consumers are entitled to request reimbursements if they are not satisfied with purchases made, even if the decision-making process involves AI algorithms.

Both the MD and DMFSD also establish mechanisms for dispute resolution between consumers and businesses relevant to AI platforms. It ensures that consumers have access to fair and efficient procedures to resolve any issues or conflicts arising during their transactions. By providing avenues for recourse in the case of disputes, the MD and DMFSD promote trust and confidence in AI platforms.

Consumer protection authorities in the Member States shall enforce such provisions by exercising their powers to investigate and act against businesses that violate consumer protection laws. While the UCPD does not explicitly acknowledge the role of digital platforms in collecting and intermediating information, insurance platforms that engage in unfair or deceptive practices are subject to its provisions.[87] In this respect, it can be argued that unfair commercial practices by insurance platforms are *per se* aggressive practices because they *implicitly* exercise undue influence on consumers' decision-making processes using the power of technologies (i.e., the case of dark patterns).

It follows that while the MD and DMFSD are not specifically tailored to AI platforms, their provisions can contribute to safeguarding insurance consumer rights in various aspects of commercial transactions, including those conducted through AI platforms. Undoubtedly, one may seriously question whether the above-described rules effectively tackle the power of insurance platforms in e-commerce.[88] While national consumer protection authorities in the EU may apply administrative sanctions such as fines and injunctions to prevent and reduce the proliferation of harmful practices, they often need more financial, personnel and technical resources to enforce these provisions adequately. An important point here concerns the need to provide the authorities with the appropriate technological solutions (also AI-based) and the human expertise required to run them so that compliance in the domain of insurance platforms can be monitored. These solutions would be more effective than the human sweeps presently done over platforms' interfaces to detect non-compliance with the existing rules. While national consumer authorities are aware of the challenge of supervising several diverse platforms and emerging ones, they need the appropriate means to cope with it. Put differently, technologies may offer new opportunities to overcome the well-known shortcomings and inconsistencies of consumer law enforcement while such instruments are at a very early stage of development in the EU.

Finally, a brief reference to the Digital Content Directive[89] should be made. It applies to consumer contracts that have digital content or service as their subject

[87] See in particular point 11a, UCPD Annex: 'Providing search results in response to a consumer's online search query without clearly disclosing any paid advertisement or payment specifically for achieving higher ranking of products within the search results.' This is particularly relevant with respect to platforms aggregating offers of different insurers.

[88] See Kühling and Behnke (2020).

[89] Directive (EU) 2019/770 of the European Parliament and of the Council of 20 May 2019 on certain aspects concerning contracts for the supply of digital content and digital services, OJ L 136,

matter. Nonetheless, Article 3.5. (e) of the Digital Content Directive lays down an exemption for contracts regarding financial services as defined in Article 2 (b) DMFSD, that is 'any service of a banking, credit, insurance, personal pension, investment or payment nature'.[90] The exception remains applicable to insurance platforms acting as distributors of insurance products and services, including insurance comparison websites.

6 Multiple Overlapping Legal Regimes: Gaps and Inconsistencies

6.1 *General Observations*

The overlapping application of legal regimes is primarily possible because of technological convergence. Indeed, the insurance platforms discussed here are an example of technological convergence: they leverage artificial intelligence technologies and integrate them with other functionalities.[91]

The concept of 'technological convergence' refers to the phenomenon whereby different technologies, industries, or functionalities converge and integrate with one another. It occurs when previously distinct technologies (or industries) begin to share common features, functionalities, or platforms.

The problem is that technological convergence raises several challenges for the law. It often blurs traditional sectoral boundaries, making it difficult to determine which laws apply. This can lead to inconsistencies, gaps, and overlaps in applicable legal regimes, making it challenging for lawmakers and regulators to address emerging issues effectively. Moreover, the rapid pace of technological convergence can outstrip the development of specific regulations to address the unique challenges that it poses. As a result, there may be regulatory gaps where existing laws and regulations do not adequately cover the new technological landscape. This can leave legal uncertainties and gaps in consumer protection, privacy, security, and other areas, potentially impacting individuals, businesses, and society. Technological

22.5.2019, pp. 1–27 (referred to as the Digital Content Directive).

[90] Recital 30 of the Digital Content Directive reads as follows: 'Union law relating to financial services contains numerous rules on consumer protection. Financial services, as defined by the law applicable to that sector, in particular in Directive 2002/65/EC of the European Parliament and of the Council, also cover digital content or digital services relating, or giving access, to financial services and are therefore covered by the protection of Union financial services law. Contracts relating to digital content or digital services that constitute a financial service should therefore be excluded from the scope of this Directive'. See also Schulze and Staudenmayer (2020), p. 82.

[91] Online platforms rely on various technologies to operate effectively. Some of the key technologies that power online platforms include Cloud Computing, Big Data Analytics, the Internet of Things (IoT), Application Programming Interfaces (APIs), Blockchain, Data Security and Encryption, Content Delivery Networks (CDNs), and User Interface and User Experience (UI/UX) Design.

convergence requires a multidisciplinary approach: expertise from various fields, including the law, technology, ethics, and social sciences. To develop effective and balanced regulations, policymakers and regulators must understand the technical aspects, societal implications, and ethical considerations associated with converging technologies. The interdisciplinary nature of the challenges makes it necessary to bridge knowledge gaps and foster collaboration among different stakeholders. Indeed, enforcing laws and regulations in the context of technological convergence can be challenging: such technologies often operate across borders, making enforcement efforts more complex. Moreover, compliance with multiple and potentially divergent regulatory frameworks can be burdensome for businesses operating in the converged space.

While the AI Act addresses AI systems, the DSA encompasses online platform design, interfaces and technologies. Both regimes may apply to insurance platforms resulting from technological convergence. Further, these regimes apply in parallel with a general legal regime for consumer protection comprising a set of norms that were not designed to govern consumer markets that are now driven by digital technologies.

The AI Act aims to regulate the development and deployment of AI systems in the EU. It includes provisions to ensure AI's ethical and trustworthy use while safeguarding fundamental rights. The AI Act seeks to protect consumers from potential risks associated with AI technologies by imposing obligations on AI system developers and operators. This concerns addressing issues such as transparency, accountability, and mitigating high-risk AI practices that could harm consumers.

The DSA, on the other hand, primarily targets digital services, including online platforms. It aims to update and modernise the legal framework governing digital services to ensure user safety, address issues related to online content moderation, and promote the accountability and transparency of online platforms. Although the DSA is not specifically tailored for AI platforms, it includes provisions serving to ensure the accountability and responsibility of online platforms in protecting consumers. It addresses issues such as content moderation, advertising practices, transparency in terms and conditions, and user safety. Compliance with the DSA would require insurance platforms to meet the obligations set forth by the Act concerning transparency, user protection, and fair practices. Indeed, while the AI Act and the DSA are not consumer protection measures, they may positively impact transparency and accountability for platforms and AI platforms.

Most importantly, the lack of clarity and coordination with respect to the interplay of overlapping legal regimes can be particularly problematic for enforcing consumer rights in relation to AI platforms. These platforms heavily rely on AI algorithms and automated decision-making processes, which may intersect with consumer rights, privacy regulations, and algorithmic transparency requirements. The overlapping frameworks may provide ambiguous guidelines or fail to address specific challenges unique to AI technology. This uncertainty can hinder effective compliance, increase legal risks, and create challenges in interpreting and applying the rules in the context of AI platforms.

The two following sections provide some examples of the problematic implications of the interplay among these legal regimes regarding the AI Act, the DSA, and consumer acquis.

6.2 Recommender Systems

Recommender systems are a significant aspect of the digital landscape, and both the Digital Services Act and the AI Act recognise their importance. However, the two legal regimes approach recommender systems in different ways. The DSA focuses on recommender systems implemented by Very Large Online Platforms (VLOPs) and large online search engines. It aims to regulate their practices and ensure transparency and accountability. On the other hand, the AI Act takes a narrower perspective, primarily targeting high-risk AI systems.

Currently, there are limited overlaps among recommender systems falling within the scope of the DSA and the AI Act. Most of the recommender systems used by VLOPs would not qualify as high-risk AI systems. Therefore, they would be subject to the rules and requirements of either the AI Act or the DSA but not both.

However, there are certain instances where recommender systems on VLOPs can fall under both laws. For example, recommender systems used by VLOPs to advertise job vacancies in an insurance company would be considered high-risk under Annex III of the AI Act. In such cases, the DSA's requirement for providing an option of a recommender system not based on profiling (Article 29 of the DSA) and the AI Act's requirements for accuracy and robustness (Article 15) would both be applicable.

It is important to note that proposed changes to the high-risk categories covered by the AI Act—such as the potential inclusion of AI systems that interact with children—could significantly expand the number of recommender systems falling under both the DSA and the AI Act. This expansion would result in more significant overlap and the need for comprehensive compliance with the requirements of both regulations.

Thus, recognising the requirements related to recommender systems introduced by the DSA and incorporating provisions for researchers' data access within the AI Act would give rise to a more comprehensive and coherent regulatory framework. This alignment would ensure that recommender systems across various online platforms are regulated consistently and that researchers can effectively contribute to oversight and accountability in the AI domain.

6.3 Information and Disclosure Policies

Given that they pursue different goals and objectives, the DSA and EU Consumer Law are not aligned. First, it has been noted that the DSA does not fully align itself with earlier regulations on consumer protection regarding mandatory disclosures in online contracts, specifically Directive 2002/65/EC concerning the distance marketing of consumer financial services, which is currently under review.[92] This lack of alignment raises concerns about inconsistencies within the EU legal framework. Harmonising regulations and ensuring consistency across different legislative measures is crucial for a coherent and effective legal system.

Second, the DSA largely maintains the protection offered to intermediary service providers under the E-Commerce Directive.[93] This ensures that these service providers are not held directly responsible for their users' content and actions. Moreover, the DSA provides legal certainty to intermediaries, assuring them they will not face negative consequences if they voluntarily monitor their platforms. However, the responsibility for protecting service recipients, such as consumers or individuals, is primarily outsourced to private parties.

Furthermore, it has also been observed that enforcement is to a large extent entrusted to private entities. This approach raises concerns about due process and the potential implications it may have for affected individuals. While the DSA grants powers of investigation and remediation to Digital Services Coordinators and the Commission, it remains to be seen whether these provisions are sufficient to adequately protect the interests of intermediary service recipients, particularly consumers. Balancing the need for effective enforcement with ensuring proper procedural safeguards is essential for maintaining a fair and just regulatory environment.

Lastly, the digital enforcement and cooperation frameworks proposed by the DSA may raise concerns. Given the potential challenges Member States may face in complying with DSA enforcement obligations from a technical perspective, the cooperation frameworks between Member States and the Commission play a crucial role. These frameworks provide the support and assistance necessary to ensure that digital enforcement is effective and that the harmonising impact expected from the DSA is not undermined. Collaboration and coordination among stakeholders are essential for addressing the complexities of digital enforcement and mitigating any potential disparities of compliance across different jurisdictions.

Thus, the DSA raises important considerations regarding the internal coherence of EU law, intermediary liability, enforcement mechanisms, and cooperation frameworks for digital enforcement. Balancing the interests of different stakeholders,

[92] Directive 2002/65/EC was repealed and replaced by Directive (EU) 2023/2673 of the European Parliament and of the Council of 22 November 2023 amending Directive 2011/83/EU as regards financial services contracts concluded at a distance and repealing Directive 2002/65/EC. The new Directive 2023/2673 must be transposed into the legal systems of Member States by 19 June 2026.

[93] Directive 2000/31/EC of the European Parliament and of the Council of 8 June 2000 on certain legal aspects of information society services, in particular electronic commerce, in the Internal Market ('Directive on electronic commerce') OJ L 178, 17.7.2000, pp. 1–16.

including service providers, consumers, and regulatory authorities, is crucial for developing an effective and fair regulatory framework that upholds the principles of accountability, transparency, and due process in the digital realm.

7 Conclusions

The convergence of technologies is rapidly reshaping insurance markets. Businesses increasingly leverage advanced technologies to enhance insurance customer experiences, streamline operations, and drive sales.[94]

One of the most significant ways AI is revolutionising insurance is through personalised customer experiences. By analysing vast amounts of data on consumer behaviour, preferences, and purchasing patterns, AI algorithms generate closely targeted product recommendations and marketing messages that resonate with individual shoppers.[95]

In addition to enhancing insurance customer experiences, AI is streamlining insurance operations through automation and optimisation. AI-powered chatbots, for example, handle routine insurance customer inquiries and support tasks, allowing human agents to focus on more complex issues and providing a more efficient and cost-effective solution for businesses. Similarly, AI-driven inventory management systems analyse sales data and trends to optimise stock levels and minimise the risk of overstocking or stockouts, thus improving operational efficiency and reducing costs.

AI significantly affects insurance pricing and promotions. Dynamic pricing algorithms analyse real-time market data, competitor pricing, and insurance customer demand to determine the optimal price for a given product at any given time. This enables retailers to maximise profits and stay competitive. AI can also optimise promotional strategies by identifying the most effective offers and discounts for specific insurance customer segments, further driving sales and revenue growth.

Despite the benefits of personalised insurance services, some concerns must also be addressed. The expanding presence of insurance platforms raises significant challenges to consumer information and autonomy. While the personalised nature of these platforms enhances user experiences, it can result in filter bubbles and limited exposure to diverse choices. Targeted advertising and data collection practices may infringe on privacy rights and restrict consumers' exploration of alternative products and services.[96] Biased algorithms and content moderation decisions can limit access to diverse perspectives and impede freedom of expression.

[94] See Chen et al. (2022).

[95] See in this volume on how insurance consumers view the use of digital technologies in the insurer-customer relationship: Cichowicz and Tereszkiewicz (this volume).

[96] See Jabłonowska (2022).

This chapter has discussed the overlap and interplay among three main legal regimes—i.e., sectorial rules, the Digital Acquis (i.e., the DSA, the AI Act) and the Consumer Acquis—in regulating digital insurance and platforms. Addressing the challenges of overlapping legal regimes in the EU's rapidly evolving digital insurance sector calls for a multi-faceted approach that coordinates legislation, offers regulatory guidance, employs technological solutions, and actively engages stakeholders. Regulatory guidance can further facilitate this alignment. Regulatory bodies can issue clarifying notes or guidelines that spell out the relationships between different legal frameworks, their application in various digital insurance contexts, and how companies can achieve compliance. Given the specialised nature of the insurance sector, a centralised EU-wide regulatory body—EIOPA—and national supervisory bodies—have a crucial role in issuing guidelines and overseeing digital insurance markets. EIOPA is well-placed to ensure coherence and uniformity across Member States. Further, the jurisprudence of the CJUE will continue to shape the EU legal framework applicable to the insurance business.

Stakeholder engagement remains crucial in ensuring the legal frameworks are pragmatic and responsive to real-world needs. Forums should be established where regulators, industry representatives, and consumer protection agencies convene to share insights and work collaboratively to address existing challenges. Public consultations could offer an additional layer of scrutiny and input, allowing for a broader range of stakeholders, including consumers, to have their say on proposed legal and regulatory changes. One should welcome recent initiatives led by the EIOPA in this respect.[97]

Finally, any framework must remain adaptive to technological and market changes. This calls for the establishment of mechanisms for periodic audits and reviews. These audits would ensure that the legal landscape remains appropriate and adapts to new developments in technology and market behaviour. Moreover, feedback loops could be instituted so that the regulatory body can continuously receive updates from industry players, facilitating timely adjustments to regulations as needed.

Through this multi-pronged approach, we can aspire to create a more cohesive and transparent legal framework that nurtures the insurance industry's digital transformation while robustly protecting insurance consumer rights.

[97] The European Insurance and Occupational Pensions Authority (EIOPA) held a public event about the application of the Insurance Distribution Directive (IDD) on 9–10 March 2023. One of the key topics concerned the digitalisation of insurance and new distribution models. The event organisers concluded that 'even if digitalisation could help consumers to interact with insurance distributors, the human interaction, including in hybrid models, in terms of insurance sales such as life insurance, is not likely to disappear soon', see: https://www.eiopa.europa.eu/media/events/five-years-insurance-distribution-directive-idd-time-take-stock-2023-03-09_en.

References

BEUC (2022) Dark patterns and the EU consumer law acquis. Brussels

Bogucki A, Engler A, Perarnaud C, Renda A (2021) The AI Act and emerging EU digital acquis. Overlaps, gaps, and inconsistencies. CEPS-in-depth analysis (London-Brussels). file:///D:/LIBRARY/CEPS-In-depth-analysis-2022-02_The-AI-Act-and-emerging-EU-digital-acquis.pdf. Accessed 21 Oct 2024

Cappiello A (2018) Technology and the insurance industry. Palgrave Macmillan

Cauffman C, Goanta C (2021) A new order: the Digital Services Act and consumer protection. Eur J Risk Regul 12:758–774

Ceylan IE (2022) The effects of artificial intelligence on the insurance sector: emergence, applications, challenges, and opportunities. In: Bozkuş Kahyaoğlu S (eds) The impact of artificial intelligence on governance, economics and finance, vol 2. Springer

Chen L, Jiang M, Jia F, Liu G (2022) Artificial intelligence adoption in business-to-business marketing: toward a conceptual framework. J Bus Ind Mark 37(5):1025–1044

Cichowicz E, Tereszkiewicz P (this volume) How do consumers inform themselves about insurance products in the digital age? Analysing the results of a consumer survey. In: Poncibò C, Tereszkiewicz P (eds) European insurance law within the digital age. Springer, Cham

Das S, Gao G, Lim E-P (2021) Explainability in AI and its challenges to legal responsibility. AI Soc 35:821–832

De Maesschalck N (2017) The insurance distribution directive: what does it change for intermediaries and for others? In: Pierpaolo M, Michelle S (eds) Insurance regulation in the European Union. Springer, Cham, pp 59–74

Dequen G, Birot F (2020) Artificial intelligence in e-commerce: focus on data protection law. Comput Law Secur Rev 38:105441

Duivenvoorde B (2022) The liability of online marketplaces under the unfair commercial practices directive, the E-commerce Directive and the Digital Services Act. J Eur Consum Mark Law 11

Durovic A (this volume) Smart contracts in insurance law. In: Poncibò C, Tereszkiewicz P (eds) European insurance law within the digital age. Springer, Cham

Durovic M, Kaprou E (2024) The new concept of digital vulnerability and the European rules on unfair commercial practices. In: Crea C, de Franceschi A (eds) Digital vulnerability in European private law. Nomos. Baden-Baden

Ebers M (2021) Liability for artificial intelligence and EU consumer law. J Intellect Prop Inf Technol Electr Commerce Law 1. https://ssrn.com/abstract=3855110. Accessed 21 Oct 2024

Ebers M (2022) Standardising AI - the case of the European Commission's proposal for an Artificial Intelligence Act. In: Di Matteo L, Cannarsa M, Poncibò C (eds) The Cambridge handbook of artificial intelligence: global perspectives on law and ethics. https://ssrn.com/abstract=3900378 or https://doi.org/10.2139/ssrn.3900378

Eling M, Lehmann M (2018) The impact of digitisation on the insurance value chain and the insurability of risks. Geneva Pap Risk Insur Issues Pract 43:359–396

Haluza D, Jungwirth D (2023) Artificial intelligence and ten societal megatrends: an exploratory study using GPT-3. Systems 11(3):120

Heiss H (2023) European business law: insurance law as regulatory private law. In: Andre J, Matthias L, Reiner S (eds) The future of European private law. Nomos, Baden-Baden

Hellwege P (this volume) Innovation and insurance law in legal history. In: Poncibò C, Tereszkiewicz P (eds) European insurance law within the digital age. Springer, Cham

Howells GG, Twigg-Flesner C, Wilhelmsson T (2018) Rethinking EU consumer law. Routledge, London

Infantino M (this volume) Automated personalisation and consumer insurtech in European law: prospects and challenges. In: Poncibò C, Tereszkiewicz P (eds) European insurance law within the digital age. Springer, Cham

Jabłonowska A (2022) Consumer protection in the age of data-driven behaviour modification. J Eur Consum Mark Law 11:2

Jabłonowska A, Lagioia F, Liepiņa R, Micklitz H-W, Sartor G (this volume) Automating compliance assessment of insurance contracts using AI: promises and challenges. In: Poncibò C, Tereszkiewicz P (eds) European insurance law within the digital age. Springer, Cham
Knetsch J (this volume) Data protection rights and automated decision-making in the field of insurance. In: Poncibò C, Tereszkiewicz P (eds) European insurance law within the digital age. Springer, Cham
Kohne T, Brommelmeyer C (2018) The new insurance distribution regulation in the E.U.—a critical assessment from a legal and economic perspective. Geneva Pap Risk Insur Issues Pract 43(4):704–739
Kühling J, Behnke J (2020) Legal challenges of AI-based automated decision-making in e-commerce. Eur J Law Technol 11:1–22
Kumar S, Grover A (2020) Artificial intelligence and data protection: challenges and opportunities in the era of algorithmic decision-making. J Enterp Inf Manag 33(4):651–668
Loos MBM (2020) The modernization of European consumer law (continued): more meat on the bone after all. Eur Rev Priv Law 28(2):407–424
Mak V, Busch C (2021) Putting the Digital Services Act in context. J Eur Consum Mark Law 10
Marano P (2019) Navigating InsurTech: the digital intermediaries of insurance products and customer protection in the E.U. Maastricht J Eur Comp Law 26:294–315
Maultzsch F (2022) Paradigms of EU consumer law in the digital age. In: Kettemann MC, Peukert A, Spiecker gen. Döhmann I (eds) The law of global digitality. Routledge
Mik E (this volume) Smart contracts and the “Oracle Problem” in the context of InsurTech. In: Poncibò C, Tereszkiewicz P (eds) European insurance law within the digital age. Springer, Cham
Mischau L (2022) The concept of digital content and digital services in European contract law. J Eur Consum Mark Law 11
Nicoletti B (2016) Digital insurance. Business innovation in the post-crisis era. Palgrave Macmillan
Nicoletti B (2021) Insurance 4.0. Benefits and challenges of digital transformation. Springer
Ocampo DG, Taneja J, Yong J, Zhu J (2023) From clicks to claims: emerging trends and risks of big techs’ foray into insurance. Bank for International Settlements. FSI Insights on policy implementation 51
Ostrowska M (this volume) The impact of technology on information asymmetry in insurance. What does it mean for the pre-contractual duty of disclosure? In: Poncibò C, Tereszkiewicz P (eds) European insurance law within the digital age. Springer, Cham
Pałka P, Wiśniewska K (this volume) Normative considerations in data-driven personalization of consumer insurance contracts. In: Poncibò C, Tereszkiewicz P (eds) European insurance law within the digital age. Springer, Cham
Paolini A (this volume) Robo-directors and D&O insurance markets: an assessment. In: Poncibò C, Tereszkiewicz P (eds) European insurance law within the digital age. Springer, Cham
Pisoni G (2021) Going digital: case study of an Italian insurance company. J Bus Strateg 42:106–115. https://doi.org/10.1108/JBS-11-2019-0225
Południak-Gierz K (this volume) Problematic consequences of personalization of advertisement – the case of insurance contracts. In: Poncibò C, Tereszkiewicz P (eds) European insurance law within the digital age. Springer, Cham
Schulze R, Staudenmayer D (eds) (2020) EU digital law. Article-by-article commentary. Beck Hart Nomos
Soyer B (2022) Use of big data analytics and sensor technology in consumer insurance context: legal and practical challenges. Camb Law J 81(1):165–194
Talonen A (this volume) Supervisory authorities as value creators in the age of digitalization: towards an ecosystem view of the insurance industry. In: Poncibò C, Tereszkiewicz P (eds) European insurance law within the digital age. Springer, Cham
Tereszkiewicz P (2020) Digitalisation of insurance contract law: preliminary thoughts with special regard to insurer’s duty to advise. In: Marano P, Noussia K (eds) InsurTech: a legal and regulatory view. Springer, Cham, pp 127–146
Tereszkiewicz P, Południak-Gierz K, Walczak P (2024) Digital vulnerability of insurance consumers and personalised pricing of insurance products under GPDR and UCPD. In: Crea C, de Franceschi A (eds) Digital vulnerability in European private law. Nomos. Baden-Baden

Thouvenin F, Suter F, George D, Weber RH (2019) Big data in the insurance industry: Leeway and limits for individualising insurance contracts. JIPITEC 10:209

Tournaire V (this volume) Insurance contract law and smart vehicles under French law. In: Poncibò C, Tereszkiewicz P (eds) European insurance law within the digital age. Springer, Cham

Twigg-Flesner C (2018a) Regulation of unfair commercial practices. In: Howells GG, Twigg-Flesner C, Wilhelmsson T (eds) Rethinking EU consumer law. Routledge, London, pp 46–93

Twigg-Flesner C (2018b) Pre-contractual information duties and the right of withdrawal. In: Howells GG, Twigg-Flesner C, Wilhelmsson T (eds) Rethinking EU consumer law. Routledge, London, pp 94–128

Zenner K, Scott Markus JS, Sekut K (2023) A dataset on EU legislation for the digital world. Bruegel Publications. https://www.bruegel.org/sites/default/files/2023-07/Tables_Scott_Kai.pdf. Accessed 21 Oct 2024

Cristina Poncibò is a professor of Comparative Private Law at the Law Department of the University of Turin and a Fellow at Collegio Carlo Alberto. Cristina is the Scientific Director of the Master's Degree Programme in International Trade Law, organised with ITC-ILO, Uncitral and Unidroit. Cristina has been a Marie Skłodowska-Curie Fellow from the European Commission at Université Panthéon-Assas and a Max Weber Fellow at the European University Institute, Italy.

Piotr Tereszkiewicz Ph.D. (Jagiellonian University in Kraków), M.Jur (Oxford) is a professor at the Jagiellonian University Private Law Department, and a senior affiliated researcher at the University of Leuven (KU Leuven). His research interests include private law, law and economics, insurance law and financial services in a comparative and international perspective. He was Deputy Chair of the Scientific Advisory Committee at the Financial Ombudsman in Poland (2019–2021), and is a board member of the Polish Association of Law and Economics in Warsaw.

Innovation and Insurance Law in Legal History

Phillip Hellwege

1 Introduction

1.1 Innovation and Insurance Law in Legal History: Reflections on How to React in Law to Innovation

When the editors asked me to contribute to the present volume on "European Insurance Law within the Digital Age", I was at first hesitant to accept the invitation. After all, what is a legal historian able to say on digitalization? My fear was that my paper will suffer the same fate as many introductory chapters authored by legal historians in volumes on present legal issues: They are decorative, at best a sort of appetizer, but at the same time they are rather irrelevant and, for that reason, largely ignored. After some consideration, I nevertheless accepted the invitation but at the same time decided to give my contribution a different focus than the other papers to the present volume have. Its primary focus is on *innovation* and law, not on *digitalization* and law. The reason for this broader focus is simple: Digitalization is an innovation. Furthermore, digitalization is an innovation that has already for some decades been, and still is today, a great challenge not only to insurance contract law, but to the entire insurance law, the entire contract law, the entire private law, and the entire legal system. However, it is not the first innovation that the law, and insurance law in particular, had to face. Legal history and insurance legal history have seen countless innovations of different types. In the present contribution, I wish to discuss, by way of example, two such innovations, to analyse their effects on insurance law and the law in general, and to reflect on what these lessons from history may teach us for the general theme of the present volume: "European

P. Hellwege (✉)
University of Augsburg, Faculty of Law, Augsburg, Germany
e-mail: phillip.hellwege@jura.uni-augsburg.de

C. Poncibò, P. Tereszkiewicz (eds.), *European Insurance Law within the Digital Age*, AIDA Europe Research Series on Insurance Law and Regulation 14,
https://doi.org/10.1007/978-3-031-96496-1_2

Insurance Law within the Digital Age". Thus, the present chapter focuses, in essence, on the questions of how the law and lawyers have reacted in the past to innovations and what we can learn from history how to approach today the many challenges that digitalization poses. The present chapter is, therefore, an exercise of self-reflection.

1.2 Classifying Innovation

Before turning to the two examples of innovations in insurance legal history which I wish to discuss, two points need clarification. In the last paragraph, I have written that (insurance) legal history has seen countless innovations of "different types", and it is—this is the first point that needs clarification—necessary to make explicit what I mean when speaking of different types of innovations. If the present chapter's focus is on how the law and lawyers have reacted in the past to innovations and if it wishes to reflect on the lessons that we can learn from history how to face innovations such as digitalization today, we need a clear understanding of how heterogeneous the category "innovation" is.[1]

Some innovations may be characterised as *legal* innovations. The very beginning of private insurance was marked by such a legal innovation: the singling out of the risk element in sea loan contracts and its transformation into a separate type of contract, the marine insurance contract.[2] Even though something is characterised as a legal innovation, does not mean that there is no need for the law to react to it, and indeed it took centuries until the judiciary, the legislature, and legal academia had fully developed a regulatory framework for this new type of contract.[3] *Prima facie* it may seem paradox that there is the necessity for the law to react to legal innovation. However, even today this is something that occurs again and again, and the reason for this phenomenon is simple: Different legal actors are involved. In a first step a new type of contract is designed by in-house counsels or, in the historic example of the invention of marine insurance, by notaries, and thereafter the judiciary, the legislature, and legal academia will try to find answers to the many legal problems this new type of contract poses.[4]

---

[1] There are numerous publications that deal with single innovations and their effects on the law, see, e.g., the contributions in Meier et al. (2020). Furthermore, there is abundant literature on single areas of law and how they deal with, react to, or create a legal framework for the development of innovation, foremost in intellectual property law, tort law, data protection law, or contract law, see, e.g., the contributions in Maute and Mackenrodt (2019) and Grundmann and Möslein (2020). A more general approach can be found in Hoffmann-Riem (2016), who, at pp. 23–26, also discusses possible classifications of innovation.

[2] See on the resulting academic debates Lohsse (2016).

[3] There is abundant literature on the history of marine insurance and marine insurance law. On the development of marine insurance law, see, e.g., Nehlsen-von Stryk (1986), van Niekerk (1998), Rossi (2016), and Merkin (2021).

[4] See, e.g., Martinek (1991–1993) and Bartsch (2000).

Legal innovations may be contrasted with *extra-legal* innovations. An example of such extra-legal innovations are *commercial* innovations. One would think that it is always possible to clearly distinguish legal innovations from extra-legal innovations. Yet, the example concerning the beginning of marine insurance already hints that such distinction may be difficult: Was the singling out of the risk element in sea loan contracts and its transformation into a separate type of contract a legal innovation or was it not rather an innovation in the business model of mediaeval commerce resulting in the invention of a new financial product? Was it, thus, a commercial innovation? The answer to this question will probably depend on who develops it. A legal historian will claim that it was a legal innovation, whereas an economic historian will insist that it was a commercial innovation. In essence, it was both. Insurance is, as has been pointed out by Dreher, a "legal product".[5] It follows that an innovation in an insurer's business model, the invention of a new insurance product, and thus a commercial innovation is always reflected in the insurer's insurance contracts defining the very product and that this innovation is therefore necessarily reflected in the legal sphere. And it also follows that, *vice versa*, an innovation in insurance law will often change the very product which insurers offer and will thus result in a commercial innovation. In the case of insurance as a legal product, legal and commercial innovations will therefore often go hand in hand.[6]

With other innovations in insurance history, it is possible to say that they were truly extra-legal, even though they nevertheless may have had an impact on both the insurers' business models and the legal sphere. Numerous examples come to mind: advancements in fire fighting and fire prevention, advancements in actuarial mathematics, medical innovations such as the invention of the vaccine against smallpox, or the invention of new and quicker forms of communication. As long as fire fighting and fire prevention were underdeveloped and, consequently, the smallest fire was able to develop into a large-scale catastrophe, fire insurance was not able to flourish as insurers would not have been able to assess the risk and as the insured would not have been able to afford the premiums.[7] Advancement in actuarial mathematics was a precondition for modern life insurance to develop.[8] Medical innovations allowed, for example, life insurers to better select and assess the risks against which they offered coverage.[9] The development of new and quicker forms of communication were, for example, of great relevance in marine insurance where information needed to be exchanged between distant places.[10] In distinction to commercial innovations, one may speak of mathematical and technical innovations as well as of innovations in the natural sciences including the life sciences.

---

[5] Dreher (1991).

[6] Hellwege and Rossi (2021), pp. 9–14.

[7] See, e.g., Caja (2021), pp. 76–90, 78; Clayton (1971), p. 36.

[8] For a detailed discussion see section 2.1, below.

[9] See, e.g., Heuermann (2023), p. 185.

[10] For a detailed discussion see section 3.1, below.

1.3 Legislation and the Lex Contractus

The second point that needs clarification concerns the question of what a legal historian working in insurance legal history means when speaking of law. The title of the present volume "European Insurance Law within the Digital Age" presumably uses the term "European Insurance Law" in the meaning of legislation and case law. By contrast, in a paper on insurance legal history that includes the early modern period as well as the nineteenth century, the meaning of law cannot be reduced to legislation and case law, but it is necessary to use a broader understanding. Heuermann opens his dissertation on the history of English and German life insurance law with a quote from a nineteenth-century monograph authored by Jung:[11]

> Ehe Sprachregeln waren, gab es Sprachen; ehe Gesetze waren, gab es Rechtsverhältnisse.
>
> Before there were rules on language [i.e. grammar rules], languages existed; before there was legislation, legal relationships existed.

In the early modern period and the nineteenth century, insurance legislation was still in the making. If we want to understand how the relationship between insurers and policyholders was regulated, we thus have to turn to insurers' statutes and individual insurance contracts.[12] It is, to apply a term which was widely used in nineteenth-century German legal literature,[13] the *lex contractus* which we have to focus on. In a similar vein Art. 1103 of the French *Code civil* states:[14]

> Les contrats légalement formés tiennent lieu de loi à ceux qui les ont faits.
>
> Contracts which are lawfully formed have the binding force of legislation for those who have made them.

Thus, whereas the other contributions to the present volume will most probably observe how the case law and the legislature react, or should react, to digitalization, the present chapter will primarily, but not exclusively, focus on the insurers' statutes and insurance contracts and assess what impact innovations had on them.

However, such a broader view may even be valuable for the other contributions to the present volume: It may be an important observation how in-house counsels working for insurers and drafting insurance contracts react to digitalization, as this may in turn necessitate a reaction by the legislature and the courts and as this may in turn stimulate academic debates. After all, the first legal actors who will face an innovation in the insurance industry are counsels drafting contracts.

In summary, for the general aim of the present chapter—that is to reflect on how the law and lawyers have reacted in the past to innovations and what we can learn

[11] Heuermann (2023), p. 19, citing Jung (1840), p. iii (author's translation).

[12] See already Hellwege (2021a), pp. 139–140.

[13] On this term see already Hellwege (2010), pp. 39–41.

[14] Translation by Cartwright et al. (2016). On the cited provision see Ferid and Sonnenberger (1994), para 1 B 89.

from history of how to approach today the many challenges that digitalization poses—the inclusion of contract practice seems to be valuable.

2 Advancements in Actuarial Mathematics

The seventeenth and eighteenth centuries witnessed great advancements in mathematics, especially the theory of probabilities and actuarial mathematics.[15] These advancements affected not only modern life insurance, but also life annuities and tontines, the traditional support funds for the benefit of widows and orphans as they had existed for example in Germany since the sixteenth century as well as the law in general.[16]

2.1 Advancements in Actuarial Mathematics and the Life Annuity Market

Life annuity contracts existed since the Middle Ages.[17] In a nutshell, an investor pays at the commencement of the contract a sum of money (the capital) to the seller. In return, the seller promises to make annual payments of a fixed sum of money (the annuities) to the annuitant. With the death of the annuitant, the obligation to pay the annuities terminates, and the seller is allowed to keep the capital. However, all of these elements may vary: The investor and the annuitant are often, but not necessarily, the same person. Instead of paying over a capital to the seller, the investor may transfer immovable property to him. Instead of recurring payments, the seller may promise other forms of recurring support to the annuitant. And the parties may also choose that the recurring payments are not contingent on the annuitant's life but are dependent on some other condition. Tontines are a further variation: They are pooled life annuity transactions where the interest on the entire capital paid in by all investors is split between all surviving annuitants in the pool until the last surviving annuitant deceases.[18]

For annuitants, traditional life annuities and tontines are pension products; for sellers, they serve the function of raising capital.[19] Whether life annuities and tontines are able to serve these functions and meet the expectations of both sides to the contract, depends on the calculation of the recurring payments to the annuitant. As a life annuity transaction was, in the regular case, a life contingent investment, it

[15] See, e.g., Wußing (2009), pp. 19–82.

[16] Koch (1998), pp. 25–42; Hellwege (2018), pp. 111–112; Hellwege (2020), pp. 227–228.

[17] On what follows see Ogris (1961).

[18] On early tontine designs see Gallais-Hamono and Rietsch (2018).

[19] On the different functions which tontines served see Hellwege (2018), pp. 106–110.

was the annuitant's life expectancy which should have been the single most important factor for calculating the recurring payments. However, at a time when actuarial mathematics was still underdeveloped and the necessary data not available the calculations were often inexact—often to the disadvantage of the sellers who had promised too high annuities in order to attract investors and raise the needed capital.[20] When life annuities were sold at a large scale, the resulting negative effects for sellers multiplied. Furthermore, this multiplying effect was inherent in tontines as they were pooled life annuity transactions with a large number of investors. With some life annuities and tontines, the resulting financial problems lead to legal problems as sellers, after the conclusion of the contract, tried to modify the scheme's terms, for example to reduce the interest rate they had promised to pay.[21]

The effects that the advancements in actuarial mathematics had on the life annuity market including the market for tontine products were thus simple: Before these advancements were made, unsound life annuity and tontine products had caused manifold financial and legal problems. Now, the sellers of life annuity and tontine products were able to offer financially sound products, thus, avoiding these problems.

2.2 *Advancements in Actuarial Mathematics and Modern Life Insurance*

The effect that the advancements in actuarial mathematics had on the life insurance market was different: These advancements were a precondition for the modern life insurance market to develop. It is usually claimed that the modern life insurance business was invented in eighteenth-century England when the *Equitable Life Assurance Society* was founded in 1762.[22] From England modern life insurance spread to continental Europe with English life insurers entering the continental European markets and with modern life insurance companies being established outside England.

An important, but not the only, motivation for policyholders to enter into life insurance contracts is to provide for dependants. A husband—in the early modern period it was usually the husband who was a family's breadwinner—wants to ensure that his wife and children are provided for in case of his death. Yet, it was possible to provide for dependents even before the invention of modern life insurance. The aforementioned life annuity and tontine products were such options. However, with them the annuitant usually had a right to the annuities immediately after the investor

[20] An example where the issuer of the tontine decided to increase the promised interest rate in the course of marketing the tontine in order to attract more investors, see Hellwege (2018), pp. 74–75, 108–109.

[21] See the examples discussed by Delbrel (2018), pp. 115–116; Pearson (2018), p. 88; Gallais-Hamono and Rietsch (2018), p. 65; Hellwege (2018), p. 95.

[22] Ibbetson (2009), p. 253.

had paid the capital to the seller: Payments usually ended with the annuitant's death, but they did not commence with the investor's death. Life annuities and tontines were a tool to provide for dependents because they were a means to protect an annuitant against the risk that her savings were not sufficient to provide for her until her death as she may have lived longer than anticipated. However, they were not a means to protect against the risk of an early death of a family's breadwinner.

In continental Europe, another option were the aforementioned funds for the provision of widows and orphans that had existed in Germany at least since the second half of the sixteenth century.[23] German literature speaks of *Witwen- und Waisenkassen*. It is likely that these funds were inspired by the support offered by miners' guilds to miners' widows and orphans.[24] In German literature these guilds are called *Knappschaften*. Unlike life annuities and tontines, these *Witwen- und Waisenkassen* and *Knappschaften* were a means to protect dependents against the risk of an early death of a family's breadwinner. However, unlike modern life insurance, they followed a collective risk model:[25] All insured had to make identical contributions, and their dependents received identical support, regardless of the individual risk of death. Thus, the member's age at the time of joining the scheme was irrelevant for calculating the contributions which he owed towards the scheme. The details then varied among the different schemes. With some, the insured had to make fixed contributions and whatever sum was raised was split between all eligible beneficiaries so that the pension, which beneficiaries received, differed according to how many eligible beneficiaries existed. With other schemes, the beneficiaries were promised a predefined sum of money, and the insured had to contribute whatever was necessary to raise the sum to which beneficiaries had a right to. The fact that either the income or the expenses were not predefined guaranteed the financial stability of these schemes. Nevertheless, with both variants the total amount raised simply equalled all bundled risks in the fund. That is why one is able to say that these funds followed a collective risk model: Even though the individual premium did not reflect the insured's individual risk, the totality of the raised income reflected the entirety of all risks. Yet, this statement needs to be qualified as it is an oversimplification. Until the middle of the eighteenth century, the collective risk model was not strictly adhered to. Miners' guilds often did not have separate funds financing the support for widows and orphans.[26] Consequently, it was not only the miners' contributions that financed the support for their widows and orphans. Guilds may have also used their other income to provide for widows and orphans. The *Witwen- und Waisenkassen* were, at least in Germany, often initiated by the sovereigns of the many German principalities for the benefit of, at first, the widows and orphans of Protestant pastors and, later, for the widows and orphans of schoolteachers and civil

---

[23] On such funds for the provision of widows and orphans in Germany, see Wunder (1985).

[24] Hellwege (2020), pp. 241–242.

[25] On what follows see Hellwege (2021b), pp. 81–82; Hellwege (2022), pp. 453–460; Hellwege (2020), pp. 238–266.

[26] Hellwege (2020), pp. 164–167, 224–225.

servants.[27] These funds relied not only on the contributions of their members, but also on offerings collected in churches and on subsidies made by the sovereigns.[28]

By contrast, modern life insurance as invented by the *Equitable Life Assurance Society* in 1762 followed an individual risk model:[29] The premium which each policyholder had to pay reflected the individual risk of death of each insured life. And the most important factor to assess the individual risk of death was the age of the insured life at the time of the conclusion of the contract. Of course, the *Equitable* did not invent the individual risk model. Marine insurance had always followed it.[30] Yet in marine insurance, the individual risk insured was at first not mathematically calculated. It was roughly estimated relying on experience taking into account, among other factors, the type and condition of the vessel, the time of the year, the length of the journey and its destination, the risk of piracy for the planned route, as well as the political situation. Under marine insurance contracts, it was also possible to insure the lives of mariners and passengers.[31] Again, the individual risk of death was decisive for specifying the premium. However, in the marine insurance sector it was only possible to insure a life for a short period of time, for example for a year or for a specific journey. Consequently, it was again the aforementioned factors that defined the insured's individual risk of death. His or her age was largely irrelevant.

The individual risk model was adopted by the newly founded English fire insurance companies already in the late seventeenth century.[32] By contrast, the traditional fire funds, as they existed for example in Germany, again applied the collective risk model. The individual contributions were calculated only on the basis of the value insured, and the individual risk of fire of the insured building was irrelevant for defining the individual contributions. The newly founded English fire insurance companies then calculated the individual premiums on the basis of the single most important factor defining a building's individual risk of fire: the material of which the insured building was made.[33]

The life insurance product offered by the *Equitable* and by all the English and continental European life insurance companies following the example of the *Equitable* differed in many respects, on the one hand, from the protection offered by the *Witwen- und Waisenkassen* and *Knappschaften* in Germany and, on the other hand, from life insurance as it had traditionally been offered throughout Europe in the marine insurance sector:[34] (1) Modern life insurance offered more flexibility to policyholders. The only purpose which the *Witwen- und Waisenkassen* and *Knappschaften* served was to provide for widows and orphans. By contrast, under

---

[27] Hellwege (2020), p. 239.

[28] Hellwege (2020), pp. 238–266.

[29] Bogner (2022), p. 124; Heuermann (2023), p. 145; Hellwege (2022), pp. 460–463.

[30] Hellwege (2022), pp. 460–463.

[31] Hellwege (2022), p. 462.

[32] On what follows see Bogner (2022), pp. 67, 70, 127; Bogner (2021), pp. 29–64.

[33] Ogis (2021), pp. 65–75; Caja (2021), pp. 76–90; Siegwart (2021), pp. 19–27.

[34] On what follows see Hellwege (2021b), pp. 78–84.

modern life insurance the policyholder himself defines the detrimental pecuniary consequences which the death of the insured may have for the beneficiary. In the marine insurance sector, life insurance had always offered such flexibility to the policyholder. (2) In the marine insurance sector, it was only possible to insure a live for a short period of time, for example for a year or for a specific journey. The *Equitable* now offered life insurance for a whole life. In this respect, the modern life insurance products as offered by the *Equitable* are in line with the protection provided by *Witwen- und Waisenkassen* and *Knappschaften* in Germany. (3) Furthermore, the *Equitable* had turned the flexible life insurance product, which had remained in the marine insurance sector a niche product, to its core product. (4) Finally, the *Equitable* promised the payment of a predefined insurance sum against the payment of a predefined premium. In this respect, the product developed by the *Equitable* was comparable to life insurance products in the marine insurance sector. By contrast, the German *Witwen- und Waisenkassen* and *Knappschaften* either promised to pay predefined benefits, but then every member was obliged to contribute whatever was necessary in order to meet the claims of eligible widows and orphans; or they predefined the members' contributions, but then only the existing income was split between eligible widows and orphans.

These changes were only possible because the *Equitable* applied exact premium tables and was, due to the advancements in actuarial mathematics and the availability of more exact data, able to calculate the individual risk of the insured life on the basis of his or her individual age. Of course, the statement that the individual premium reflects the individual risk needs to be qualified. The individual risk is always typified. In the fire insurance sector, the most important factor for typifying the individual risk of a building was the material of which the building was made. In the life insurance sector, the most important factor for typifying the individual risk of the insured life is the age. However, even after the *Equitable* had developed the first modern life insurance product, the advancements in actuarial mathematics did not come to a halt. More exact data allowed insurers to put a price on other risk factors such as specific illnesses of which the insured life suffered at the time of the conclusion of the contract.[35]

In essence, the advancements in actuarial mathematics made possible a commercial innovation: the invention of a new insurance product, i.e. modern life insurance. However, this also had an immediate impact on the law.[36] In Germany, *Witwen- und Waisenkassen* and *Knappschaften* did not need to assess the individual risk of the insured as it was not relevant for calculating the individual contributions which the insured had to pay. Furthermore, these schemes often had compulsory membership. Everybody working as pastor, schoolteacher, civil servant, and miner had to contribute. Consequently, these institutions did not exclude bad risks from coverage. By contrast, the first modern life insurance companies now had to assess the individual risk factors of each assured. Furthermore, they were private companies that did not

[35] Heuermann (2023), pp. 151–161.

[36] Heuermann (2023), pp. 162–237.

have compulsory membership. Rather, they had an interest to insure only those who did not exhibit a high risk of an early death. Consequently, modern life insurance companies, in a first step, had to develop legal rules on how to ascertain the relevant risk factors, and in a second step, the judiciary, the legislatures, and legal academia reacted to the insurers' contract practices.

2.3 Advancement in Actuarial Mathematics and the Insurers' Operating Radius

Advancements in actuarial mathematics had a further impact on modern life insurance. As their business model was based on sound data and on sound calculations, modern life insurers were able to expand their business and their operating radius. By contrast, *Witwen- und Waisenkassen* and *Knappschaften* at first operated locally, only. Again, the expansion of the operating radius had an important effect on the law. Funds that operated only locally usually had knowledge of a member passing away. There was no need for legal rules on how the death of the insured had to be proven to these funds.[37] By contrast, modern life insurance companies had to develop such rules early on.[38] And again, we are able to observe a two-tiered legal reaction to the insurers expanding their operating radius. In a first step, insurers' in-house counsels introduced legal rules in the insurers' statutes and standard contract terms, and in a second step, the judiciary reacted to the corresponding practice.

2.4 Advancements in Actuarial Mathematics and Social Insurance

Witwen- und Waisenkassen and *Knappschaften* were, together with other comparable schemes, an important source of inspiration for Germany's modern social insurance system as established in the second half of the nineteenth century.[39] Germany's modern social insurance system, too, follows the collective risk model. Even though most *Witwen- und Waisenkassen* and *Knappschaften* adhered to the collective risk model even after the reception of the individual risk model by modern life insurance companies, these schemes were nevertheless affected by the advancements in actuarial mathematics. As pointed out above, with some of these schemes, members had to make fixed contributions and whatever sum was raised was split between all eligible beneficiaries so that the pension, which beneficiaries received, differed depending on how many eligible beneficiaries existed. With other schemes, the

[37] Heuermann (2023), p. 125.

[38] Heuermann (2023), p. 251.

[39] Hellwege (2020), pp. 276–315.

beneficiaries were promised a predefined sum of money, and the members had to contribute whatever was necessary to raise the sum to which beneficiaries had a right to. Both systems proved to be unsatisfactory. With the first system, benefits were not predictable, and with the second system, members may have been overly burdened. In the second half of the eighteenth century, these schemes started to promise predefined benefits in exchange for predefined contributions. Even though these schemes still followed the collective risk model, they now had to apply actuarial mathematics in order to see that the total income reflected the entirety of risks.[40] However, for them the task was more difficult than for modern life insurance companies. They could not rely on the standard mortality tables as these schemes covered special professional risks which, for example, miners were exposed to.

2.5 *Advancements in Mathematics and the Law*

The advancements in actuarial mathematics further impacted insurance law: When it became possible to establish financially sound life insurance companies, regulatory debates started that life insurance companies should actually be required to base their business model on sound calculations for the protection of the insured.[41] However, the advancements in mathematics, the theory of probabilities and actuarial mathematics in the seventeenth and eighteenth centuries not only affected insurance law. They had an impact on general private law and on legal methods as Dajczak has recently pointed out.[42]

3 Advancements in Communications: Telegraphy

Telegraphy allows the transmission of messages over long distances. Optical telegraphy had been known since the antiquities but was modernised during the seventeenth and eighteenth centuries.[43] Cable-based electrical telegraphy was invented in the late eighteenth century, it was further developed during the nineteenth century, and since the middle of the nineteenth century a system of undersea telegraphic cables was built revolutionising communications. Now it was possible to transmit information over long distances at great speed—first between cities, then between countries, and later even between continents.

---

[40] Hellwege (2020), pp. 225–228.

[41] With respect to tontines Hellwege (2018), pp. 128–139; with respect to widows' and orphans' funds Hellwege (2020), pp. 265–266.

[42] Dajczak (2024).

[43] On the history of telegraphy Griesbach and Beil (2014); Schneider (1999); Seidel (1980), pp. 16–107.

3.1 Advancements in Telegraphy and Marine Insurance Practice

Even though the advancements in telegraphy were of great importance for insurance practice, their impact on the legal sphere was minor. In marine insurance, insurers never had restricted themselves to offer coverage for vessels and cargo located at the place of their offices. Marine insurance had always been an international business. Early on, a shipowner situated in one port may have sought insurance with a marine insurer based in another port for a ship lying at anchor in yet a third port, a port that was perhaps even located on another continent. This practice raised an immediate problem at a time when information passed only very slowly from one place to another. In principle, an insurance contract was void if the vessel or the cargo had, at the time of the conclusion of the contract, already been lost.[44] Yet, there was an important exception to this principle reflecting the necessities of the insurance market: if both the insurer and the insured were, at the time of concluding the insurance contract, ignorant of the fact that the object to be insured was already lost, the contract was valid. This exception opened the door to possible fraud on the side of the insured. He may have taken out insurance at a point of time when he already knew that the object was lost without disclosing his knowledge to the insurer—a typical situation of an information asymmetry. Actual knowledge is however hard to prove. Consequently, the contract was void not only if the insured knew, but also if he ought to have known of the ship's/cargo's loss at the time of the conclusion of the contract. But when exactly was knowledge to be presumed? Insurance practice took into consideration the time when the ship was lost, the time when the contract was concluded, the distance between the places where the ship was lost and where the insured was located, and the speed with which information could travel by sea and by land. If, on the basis of this data, the information could have reached the insured before taking out insurance, it was taken that he ought to have known of the loss, and the contract was void. This presumption was highly relevant in early insurance practice. Before the advancements in telegraphy, the speed with which information could travel by sea was rather slow, for example three miles per hour. Consequently, the situation that insurance coverage was taken out for a ship or for cargo that had already been lost must have occurred regularly. The situation, however, lost its significance with the advancements in telegraphy.

3.2 Advancements in Telegraphy and General Contract Law

However, telegraphy not only affected marine insurance practice. It also impacted the general contract law. And even though in insurance practice the advancements in telegraphy simply solved a notorious problem, in other areas of law, telegraphy

[44] On what follows see van Niekerk (1998), vol. 1, p. 274, vol. 2, pp. 857–891.

caused problems. In most German territories, it was only public authorities which were allowed to operate telegraphs; in other territories, private companies were allowed to operate telegraphs, too, but only if they had a concession to do so.[45] If telegraphs were operated by public authorities, private individuals were nevertheless allowed to use them: Public authorities offered to contract for the use of telegraphs by private individuals. Even though one of the contracting parties was a public authority, the parties concluded a private law contract. This raised numerous problems and questions in contract law.

3.2.1 Contracting with Telegraph Operators

The question of how to classify a contract is of importance as the classification defines its legal framework. There was a strong view that a contract for the use of telegraphs was, or had to be treated analogous to, a contract of carriage.[46] It was argued that even though the message was not physically transported from one place to another, its content was. The view, that a contract for the use of telegraphs was to be treated as a contract of carriage, had important implications: Under a contract of carriage, a carrier is strictly liable for any damage to, or loss of, the carried goods. Consequently, telegraph operators were strictly liable in case a message was lost, or changed its content, in the process of being transmitted from one place to the other. In order to escape such liability, telegraph operators picked up the practice of other carriers. They used standard contract terms in order to limit, or even exclude, their liability.[47]

3.2.2 Using Telegraphs for the Conclusion of Contracts

One of the many purposes for which private individuals may have used telegraphy was for the conclusion of contracts. Parties located in different places used telegraphs in order to transmit their offers and acceptances. This raised the question of how the contract is concluded when using telegraphs. Contract law scholars distinguish the formation of contract through instantaneous forms of communication and its conclusion through non-instantaneous forms of communication. The only examples of non-instantaneous forms of communication prior to the invention of telegraphs were letters and the use of messengers. In Germany, nineteenth-century lawyers discussed how the existing legal rules on the formation of contracts through non-instantaneous forms of communication could be applied to contracts concluded through telegraphs.[48] Eventually, it was accepted that the existing legal framework

---

[45] On what follows see, e.g., Reyscher (1859), pp. 282–286, 296–298.

[46] See the discussion by Gareis and Fuchsberger (1891), Art. 390 para 4.

[47] Hellwege (2010), pp. 49–50.

[48] See, e.g., Meili (1873), pp. 65–89.

was able to satisfactorily answer all problems relating to the formation of contracts through this new form of communication.

3.3 Advancements in Telegraphy and General Private Law

The famous *Kölner Telegraphenfall* (Cologne telegraphy case), also known as the *Frankfurter Telegraphenfall* (Frankfurt telegraphy case), of 1856 raised another interesting issue.[49] The Cologne banking house Oppenheim had sent a telegram to the Frankfurt banking house Weiller ordering the *purchase* of certain shares. Through the fault of the telegraph operator, Weiller however received a telegram ordering the *sale* of these shares. After Weiller had sold the shares, the mistake was discovered, and Weiller had to repurchase the shares at a loss. As telegraph operators always excluded their liability, the question arose who—Weiller or Oppenheim—had to shoulder the loss. The court in Cologne held that Oppenheim had to make good the loss to Weiller. However, the court also found that there was no contract between Weiller and Oppenheim as the contract was void for mistake. Rather, Oppenheim was liable for damages on the basis that it had used an unreliable means of communication. The case was widely discussed, and today it is primarily remembered because von Jhering saw in it an application of a liability for *culpa in contrahendo*, a basis of liability which he is thought to have invented, thereby analysing the case from the perspective of the *ius commune* even though the Cologne court had applied Rhenish law which was in essence French law.[50] The Cologne telegraphy case draws attention to one final point that is worth mentioning: Telegraphy was not an overnight innovation. Over a long period of time, it was constantly improved. This in turn had an impact on the lawyers' attitude towards telegraphy: In 1856 the Cologne court held that telegraphy was an unreliable means of communication so that the party using it had to make good any loss resulting from it being used in a pre-contractual setting. Today, lawyers would not assess telegraphy as an unreliable means of communication the use of which gives rise to precontractual liability.

3.4 Advancements in Telegraphy and Public Law

Finally, telegraphy raised, at least in nineteenth-century Germany, regulatory questions belonging to the sphere of public law:[51] As already mentioned, in many German territories, it was only public authorities which were allowed to operate

[49] See, e.g., Haferkamp (2008), pp. 254–265.
[50] von Jhering (1861), pp. 6–7, 83–84, 106–112.
[51] See, e.g., Kilger (1993), pp. 81–118.

telegraphs; in other territories, private companies were allowed to operate telegraphs, but they needed a public law concession to do so.

4 Learning from the Past: Digitalization and Insurance Contract Law

The aim of the present contribution is to identify two historical innovations, to point out their manifold effects on the law, and to reflect on what history may teach us for the great challenge which we face today in insurance contract law, insurance law, and the law in general: digitalization. Of course, a legal historian is not able to formulate any recommendation for action let alone any sort of solution ready for implementation. That is trite. Reflecting on history serves in the present context a different purpose. Retrospectively, it is easy to understand a problem, to analyse its implications, to reconstruct how actors facing it reacted, and to evaluate these reactions. By contrast, amidst being confronted with a problem, it may be difficult to understand it in all its complexity. Historical experience may allow us to develop a clearer, more differentiated, and more nuanced view on a present-day problem and thus to better understand the challenge we currently face in the process of digitalization. In summary, the present chapter is foremost an exercise of self-reflection: How have the law and lawyers reacted to innovations in the past? And what lesson can we learn from history of how to approach today the many challenges that digitalization poses? In this last part of my contribution, I will proceed in two steps. In a first step, I will draw the reader's attention to some similarities and differences between the advancements in actuarial mathematics and telegraphy on the one hand and digitalization on the other hand. Against this background, I will then formulate six general propositions on how to react in law to innovation. In the course of this last part of my paper, I will, where suitable, refer to further historical examples—examples that do not necessarily come from insurance history.

4.1 Advancements in Actuarial Mathematics, Telegraphy and Digitalization Compared

4.1.1 Digitalization as a "Querschnittsphänomen"

As digitalization affects every aspect of modern life, it consequently affects all branches of law as much as it affects all disciplines taught in universities. Digitalization is thus an innovation that is a challenge not only to insurance contract law, but to the entire insurance law, the entire contract law, the entire private law, and the entire legal system. For this reason, German lawyers often refer to digitalization in personal discussions as a legal *Querschnittsmaterie*. The German language allows to express complex ideas in compound nouns, and a German lawyer uses the term legal *Querschnittsmaterie* in order to describe a legal discipline (*Materie*) that cannot be classified as belonging to one specific area of law, but that cuts across (*Querschnitt*) different areas of law. However, we have to be careful when using the term *Querschnittsmaterie* in the present context. The reason for being cautious becomes clear when we compare digitalization with other legal *Querschnittsmaterien*.

Modern medical law is a specific legal discipline.[52] However, it is impossible to put medical law as an independent area of law next to the three traditional pillars of continental European legal systems—private law, public law, and criminal law—or to understand it as belonging exclusively to one of these three pillars. Medical law is private law when it discusses the contractual relationship between doctors and patients or when it discusses the doctor's liability in damages for malpractice. It is public law when it discusses the legal framework for the regulatory evaluation of medical products. And it is criminal law when it discusses the doctor's criminal responsibility for malpractice. Medical law is a legal *Querschnittsmaterie* cutting across private, public, and criminal law. Another such *Querschnittsmaterie* is sports law.[53]

Digitalization is different. This is already signalled by the fact that lawyers do not speak of digital law, and if they do so, they presumably mean something different. Of course, there is a specific legal discipline called IT law. IT law is again a legal *Querschnittsmaterie* merging all legal aspects of modern information technology together.[54] With respect to digitalization, lawyers speak of "law and digitalization". They do so in order to signal that they are not limiting themselves to a specific body of law regulating digitalization, but that they are discussing all effects of the extra-legal phenomenon digitalization on the law and that they are analysing all legal aspects of digitalization.[55] In a similar vein, the title of the present volume is "European Insurance Law within the Digital Age". It is not "The Evolution of European Digital Insurance Contract Law", as this would mean something totally different. Yet, as the effects of digitalization cannot be limited to a specific area of law, one could probably speak of a *Querschnittsphänomen*. Traditionally, German lawyers speak of a *Querschnittsmaterie* when they refer to a *legal discipline* that cuts across the different areas of law. By contrast, digitalization is not a legal discipline. It is an extra-legal *phenomenon* that nevertheless cuts across all areas of law. It may, thus, be referred to as a *Querschnittsphänomen*. However, the present volume does not discuss the effects that digitalization has on all areas of law. It does not even discuss the effects of digitalization on the entire insurance law. It has a very specific focus: insurance contract law.

The two examples of innovations from insurance history which I have discussed above, too, were *Querschnittsphänomene*. Actuarial mathematics and telegraphy are not areas of law or legal disciplines, but they are extra-legal phenomena, even

---

[52] Janda (2019), p. 27; Quaas and Zuck (2018), p. vi.

[53] Singbartl and Dziwis (2014), p. 407; Korff (2014), p. v.

[54] Klein (2020), p. 218.

[55] Heckmann and Paschke (2021), Vorwort.

though some nineteenth-century publications actually used the term *Telegraphenrecht* (telegraphy law) in their titles.[56] Nevertheless, these extra-legal phenomena had an impact on different areas of law.

4.1.2 Digitalization as a Long-Lasting Process, Rather than a Single Innovation

The advancements in actuarial mathematics and in telegraphy did not happen overnight. Rather, these advancements were long-lasting processes. In the middle of the eighteenth century, the available data only allowed calculating the mortality risk in relation to the age of the insured at the time of the conclusion of the contract. With the data available in the first half of the nineteenth century it was then possible to understand what impact different illnesses had on the risk of death. This continual progress in actuarial mathematics resulted in a continual adaptation of the standard contract terms of modern life insurers in the eighteenth and nineteenth centuries. When cable-based telegraphy was first used, the Cologne court in the famous Cologne telegraphy case of 1856 held that it was an unreliable means of communication. Today, such reservations have vanished. Similarly, digitalization is a long-lasting process, and at this point it is (at least to a legal historian) not foreseeable what this process is still to bring.

4.1.3 Digitalization: Not One Innovation, but Many Innovations

There is one fundamental difference between the advancements in actuarial mathematics and the development of telegraphy on the one hand and digitalization on the other hand. The former were single innovations even if they experienced continuous improvements. By contrast, digitalization is a label summarising uncountable innovations. For the advancements in actuarial mathematics and telegraphy I have above used the term *Querschnittsphänomen* in the singular. For digitalization it is probably necessary to use the term in the plural: the term digitalization refers to numerous *Querschnittsphänomene*.

4.1.4 Digitalization as Technical Innovations Leading to Numerous Commercial and Legal Innovations

The advancements in mathematics, the theory of probabilities and actuarial mathematics were mathematical innovations. However, they affected the law, and these effects on the law were complex and multi-layered.[57] The advancements in actuarial

[56] See, e.g., Meili (1873).

[57] See section 2, above.

mathematics allowed the sellers of life annuity and tontine products to offer sound products thereby avoiding the many financial and legal problems of the past. Furthermore, they paved the ground for a commercial innovation: the invention of modern life insurance. This new financial product in turn raised numerous new problems which needed to be addressed in insurance contract law, but these advancements also initiated regulatory debates whether it should be required that modern life insurance companies base their business model on sound calculations. The impact in insurance contract law was a two-tiered process: In a first step, in-house counsels solved the numerous problems raised by this new financial product in the insurers' statutes and standard terms of business; in a second step, the judiciary, the legislature, and legal academia had to deal with these developments in legal practice. In addition, the traditional *Witwen- und Waisenkassen* and *Knappschaften* were now able to promise predefined benefits in return for predefined contributions, thereby paving the ground to Germany's modern social security system. Finally, the advancements in mathematics during the seventeenth and eighteenth centuries had an impact on general private law and on legal methods.

Telegraphy was a technical innovation. Yet again, the example of telegraphy proves how multifaceted the implications of a technical innovation on the law may be:[58] Lawyers had to answer the question of how to classify a contract for the use of this new technology. In this particular case, German lawyers decided that it was not a contract *sui generis*, but they treated it analogously to a contract of carriage. They then analysed the legal implications of such classification: Telegraph operators were strictly liable for the loss of, or damage caused to, the message. Telegraph operators, i.e. their in-house counsels, then reacted to the implication of treating the contract for the use of a telegraph analogously to a contract of carriage by excluding their liability in standard contract terms. If telegraph operators were able to exclude their liability, the question arose who had to shoulder the loss caused by the loss of, or damage to, a message: its sender or its recipient. This question in turn supported von Jhering's argument for introducing a liability for *culpa in contrahendo*, the *culpa in contrahendo* being a legal innovation. On a totally different level, the advancements in telegraphy solved a practical problem in marine insurance practice and thereby led to a change in the standard contract terms of marine insurers. Furthermore, we saw that telegraphy had an impact not only on private law, but also on public law.

Digitalization is a label summarising numerous technical innovations. Together, they affect every aspect of our modern lives, and each of these technical innovations may have complex and multi-layered effects on the law. Countless commercial innovations as well as countless legal innovations are based on digitalization as a technical innovation: platform economy, sharing economy, digital payment services, crypto tokens, cloud computing, esports, algorithmic trading, high-frequency trading, robo-advising, digital health services, legal tech, smart contracts, autonomous driving, "work 4.0", and "industry 4.0", to name just some. Each of these innovations may have the same complex and multi-layered effects on the law as the

[58] See section 3, above.

advancements in actuarial mathematics and telegraphy had in the past. And with respect to the effects of digitalization on the law, we may again find a two-tiered, or even multi-tiered, process with in-house counsels of providers of the respective digital solutions implementing legal solutions in the providers' business practices and with the judiciary, the legislature, regulatory bodies, and legal academia reacting to these business practices.

4.1.5 Digitalization as the Fourth Industrial Revolution

Digitalization is often referred to as the fourth industrial revolution.[59] The use of the word revolution signals the disruptive effects digitalization has. However, when referring to digitalization as an industrial revolution, we focus on the impact digitalization has on modern industry. Yet, as pointed out, digitalization affects all aspects of our modern lives. The oft-used term digital revolution thus seems more apt.

4.2 Six General Proposition on How to React in Law to Innovation

In a nutshell, digitalization seems to be a far more complex and far more multi-layered innovation than the innovations we have experienced in the past. This does not mean that our historical experience is of no value. To the contrary, our historical experience is more important than ever. It reminds us of our task in the age of digitalization so that the complexities of digitalization do not bewilder us. Against this background, I would like to formulate six propositions on how to react in law to innovation in general and to digitalization in particular.

4.2.1 We Need to Understand the Problems that Digitalization Cause and that Call for a Reaction in Law as the Single Problem May Not Be Digitalization Itself

The first proposition follows directly from the above comparison with the advancements in actuarial mathematics and telegraphy in legal history: Digitalization is a label summarising numerous technical innovations. These innovations may have complex and manifold effects that need to be addressed by the law and by lawyers as much as actuarial mathematics and telegraphy had diverse effects on the law that evoked reactions in law. In order to react, lawyers need an understanding of these problems: (1) At times, digitalization has led to new business models, and it is these business models which need a reaction in law: platform economy, sharing economy,

[59] Bai et al. (2020), pp. 1–15.

digital payment services, algorithmic and high-frequency trading, robo-advising, and many more. The problems these business models raise are diverse, and they need different answers in law: Algorithmic and high-frequency trading may cause flash crashes resulting in damage to third parties.[60] By contrast, the digital economy may have disruptive effects on individual labour relationships between two parties.[61] In both examples, the effects of a business model based on digitalization which call for a reaction in law are totally different. Or to put it differently: It is not digitalization that causes problems which need to be addressed in law. It is rather different business models based on digitalization that cause problems which need to be addressed in law. (2) At times, in-house counsels may have drafted standard contract terms for a provider of such a digital business model. Then it may become necessary for the judiciary, the legislature, or regulatory bodies to react to the problems raised by such standard contract terms, and legal academia needs to discuss these problems thereby paving the ground for the judiciary, the legislature, or regulatory bodies to act. In these examples, we do not directly react to digitalization but to legal problems caused in the context of digitalization. And as much as the business models based on digitalization are diverse, so are the standard contract terms used by the providers of such services. In each case, we will face very different problems. (3) At times, digital tools may be used in law as much as telegraphy was used for the purpose of concluding contracts. Again, the examples are manifold and go beyond legal tech and smart contracts: In medical law, a patient needs to give an informed consent to his medical treatment, and this raises the question as to how far digital tools may be applied in order to assist the patient to give his or her informed consent.[62] The problem we need to solve here is not defined by digitalization, but by the legal context in which digital tools are applied: medical law. (4) Finally, digital advancements may directly be the object of law. Digital content may be the object of a contract of sale. This raises the question whether, for example, the traditional sales law is apt to handle such situations.[63]

Digitalization is a label summarizing countless technical innovations leading in turn to countless commercial and legal innovations, and each of these single technical, commercial, and legal innovations raises socio-economic or legal problems that may need a reaction in law. These problems are so diverse that it is questionable whether it is of any epistemological value to pull all these problems together under the label of digitalization. The use of the term digitalization somehow implies that there is a common denominator to all these problems. The common denominator is that all these problems are somehow connected to digitalization and that lawyers will need at least some basic understanding of digitalization in order to analyse them. However, it seems that the term digitalization does not refer to a specific type

---

[60] See, e.g., Kollmann (2019).

[61] See, e.g., Riesenhuber (2021), pp. 5–43; Schneider-Dörr (2021).

[62] See, e.g., Stellpflug (2019), pp. 76–81; Spickhoff and Bleckwenn (2013), pp. 1350–1364.

[63] See, e.g., Directive (EU) 2019/770 of the European Parliament and of the Council of 20 May 2019 on certain aspects concerning contracts for the supply of digital content and digital services, Official Journal of the European Union L 136, 22 May 2019, 1–27.

of problem. And the term digitalization also does not refer to any specific solution to these problems. It only refers to the problem's context or its ultimate cause. In a nutshell, we need to rethink the entire legal system in the light of digitalization. If that is all that the word digitalization refers to when we use it in academic legal debate, then its epistemological value is indeed minor. However, one could argue that the use of the term digitalization signals that it is a new problem that may need an innovative answer in law. That brings me to the second proposition: Lawyers must beware of being themselves overly innovative.

4.2.2 We Must Beware of Being Ourselves Overly Innovative

But how do lawyers address the many problems raised by digitalization? Let us be clear: Lawyers themselves are usually not innovative. When facing a novel problem for which a lawyer needs to find a legal solution, the lawyer usually first looks around whether there are any existing legal solutions, legal rules, or legal tools that could be applied to the new problem. The contract for the transmission of a message via telegraphy was treated like a contract of carriage. The traditional rules on the formation of contract through non-instantaneous forms of communication were simply applied to the formation of contract via telegraphy. Equally, in the 1990s there was discussion whether it is possible to apply the traditional rules on the formation of contracts to situations in which contracts are concluded via the internet and in online auctions or whether it is necessary to develop new rules for these situations. In the end it was not deemed necessary to develop new rules.[64] Many people criticise lawyers for always thinking in traditional categories. However, there is an advantage to such a method: It has a stabilising effect. Each new problem puts centrifugal forces on the legal system if we follow the impetus that every new problem needs a novel answer. If we follow that impetus, a legal system will be fragmented. Thus, with each problem we should first ask ourselves whether there is already an answer which we can simply apply. Only when we see that there is none, a lawyer needs to be innovative.

4.2.3 We Will, at First, Find Fragmented Solutions, Only

Nevertheless, innovation always causes a degree of fragmentation in our legal system. The effects of the advancements of actuarial mathematics on the law were, at first, a topic discussed only by specialised lawyers. Similarly, lawyers at first published monographs on "telegraphy law" pulling together and discussing all legal aspects of telegraphy in an isolated fashion.[65] It is also possible to identify such tendencies of fragmentation with other innovations and in situations in which the

[64] See, e.g., Mehrings (1998), pp. 30–33.

[65] See, e.g., Meili (1873).

law faces other types of new problems: In the nineteenth-century, instalment contracts became widely used, leading to a new type of contract and thus to a legal and commercial innovation, the contract being called in German *Abzahlungsgeschäft*. In reaction to the many problems caused by the contract practice surrounding *Abzahlungsgeschäfte*, the German legislature passed the *Abzahlungsgesetz* in 1894.[66] It was a short act of parliament addressing specific problems in a fragmented way. In 1991 it was replaced by the *Verbraucherkreditgesetz* (Consumer Credit Act)[67] that was also based on the respective European directive.[68] As a reaction to new forms of marketing goods to consumers such as door-step-selling or distant selling, legislatures passed in the second half of the twentieth century fragmented legislation addressing the problems caused by these marketing strategies. In Germany, these acts were the *Haustürwiderrufsgesetz* of 1986[69] and the *Fernabsatzgesetz* of 2000,[70] again reflecting corresponding European directives.[71] When standard contract terms became in the nineteenth century a mass phenomenon, the German legislatures reacted in a piecemeal fashion by developing different solutions in the different contexts in which standard contract terms were used, and it took until the second half of the twentieth century until the legislature found a general answer to the use of standard contract terms.[72] In Germany it was the *Gesetz zur Regelung des Rechts der Allgemeinen Geschäftsbedingungen* of 1976[73] which later came under the influence of European legislation.[74] In the 1990s, legal academia pointed to the fragmentary character of these pieces of consumer legislation and demanded a revision on national and European level.[75] In Germany, the fragmentary *status quo* was at least formally ended when in 2002 these diverse acts

---

[66] Gesetz, betreffend die Abzahlungsgeschäfte, 16 May 1894, Deutsches Reichsgesetzblatt 1894, no. 23, 450–451.

[67] Verbraucherkreditgesetz, 17 December 1990, Bundesgesetzblatt 1990 I, 2840–2844.

[68] Council Directive 87/102/EEC of 22 December 1986 for the approximation of the laws, regulations and administrative provisions of the Member States concerning consumer credit, Official Journal of the European Union L 42, 12 February 1987, 48–53.

[69] Gesetz über den Widerruf von Haustürgeschäften und ähnlichen Geschäften, 16. January 1986, Bundesgesetzblatt 1986 I, 122–123.

[70] Fernabsatzgesetz, 27 June 2000, Bundesgesetzblatt 2000 I, 897–899.

[71] Council Directive 85/577/EEC of 20 December 1985 to protect the consumer in respect of contracts negotiated away from business premises, Official Journal of the European Union L 372, 31 December 1985, 31–33; Directive 97/7/EC of the European Parliament and of the Council of 20 May 1997 on the protection of consumers in respect of distance contracts, Official Journal of the European Union L 144, 4 June 1997, 19–27.

[72] In detail Hellwege (2010).

[73] Gesetz zur Regelung des Rechts der Allgemeinen Geschäftsbedingungen, 9. December 1976, Bundesgesetzblatt 1976 I, 3317–3324.

[74] Council Directive 93/13/EEC of 5 April 1993 on unfair terms in consumer contracts, Official Journal of the European Union L 95, 21 April 1993, 29–34.

[75] See, e.g., Zimmermann (1994–1995), pp. 73–80.

were finally integrated into the German Civil Code, the *Bürgerliches Gesetzbuch.*[76] When in the second half of the nineteenth century industrial labour caused grieve social problems, the German legislature equally did not react in the *Bürgerliches Gesetzbuch*, that was then in the making, but legislatures tried to address these problems in special legislation which is again a sign of fragmentation.[77] In Germany, modern labour law only developed after the enactment of the *Bürgerliches Gesetzbuch.*[78] In conclusion, it is a recurring phenomenon in legal history, that a new problem, whether it is caused by technological, scientific, commercial, or legal innovation or whether it is a new socio-economic problem, will at first find a fragmented answer only. It is only at a later stage of the development that lawyers will revise these fragmented answers, that they will embed these solutions into the general legal framework and that they will work out the fundamental principles underlying the single solutions. Fragmentation is always followed by generalisation. With respect to digitalization, we are currently experiencing the first phase of this recurring historical phenomenon.

4.2.4 We May, at First, Find Tentative Answers, Only

Consequently, most substantive answers to legal questions raised by innovation will at first be tentative, only. The reasons are manifold: (1) At first, we identify a single new phenomenon which we as lawyers think needs to be legally addressed, for example bitcoins. Lawyers will try to find answers to the legal problems raised by bitcoins. Only in a second step, lawyers realise that bitcoins are only one example of crypto tokens and that the legal problems raised by crypto tokens may need general answers.[79] Similarly, when lawyers first discussed the liability problems arising from the use of intelligent and autonomous agents, they primarily had autonomous driving systems in mind. Only in a second step, they began to realise that the problem is much wider.[80] (2) Digitalization is, as much as the advancements in actuarial mathematics and telegraphy, a long-lasting process. Digital services and products have seen improvements as is, for example, the case with online banking services. These improvements will necessarily change the legal problems that lawyers need to solve. Consequently, the legal solutions that had already been developed need to be revised, too, due to technical progress. (3) Lawyers have always been criticised for ignoring new problems. However, that is, at least to a certain extent, simply inherent in a lawyers' job description: Lawyers develop legal solutions to problems in real life, and they can only do so after the problem has arisen. In order to be able

[76] Gesetz zur Modernisierung des Schuldrechts, 26 November 2001, Bundesgesetzblatt 2001 I, 3138–3188.

[77] Rückert (2003), p. 751.

[78] Dütz and Thüsing (2021), paras 9–10.

[79] See the contributions in: Maute and Maume (2020) and Maume et al. (2022).

[80] Sommer (2020), p. 71.

to offer a good solution, they then first need to carefully analyse the problem. Lawyers react with a time gap. The covid pandemic has proven the problems of legislation that has been drafted too hastily when lawyers have not taken the time necessary to fully analyse the problem they need to regulate. However, the opposite strategy—that is to wait with developing a legal solution until the problem has fully developed—should also not be followed. In nineteenth-century Germany, a standard argument against codifying insurance contract law was that the insurance market, insurance products, and insurance practice first need to fully develop before a legislature can regulate insurance contracts.[81] Today, we simply cannot wait until we see the outcome of digitalization before starting legal debates. Above, I have claimed that the word digitalization has no epistemological value. The reason why the term is nevertheless widely used in legal academia is perhaps that lawyers want to signal to society that they have started to fulfil their societal duty to find legal solutions to the problems of our time. In all, a tentative answer is better than no answer. However, we need to be willing to critically revisit and revise these tentative answers. Then, it is not a problem that we will, in a first step, develop such tentative answers, only. Or to look at what has been said from yet a different perspective: Our approach to codification has changed over time. In the nineteenth century, codifiers wanted to create codifications that solved legal problems in the most abstract and principled way[82] and that would be in force for generations. Today, it seems that legislatures are expected to react immediately after a problem has arisen. Consequently, we have to accept that the solutions implemented by the legislature may need to be revised soon after they have been enacted, and this also impacts on academic debates.

4.2.5 Digitalization Requires Us to Think Beyond the Limits of Traditional Legal Disciplines

The next point may be short: As much as the advancements in actuarial mathematics and telegraphy were *Querschnittsphänomene* affecting both private law and public law, so are the numerous effects of digitalization. Today, it is at times claimed that the distinction of legal scholarship into private law, public law and criminal law needs to be overcome.[83] In order to develop holistic solutions for the problems caused by digitalization each lawyer, indeed, needs to look beyond his field of specialisation. There is a need for interdisciplinary research. Nevertheless, I personally am a strong proponent of the tripartite division as the principles underlying private, public, and criminal law are fundamentally different.

[81] Compare the discussion by von Kübel (1866), p. 331.

[82] Rückert (2003), p. 571.

[83] Honsell and Mayer-Maly (2015), p. 224.

4.2.6 Law Is a Discursive Discipline

Finally, at a time when we experience the disruptive effects such as those caused by digitalization on the law, we need to remember the essence of law as an academic discipline. First, law is a dogmatic discipline.[84] This links to the observation from above that fragmentation is always followed by generalisation. At least in continental Europe, legal scholarship is based on the assumption that the legal system is a coherent and consistent whole. That is why continental European lawyers feel uneasy with fragmented solutions and why legal scholarship is always working towards generalisation. This is not simply *l'art pour l'art* but is a manifestation of a fundamental principle of justice: to treat like cases alike. In a fragmented legal system, two cases may be decided differently only because they are regulated by two distinct sets of rules and even though they involve exactly the same policy considerations. Overcoming fragmentation in law is a long-lasting process. In doing so, lawyers can apply different methodologies: They may apply the method of legal dogmatics, of legal history, of comparative law, or they may assess the economic and social effects of certain sets of rules. In the case of rules regulating digitalization, they also need to understand the technical side. It is unlikely that any single legal academic will be able to fulfil this task. That is why we need to remember that law is not only a dogmatic discipline, but also a discursive discipline. Different lawyers look onto the same problem from different angles, applying different methodologies thereby furthering legal scholarship. Unlike in other scientific disciplines, legal scholarship is rarely about presenting novel results. Legal history may present novel results. However, in the course of an academic discourse striving towards the solution of a novel problem, legal scholarship is about adding further views and arguments for or against a certain solution. And unlike in other scientific disciplines, in legal scholarship the repetition of arguments has a certain value if it brings out the making of a predominant view or if an argument is rephrased more pointedly, more vividly, and more powerful. When the law and lawyers have to react to innovations and to new challenges, legal scholarship is a debate—it has been in the past as the discussions on the effects of the advancements in actuarial mathematics and in telegraphy on the law have proven, and it is today when we face the digital revolution.

References

Bai C, Dallasega P, Orzes G, Sarkis J (2020) Industry 4.0 technologies assessment: a sustainability perspective. Int J Prod Econ 229:1–15

Bartsch M (2000) Das BGB und die modernen Vertragstypen. Computer und Recht. Zeitschrift für die Praxis des Rechts der Informationstechnologien 3–11

Bogner M (2021) Germany. In: Hellwege P (ed) Essays on a comparative history of fire insurance. Duncker & Humblot, pp 29–64

[84] Compare Rüthers et al. (2021), paras 309–312; Kaufmann (2016), p. 1.

Bogner M (2022) Das Versicherungsvertragsrecht – ein Spiegel der vorgesetzlichen Praxis? Das Binnenversicherungsrecht und seine Quellen vom Preußischen Allgemeinen Landrecht (1794) bis zum Versicherungsvertragsrecht (1908). Duncker & Humblot

Caja E (2021) England. The development of fire insurance after the Great Fire of London. In: Hellwege P (ed) Essays on a comparative history of fire insurance. Duncker & Humblot, pp 76–90

Cartwright J, Fauvarque-Cosson B, Whittaker S (2016) The law of contract, the general regime of obligations, and proof of obligations. The new provisions of the Code civil created by Ordonnance n° 2016-131 of 10 February 2016 translated into English. http://www.textes.justice.gouv.fr/art_pix/THE-LAW-OF-CONTRACT-2-5-16.pdf. Last visited 29 Apr 2022

Clayton G (1971) British insurance. Elek

Dajczak W (2024) Law and mathematics: old problems in the digital era. A plea for reforming today's law school curricula. In: Hellwege P, Soniewicka M (eds) Law and interdisciplinarity. Mohr Siebeck, pp 499–515

Delbrel S (2018) Tontines in France from the Ancien Régime to the Third Republic. In: Hellwege P (ed) The past, present, and future of tontines. A seventeenth century financial product and the development of life insurance. Duncker & Humblot, pp 109–120

Dreher M (1991) Die Versicherung als Rechtsprodukt. Die Privatversicherung und ihre rechtliche Gestaltung. Mohr Siebeck

Dütz W, Thüsing G (2021) Arbeitsrecht, 26th edn. CH Beck

Ferid M, Sonnenberger HJ (1994) Das Französische Zivilrecht, vol 1/1, 2nd edn. Verlag Recht und Wirtschaft

Gallais-Hamono G, Rietsch C (2018) Financial engineering in the 17 and 18 centuries – tontines in England, France, and Ireland. In: Hellwege P (ed) The past, present, and future of tontines. A seventeenth century financial product and the development of life insurance. Duncker & Humblot, pp 49–77

Gareis C, Fuchsberger O (1891) Das Allgemeine Deutsche Handelsgesetzbuch. Guttentag

Griesbach A, Beil B (2014) Telefon/Telegraphie. In: Schröter J (ed) Handbuch Medienwissenschaft. JB Metzler, pp 262–267

Grundmann S, Möslein F (2020) Innovation und Vertragsrecht. Mohr Siebeck

Haferkamp H-P (2008) Der Kölner Telegrafenfall. In: Falk U et al (eds) Fälle aus der Rechtsgeschichte. CH Beck, pp 254–265

Heckmann D, Paschke A (2021) Juris Praxis-Kommentar Internetrecht, 7th edn. Juris

Hellwege P (2010) Allgemeine Geschäftsbedingungen, einseitig gestellte Vertragsbedingungen und die allgemeine Rechtsgeschäftslehre. Mohr Siebeck

Hellwege P (2018) A history of tontines in Germany. From a multi-purpose financial product to a single-purpose pension product. Duncker & Humblot

Hellwege P (2020) From Guild Welfare to Bismarck Care. Professional guilds and the origins of modern social security law and insurance law in Germany. Duncker & Humblot

Hellwege P (2021a) Eine europäische Versicherungsrechtsgeschichte. Ausgangspunkt, Ergebnisse und Perspektiven eines Augsburger Forschungsprojektes. In: Koch A et al (eds) 50 Jahre Juristische Fakultät Augsburg. Mohr Siebeck, pp 129–155

Hellwege P (2021b) Germany. In: Hellwege P (ed) Widows and the history of insurance. Duncker & Humblot, pp 47–94

Hellwege P (2022) Der Beitrag der englischen Privatversicherungspraxis zur Entstehung der deutschen Sozialversicherung. In: Jansen N et al (eds) Iurium itinera. Mohr Siebeck, pp 445–466

Hellwege P, Rossi G (2021) Maritime risk management: marine insurance, general average, sea loan. In: Hellwege P, Rossi G (eds) Maritime risk management. Essays on the history of marine insurance, general average and sea loan. Duncker & Humblot, pp 9–16

Heuermann T (2023) Englisches Lebensversicherungsrecht als Leitbild für deutsches Lebensversicherungsrecht. Entwicklungslinien des selbstgeschaffenen Rechts englischer und deutscher Lebensversicherer im 18. und 19. Jahrhundert. Duncker & Humblot

Hoffmann-Riem W (2016) Innovation und Recht – Recht und Innovation. Recht im Ensemble seiner Kontexte. Mohr Siebeck
Honsell H, Mayer-Maly T (2015) Rechtswissenschaft. Eine Einführung in das Recht und seine Grundlagen, 6th edn. Springer
Ibbetson D (2009) Insurance. English common law. In: Katz SN (ed) The Oxford international encyclopedia of legal history, vol 3. Oxford University Press, pp 252–254
Janda C (2019) Medizinrecht, 4th edn. UVK Verlag
Jung L (1840) Ueber rechtliche Natur und zweckmässige Benutzung der Preußischen Renten-Versicherungs-Anstalt zu Berlin, 2nd edn. Jonas
Kaufmann A (2016) Rechtsphilosophie, Rechtstheorie, Rechtsdogmatik. In: Hassemer W et al (eds) Einführung in die Rechtsphilosophie und Rechtstheorie der Gegenwart, 9th edn. CF Müller, pp 1–22
Kilger F (1993) Die Entwicklung des Telegraphenrechts im 19. Jahrhundert mit besonderer Berücksichtigung der technischen Entwicklung. Telegraphenrecht im 19. Jahrhundert. Peter Lang
Klein UA (2020) Rechtsrealismus und Digitalwirtschaft. Einfluss amerikanischer Rechtstheorie auf Rechtsverständnis und Praxis. Mohr Siebeck
Koch P (1998) Geschichte der Versicherungswissenschaft in Deutschland. Verlag Versicherungswirtschaft
Kollmann H-P (2019) Autonome und intelligente Wertpapierhandelssysteme. Analyse, Regulierung und Haftung. Mohr Siebeck
Korff N (2014) Sportrecht. Kohlhammer
Lohsse S (2016) Vom Seedarlehen zur Versicherung in der mittelalterlichen Rechtswissenschaft. Zeitschrift der Savigny-Stiftung für Rechtsgeschichte. Romanistische Abteilung 133:372–399
Martinek M (1991–1993) Moderne Vertragstypen, 3 vols. CH Beck
Maume P, Maute L, Fromberger M (2022) The law of crypto assets. A handbook. CH Beck
Maute L, Mackenrodt M-O (2019) Recht als Infrastruktur für Innovation. Nomos
Maute L, Maume P (2020) Rechtshandbuch Kryptowert – Blockchain, Tokenisierung, Initial Coin Offerings. CH Beck
Mehrings J (1998) Vertragsabschluß im Internet. Eine neue Herausforderung für das "alte" BGB. MultiMedia und Recht. Zeitschrift für IT-Recht und Recht der Digitalisierung 30–33
Meier J, Zurkinden N, Staffler L (2020) Recht und Innovation. Innovation durch Recht, im Recht und als Herausforderung für das Recht. Dike Verlag
Meili F (1873) Das Telegraphen-Recht. Eine civilistische Abhandlung, 2nd edn. Füssli & Comp
Merkin R (2021) Marine insurance. A legal history, 2 vol. Edward Elgar
Nehlsen-von Stryk K (1986) Die venezianische Seeversicherung im 15. Jahrhundert. Gremer
Ogis S (2021) England. Fire assistance, prevention, and insurance before 1666. In: Hellwege P (ed) Essays on a comparative history of fire insurance. Duncker & Humblot, pp 65–75
Ogris W (1961) Der mittelalterliche Leibrentenvertrag. Ein Beitrag zur Geschichte des deutschen Privatrechts. Herold
Pearson R (2018) The socio-economic setting for developing tontines from the 17th to the 19th centuries. In: Hellwege P (ed) The past, present, and future of tontines. A seventeenth century financial product and the development of life insurance. Duncker & Humblot, pp 79–105
Quaas M, Zuck R (2018) Aus dem Vorwort der 1. Auflage. In: Quaas M et al (eds) Medizinrecht. Öffentliches Medizinrecht – Pflegeversicherungsrecht – Arzthaftpflichtrecht – Arztstrafrecht, 4th edn. CH Beck
Reyscher AL (1859) Das Telegraphenrecht, insbesondere die Haftpflicht aus unrichtiger oder verspäteter Telegraphierung. Zeitschrift für deutsches Recht und deutsche Rechtswissenschaft 19:271–320
Riesenhuber K (2021) Arbeitnehmer(ähnlicher) Schutz von Crowd-Dienstleistern? Zeitschrift für Arbeitsrecht 5–43
Rossi G (2016) Insurance in Elizabethan England. The London Code. Cambridge University Press

Rückert J (2003) Das Bürgerliche Gesetzbuch – ein Gesetzbuch ohne Chance? JuristenZeitung 58:749–760
Rüthers B, Fischer C, Birk A (2021) Rechtstheorie mit Juristischer Methodenlehre, 12th edn. CH Beck
Schneider V (1999) Staat und technische Kommunikation. Die politische Entwicklung der Telekommunikation in den USA, Japan, Großbritannien, Deutschland, Frankreich und Italien. Westdeutscher Verlag
Schneider-Dörr A (2021) Crowd work und Plattformökonomie. Eine arbeitsrechtliche Fallstudie. Nomos
Seidel R (1980) Verkehrsmittel Telegraph. Zur Geschichte der Telegraphie im 19. Jahrhundert bis 1866 unter besonderer Berücksichtigung des Raumes Hannover-Bremen
Siegwart F (2021) Englische und französische Feuerversicherungsbedingungen vor 1900. Gemeinsamkeiten – Einflussnahmen – Unterschiede. Duncker & Humblot
Singbartl J, Dziwis T (2014) "Nach dem Spiel ist vor dem Spiel": Einführung in das Sportrecht am Beispiel des Fußballs. Juristische Arbeitsblätter 407–412
Sommer M (2020) Haftung für autonome Systeme. Verteilung der Risiken selbstlernender und vernetzter Algorithmen im Vertrags- und Deliktsrecht. Nomos
Spickhoff A, Bleckwenn E (2013) Zum Beweiswert digitaler Aufklärungsbögen bei Verwendung elektronischer Signaturen. Versicherungsrecht. Zeitschrift für Versicherungsrecht, Haftungs- und Schadensrecht 1350–1364
Stellpflug MH (2019) Arzthaftung bei der Verwendung telemedizinischer Anwendungen. GesundheitsRecht. Zeitschrift für Arztrecht, Krankenhausrecht, Apotheken- und Arzneimittelrecht 76–81
van Niekerk JP (1998) The development of the principles of insurance law in the Netherlands from 1500 to 1800, 2 vols. Juta
von Jhering R (1861) Culpa in contrahendo oder Schadensersatz bei nichtigen oder nicht zur Perfection gelangten Verträgen. Jahrbücher für die Dogmatik des heutigen römischen und deutschen Privatrechts 4:1–112
von Kübel FP (1866) Die Verhandlungen der Dresdener Bundeskommission zur Ausarbeitung eines allgemeinen deutschen Obligationenrechts über den Versicherungsvertrag. Zeitschrift für Versicherungsrecht 1:321–407
Wunder B (1985) Pfarrwitwenkassen und Beamtenwitwen-Anstalten vom 16.–19. Jahrhundert. Die Entstehung der staatlichen Hinterbliebenenversorgung in Deutschland. Zeitschrift für Historische Forschung 12:429–498
Wußing H (2009) 6000 Jahre Mathematik, vol 2. Springer
Zimmermann R (1994–1995) Civil code and civil law – the "Europeanization" of private law within the European community and the re-emergence of a European legal science. Columbia J Eur Law 1:63–105

Phillip Hellwege is Full Professor and holder of the Chair for Private Law, Business Law and Legal History at the University of Augsburg, Augsburg, Germany. His main research interests are legal history, comparative legal history and insurance legal history.

Normative Considerations in Data-driven Personalisation of Consumer Insurance Contracts

Przemysław Pałka and Katarzyna Wiśniewska

1 Introduction[1]

In the data analytics society, insurance companies can (potentially) access previously unimaginable amounts of data about consumers, both personal data concerning individuals and statistical data concerning various communities.[2] This chapter asks a provocative question: is this bad?

Put in a more intellectually rigid manner, this chapter ponders what uses of data about humans, undertaken by insurance companies when dealing with consumers, should be assessed negatively, and what positively, under various normative theories of consumer law. Is every situation of corporations obtaining access to data concerning consumers detrimental to the latter? Are there data-related practices of insurance companies that might benefit consumers from one viewpoint and, simultaneously, threaten their rights or interests from another?

The motivation behind the chapter is dual.

On the one hand, in law & technology scholarships, the affirmative answer to the first question – "yes, it is bad that insurance companies get access to consumer data" – seems to be almost universally assumed, although almost never argued explicitly. Numerous works scrutinizing the developments in data analytics, when identifying why pervasive data collection and use is problematic (in general),

[1] This chapter is based on a Polish-language text by the authors: Wiśniewska and Pałka (2025). It has been slightly adapted for the international audience.

[2] E.g., Alpaydin (2016), pp. 9–20; Igual and Seguí (2017). pp. 1–3.

P. Pałka (✉) · K. Wiśniewska
Jagiellonian University, Krakow, Poland
e-mail: przemyslaw1.palka@uj.edu.pl; kat.wisniewska@doctoral.uj.edu.pl

C. Poncibò, P. Tereszkiewicz (eds.), *European Insurance Law within the Digital Age*, AIDA Europe Research Series on Insurance Law and Regulation 14,
https://doi.org/10.1007/978-3-031-96496-1_3

mention insurance companies obtaining information only in passing,[3] alongside the threats of discrimination,[4] manipulation,[5] or privacy.[6] However, upon closer examination, this value judgment seems too simplistic. In fact, consumer law's stance on corporations accessing information about humans (as a whole, not only insurance companies) is much more complex than a direct "good" or "bad" evaluation. This is because consumer law attempts to realize several objectives at the same time: lower prices,[7] broader consumer choice,[8] socialization of risk,[9] decisional and contractual autonomy,[10] and overall efficiency.[11] And data's availability to the traders might help advance some of these while complicating others. Hence, firstly, there is a need for scholars to scrutinize the possible effects of data-driven insurance from the point of view of several normative theories.

On the other hand, when pondering policy interventions, some legal scholars have a tendency to treat the choice between various options as legal, and not political, in character. Methodologically, they approach the balancing of different values the way a judge would approach a case; as if one correct and legally determined decision was available in the law. However, in data law in general, and insurance law in particular, there are many equally lawful, possible policy choices. When deciding to intervene in one way or another, the lawmaker acts within the boundaries of the law (constitutional and fundamental rights) but is free to regulate based on political considerations. Of course, this does not mean that every policy choice is equally good. However, the threshold for comparison stems from the adopted normative theories, and not from the existing law. Hence, secondly, there is a need to flush out the political choices inherent in the (potential) reform of the law governing data-driven consumer insurance contracts.

The chapter proceeds in four stages. First, we investigate the socio-technological foundations—specific technical advances and social practices of technological adoption—that make it possible for insurance companies to collect and analyze vast amounts of consumer data. Second, we survey the normative considerations, specifically consumer law and data protection law, both from the point of view of how they facilitate widespread data collection and analysis, and how their principles could guide the evaluation of various data-driven practices. Third, we engage in a thought experiment and imagine a world in which insurance companies possess all the possible data about consumer behavior, discuss various ways in which they could use this data, and assess the pros and cons of such uses under different

[3] Barocas and Selbst (2016) p. 677; Cohen (2019), p. 19; Viljoen (2021), p. 589.

[4] E.g., generally, Ali et al. (2019); Xenidis (2020)

[5] E.g., generally, Calo (2013); Mik (2016); Susser et al. (2019).

[6] E.g., generally, Citron and Solove (2022).

[7] Van Loo (2019), p. 213.

[8] Generally, Dagan and Heller (2017); Osmola (2022).

[9] Howells et al. (2017), pp. 7–8.

[10] Generally, Weatherill et al. (2017); Jagielska (2017), p. 29; Południak-Gierz (2018), pp. 90–92.

[11] Herrine (2022), p. 4.

normative theories. Fourth, we distinguish between the legal and political considerations of a potential legal reform. Finally, we draw our conclusions.

2 The Sociotechnical Underpinnings of the Problem

Even though the considerations of this chapter are based on a thought experiment—the assumption that insurance companies can obtain access to all data documenting consumer behavior—this imagined world is not such a far-fetched, science-fiction-like future. On the contrary, already today, given the changes in technology and social practices of using technology,[12] corporations' factual abilities to collect information are vast. Hence, before moving to the core of the argument, it makes sense to devote several paragraphs to understanding how exactly modern data collection and analytics function.

As of the early 2020s, technology mediates a growing number of once-analog activities. We have apps and platforms for work, shopping, communication, transport, entertainment, exercise, food delivery, and even meditation or prayer.[13] A vast majority of these apps are designed to record user behavior in the form of data.[14] They did not have to be designed this way—something scholars have been pointing out since the 1990s—but online service providers choose to do so as data is a source of value.[15] In what sense?

Data can be directly monetized in many ways, both by increasing profits and lowering costs. In particular, data can be used to personalize commercial communications, especially offers and ads,[16] optimize various processes, including by automation,[17] or gain insights about the market, including monitoring the demand for new products and people's preferences.[18] For example, a company knowing which consumers are potentially interested in buying its product can spend less on advertising and still achieve more sales than in a regular advertising campaign. Similarly, a corporation having access to historical data about fraudulent or risky behavior can use it to automate the processes of fraud detection or risk assessment.[19]

Data can also be monetized indirectly, by selling it, or by selling access to the insights derived from it. Even if a corporation is unable to collect behavior data itself, it might still have an incentive to pay for access, if the price is lower than the expected benefit. Hence, in the case of insurers, one can imagine both a scenario in

[12] Balkin (2015), pp. 46–49.

[13] Generally, Collins et al. (2017); Mahlo and Windsor (2021).

[14] Cohen (2019), pp. 15–25.

[15] Lessig (1999), pp. 543–545.

[16] Mik (2016), pp. 14–16; Hwang (2020), pp. 15–27.

[17] Generally, Susskind and Susskind (2015); Alpaydin (2016); Mcafee and Brynjolfsson (2018).

[18] Generally, Mayer-Schönberger and Ramge (2018).

[19] Generally, Gee (2014).

which they create data-collecting-apps and incentive/mandate policyholders to install them, and a scenario in which they obtain data from third parties.[20]

Importantly, given the advances in data analytics technologies, analyzed in the literature under the heading "big data"[21] or "data science,"[22] one can derive much more knowledge from data than is immediately apparent. This is because in addition to analyzing data about a particular individual (What websites do they visit? What food do they order? Do they meditate? How often do they exercise? Etc.), one can also try to detect patterns by studying this information in the context of data about millions of others.[23] In this sense, a significant amount of data can serve as proxy data for insights visible only on the population-scale.[24] For example, scholars have shown how the music one listens to correlates with race,[25] or the food one likes is linked to political convictions.[26] Of course, this only concerns probability, never certainty; nevertheless, knowing that an individual has a 7% or 81% chance of engaging in risky behavior is already valuable from the point of view of insurance companies.

3 The Normative Underpinnings of the Problem

The process of corporate collection and use of consumer data is governed by several legal regimes, most importantly data protection law (in the EU, enshrined in the General Data Protection Regulation[27]) and consumer law.[28] However, the mere fact that these regulations are in place does not mean that all the possible policy problems are solved. In fact, not only does the existing regime provide less protection than one could assume but also, given the sometimes-contradictory goals of these laws, it is not always clear what "protection" would even mean.

The GDPR aims to secure the fundamental rights of individuals whose data is processed[29] and, simultaneously, facilitate the free movement of personal data within the European Union.[30] It does so by instituting several general principles,[31]

[20] From the technical standpoint. The legal constraints are discussed in the next section.

[21] Generally, Vogl (2021).

[22] Generally, Mak et al. (2018).

[23] Alpaydin (2016), pp. 9–20; Igual and Seguí (2017), pp. 1–3.

[24] Generally, Barocas and Selbst (2016); Prince and Schwarcz (2019).

[25] Generally, Marshall and Naumann (2018).

[26] Generally, DellaPosta et al. (2015).

[27] Regulation (EU) 2016/679 of the European Parliament and of the Council of 27 April 2016 on the protection of natural persons with regard to the processing of personal data and on the free movement of such data, and repealing Directive 95/46/EC (General Data Protection Regulation), OJ L 119, 4.5.2016, pp. 1–88 (hereinafter GDPR).

[28] On the intersections of consumer law and data protection law, see Helberger et al. (2017).

[29] Article 1(2) GDPR; Lynskey (2014).

[30] Article 1(1) GDPR; Article 1(3) GDPR.

[31] See Articles 5-11 GDPR.

endowing individuals with rights,[32] and imposing obligations on the data controllers.[33] Most importantly from the point of view of this chapter, the GDPR requires that for every operation undertaken on personal data, there is a legal basis from Article 6, for example, consent, the necessity for the performance of the contract, the realization of a legal obligation, or legitimate interest of the controller.[34] Hence, it does not stipulate that insurance companies cannot collect and process consumer data; it merely requires that there is a legalizing basis for doing so (and other conditions, as laid out in the Regulation, are met). One can imagine a situation in which data collection and analysis is one of the contractual duties of the insurance company; in such a case, the processing is, in principle, lawful. Nothing stops the parties from agreeing that the consumer must install some app on their phone as a part of their contractual obligations. Or, one can argue that some data-related-activities (like fraud detection), belong to the insurer's legitimate interest.[35] Or, one can imagine the lawmaker placing obligations on the insurers (regarding, e.g., detailed risk assessment) in which case processing would be legal as well. Moreover, the GDPR concerns only the processing of "personal" data, excluding its application from anonymous information, including for statistical or research purposes, i.e., a significant portion of the information valuable to insurers.[36] In summary, even though the GDPR makes data collection and analysis more difficult and costly, it does not—in principle—forbid the insurers from collecting and analyzing policyholders' data. The overall attitude of the GDPR might be that of "data minimization" but the actual rules make it harder, but not impossible, to process vast amounts of data

As for consumer law,[37] its goals are diverse. In continental Europe, especially among civil lawyers, there is a tendency to focus on the protection of the contractual

---

[32] See Articles 12-23 GDPR.

[33] See Articles 24-31 GDPR.

[34] Article 6 GDPR.

[35] Article 29 Data Protection Working Party (2014), Opinion 06/2014 on the notion of legitimate interests of the data controller under Article 7 of Directive 95/46/EC, 844/14/EN WP 217.

[36] Recital 26 GDPR.

[37] In the EU, this means mostly the directives: Council Directive 93/13/EEC of 5 April 1993 on unfair terms in consumer contracts, OJ L 95, 21.4.1993, pp. 29–34 (hereinafter UTD), Directive 2005/29/EC of the European Parliament and of the Council of 11 May 2005 concerning unfair business-to-consumer commercial practices in the internal market and amending Council Directive 84/450/EEC, Directives 97/7/EC, 98/27/EC and 2002/65/EC of the European Parliament and of the Council and Regulation (EC) No 2006/2004 of the European Parliament and of the Council ('Unfair Commercial Practices Directive'), OJ L 149, 11.6.2005, pp. 22–39 (hereinafter UCPD), Directive 2011/83/EU of the European Parliament and of the Council of 25 October 2011 on consumer rights, amending Council Directive 93/13/EEC and Directive 1999/44/EC of the European Parliament and of the Council and repealing Council Directive 85/577/EEC and Directive 97/7/EC of the European Parliament and of the Council Text with EEA relevance, OJ L 304, 22.11.2011, pp. 64–88 (hereinafter CRD), Directive (EU) 2019/771 of the European Parliament and of the Council of 20 May 2019 on certain aspects concerning contracts for the sale of goods, amending Regulation (EU) 2017/2394 and Directive 2009/22/EC, and repealing Directive 1999/44/EC, OJ L 136, 22.5.2019, pp. 28–50 (hereinafter SGD) and DCD.

autonomy of the weaker party,[38] e.g., by introducing mandatory rights,[39] information obligations, [40] and policing the unfair boilerplate clauses[41] or unfair commercial practices.[42] This individualist perspective is warranted but nothing in the text of these laws suggests its primacy over other policy objectives, especially macro and collective. These include, among others, broadening consumer choice,[43] lowering prices,[44] increasing overall efficiency,[45] and socialization of risk inherent in dangerous products.[46]

Importantly, the realization of some of these macro and collective goals is actually helped by the wide availability of information about consumer behavior. Starting with choice, the ability to monitor consumer online and offline behavior might facilitate the creation of new products for which there is demand, or targeted offers fine-tuned to consumer needs. Regarding prices, the fact that for the purpose of defining the scope of the Digital Content Directive,[47] the consumer may provide or undertake to provide personal data to the trader instead of paying the price,[48] helps lower the monetary price or even eliminate it entirely, as is the case with products like Facebook or Twitter. Regarding efficiency, one should remember that the "perfect competition" ideal assumes the situation of "perfect information," where not only do consumers have full knowledge of available goods and services but also all the traders have information about all the consumers' preferences.[49] This is the policy rationale for consumer-oriented disclosures[50] and prohibitions of inserting false information into circulation[51] which, simultaneously, encourages broadening access to data by the traders, as seen in the EU's new legislative instruments, like the Data Governance Act.[52] Further, more information allows to transform uncertainties

---

[38] Generally, Weatherill et al. (2017); Jagielska (2017), p. 29; Południak-Gierz (2018), pp. 90–92.

[39] See Article 9 CRD, Article 13 SGD, Article 14 DCD.

[40] See Article 6 CRD.

[41] See Article 3 UTD.

[42] See Article 5 UCPD.

[43] Generally, Dagan and Heller (2017); Osmola (2022).

[44] Van Loo (2019), p. 213.

[45] Herrine (2022), p. 4.

[46] Howells et al. (2017), pp 7–8.

[47] Directive (EU) 2019/770 of the European Parliament and of the Council of 20 May 2019 on certain aspects concerning contracts for the supply of digital content and digital services, OJ L 136, 22.5.2019, pp. 1–27 (hereinafter DCD).

[48] Article 3(1) DCD.

[49] Generally, Stigler (1957); Varian (2009).

[50] Generally, Ben-Shahar and Schneider (2014); Namysłowska and Jabłonowska (2019).

[51] See Article 6 UCPD.

[52] Regulation (EU) 2022/868 of the European Parliament and of the Council of 30 May 2022 on European data governance and amending Regulation (EU) 2018/1724 (Data Governance Act), OJ L 152, 3.6.2022, pp. 1–44; the Act seeks to improve the conditions for data sharing in the internal market, by creating a harmonized framework for data exchanges and laying down certain basic requirements for data governance, paying specific attention to facilitating cooperation between Member States (Recital 3 Data Governance Act).

about the future into calculable risk,[53] lowering costs of operation and—in the competitive markets—lowering the consumer prices. Finally, the protection of health and safety, and socialization of risk, might be easier and more effective when risky behavior can be predicted using data.

For all these reasons, the mere fact that insurance companies collect, analyze, and use data about (potential) policyholders is not *prima facie* problematic. Some of the uses might clearly be illegal, e.g., if data is publicized without consent or processed in non-secure environments (violating one's right to privacy), or if some practices, like risk assessment or price differentiation, lead to discriminatory outcomes. However, in many other cases, the evaluation of possible data practices is much less evident and will be contingent on the prioritizing of one normative theory over the other. Let us now look at these possible uses.

4 Personal-data-driven Insurance Sector: Pros and Cons for Consumers

One should remember that insurance has always been a data-heavy sector.[54] The very essence of the business is the ability to assess the probability of future risk and calculate the premium in a way that presents competitive market prices while still guaranteeing the corporate profit. This has been done with the use of statistical and demographic data, where long before the advent of modern information technology it was possible to calculate how many accidents would, statistically speaking, occur.[55]

What has changed with the emergence of a society with pervasive data collection is the speed, amount, depth, and granularity of available data. With almost everyone regularly carrying data-collecting, internet-connected devices (like smartphones or wearables) almost always, insurance companies can get access to real-time information about the behavior of individuals, not only the population at large. It is, in principle, possible to know that Przemysław Pałka is riding his bike on an icy road, without a helmet, now, and three times a week; and not only that; 0.7% of males between the ages of 25 and 35 have gotten into bike accidents in the last ten years.

For the purposes of this section—where we scrutinize the possible ways in which insurance companies can use data about (potential) policyholders, under various possible normative theories – we assume that, hypothetically, they can learn everything about the consumers' behavior. This counterfactual, by simplifying the model, prepares the ground for the ideal-type analysis, without having to account for the nitty-gritty of technological and legal preconditions necessary to enable the situations under consideration. In this sense, some horizontal problems—like that of potential privacy breaches, stemming either from intentional disclosure by

[53] Generally, Knight (1921).

[54] Hussain and Prieto (2016), p. 209.

[55] Generally, Calabresi (1965).

corporations to negligent behavior like processing data without proper security and enabling data breaches—should be in the back of our minds for every single case study. These are serious problems and should not be neglected; however, for the purposes of this section, we take them out of the normative equation.

Among many possible ways in which insurance companies could use data about consumers, five will be analyzed:

1. *Product creation*
2. *Consumer acquisition / personalized products*
3. *Risk assessment / personalized pricing*
4. *Influencing policyholders' behavior*
5. *Complaint handling / fraud detection*

Let us now analyze them in the above order.

4.1 Product-creation

When insurance companies know what kinds of risky activities consumers engage in, they can potentially create new insurance products, previously unavailable, for which there might be demand.

Imagine, for example, that in some populations, e.g., young professionals working in Polish cities, there is a significant increase in using bicycles to commute. Suddenly, many more individuals are potential victims of bike theft or accidents, creating a demand for property insurance, accident insurance, or life insurance. Of course, this trend could be noticed without monitoring individuals' behavior; however, with the availability of data, not only can it be noticed faster but also the understanding of the phenomenon (what routes people take, how often they bike, at what time, how do they lock their bikes, etc.) will be greater.

Or consider another example: direct investment in cryptocurrencies. With rising inflation,[56] many people without enough savings to invest in real estate might be tempted to play on the cryptocurrency markets and, with the big exchanges defaulting,[57] opt for storing them in their own individual wallets, bypassing the intermediaries. Such a trend would create new risks of crypto theft if the coinholders do not pay enough attention to cybersecurity, or of getting locked out of their wallets (if they lose the seed phrase necessary to recover it). With these risks might come a demand for new types of property insurance, or even insurance for

[56] At the time of writing this chapter, the inflation rates for Poland, the EU, and the US were 17.5%, 11.10%, and 7.1%, respectively. https://tradingeconomics.com. Accessed December 23, 2022.

[57] Yaffe-Bellany (2022).

previously nonexistent risks, like lock-out insurance. The same considerations as in the previous example apply: such trends are noticeable without direct data collection, but the speed and granularity of data enable the insurance companies to respond to the market demand quicker and with better products.

From the point of view of consumer law, this would be a good development. Not only would it broaden consumer choice but also facilitate the limiting of risk through private insurance.

4.2 Consumer Acquisition/Personalized Products

One of the most popular ways to monetize data is through targeted advertising.[58] The idea behind this is that, given the data about consumers' day-to-day behavior, one can infer information about their interests and preferences not only from purchasing activities (as was assumed under the so-called revealed preferences theory)[59] but also from what sites they visit, how they spend their free time, etc. This enables the advertisers to reach the consumers with the highest probability of wanting to buy their product, while the consumers who would see some ads anyway are exposed to products they might actually need, thereby limiting their search- and other transaction costs.[60]

Insurance companies can clearly benefit from personalized commercial communications. Suddenly, instead of (only) running generic ads, they can propose very specific kinds of insurance products to consumers who need them. A driver-turned-biker might receive an offer for property or accident insurance, an individual crypto-investor, for lock-out insurance, almost immediately after they start engaging in these risky activities. Furthermore, the range of offered products can be broader, given the possibility to move from generic products (e.g., for the entire state) to products tailored to the needs of very specific customers (e.g., property insurance for bicycles just in the city of Warsaw, lock-out insurance just for the Metamask wallet, etc.). As the risk of theft might vary from city to city, or the lockout risk from wallet to wallet, the personalized product might be more suitable than an off-the-shelf version.

Such a development would clearly come with many benefits to consumers. Suddenly, information about the supply-side becomes cheaper, lowering transaction costs, and increasing individual-level efficiency. Wider consumer choice is facilitated, while the measures necessary to avert risk to property or health and safety are available. Prices are lower for consumers living in cities with less theft.

However, such a development also comes with visible threats. As with all personalized ads, there is a danger of manipulation coming from tricking consumers into purchasing products they do not really need, e.g., by displaying the ads at a time

---

58 Mik (2016), pp. 14–16; Hwang (2020), pp. 15–27.

59 Kornhauser (2003), pp. 724–725.

60 For a critical view on the matter, see, generally, Woodcock (2017).

when they are cognitively vulnerable,[61] or exaggerating the level of risk. In such a world, consumers can act against their long-term preferences.[62] The line between manipulation and really good advertising—between coercing consumers into purchases and having them buy things they actually want at a given time, which they later regret purchasing—is admittedly blurred and the scholars are yet to demarcate it properly. Nonetheless, we should be mindful of the risks to contractual autonomy.

4.3 Risk Assessment/Personalized Pricing

Probably the most insurance-specific use of consumer data concerns personalized underwriting, i.e., the risk assessment concerning the specific individual.

For example, regarding accident insurance, companies can now not only obtain general demographic information about the potential policyholder (e.g., that Przemysław Pałka is young and healthy) but also about individual-specific behavior (e.g., that Przemysław Pałka likes to listen to music while biking, is generally prone to distraction, and is so obsessed with his haircut as to, potentially, choose not to wear a helmet). In this sense, he might present a much higher risk of getting into an accident than his colleague of the same age, health, and class, who acts in a way suggesting she is vigilant and risk averse. Or, conversely, he might be obsessed with cybersecurity, reading a lot about the ways to keep the crypto-wallet and the seed-phrase safe, thereby suggesting that the risk of having funds stolen or getting locked out is low. Personalized risk assessment can be directly linked to personalized pricing. Again, premiums of policyholders deemed to present different levels of risk have already varied sometimes, however, with such detailed information available, insurance companies can tailor the price to the specific individual.

This comes with benefits to consumers who behave diligently, in the form of lower prices. Moreover, price discrimination, if occurring in a competitive market and based on calculable risks, can increase overall efficiency,[63] possibly lowering prices even for those who are not the direct beneficiaries of individualized discounts.

However, those individuals deemed to present higher levels of risk would see an increase in premiums that—on top of always being bad for these individuals—could lead to unfair distributive outcomes. What about consumers who, for example, are more prone to distraction not due to conditions they control but simply the personal characteristics of their minds? Is it fair to shift the costs onto them, even if there is nothing they can do to change their behavior? This consideration echoes the very heated debates that, especially in the US, insurance scholars have had regarding so-called "preexisting conditions" in health insurance.[64] Isn't the purpose of insurance

---

[61] Helberger et al. (2021), pp. 5–27.

[62] Porat (2021); Liscow and Markovits (2022), pp. 43–46.

[63] Generally, Bar-Gill (2019).

[64] Generally, Sanford (2013).

to socialize risk in a distributively fair manner? Under some theories of consumer law, this is exactly the goal (Howells et al., 2017).[65] Hence, we see how lowering prices for some consumers, potentially even increasing the overall efficiency, could lead to limiting the choice for others and even denying them insurance protection.

4.4 Influencing Policyholders' Behavior

The risk that individuals face comes not only from unchangeable characteristics but also from day-to-day choices. For example, when getting on a bike well-rested, sober, without earphones, and with a helmet on, the risk of an accident during this one trip goes down. When eating healthily and exercising, the risk of future heart disease goes down. When investing in proper cybersecurity measures, the risk of a hack goes down.

Given that insurance companies can not only obtain data but also send communication, we could imagine a world in which they take measures to incentivize consumers into engaging in safer behavior. This could take place on many different levels of intrusiveness, ranging from soft measures (like sending reminders; "remember to have a helmet on while biking"), to increasing or decreasing premiums depending on the day-to-day behavior (when biking with music on, the premium goes up, when biking without listening to music, the premium goes down), to denying coverage in some situations and informing the consumer about it (you just spent three hours in a bar, paid for several beers with your credit card, if you ride a bike now, you won't be compensated for an accident).

Here, the normative evaluation seems to trigger the strongest intuitive judgments, as we are moving ever closer to the world of "commercial surveillance,"[66] bringing to one's mind the dystopian images from the *Minority Report* or the *Black Mirror.* Indeed, on top of the evident intrusion into one's privacy, the very concept of individual autonomy—central to many conceptions of consumer law—is in clear jeopardy. Not only do consumers become barred from acting upon some of their preferences (what if I like biking after one beer or while listening to a podcast?) but suddenly some external entity, with high market power, is telling them what to do.

And yet, one cannot exclude the possibility that, in some cases, this might actually increase consumer satisfaction. In some general sense, I might have a preference for not breaking my arm, or dying in an accident, over receiving monetary compensation when such an unfortunate event occurs. Discussions about using data to prevent risky behavior have been taking place at least since the 1970s, have taken up new life with the concept of "nudging" gaining prominence,[67] and are far from resolved. Yet, given the increased ability of insurers to collect information about the

[65] Howells et al. (2017), pp. 7–8.

[66] BEUC, The European Consumer Organisation (2022).

[67] Generally, Thaler and Sunstein (2008).

policyholders, and the real prospect of using it to decrease risky behavior (and thereby prices) at the expense of individual autonomy, this trade-off should not escape the minds of those who ponder the regulation of personal-data-driven insurance.

4.5 Complaint Handling/Fraud Detection

The availability of all this information about consumer behavior means not only that their potentially risky activities are documented but also that vast records of the interaction they have with insurance companies emerge. This data, given the rapid uptake of technologies like machine learning, can be used to automate many tasks that, until recently, had to be handled by human employees of insurance companies such as complaint handling or fraud detection. The drive towards automation can be seen in many sectors where knowledge-work is widespread,[68] triggering further discussions from a labor perspective as well as heated debates about the regulation of automated decision-making. Hence, there is a lot of material to learn from when pondering sector-specific regulations in insurance.

As for the benefits for consumers, in a competitive market, automation of work and less fraud (translating into lowering of operation costs) could lead to lower market prices. In addition, if done properly, automation can increase the speed of the interactions with the insurance and, under strict conditions, increase the fairness of the process. However, if done badly, automation can also make it much harder to communicate with the insurers, as well as deny coverage to those who are, mistakenly, deemed to engage in fraud.

5 Legal and Political Considerations in Data-driven Insurance for Consumers

As the discussion from the previous section makes clear, a world in which insurance companies have access to all the available information about consumers' day-to-day behavior would be difficult to assess simply as "good" or "bad." This is the case both because a lot would depend on the exact implementation—as always—but also because some elements of this world would seem beneficial to consumers under one normative theory while detrimental under another.

Moving from philosophical normative considerations into legal and policy ones, we would like to refrain from making very specific recommendations on what the lawmakers, in our view, should do. This is because, as we demonstrate below, while some action might be legally required (by higher-level norms, e.g., the European

[68] Generally, Susskind and Susskind (2015); Alpaydin (2016); Mcafee and Brynjolfsson (2018).

Charter of Fundamental Rights[69]) there are many, equally-legally-acceptable, choices to be made. This does not mean that all these choices are equally good. However, what we would like to offer in this last section is a distinction between the legal questions and the political ones. In a liberal, democratic society, the decisions made by the policymakers—as a matter of fact and principle—could trump the technocratic recommendations. Facilitation of the former, not prescribing the latter, is our ambition.

5.1 *Legally Required Interventions*

There are certain fundamental protections that the policymakers, as a matter of law, must guarantee. For example, given Articles 8 and 9 of the ECFR, European and national law must provide for some privacy and data protection mechanisms in the data-agile economy. Similarly, given the primary law of the EU, the law must guarantee a "high level of consumer protection."[70]

Hence, there will be situations where the goal of regulation is clear. For example, the law must make sure that mechanisms preventing unwanted disclosure of personal data are in place. If an insurance company sitting on a large dataset documenting the behavior of an individual, intentionally communicates this information without a legal basis, this must be illegal and prevented, including by technical means.[71] Similarly, some guarantees for cybersecurity of the data processing systems—aimed at preventing the unintentional disclosure resulting, e.g., from a breach—are necessary. Accountability and transparency of processing, similarly, must be provided for by the law. The question as to what extent the existing regulations, especially the GDPR, already provide for what the law requires is an open one and should be answered not only by looking at the text of provisions but also, or especially, by relying on the empirical data about the efficacy of these norms on the ground.

Similarly, some levels of consumer protection must be guaranteed in the legislation, and actually available as a matter of practice. Especially given the recent developments, increased protection against deception and fraud[72] (on the supply side) is a must, essentially under all the theories of consumer law. Again, the existing regulations do a lot of the heavy lifting already and their actual efficacy, not just the law on the books, must be scrutinized to assess if reform is necessary.

The list could go on: some protection against discrimination must be in place, some checks on automated decision-making must be implemented, etc. Clearly,

---

[69] Charter of Fundamental Rights of the European Union, OJ C 326, 26.10.2012, pp. 391–407 (hereinafter ECFR).

[70] Article 169(1) Consolidated version of the Treaty on the Functioning of the European Union, OJ C 326, 26.10.2012, pp. 47–390.

[71] Generally, Tamò-Larrieux (2018).

[72] Generally, Willis (2020).

however, the law—as a normative threshold—provides only the high-level guidance for the lawmakers, the general lists of "must" and "must not." Their actual implementation is open to discussion. And, in addition, some goals of regulation—when competing values must be assessed vis a vis one another—are up for debate.

5.2 *Political Choices for the Legislature*

Once the fundamental protections are in place, the freedom of choice for the legislature is much broader than many legal scholars tend to assume.[73] Here, we analyze three such choices.

First, regarding targeted advertising: what constitutes manipulation, and what is just really good marketing? The ability to fine-tune commercial communications to specific consumers lowers the transaction costs while, simultaneously, putting consumer autonomy in danger. However, the problem escapes the existing threshold in the UCPD, namely the "misleading" ads. The questions become interesting and difficult when the ads do not contain any untrue information but they are served to consumers in such a manner as to affect their behavior. This is a general challenge that the advertising law must tackle but insurance, with all its specificity, might need a sectoral addition.

Second, when it comes to personalized underwriting and price discrimination, the question the policymakers must answer is: to what extent is the role of insurance law to facilitate subsidies from low-risk policyholders to high-risk ones and, conversely, to what extent should persons be rewarded/punished for presenting high or low levels of risk? Should the answer depend on whether the characteristics in question are malleable or stable? Arguably, answers in both directions are legally admissible, and which one is evaluated as the optimal one will depend on the focus: individual well-being or distributive fairness.

Third, and by far the hardest choice, is to what extent insurance companies should be allowed to use carrots and sticks to nudge (coerce?) consumers into behaving one way or another. This idea clearly triggers an intuitive opposition, given the dystopian images it brings to mind. However, are we so sure that in all cases the private actors (like insurance companies), with the knowledge and means necessary to make the world a safer place, should refrain from doing so? Shouldn't insurers alert consumers when they're driving too fast, seem sleepy behind the wheel, or are about to invest in a very sketchy crypto scheme? Notice that, as a matter of law today, consumers can freely choose to enter contracts where insurance companies do this. So, the question for legal reform is not what the lawmakers should allow but rather what they should prevent. And it is not clear that they should prevent everything. The trade-off, again, boils down mostly to the primacy of

[73] Take, for example, the practice of the ELI to draft "model rules" for the digital economy, as if this was a scientific and not a political exercise; see European Law Institute (2019) and European Law Institute – UNIDROIT (2021).

autonomy or socialization of risk, efficiency, and safety. However, it is more than a technical exercise; it touches upon the very vision of the society we want to live in.

6 Conclusion

In this chapter, we have imagined a world in which insurance companies obtain access to all the data about policyholders' behavior—having scrutinized the technological and legal foundations indicating that this world is not a sci-fi-like thought experiment but actually a possible reality—and assessed this world under various theories of consumer law. We have done so by analyzing five types of uses that insurers can put data to the creation of new products, personalized offers and products, personalized underwriting, influencing policyholders' behavior, and automation of tasks like complaint handling or fraud detection.

We have demonstrated that such a world, contrary to the commonly accepted view, would not necessarily be bad for consumers. How to assess its various elements would very much depend on the adopted normative theory. Personal autonomy might lead to seeing a practice as negative, while efficiency, social solidarity, or lowering of prices make us judge the exact same practice as positive.

Consequently, when pondering the regulation of data-driven consumer insurance contracts, policymakers have some tough choices to make. We have shown how the law provides some general guidance on what must, and must not, find itself in the law. However, some fundamental questions arise regarding the shape of the society we want to live in—what is still good marketing and what is manipulation? To what extent should insurance law be treated as a tool for social redistribution? Or: how far can insurance companies go in influencing the behavior of policyholders?—are up for debate. This debate will be political, and not legal, in character. And the lawmakers should not shy away from holding it openly.

References

Ali M, Sapiezynski P, Bogen M, et al (2019) Discrimination through optimization: how Facebook's Ad delivery can lead to biased outcomes. Proc ACM Hum-Comput Interact 3:199:1–199:30. https://doi.org/10.1145/3359301

Alpaydin E (2016) Machine learning: the new AI. The MIT Press

Article 29 Data Protection Working Party (2014) Opinion 06/2014 on the notion of legitimate interests of the data controller under Article 7 of Directive 95/46/EC, 844/14/EN WP 217

Balkin JM (2015) The path of Robotics law. Calif Law Rev Circuit 6:45

Bar-Gill O (2019) Algorithmic price discrimination when demand is a function of both preferences and (Mis)Perceptions. University of Chicago Law Review 86

Barocas S, Selbst AD (2016) Big data's disparate impact. Calif Law Rev 104:671–732

Ben-Shahar O, Schneider CE (2014) More than you wanted to know: the failure of mandated disclosure. Princeton University Press

BEUC, The European Consumer Organisation (2022) Time to #StopCommercialSurveillance! https://www.beuc.eu/news/time-stopcommercialsurveillance. Accessed December 23, 2022
Calabresi G (1965) The decision for accidents: an approach to non-fault allocation of costs. Faculty Scholarship Series
Calo R (2013) Digital market manipulation. Geo Wash Law Rev 82:995–1051
Citron D, Solove DJ (2022) Privacy harms. BU Law Rev 102:793–864
Cohen JE (2019) Between truth and power: the legal constructions of informational capitalism. Oxford University Press, Oxford, New York
Collins SG, Durington M, Favero P et al (2017) Ethnographic apps/apps as ethnography. Anthropol Now 9:102–118. https://doi.org/10.1080/19428200.2017.1291054
Dagan H, Heller M (2017) The choice theory of contracts. Cambridge University Press, Cambridge
DellaPosta D, Shi Y, Macy M (2015) Why do liberals drink lattes? Am J Sociol 120:1473–1511. https://doi.org/10.1086/681254
European Law Institute (2019) Model Rules on Online Platforms. https://www.europeanlawinstitute.eu/fileadmin/user_upload/p_eli/Publications/ELI_Model_Rules_on_Online_Platforms.pdf, Accessed 23 Dec 2022
European Law Institute – UNIDROIT (2021) Model European Rules of Civil Procedure. https://www.unidroit.org/english/principles/civilprocedure/eli-unidroit-rules/200925-eli-unidroit-rules-e.pdf. Accessed 23 Dec 2022
Gee S (2014) Fraud and fraud detection: a data analytics approach. John Wiley & Sons
Helberger N, Borgesius FZ, Reyna A (2017) The perfect match? A closer look at the relationship between EU consumer law and data protection law. Common Mark Law Rev 54
Helberger N, Lynskey O, Micklitz H-W, et al (2021) EU consumer protection 2.0: structural asymmetries in digital consumer markets.
Herrine L (2022) What is consumer protection for? Loyola Consumer Law Rev 33. https://doi.org/10.2139/ssrn.3781762
Howells G, Twigg-Flesner C, Wilhelmsson T (2017) Rethinking EU consumer law, 1st edn. Routledge, Milton Park, Abingdon, Oxon New York
Hussain K, Prieto E (2016) Big data in the finance and insurance sectors. In: Cavanillas JM, Curry E, Wahlster W (eds) New horizons for a data-driven economy: a roadmap for usage and exploitation of big data in Europe. Springer International Publishing, Cham, pp 209–223
Hwang T (2020) Subprime attention crisis: advertising and the time bomb at the heart of the internet. FSG Originals, New York
Igual L, Seguí S (2017) Introduction to data science. Springer International Publishing, Cham
Jagielska M (2017) Prawo konsumenckie w przyszłym kodeksie cywilnym. Transformacje Prawa Prywatnego 2:23–36
Knight F (1921) Risk, uncertainty and profit. University of Chicago Press
Kornhauser LA (2003) The domain of preference. Univ Pennsylvania Law Rev 151:717–746. https://doi.org/10.2307/3312876
Lessig L (1999) The law of the horse: what cyberlaw might teach. Harv Law Rev 113:501–549. https://doi.org/10.2307/1342331
Liscow Z, Markovits D (2022) Democratizing behavioral economics. Yale Law Economics Research Paper Forthcoming. https://doi.org/10.2139/ssrn.4012996
Lynskey O (2014) Deconstructing data protection: the 'added-value' of a right to data protection in the EU legal order. Int Comp Law Quart 63:569–597. https://doi.org/10.1017/S0020589314000244
Mahlo L, Windsor TD (2021) Feasibility, acceptability, and preliminary efficacy of an app-based mindfulness-meditation program among older adults. The Gerontologist 61:775–786. https://doi.org/10.1093/geront/gnaa093
Mak V, Tai ETT, Berlee A (2018) Research handbook in data science and law. Edward Elgar Publishing
Marshall SR, Naumann LP (2018) What's your favorite music? Music preferences cue racial identity. J Res Personal 76:74–91. https://doi.org/10.1016/j.jrp.2018.07.008

Mayer-Schönberger V, Ramge T (2018) Reinventing capitalism in the age of big data. Basic Books, New York

Mcafee A, Brynjolfsson E (2018) Machine, platform, crowd: harnessing our digital future. New York London

Mik E (2016) The erosion of autonomy in online consumer transactions. Law Innov Technol 8:1–38. https://doi.org/10.1080/17579961.2016.1161893

Namysłowska M, Jabłonowska A (2019) Information obligations and disinformation of consumers: polish law report. In: Straetmans G (ed) Information obligations and disinformation of consumers. Springer International Publishing, Cham, pp 301–337

Osmola S (2022) Reflective choices: a liberal theory of consumer law. Thesis, European University Institute

Południak-Gierz K (2018) Instrumenty indywidualnej ochrony konsumenta w ustawie o przeciwdziałaniu nieuczciwym praktykom rynkowym a "Nowy ład dla konsumentów". internetowy Kwartalnik Antymonopolowy i Regulacyjny 7(6):88-103. doi:https://doi.org/10.7172/2299-5749.IKAR.6.7.7

Porat A (2021) Changing people's preferences by the State and the Law. Theor Inq Law 22:215–246. https://doi.org/10.1515/til-2021-0022

Prince AER, Schwarcz D (2019) Proxy discrimination in the age of artificial intelligence and big data. Iowa Law Rev 105:1257–1318

Sanford ST (2013) The struggle to bury pre-existing condition consideration. St Louis Univ J Health Law Policy 7:405

Stigler GJ (1957) Perfect competition, historically contemplated. J Polit Econ 65:1–17

Susser D, Roessler B, Nissenbaum H (2019) Online manipulation: hidden influences in a digital world. Georgetown Law Technol Rev 4:1–45

Susskind R, Susskind D (2015) The future of the professions: how technology will transform the work of human experts, Reprint edition. OUP, Oxford

Tamò-Larrieux A (2018) Designing for privacy and its legal framework: data protection by design and default for the internet of things, 1st edn. 2018 edition. Springer

Thaler R, Sunstein C (2008) Nudge: improving decisions about health, wealth and happiness, 1st edn. Penguin, London

Van Loo R (2019) Broadening consumer law: competition, protection, and distribution. Notre Dame Law Rev 95:211

Varian HR (2009) Intermediate microeconomics: a modern approach, 8th edn. W. W. Norton & Company, New York

Viljoen S (2021) A relational theory of data governance. Yale Law J 131:573

Vogl R (2021) Research handbook on big data law. Edward Elgar Publishing

Weatherill S, Vogenauer S, Weingerl P (2017) Private autonomy and protection of the weaker party. In: Weatherill S, Vogenauer S (eds) General principles of law: European and comparative perspectives. Hart Publishing

Willis L (2020) Deception by design. Harv J Law Technol 34:116–190

Wiśniewska K, Pałka P (2025) Wykorzystanie danych konsumentów przez ubezpieczycieli: perspektywa normatywna. In: Tereszkiewicz P, Południak-Gierz K (eds) Umowa ubezpieczenia: nowe technologie i prawo konsumenckie. C.H. Beck, Warsaw.

Woodcock RA (2017) The obsolescence of advertising in the information age. Yale Law J 127:2270–2341

Xenidis R (2020) Tuning EU equality law to algorithmic discrimination: three pathways to resilience. Maastricht J Eur Comp Law 27:736–758. https://doi.org/10.1177/1023263X20982173

Yaffe-Bellany D (2022) How Sam Bankman-Fried's Crypto Empire Collapsed. The New York Times. https://www.nytimes.com/2022/11/14/technology/ftx-sam-bankman-fried-crypto-bankruptcy.html. Accessed 23 Dec 2022

Przemysław Pałka is an assistant professor at the Faculty of Law and Administration at Jagiellonian University in Krakow, Poland, and an affiliated fellow at Yale Information Society Project. He is the principal investigator in two projects: "Private Law of Data" (Norway Grants) and "Consumer Law and the Attention Economy" (National Science Center, Poland). He holds a PhD and an LL.M. from the European University Institute in Florence, Italy, and a master's in law from the University of Warsaw, Poland. Before joining Jagiellonian, he was the Fellow in Private Law at Yale Law School (2018–2020) and a researcher at the EUI (2016–2018). His research focuses on economic law, technology, and psychology. The research leading to these results has received funding from the Norwegian Financial Mechanism 2014–2021, project no. 2020/37/K/HS5/02769, titled "Private Law of Data: Concepts, Practices, Principles & Politics."

Katarzyna Wiśniewska is the principal investigator of the project titled "The End of the Consumer – Protecting the Weaker Party in Contractual Relationships in the Digital Market" funded by the National Science Center, Poland. She also served as a researcher in the "Private Law of Data" project (Norway Grants) and the "Consumer Law and the Attention Economy" project (National Science Center, Poland). All of these projects are hosted by the Jagiellonian University in Krakow. Currently, she is pursuing her doctoral studies in Legal Sciences at the University's Doctoral School in the Social Sciences while also practicing as an attorney-at-law. Her research covers a range of topics including private law, new technologies, consumer protection, EU law, and Japanese law. She earned her Master of Arts in 2020 from the Jagiellonian University in Krakow, where she wrote her thesis on cloud computing and the EU's Digital Content Directive, under the supervision of Prof. Dr. Hab. Fryderyk Zoll at the Chair of Civil Law, where she also teaches. Additionally, she holds a postgraduate certificate in IT Resource Management from the Warsaw University of Technology.

Automated Personalisation and Consumer Insurtech in European Law: Prospects and Challenges

Marta Infantino

1 Introduction

The aim of this chapter is to explore the extent to which European is experiencing a trend towards automated personalisation in consumer insurance contracts (with Europe being taken to include continental countries belonging to the European Union) and to draw some observations on the prospects and challenges that this trend raises.

It is well known that big data analytics (BDA), often coupled with artificial intelligence (AI) techniques, affects the insurance value chain through all its stages (marketing, underwriting, risk selection, pricing, claims management), fostering the increasing personalisation of a variety of insurance products and services.[1] In common law jurisdictions, empirical data and critical studies have triggered a substantial debate on the risks of automated personalisation for individuals and the insurance sector as a whole. One can for instance read that, in Australia, supermarket chains operate customer loyalty programs that collect information (not only about spending habits, but also) about members' health and fitness through smartphones and smartwatches, and are "associated with a major private health-insurance company that offers benefits to insured clients who regularly upload health and fitness data onto their platform".[2] In the United Kingdom, it has been noted that "[a]lgorithms are now available to insurers to identify which prospective insureds would be a good

[1] International Association of Insurance Supervisors (IAIS) (2020), p. 4.

[2] Lupton (2016), p. 123.

M. Infantino (✉)
University of Trieste, Department of Political Science, Trieste, TS, Italy
e-mail: minfantino@units.it

C. Poncibò, P. Tereszkiewicz (eds.), *European Insurance Law within the Digital Age*, AIDA Europe Research Series on Insurance Law and Regulation 14,
https://doi.org/10.1007/978-3-031-96496-1_4

bet and which should be avoided. […] Because predictive analytics operates by reference to correlation and not causality, there is a risk of prospectively punishing people for their propensities and not their actions".[3] Again, in the United Kingdom, another commentator observes that "[t]he real-time data obtained from individuals with high health-related risks (not induced by their own lifestyle choices) would mean that they will face high and potentially unaffordable premiums which would no doubt limit their access to basic medical service provision, leading to a further deterioration of their condition".[4] In the United States, a best-selling author wrote more than 5 years ago that "already insurers are using data to divide us into smaller tribes, to offer us different products and services at varying prices",[5] and predicted that "[a]s insurance companies learn more about us, they'll be able to pinpoint those who appear to be the riskiest customers and then either drive their rates to the stratosphere or, where legal, deny them coverage".[6] As another authoritative scholar has commented, "[a]s certainty replaces uncertainty, premiums that once reflected the necessary unknowns of everyday life can now rise and fall from millisecond to millisecond […] Rates based on actual behavior are a big advantage in being able to price appropriately. This kind of certainty means that insurance contracts designed to mitigate risk now give way to machine processes that respond "almost immediately" to nuanced infractions of prescribed behavioral parameters and thus substantially decrease risk or eliminate it entirely".[7] A number of real-world successful experiments with 24/7 behavioral insurance confirm this trend. Consider the commercial success of the US-based company Lemonade Inc., which provides policyholders who are permanently connected with personalised property and casualty insurance.[8] Even more astonishingly, Vitality, a branch of the South-African financial service group Discovery Limited, now sells its self-tracking products for health and life insurance in the US, the UK, and Australia.[9]

From the continental perspective, a question arises as to whether a similar trend is taking place in Europe and whether there are any issues that we, as European consumers and legal scholars, should be concerned about. The hypothesis proposed in this chapter is that the growth of personalised insurtech in common law jurisdictions has been made possible not only by advances in technology but also by local cultural and legal features, which include the weakness of the welfare state and the high costs of private alternatives, lenient approaches to privacy and data circulation, minimal consumer protection and virtually non-existent regulatory oversight of

[3] McGurk (2018), p. 27.

[4] Soyer (2022), p. 186.

[5] O'Neil (2016), p. 164.

[6] O'Neil (2016), p. 171.

[7] Zuboff (2019), p. 213.

[8] See https://www.lemonade.com/fr/en; as well as Talesh and Cunningham (2021), pp. 978–980; McFall et al. (2020), pp. 3–4.

[9] Vitality has also expanded into a number of Asian countries and entered into partnership agreements with a few continental European insurance companies: see https://vitality.international. For an analysis of the history of the company, see Jeanningros and McFall (2020), pp. 6–12; Couldry and Mejias (2019), pp. 134–137.

BDA. Considering that these and other features are either lacking or remarkably different in European countries, it is argued here that any discussion of the opportunities and perils raised by insurtech-driven automated personalisation should take into consideration the specificities of the European legal framework.

Before examining some of these specificities, it is necessary to clarify what is meant by automated personalisation (Sect. 2) and also the hopes and fears associated with its insurtech growth in the common law world (Sect. 3). After a brief description, on the basis of the few empirical data available, of the state-of-the-art of automated personalisation in the European insurance market (Sect. 4), it will be possible to consider some of the distinguishing characteristics of the continental legal framework (Sect. 5). For the sake of clarity, acknowledging the current differences between common law and civil law approaches to automated personalisation and consumer insurtech does not imply that European countries are and will be insulated from the opportunities and challenges opened up by developments on the insurance market (Sect. 6). The important point is that these developments should be appreciated and monitored, embraced or criticised in light of the strengths and weaknesses of the continental legal framework, rather than on the basis of borrowed hopes and imagined fears stemming from common law jurisdictions (Sect. 7). In a world of increased globalization of products and risks, our answer can—and perhaps should—be distinctively European.

2 What Is Automated Personalisation?

Before proceeding further, a few caveats on the very notion of 'automated personalisation' are in order, since the contours of the notion are both ambiguous and misleading.

This is partly due to the "under-specification of personalisation as a concept",[10] which leaves open a number of questions about what exactly is personal, what makes a contract personalized, and what the relationship is between personalization, individual identity and contractual autonomy.

When personalization becomes automated, a further layer of ambiguity is added to the picture. The notion of automated personalization evokes a scenario in which data-fed, machine-driven algorithms capture individuals' unique traits and adapt the contractual response accordingly, offering products, services and conditions that match up with what those individuals (know or do not know they) want. However, such an understanding of the notion falls short of describing how BDA-powered personalizing techniques work.

BDA does not enable people's identities to be found: they are on the contrary constructed. Rather than representing any given individual, algorithmic processing generates "abstracted and decorporealized 'data doubles' that figure or signify

[10] McFall and Moor (2018), p. 209; but see also, with regard to contractual personalization in general, Lynskey et al. (2021), pp. 92, 94–112.

individual actions",[11] many of which have little to do with what one would classify as personal—such as patterns of screen activity and typing speed average, speed of the internet connections used, or the name and version of the operating system installed on a device. These algorithmic data doubles have at best tenuous factual linkages with the individuals to whom information is attached, being based on automated correlations and stereotyping that might (or might not) be reasonable for large numbers but are completely detached from real people (such as 'a person using the X version of the Y browser is more likely to pay a higher price').[12] This is why the notion of automated personalization is misleading: contrary to what the term might suggest, automated personalisation does not lead to individualization; it rather "puts an end to individualisation [...]; treating the person as a commodity or as a product de-individualises them through standardisation techniques".[13] In legal terms, far from offering personalized legal terms and conditions, BDA-driven algorithms "may be seen as offering radically depersonalized law".[14]

Personalization is thus best understood as a form of mass customisation. In the words of the International Association of Insurance Supervisors, mass customization in insurance "involves products/bundles that are designed for mass markets, but which are adjusted slightly for different customers based on individual customer insights obtained through the application of BDA. At their core, these products are not truly individualized, in that they simply follow a mass targeted design template, with minor refinements being made based on the preferences of particular customers".[15] In other words, automated personalization is a misnomer: it hides standardized mass contracting behind the veil of individually-tailored insurance contracts. Moreover, when coupled with constant monitoring, behavioral nudges and real-time adjustment of contractual conditions, personalisation in mass contracts raises further challenges, as the next section will seek to show.

3 Hopes and Fears (from the Common Law World)

Scholarly literature in common law jurisdictions has long highlighted how the reliance on BDA and automated personalization in insurance creates a number of opportunities and concerns for consumers.[16] Opportunities include individual

[11] Burk (2021), p. 1160; see also Lynskey et al. (2021), pp. 94, 104–106; Couldry and Mejias (2019), pp. 128–131; Calo (2017), p. 1021. With specific regard to insurance, cf. Jeanningros and McFall (2020), p. 3–4; Lury and Day (2019); McGurk (2018), pp. 54–55.

[12] Burk (2021), p. 1165; see also Lynskey et al. (2021), p. 104; Couldry and Mejias (2019), pp. 128–131; with specific regard to insurance, McFall and Moor (2018), p. 208.

[13] Lynskey et al. (2021), p. 104.

[14] Burk (2021), p. 1165; see also Lynskey et al. (2021), p. 104.

[15] IAIS (2020), p. 15. Cf. Barsan (2020), p. 59; Cappiello (2020), p. 9; see also Infantino (2022), pp. 615–620; Lynskey et al. (2021), p. 94; Tereszkiewicz and Południak-Gierz (2021), p. 1.

[16] Cf. Talesh and Cunningham (2021), pp. 984–989; Zuboff (2019), pp. 3–4, 200–206; Eubanks (2016), pp. 1–12; McGurk (2018), pp. 6–7, 26–29, 268–269; O'Neil (2016), pp. 161–178; Lupton (2016), pp. 119–127; Swedloff (2014). See also IAIS (2020), pp. 7–8, 14–30.

advertising, more granular segmentation of risks, more risk-sensitive pricing and dynamically-adjusted premiums, as well as the opening up of insurance to previously uninsured groups. However, automated personalization also reduces consumer autonomy in decision-making due to aggressive nudging, solicited (self-) measurements and continuous monitoring through ubiquitous sensors. The inaccuracy of data and the opacity of the algorithms relied upon by insurers risk perpetuating historical biases, ultimately resulting in the financial exclusion of customers who are presumptively classified by algorithms as riskier. It has for instance been noted that “the remote sensate monitoring systems of modern telematics can provide a continuous stream of data about where we are, where we’re going, the details of our [...] behavior [...]. App-based telematics can also calculate how we are feeling and what we are saying by integrating dashboard and even smartphone information”.[17] This allows insurance companies not only to address their current and prospective customers with micro-targeted ads and behavioral nudges, but also to scrape “big data sets to develop customer profiles, with the result that disadvantaged groups suffer further disadvantage by being targeted for differential offers or excluded altogether because they are not viewed as profitable or as poor credit risks”.[18] According to another commentator, “[i]nstead of smoothing out life’s bums, insurance companies will demand payment for those bumps in advance. This undermines the point of insurance, and the hits will fall especially hard on those who can least afford them”.[19]

These accounts are extremely persuasive, as far as common law jurisdictions are concerned.[20] They essentially describe a world of surveillance capitalism, in which incumbent and non-incumbent insurance companies compete in monitoring individuals 24/7 through a myriad of interconnected objects (smartphones, laptops, sensors and cameras), resulting in a 360-degree exposure of the underwriters, submerging consumers with profiled offers and behavioral reward programs.

Do these very same accounts fairly describe the state of the art in Europe? Given the current absence of clear empirical data concerning the European market for automated personalized insurance,[21] the debate by European supervisory agencies and scholars largely consider the above “scenarios of intensely surveillant, personalised insurance use cases [...] as the ubiquitous, nearly present, already unavoidable, now”,[22] and then replicate the arguments put forward by fellow authorities and

[17] See for instance Zuboff (2019), p. 213.

[18] Lupton (2016), p. 120.

[19] O’Neil (2016), p. 171.

[20] Of course, the developments mentioned in the text affect common law jurisdictions in different ways and to a different extent; for instance it is clear that the legacy of EU law and the participation in the Council of Europe’s human rights system by the United Kingdom make much of the above considerations less persuasive for common law jurisdictions in the UK than for other common law countries.

[21] The lack of empirical data, especially outside the US, has been emphasized by many: see Francois and Voldoire (2022), p. 2; Frick (2020); McFall et al. (2020), p. 1; Tanninen (2020), pp. 5–6; EIOPA (2019), pp. 15–17; McFall and Moor (2018), p. 205.

[22] McFall et al. (2020), p. 6.

colleagues in common law jurisdictions.[23] However, there are several reasons to be dissatisfied with this approach, which focuses predominantly on common law jurisdictions, assumes that developments in these inevitably set out a roadmap for developments elsewhere, and overlooks current experiences in different markets and legal frameworks.[24] While it may indeed be the case that automated personalization in insurance is the future for all of us, its concrete manifestations and impact should nevertheless be appreciated in context.

4 The State-of-the-Art in Europe

As noted above, there is no clear empirical data on the actual extent to which the European insurance market already relies on BDA and specifically for which purposes.

What seems to be clear is that, for the time being, the main actors in the field are incumbent insurance companies rather than start-ups and big tech companies. These companies are increasingly experimenting with digitalization, BDA and AI, largely relying either on in-house innovation or on collaborations with partners that are subject to insurance supervision.[25] This is important because many of the developments outlined in the previous section in relation to common law jurisdictions have occurred through partnerships and cooperation agreements between insurance companies and innovative start-ups or big tech concerning the sharing of data or the supply of hardware and software (such as IoT devices and machine learning models).[26] Of course, there is also an emerging market in Europe for non-incumbent companies that are increasingly blurring the lines between insurers, insurance distributors and providers of insurance services. However, their rise seems to be less steady than it has been elsewhere.[27]

It is also clear that reliance on BDA and automated personalization by European incumbent companies is noticeable (besides in cybersecurity applications) during the pre-contractual and claims management phases, where big data helps insurers provide consumers with automatically tailored advertising, more refined individualized offers and settlement proposals, automated claims handling, and fraud detection.[28] Many of these uses are still experimental, and are being pursued either by

[23] Cf. EIOPA Expert Group (2021), pp. 22–26; EIOPA (2019), pp. 29–40; but see also Bernelin (2022), pp. 210–218; Marelli et al. (2020), pp. 451–452; Prainsack and Van Hoyweghen (2020), pp. 130–131, 144–145; Mau (2019), pp. 69–74, 151–153.

[24] Along the same lines, see Tanninen (2020), pp. 5–6; McFall and Moor (2018), p. 205.

[25] EIOPA (2021a), p. 3; see also EIOPA (2020), p. 34.

[26] Talesh and Cunningham (2021), pp. 981–982; McGurk (2018), pp. 24–25. See also EIOPA (2020), p. 7.

[27] Cf. EIOPA (2019), p. 59; see also ESA (2022), pp. 9, 101–102; EIOPA (2021a), p. 3.

[28] ESA (2022), p. 17, fn. 48; EIOPA Expert Group (2021), pp. 6, 9–10; EIOPA (2021b), pp. 16–17; EIOPA (2020), p. 10; EIOPA (2019), pp. 18–41.

insurance companies themselves or through temporary arrangements with selected partners.[29] More specifically, the use of BDA seems to be growing in online advertisement and product placement, which may be designed and framed through choice architecture, legal design, and selective highlighting to exploit potential customers' biases, weakness and emotions, and target them in a way, time, and manner that make them most prone to enter into an agreement.[30] In the sectors in which consumers tend to buy insurance products and services online, underwriting may be automated as well.[31] Some insurance companies have developed or are developing models for enhanced fraud analytics, apps and chatbots offering assistance and automated claims reporting, claims management and settlement, as well as programs that automatically assess damages and validate receipts.[32] The most advanced experiments with BDA have given rise to new species of insurance contracts, such as parametric insurance and usage-based Insurance (UBI). The former is insurance based on smart contracts where payments are automatically made when a certain parameter is met (e.g., water level on a sensor for flood insurance or duration of a delay for flight insurance).[33] UBI is much more developed. This is an insurance contract fueled by and regularly adjusted in line with consumer-generated telemetry data provided by a connected device. It is increasingly being adopted in Europe within the motor insurance sector through tracking tools installed on vehicles. However, cases in which the consumer-generated telemetry data is produced by connected home devices are still limited in number (and telemetry insurance based on wearable devices is even less common).[34] Moreover, even in telemetry motor insurance, that is the form of insurance closest to the constant surveillance models surveyed in Sect. 3, the impact of 'automated personalization' is more limited than one might think. While behavior-based motor insurance contracts are fed with real-time information associated with real people, at least for the time being premium rates in behavior-based contracts are never determined exclusively on the basis of consumer-generated data.[35] In Europe, it would appear that the "the epistemological break [brought by BDA and by the automated personalization trend] has not – at least not yet – transformed risk practices across the industry".[36]

---

[29] See the illustrations provided in Francois and Voldoire (2022), pp. 3–7; EIOPA (2021b), pp. 36–42; EIOPA (2020), pp. 13–24.

[30] EIOPA Expert Group (2021), p. 28, 37; EIOPA (2019), p. 6.

[31] EIOPA Expert Group (2021), p. 7, 10, 47; EIOPA (2020), pp. 35–36; EIOPA (2019), p. 6.

[32] EIOPA (2020), pp. 35–36; EIOPA (2019), p. 6.

[33] EIOPA (2020), p. 38.

[34] Typical UBI models are the 'pay as you drive' (PAYD) and 'pay how you drive' (PHYD) programs in the motor insurance sector, in which the insurance premium is adjusted in line with driving habits and customer behavior. Another illustration is on-demand insurance, which provides insurance coverage for specific periods of time and can be turned on and off. See EIOPA (2019), p. 10.

[35] EIOPA (2019), pp. 10–14. See also Francois and Voldoire (2022); McFall et al. (2020), p. 7; Barry and Charpentier (2020).

[36] McFall et al. (2020), p. 7.

Why is this so? Several hypotheses have been proposed to explain this apparent technological delay. Some commentators have noted that European consumers are particularly reluctant to share their data with insurers[37] or, more prosaically, that they easily become disengaged in the event that wearable devices and a commitment to self-tracking are required.[38] Others have emphasized the inherent cautiousness and conceptual resilience of the insurance market, which is grounded in the well-rooted statistical knowledge and practices of actuaries, and is therefore unlikely to be revolutionized overnight.[39] Still others have noted that the shift towards more personalized policies implies huge costs that limit its economic profitability, at least in the short term.[40] All of these reasons may be true. However, it is argued here, in line with what other scholars have suggested,[41] that perhaps contextual factors that are deeply embedded in continental European culture and legal architecture could also account for the slow embrace of BDA by insurance companies.

5 European Exceptionalism

Insurance in Europe is a highly regulated sector. It is governed by its own regulatory and supervisory requirements, as enshrined in the Solvency II Directive[42] and the Insurance Distribution Directive.[43] It has been observed in this regard that the data quality requirements under the Solvency II Directive constitute a strong limitation on the use of big data for actuarial purposes when calculating technical provisions, as they constrain the use of proxy data as predictors (such as using credit reliability

[37] Meyers and Van Hoyweghen (2020).

[38] Francois and Voldoire (2022), p. 8; Tanninen (2020), p. 8; Jeanningros and McFall (2020), pp. 9–11.

[39] Francois and Voldoire (2022); Cappiello (2020), p. 3; Barry and Charpentier (2020), p. 8–9; Barsan (2020), p. 58; Cevolini and Esposito (2020), p. 5; McFall (2019), p. 70; McFall et al. (2020), p. 4; Eling and Lehmann (2018), p. 359; McFall and Moor (2018), p. 198.

[40] Francois and Voldoire (2022), p. 8–10; McFall et al. (2020), p. 4; Barry and Charpentier (2020), p. 6–7; Jeanningros and McFall (2020), pp. 8–9, 12.

[41] Prainsack and Van Hoyweghen (2020), p. 132; Jeanningros and McFall (2020), pp. 4–5; Marelli et al. (2020), pp. 447–467; Frick (2020), p. 57; Barsan (2020), pp. 58–61; Meyers and Van Hoyweghen (2020), pp. 1–14; Thouvenin et al. (2019); EIOPA (2019), p. 56; Drechsler and Benito Sánchez (2018).

[42] Directive 2009/138/EC of the European Parliament and of the Council of 25 November 2009 on the taking-up and pursuit of the business of Insurance and Reinsurance (recast). In September 2021, the European Commission published a Proposal for a Directive of the European Parliament and of the Council amending Directive 2009/138/EC as regards proportionality, quality of supervision, reporting, long-term guarantee measures, macro-prudential tools, sustainability risks, group and cross-border supervision, COM(2021) 581 final (Solvency III proposal).

[43] Directive (EU) 2016/97 of the European Parliament and of the Council of 20 January 2016 on insurance distribution.

or, say, ownership of an orange car as a predictor of careful driving)—i.e. precisely the kind of correlation-based information that is usually obtained through BDA.[44]

Yet the legal features that matter in shaping the boundaries of insurance practices are by no means limited to those arising under special insurance legislation. Some of them arise out from institutions and practices that are incidental to consumer insurance. For instance, it is quite clear that the depth and breadth of public welfare and social insurance coverage in Europe differs substantially from the position in common law jurisdictions. Especially in the field of health and life insurance, due to the broad and accessible forms of public welfare and social insurance coverage available in Europe, European consumers often have the opportunity to rely on the state in order to reduce the risks they are facing.[45] By contrast, in many common law jurisdictions, and most notably in the US, the market is the only alternative, thus making people much more desperate for other sources of aid and more exposed to the dangers of dubious corporate deals.[46]

Other legal features that matter and that are notably distinctive vis-à-vis common law experiences—such as data sharing regimes, general legislation on consumer protection and anti-discrimination, and emerging rules on artificial intelligence (AI)—directly impinge on consumer insurtech. We shall now consider these in greater detail.

5.1 *Data Regimes*

BDA obviously relies on data: the wider and easier the availability of data, the better BDA works. On this point, the commonality of language in common law jurisdictions represents a built-in advantage. While insurance companies in mono-lingual common law jurisdictions can apply BDA on large corpora that span international borders, linguistic diversity creates a monumental barrier for infra-European data flows and analytics.[47]

Additional limitations stem from the regulations and practices in relation to data. In Europe, a vast amount of data (often not in digitalized form) is held by public entities and agencies, which often keep them for themselves; disclosure obligations have only recently been enacted through EU legislation such as the Open Data

[44] Jeanningros & McFall (2020), pp. 4–5; Verbelen et al. (2018).

[45] Consider for instance the number of social institutions and mechanisms dealing with the most statistically frequent and serious injuries, such as mandatory social insurance schemes for industrial accidents, traffic accidents and medical malpractice accidents: Jutras (2021), pp. 140–158; Fenyves et al. (2016); Oliphant and Wagner (2012); Magnus (2003).

[46] The same observation is made, in general, by Nowotny (2021), p. 11, and, as to insurance, by Jeanningros and McFall (2020), pp. 6–7; Lupton (2016), p. 124; on the breadth of public welfare and social insurance in common law jurisdictions, see the authors quoted in the fn. above.

[47] With regard to the flow of legal data, see AI4Lawyers (2021a), p. 47; AI4Lawyers (2021b), pp. 27–28.

Directive and the Data Governance Act.[48] Consider, for instance, judicial decisions: although court rulings were public documents, until recently only a few European countries had digital databases that made judicial decisions publicly available in machine-readable format.[49] As a result, European insurance companies have only recently started to explore the possibility of deploying BDA on large volumes of judicial decisions in order to predict the likelihood of litigation and infer the amount of compensation that could be obtained by the policyholder.[50] EU institutions are currently trying to favor the establishment of a supervised market for the use and sharing of non-personal data held by both public authorities and private companies.[51] Nothing of this type exists in common law jurisdictions, in which the practical legal limitations placed on big data collection, processing and use are traditionally thin.[52]

Most notably, when collecting, processing and transferring personal data, insurance companies must comply with the obligations set forth in the General Data Protection Regulation (GDPR).[53] Many of these obligations—such as rules on transparency, purpose limitation, data minimization and storage limitation—impose substantial burdens and costs on companies wishing to perform BDA.[54] By way of illustration, Article 22 GDPR provides that companies that rely on automated-decision making (ADM), including profiling, must inform consumers concerning any automated processing and must be ready to respond to consumers' transparency requests as to the ADM. This implicitly forces insurance companies to resort to explainable (and therefore simpler) forms of AI and to discard more powerful (but also less transparent) algorithms, because reliance on the latter would not allow

---

[48] See Directive (EU) 2019/1024 of the European Parliament and of the Council of 20 June 2019 on open data and the re-use of public sector information (Open Data Directive); Regulation (EU) 2022/868 of the European Parliament and of the Council of 30 May 2022 on European data governance and amending Regulation (EU) 2018/1724 (Data Governance Act), especially articles 3–9. For a general discussion of the prospects than an open data environment might open up for European insurance companies, see EIOPA (2021b).

[49] On the lack of comprehensive machine-readable and openly accessible legal databases, see D'Andrea et al. (2021).

[50] EIOPA (2019), p. 28.

[51] See Regulation (EU) 2018/1807 of the European Parliament and of the Council of 14 November 2018 on a framework for the free flow of non-personal data in the European Union; see also the Regulation (EU) 2022/868, especially articles 10–15, and the Regulation (EU) 2023/2854 of the European Parliament and of the Council of 13 December 2023 on harmonised rules on fair access to and use of data (Data Act).

[52] For an overview of the limited rules on data collection and sharing in common law jurisdictions, cf. Pittman and Levenberg (2021); Hickman and Devine (2021); Borghese (2021).

[53] Regulation (EU) 2016/679 of the European Parliament and of the Council of 27 April 2016 on the protection of natural persons with regard to the processing of personal data and on the free movement of such data (GDPR).

[54] EIOPA (2021a), p. 10. See also Bernelin (2022), p. 212; Prainsack and Van Hoyweghen (2020), p. 132; Marelli et al. (2020), pp. 447–467; Frick (2020), p. 57; Barsan (2020), pp. 58–61; Meyers and Van Hoyweghen (2020), pp. 1–14; Thouvenin et al. (2019); EIOPA (2019), p. 56; Drechsler and Benito Sánchez (2018), pp. 1–23.

them to justify the results of automated processing.[55] The principle of purpose limitation implies that insurance companies cannot reuse data that were originally collected for other purposes unless they inform the data subjects accordingly and obtain their consent.[56] While informing customers about such repurposing might be relatively easy, for insurance companies "it might be difficult or even impossible [...] to comply with this requirement if their analysis includes data about individuals who are not their customers".[57] The principles of data minimization and storage limitation further impair the reuse of data by requiring insurance companies to retain only the data that are necessary for their activity and only for the period necessary for the initial purpose of the processing. In other words, unless reuse is explicitly allowed, the data, once used, have to be deleted and are lost for future analysis.[58] These examples show how, at least on paper, compliance with the GDPR appears to clash with the core idea of BDA to gain new insights from existing data and to apply these insights to individual customers.[59]

5.2 *Consumer Protection and Anti-Discrimination Laws*

Beyond privacy, consumer insurance contracts obviously trigger the applicability of consumer protection laws.

In Europe, this implies that such contracts are subject to national and EU-derived legislation providing minimal safeguards for the weaker party in business-to-consumer (B2C) contracts. For instance, rules implementing the Unfair Contract Terms Directive (UCTD)[60] and the Unfair Commercial Practices Directive (UCPD)[61] prohibit respectively the inclusion of unfair terms in standard B2C contracts and unfair commercial practices that occur before, during and after the B2C transaction has taken place. While similar rules exist in some common law jurisdictions (such as England and Australia[62]), consumer law remains an exception in the institutional

---

[55] Ebers (2020), pp. 63–66. As recently pointed out by the Court of Justice of the European Union, Article 22 GDPR "lays down a prohibition in principle, the infringement of which does not need to be invoked individually by such a person" (Case C-634/21, *OQ v Land Hessen*, 7 December 2023, ECLI:EU:C:2023:957, paragraph 52). It should however be noted that the obligation contained in Article 22 GDPR can be bypassed by national legislation that allows ADM. For instance, in Germany, a special provision contained in the national Data Protection Act of 30 June 2017 (Bundesdatenschutzgesetz—BDSG) expressly enables insurers to process data by automated means pursuant to Article 22 GDPR: see § 37 BDSG.

[56] EIOPA (2019), p. 56; Thouvenin et al. (2019), p. 229.

[57] Thouvenin et al. (2019), p. 229; the same observation is made by Soyer (2022), p. 176.

[58] Thouvenin et al. (2019), pp. 229–230; McGurk (2018), pp. 57–58.

[59] Barsan (2020), p. 61; Thouvenin et al. (2019), pp. 229–230.

[60] Council Directive 93/13/EEC of 5 April 1993 on unfair terms in consumer contracts, as amended.

[61] Directive 2005/29/EC of 11 May 2005 concerning unfair business-to-consumer commercial practices in the internal market, as amended.

[62] Cf. the Consumer Rights Act 2015 in the United Kingdom and the federal Consumer Law (Schedule 2 of the Competition and Consumer Act 2010) in Australia.

structure of the common law, which is historically based on freedom of contract, equality of arms and individual private enforcement.[63]

Similar observations can be made with regard to the scope of anti-discrimination rules. Besides legislation covering anti-discrimination in employment contracts, all European countries have implemented the Race Equality Directive[64] and the Gender Equality Directive,[65] which prohibit both direct and indirect discrimination in access to goods and services on the grounds of racial or ethnic origin as well as gender. Complying with these laws when using BDA in insurance is hard owing to the well-known tendency of BDA to 'discriminate by proxy': BDA-powered algorithms tend to automatically discover predictive characteristics that apparently have no connection with race, ethnicity or gender, whilst being correlated to them.[66] This again distances European law from the majority of common law jurisdictions, and especially US law, under which anti-discrimination legislation is essentially confined to labor relations.[67]

5.3 *Artificial Intelligence Governance*

While the approach to AI in the majority of common law jurisdictions has so far been based on soft-law and voluntary principles,[68] EU institutions have combined the elaboration of soft-law guidelines[69] with hard-law proposals for regulating AI.[70]

According to the final text of the Artificial Intelligence Act (AIA), a huge number of AI applications in insurance qualify as non-high-risk systems,[71] since only "AI

[63] This is most notably the case in the US: see the few provisions concerning business-to-consumer (B2C) transactions in the Uniform Commercial Code (UCC), as well as the lucid analysis by Coleman (2021).

[64] Council Directive 2000/43/EC of 29 June 2000 implementing the principle of equal treatment between persons irrespective of racial or ethnic origin.

[65] Council Directive 2004/113/EC of 13 December 2004 implementing the principle of equal treatment between men and women in the access to and supply of goods.

[66] Soyer (2022), pp. 178–180; Prince and Schwarcz (2020); Marelli et al. (2020), pp. 455–456; Drechsler and Benito Sánchez (2018), pp. 3, 6–7, 11, 12–14; Barocas and Selbst (2016); Swedloff (2014).

[67] Title VII of the Civil Rights Act of 1964 in the US prohibits employment discrimination based on race, color, religion, sex and national origin. By contrast, the scope of anti-discrimination rules in the United Kingdom and Australia is broader: cf. the Equality Act 2010 in the United Kingdom with the Racial Discrimination Act 1975, the Sex Discrimination Act 1984, the Disability Discrimination Act 1992, and the Age Discrimination Act 2004 in Australia.

[68] A few attempts to regulate AI have been made at the federal level in the US, but have until now failed.

[69] See High-Level Expert Group (2019); with specific regard to the insurance sector, see EIOPA Expert Group (2021).

[70] Regulation (EU) 2024/1689 of the European Parliament and of the Council of 2024 Laying Down Harmonised Rules on Artificial Intelligence (Artificial Intelligence Act).

[71] Soyer (2022), p. 168. Unless an insurance company qualifies as a digital platform or a provider of intermediary services, it will also be unaffected by the Regulation (EU) 2022/1925 of the European Parliament and of the Council of 14 September 2022 on contestable and fair markets in

systems intended to be used for risk assessment and pricing in relation to natural persons in the case of life and health insurance" are included in the list of 'high-risk' activities.[72] This means that, except for the use of AI in risk assessment and pricing of human beings in life and health insurance (and for the possible reliance on genera-purpose AI (GPAI), which may lead to the application of the special obligations set forth by Article 53 of the AIA), insurance companies relying on AI are only subject to the voluntary application of the codes of conduct drafted under Article 95 of the AIA. Nevertheless, the European soft law instruments thus far adopted suggest a number of precautions that should be considered by both AI developers and users, including fairness, transparency, explainability, and human oversight.[73] If taken seriously, these precautions could raise the regulatory burden also for insurance companies wishing to employ AI tools.

Consider for instance the issue of algorithmic fairness (not to be confused with actuarial fairness, which refers to the adjustment of premiums to individual risks). Among its many nuances as an open concept, algorithmic fairness includes the need to avoid biases that could "lead to unintended (in)direct prejudice and discrimination against certain groups or people, potentially exacerbating prejudice and marginalisation".[74] In keeping with European anti-discrimination laws, although in broader terms, the idea of algorithmic fairness aims to ensure both that people are treated equally insofar as they possess equal characteristics and that people are not treated differently on account of characteristics that it is not fair to consider when contracting.[75] This means that insurance companies should in principle verify—both before and after data processing—that the variables and criteria highlighted are not proxies for any unfair ground, and discard any variable or criteria that might be a source of unfair discrimination.[76] As already noted, such a task is immensely complicated by the fact that BDA typically works through correlation-based information, the origins of which cannot be easily explained in causal terms. In order to comply with the requirement of algorithmic fairness, insurance companies performing BDA would thus be required to discard not only variables and criteria that are associated with (prohibited or) unfair traits, but also any variable and criteria for which there is no plausible causal link with a clearly identifiable risk or hazard, as

---

the digital sector and amending Directives (EU) 2019/1937 and (EU) 2020/1828 (Digital Markets Act), and by the Regulation (EU) 2022/2065 of the European Parliament and of the Council of 19 October 2022 on a Single Market For Digital Services and amending Directive 2000/31/EC (Digital Services Act).

[72] See Annex III, no 5, letter (c) of the Artificial Intelligence Act. Soyer (2022), p. 168.

[73] See High-Level Expert Group (2019); EIOPA Expert Group (2021). On the slow but steady emergence of these principles, see also Poncibò and Cannarsa (2022), pp. 419–428; Renda (2020), pp. 667–690; Ebers (2020); Mittelstadt et al. (2019); Floridi (2019).

[74] High-Level Expert Group (2019); EIOPA Expert Group (2021), pp. 21–39.

[75] Wachter et al. (2021).

[76] Prince and Schwarcz (2020), p. 1316; Jeanningros and McFall (2020), pp. 4–5; Marelli et al. (2020), pp. 455–456.

they might invisibly convey algorithmic unfairness.[77] The need to maintain a strong causality requirement to justify disparate treatment implies losing much of the value added by BDA-driven correlations.

6 All Quiet on the Continental Front?

The points highlighted in the previous section may help to explain the different trajectories of BDA-powered insurance and automated personalization in common law and civil law jurisdictions. In many instances, European law seems to be more inclined than the common law to shield consumers from unconstrained market power.[78] Does this mean that European law is per se well-equipped to protect consumers from the risks arising out of BDA?

The answer is obviously that it is not. Rules on AI are still in flux. Existing rules on data circulation, consumer protection and anti-discrimination, have a number of weak spots and are in urgent need of improvement.

It is sufficient to note that the notice-and-consent approach on which the most celebrated (and widely circulated) EU legislation, the GDPR, is based, assumes that people read, understand and choose whether or not to sign privacy policies. In practice, people rarely read (and, if obliged to read, rarely understand) the policies they are offered, and are generally likely to consent to any processing of their data.[79] Even if they do actually read, understand and doubt a privacy policy, consumers often have no real opportunity to opt out of data processing, as such a choice would in most cases result in denial of service.[80] Although it is indeed the case that, after a person provides consent, Articles 15–22 of the GDPR grant that person many rights, including the right to access, rectify, erase, restrict processing of and transfer her own data; in particular, in cases involving automated processing (and provided that all of the requirements set forth by Article 22 GDPR are satisfied), the data subject has the right to request information about "the existence of automated decision-making, […] and […] about the logic involved, as well as the significance and the envisaged consequences of such processing for the data subject".[81] Nonetheless, the idea that granting abstract rights to individuals is enough to protect them is quite optimistic, and is largely out of touch with reality. It is an idea that assumes that individual consumers are in a position to react—that is, that they have the time, the resources, and the willingness to ask for explanations, to interpret them, to assess

---

[77] Infantino (2024), pp. 9–11; Soyer (2022), pp. 179–180; Prince and Schwarcz (2020), p. 1316; Jeanningros and McFall (2020), p. 4–5; Marelli et al. (2020), pp. 455–456.

[78] See above, Sects. 5.1 and 5.2.

[79] Zuiderveen Borgesius et al. (2017); with specific regard to insurance, Marelli et al. (2020), pp. 456–457; Drechsler and Benito Sánchez (2018), p. 9.

[80] Marelli et al. (2020), p. 457.

[81] Article 15(1), letter h, GDPR.

whether any improper processing has occurred, and then to react accordingly.[82] It is however clear that, aside from supervisory authorities,[83] only truly motivated people and specifically dedicated associations, such as those that, according to Article 80 GDPR, can lodge complaints on behalf of multiple persons,[84] may be able to engage in such a fight.[85]

Enforcement problems also plague the application of consumer protection and anti-discrimination laws. In order to find that a standard contract term or a commercial practice is unfair under the UCTD or the UCPD, the person affected must take action before the courts or the competent administrative bodies in order to obtain a decision as to whether the term or the practice is unfair; the action can also be commenced by organizations with a legitimate interest under national law in protecting consumers or in combating unfair commercial practices.[86] Victims of discriminatory treatment are expected to sue or challenge the party responsible for the discrimination through judicial or administrative procedures[87]; EU anti-discrimination directives leave it up to national law to decide whether associations pursuing anti-discrimination objectives should be allowed to engage in these procedures on behalf or in support of complainants.[88] The point however is that BDA-customized products and services add additional layers of difficulty to the ordinary hurdles that consumers face in the individual and collective enforcement of the law.

BDA-powered personalization in contracting aims to design terms, practices and treatments for a single consumer at a single point in time and space. In situations involving automatically and individually tailored ads, offers and treatment, it becomes extremely hard for consumers and associations (as well as for supervisory authorities) to demonstrate that a given term in an insurance contract was not individually negotiated under the UCTD,[89] since by definition that term was shaped to target an individual consumer. Similarly, automated personalization makes it almost impossible to argue that a commercial practice of an insurance company is likely to materially distort the economic behavior of the 'average' consumer under the UCPD[90] or that one consumer was treated less favorably on account of her race, ethnicity or gender than another one was, or would have been treated in a compa-

---

[82] Marelli et al. (2020), p. 458; more in general, see Riefa (2022), pp. 609, 620–625.

[83] IAIS (2020), pp. 31–39, 49.

[84] Consumer associations have the right to file a collective action, even if they have not received a specific mandate from data subjects or if no individual data subjects have been specifically identified: Case C-319/20, *Meta Platforms Ireland Limited v. Bundesverband der Verbraucherzentralen und Verbraucherverbände—Verbraucherzentrale Bundesverband e.V.*, 28 April 2022, ECLI:EU:C:2022:322.

[85] Drechsler and Benito Sánchez (2018), p. 14.

[86] UCTD, article 7(2); UCPD, article 11(1).

[87] Race Equality Directive, Article 7(1); Gender Equality Directive, Article 8(1).

[88] Race Equality Directive, Article 7(2); Gender Equality Directive, Article 8(3).

[89] UCTD, Article 3(1); this is noted by Tereszkiewicz and Południak-Gierz (2021), p. 11.

[90] In particular under point (b) of Article 5(2) UCPD; on this point, see also Tereszkiewicz and Południak-Gierz (2021), p. 11.

rable situation, or that in any case she was put at a particular disadvantage compared with other persons under EU anti-discrimination directives.[91] It is also necessary to consider who an average consumer is, and how a comparable consumer can be identified in a system of one-to-one contracting. By definition, the individually-tailored experience of each consumer is unique, since any other consumer would be treated differently. Another issue is how the average or the standard, ordinary treatment can be established in a world in which companies are able to automatically micro-segment their ads, offers and practices, and in which no consumer, association or authority has the time, the resources and the competence to perform tests and collect documentation concerning thousands of unique contractual experiences.[92] However, even before considering this issue, since consumers obtain different materials through fleeting interactions with digital screens and automated chatbots, they also have difficulty in comparing one another's experiences and in realizing whether anything has gone wrong.[93]

In this regard, reliance on emerging AI standards is of little help. Consider again the case of automated discrimination, for instance by a pricing algorithm. Whenever the discriminatory price is not determined by race, ethnicity or gender, but is based on other grounds, a European consumer would have to build her case relying on the shaky authority of current European soft standards on fairness in AI applications. Even assuming that standards of AI fairness are enforceable, the consumer would have to gather evidence and to make a persuasive argument that she was a victim of a difference in treatment vis-à-vis other categories for which there was no legitimate reason. To do that, she would have to request and obtain explanations about "the existence of automated decision-making, [...] and [...] about the logic involved" under Article 22 GDPR, to reverse engineer the automated decision, and to collect evidence about the treatment of other categories. But even before that, she would need to become aware of the problem—that is, to suspect that something was wrong with what was being offered or given to her. While the Consumer Rights Directive (CRD) now obliges traders to inform consumers about whether the price offered to them "was personalised on the basis of automated decision-making",[94] the limits of the information paradigm are well-known.[95] Moreover, what characterizes automated discrimination, making it more subtle, intangible and difficult to detect than traditional forms of discrimination, is that it relies on BDA-based 'collectives' that people might not associate with (such as 'the group of consumers using version X of the Y browser'), and therefore might not even perceive to be wrongly or unfairly attributed to them. The abstract nature of digital data, the combinatorial possibilities among different data types, as well as the opacity of the categories that are used for

[91] Race Equality Directive, Article 2(2); Gender Equality Directive, Article 2.

[92] This is noted by Willis (2020), p. 157; Spencer (2020), p. 998.

[93] Infantino (2024), p. 10–11; Marelli et al. (2020), p. 458; see also Willis (2020), p. 153; Spencer (2020), p. 998. See also ESA (2022), p. 40.

[94] Directive 2011/83/EU of the European Parliament and of the Council of 25 October 2011 on consumer rights, as amended, Article 6(1), lit (ea).

[95] See the authors cited above, fn. 79.

stratification and customization make it nearly impossible for people to recognize themselves as part of a social 'group', to imagine themselves as having been discriminated against, and to even think of addressing biases that have implications for algorithmic fairness.[96]

The above problems are only set to worsen as the market evolves.[97] While the current state of the art in Europe seems to suggest that incumbent insurance companies are not likely, at least in the short term, to adopt the forms of behavioral insurance involving intense surveillance that are widespread in common law jurisdictions, the developments highlighted above show a trend towards the mass customization of the pre-contractual and management stages, that increasingly de-personalizes the insurance-customer relationship and leaves consumers in conditions of automated hardship.[98]

7 Against Automated Personalization

Many of the opportunities and risks associated in the English-speaking literature with the idea of 'automated personalization' of prices, 24/7 continuous (self-)monitoring, and real-time adjustment of contractual terms in insurance contracts are, in today's Europe, more imagined than real, especially outside the field of telemetry insurance. Yet the growing automation, mass customization and de-personalization of the sales and management phases in consumer insurance contracts raise several challenges for consumers, who are increasingly exposed to aggressive advertising, behavioral manipulation, and price discrimination. Moreover, consumers face additional difficulties in discovering whether and why something went wrong, and in complaining about it, as anyone who has tried to reason with a chatbot knows very well.

There are therefore several reasons for caution when considering automated personalization in European insurance contracts.

The expression invites us to superimpose insurtech practices that are already widespread in common law jurisdictions on the European landscape. When we talk about 'automated personalization', we overemphasize the opportunities and risks associated with insurance contracts that are fueled by continuous flows of individual data and adjusted in real-time to people's behavior. When we think in these terms, we might be tempted—as some scholars have proposed[99]—to counter business

---

[96] Prainsack and Van Hoyweghen (2020), pp. 137, 141–142; Marelli et al. (2020), p. 458; McFall and Moor (2018), p. 208.

[97] For some illustrations of the experimentations with BDA and automated personalization that are currently being carried out by European incumbent insurance companies, see EIOPA (2021b), pp. 36–42; EIOPA (2020), pp. 13–24. However, see also the new forthcoming EU rules on a smoother market for data trading cited above, fns. 48 and 51.

[98] Cappiello (2020), p. 9; see also, in general, Lynskey et al. (2021), p. 94.

[99] Busch (2021); Busch (2019); Ben-Shahar and Porat (2019); Hacker (2017).

practices of automated personalization with more personalization, by imposing on businesses working on the digital marketplace a duty to provide consumers with tailored disclosures and disclaimers matching their profile, as if adding a further layer of automated information onto already overly burdened consumers might actually help them.

Most importantly, when we think in terms of 'automated personalization', we also under-emphasize a number of real-world problems that are associated with the increasing automation and mass customization of advertisements, offers and claims handling processes. The notion of 'automated personalization' tends to conceal the fact that BDA-powered contracts are anything but personalized. A so-called 'personalized' contract might well contain terms automatically tailored to (what the company thinks is the) the individual profile of the customer, although it nevertheless remains a non-negotiated, standard-form contract. Describing BDA-powered consumer contracts in terms of 'automated personalization' risks further diluting consumers' capacity to react to misleading advertising and discriminatory treatment. This is because individually 'personalized' contractual relationships by definition cannot be compared with the treatment that an 'average' consumer or a person belonging to the same group would have received under the same circumstances. More generally, thinking in terms of 'automated personalization' obscures the mass character of BDA-powered contracts and their general capacity to exploit the pre-existing and potential vulnerabilities of consumers and to engineer their individually-tailored yet systemic disempowerment.

Understanding the specific challenges raised by the rise of insurtech in Europe is fundamental in assessing and devising strategies for safeguarding European consumers (other than submerging consumers with profiled disclosures). There are many available options. Besides prohibiting certain practices, one might consider requiring companies that rely on BDA to automate mass customization in order to abide by ex ante governance and risk-mitigation obligations, along the lines of the requirements imposed by the GDPR on data controllers as well as the AIA provision for 'high-risk' AI systems. Ex ante obligations might help to mitigate the risks of BDA contracting, and especially raise the regulatory burden for companies that are willing to adopt it. Alternatively, one might consider imposing heightened duties of care on companies that adopt BDA and mass customization techniques, or establishing against them a rebuttable presumption that automated offers, terms and treatment are exploitative of consumer vulnerability and therefore unfair.[100] Heightened duties and rebuttable presumptions would reduce the need for consumers, consumer associations and enforcement agencies to pinpoint and prove particular representations and micro-moments within a myriad of individually-tailored transactions, and would also provide companies with a substantial incentive to adopt fair algorithms and contracting models. More generally, solutions of this kind

[100] This is suggested by Lynskey et al. (2021), p. 145; see also, in Europe, Riefa (2022), pp. 621–632; in the US, Willis (2020), pp. 171–176.

would strengthen the key features of European law that already set it apart from the common law and occasionally act as a source of inspiration for other countries.

Acknowledgments This work was supported by the Italian Ministry of University and Research under the project 'Digital Vulnerability in European Private Law' (2020XBFME2).

References

Barocas S, Selbst AD (2016) Big data's disparate impact. Cal Law Rev 104:671–732

Barry L & Charpentier A (2020) Personalization as a promise: Can Big Data change the practice of insurance?. Big Data & Society 1–12. https://doi.org/10.1177/2053951720935143. Last visited June 7, 2024

Barsan IM (2020) The GDPR perspective. RTDciv:58–61

Ben-Shahar O, Porat A (2019) Personalizing mandatory rules in contract law. Univ Chi Law Rev 86:255–282

Bernelin M (2022) Tous vulnérables ? La vulnérabilité au prisme des nouvelles technologies en santé – étude en droit français et en droit européen. In: Boujeka A, Roccati M (eds), La vulnérabilité en droit international, européen et comparé. Presses Universitaires de Paris Nanterre 188–218

Borghese A (2021) Data Protection Laws and Regulations Australia, 2021–2022. https://iclg.com/practice-areas/data-protection-laws-and-regulations/australia. Last visited June 7, 2024

Burk DL (2021) Algorithmic legal metrics. Notre Dame Law Rev 96:1147–1204

Busch C (2019) Implementing personalized law: personalized disclosures in consumer law and data privacy law. Univ Chicago Law Rev 86:309–331

Busch C (2021) Algorithmic regulation and (Im)Perfect enforcement in the personalized economy. In: Busch C, De Franceschi A (eds) Algorithmic regulation and personalized law. A Handbook, Bloomsbury, pp 279–292

Calo RL (2017) Digital market manipulation. Geo Wash Law Rev 82:995–1051

Cappiello A (2020) The digital (R)Evolution of insurance business models. Am J Econ Bus Admin 1–13. https://doi.org/10.3844/ajebasp.2020.1.13. Last visited June 7, 2024

Cevolini A & Esposito E (2020) From pool to profile: social consequences of algorithmic prediction in insurance. Big Data & Society 1–11. https://doi.org/10.1177/2053951720939228. Last visited June 7, 2024

Coleman BD (2021) Endangered claims. Wm Mary Law Rev 63:345–405

Couldry N & Mejias UA (2019) The costs of connection. How data is colonizing human life and appropriating it for capitalism. Stanford University Press

D'Andrea S, Divissenko N, Fanou M, Krisztián A, Kukavica J, Potocka-Sionek N, Siems M (2021) Asymmetric cross-citations in private law: an empirical study of 28 Supreme Courts in the EU. Maastricht J Eur Comp Law 28:498–534

Drechsler L, Benito Sánchez JC (2018) The price is (not) right: data protection and discrimination in the age of pricing algorithms. Eur J Law Technol 9:1–23

Ebers M (2020) Regulating AI and Robotics: ethical and legal challenges. In: Ebers M, Navas S (eds) Algorithms and law. Cambridge University Press, pp 37–99

Eling M, Lehmann M (2018) The impact of digitalization on the insurance value chain and the insurability of risks. Geneva Papers 43:359–396

Eubanks V (2016) Automating inequality: how high-tech tools profile, police, and punish the poor. St. Martin's Press

Fenyves A, Kissling C, Perner S, Rubin D (eds) (2016) Compulsory liability insurance from a European perspective. de Gruyter

Floridi L (2019) Establishing the rules for building trustworthy AI. Nat Mach Intell 1:261–262

Francois P & Voldoire T (2022) The revolution that did not happen: telematics and car insurance in the 2010s. Big Data Soc 1–12. https://doi.org/10.1177/20539517221142033. Last visited June 7, 2024

Frick J (2020) Introduction: digitalisation and the insurance value chain. RTDciv 56–58

Hacker P (2017) Personalizing EU private law: from disclosures to nudges and mandates. Eur Rev Priv Law 25:651–677

Hickman T, Devine J (2021) Data Protection Laws and Regulations United Kingdom 2021-2022. https://iclg.com/practice-areas/data-protection-laws-and-regulations/united-kingdom. Last visited June 7, 2024

Infantino M (2022) Big data analytics, insurtech and consumer contracts: a European appraisal. Eur Rev Priv Law 30:613–634

Infantino M (2024) A comparative study of automated quantification in digital insurance. Int J Digit Law Gov 1:1–27

Jeanningros H & McFall L (2020) The value of sharing: branding and behaviour in a life and health insurance company. Big Data Soc 1–15. https://doi.org/10.1177/2053951720950350. Last visited June 7, 2024

Jutras D (2021) Alternative compensation schemes from a comparative perspective. In: Bussani & Sebok AJ (eds) Comparative tort law. Global perspectives, 2nd edn. Edward Elgar, pp 140–158

Lupton D (2016) The Quantified self: a sociology of self-tracking. Polity

Lury C, Day S (2019) Algorithmic personalization as a mode of individuation. Theory Cult Society 36:17–37

Lynskey O, Micklitz H-W, Rott P (2021), Part II. Personalised pricing and personalised commercial practices. In: BEUC (ed) EU Consumer Protection 2.0. Structural asymmetries in digital consumer markets. https://www.beuc.eu/publications/beuc-x-2021-018_eu_consumer_protection.0_0.pdf. Last visited June 7, 2024

Magnus U (ed) (2003) The impact of social security law on tort law. Springer

Marelli L, Lievevrouw E, Van Hoyweghen I (2020) Fit for purpose? The GDPR and the governance of European digital health. Policy Stud 41:471–467

Mau S (2019) The metric society. Polity

McFall L (2019) Personalizing solidarity? The role of selftracking in health insurance pricing. Econ Society 48:52–76

McFall L, Moor L (2018) Who, or what, is insurtech personalizing?: Persons, prices and the historical classifications of risk. Distinktion J Soc Theory 19:193–213

McFall L, Meyers G, Van Hoyweghen I (2020), Editorial: the personalisation of insurance: data, behavior and innovation. Big Data Society 1–11, https://doi.org/10.1177/2053951720973707. Last visited June 7, 2024

McGurk B (2018), Data profiling and insurance law. Hart

Meyers G, Van Hoyweghen I (2020) 'Happy failures': experimentation with behavior-based personalisation in car insurance. Big Data Society 1–14. https://doi.org/10.1177/2053951720914650. Last visited June 7, 2024

Mittelstadt B, Russell C, Wachter S (2019) Explaining explanations in AI. Proceedings of the conference on fairness, accountability, and transparency 279–288

Nowotny H (2021) In AI We Trust. Power, illusion and control of predictive algorithms. Polity

O'Neil C (2016) Weapons of math destruction. Crown

Oliphant K, Wagner G (eds) (2012) Employers' liability and workers' compensation. de Gruyter

Pittman FP, Levenberg K (2021) Data Protection Laws and Regulations USA 2021-2022, at https://iclg.com/practice-areas/data-protection-laws-and-regulations/usa. Last visited June 7, 2024

Poncibò C, Cannarsa M (2022) AI and the law: interdisciplinary challenges and comparative perspectives. In: DiMatteo L, Poncibò C, Cannarsa M (eds) The Cambridge handbook of artificial intelligence: Global perspectives on law and ethics. Cambridge University Press, pp 419–428

Prainsack B, Van Hoyweghen I (2020) Shifting solidarities: personalisation in insurance and medicine. In: Van Hoyweghen I, Pulignano V, Meyers G (eds) Shifting solidarities. Trends and developments in European Societies. Palgrave Macmillan, pp 127–151

Prince AER, Schwarcz D (2020) Proxy discrimination in the age of artificial intelligence and big data. Iowa Law Rev 105:1257–1318

Renda A (2020) Moral machines: the emerging EU policy on "Trustworthy AI". In: Barfield W (ed) The Cambridge handbook of the law of algorithms. Cambridge University Press, pp 667–690

Riefa C (2022) Protecting vulnerable consumers in the digital single market. Eur Bus Law Rev 33:607–634

Soyer B (2022) Use of big data analytics and sensor technology in consumer insurance context: legal and practical challenges. Cambridge Law J 81:165–194

Spencer SB (2020) The problem of online manipulation. Univ Ill Law Rev:959–1005

Swedloff R (2014) Risk classification's big data (r)evolution. Conn Insurance Law J 21:339–374

Talesh SA, Cunningham B (2021) The technologization of insurance: an empirical analysis of big data and artificial intelligence's impact on cybersecurity and privacy. Utah Law Rev:967–1027

Tanninen M (2020) Contested technology: social scientific perspectives of behaviour-based insurance. Big Data Soc 1–14. https://doi.org/10.1177/2053951720942536. Last visited June 7, 2024

Tereszkiewicz P, Południak-Gierz K (2021) Liability for incorrect client personalization in the distribution of consumer insurance, Risks 9(83)1–15. https://doi.org/10.3390/risks9050083 Last visited June 7, 2024

Thouvenin F, Suter F, George D, Weber RH (2019) Big data in the insurance industry: Leeway and limits for individualising insurance contracts. J Intell Prop Inform Technol Elec Comm Law 10(29):209–243

Verbelen R, Antonio K, Claeskens G (2018) Unraveling the predictive power of telematics data in car insurance pricing. J Royal Stat Society Series C (Appl Stat) 67(5):1275–1304

Wachter S, Mittelstadt B, Russell C (2021) Why fairness cannot be automated: bridging the gap between EU non-discrimination law and AI. Comput Law Sec Rev 41. https://doi.org/10.1016/j.clsr.2021.105567. Last visited June 7, 2024

Willis LE (2020) Deception by design. Harv J Law Technol 34:115–190

Zuboff S (2019) The age of surveillance capitalism. Public Affairs

Zuiderveen Borgesius FJ, Kruikemeier S, Boerman SC, Helberger N (2017) Tracking walls, take-it-or-leave-it choices, the GDPR, and the ePrivacy regulation. Eur Data Prot Law Rev 3:353–368

Documents

AI4Lawyers (European Lawyers Foundation (ELF) and the Council of Bars and Law Societies of Europe (CCBE)) (2021a) Overview of the "Average State of the Art" IT Capabilities of Law Firms in the European Union and Gap Analysis Compared to US/UK/Canada Best Practices. http://elf-fae.eu/wp-content/uploads/2021/03/Overview-of-the-average-state-of-the-art-IT-capabilities-in-the-EU.pdf. Last visited June 7, 2024

AI4Lawyers (European Lawyers Foundation (ELF) and the Council of Bars and Law Societies of Europe (CCBE)) (2021b) Opportunities and Barriers in the Use of Natural Language Processing Tools in SME Law Practices. https://elf-fae.eu/wp-content/uploads/2021/12/Report-on-opportunities-and-barriers-in-the-use-of-NLP-tools-in-SME-law-practices.pdf. Last visited June 7, 2024

EIOPA's Consultative Expert Group on Digital Ethics in insurance [EIOPA Expert Group] (2021) Artificial Intelligence Governance Principles: Towards Ethical and Trustworthy Artificial Intelligence in the European Insurance Sector. https://www.eiopa.europa.eu/document-library/report/artificial-intelligence-governance-principles-towards-ethical-and_en. Last visited June 7, 2024

European Insurance and Occupational Pensions Authority (EIOPA) (2019) Big Data Analytics in Motor and Health Insurance. https://www.eiopa.europa.eu/document-library/fact-sheet/big-data-analytics-motor-and-health-insurance_en. Last visited June 7, 2024

European Insurance and Occupational Pensions Authority (EIOPA) (2020), Discussion Paper on the (Re)insurance Value Chain and New Business Models Arising from Digitalisation (EIOPA-

BoS-20.276). https://www.eiopa.europa.eu/document-library/consultation/discussion-paper-reinsurance-value-chain-and-new-business-models_en. Last visited June 7, 2024

European Insurance and Occupational Pensions Authority (EIOPA) (2021a) (Re)insurance Value Chain and New Business Models Arising from Digitalisation: Feedback statement to the Discussion Paper (EIOPA-BoS-21-219). https://www.eiopa.europa.eu/document-library/consultation/discussion-paper-reinsurance-value-chain-and-new-business-models_en. Last visited June 7, 2024

European Insurance and Occupational Pensions Authority (EIOPA) (2021b) Open Insurance: Accessing and Sharing Insurance-Related Data. Discussion Paper. https://www.eiopa.europa.eu/document-library/consultation/open-insurance-accessing-and-sharing-insurance-related-data_en. Last visited June 7, 2024

European Supervisory Authority (ESA) (2022) Joint European Supervisory Authority Response to the European Commission's February 2021 Call for Advice on digital finance and related issues (ESA 2022 01). https://www.eba.europa.eu/sites/default/documents/files/document_library/Publications/Reports/2022/1026595/ESA%202022%2001%20ESA%20Final%20Report%20on%20Digital%20Finance.pdf. Last visited June 7, 2024

High-Level Expert Group on Artificial Intelligence (2019) Ethics Guidelines for Trustworthy Artificial Intelligence. https://digital-strategy.ec.europa.eu/en/library/ethics-guidelines-trustworthy-ai. Last visited June 7, 2024

International Association of Insurance Supervisors (IAIS) (2020) Issues Paper on the Use of Big Data Analytics in Insurance. https://www.iaisweb.org/page/supervisory-material/issues-papers. Last visited June 7, 2024

Marta Infantino Ph.D. (Palermo), LL.M. (NYU School of Law), is Associate Professor of Comparative Law at the University of Trieste, Italy, and Associate Member of the International Academy of Comparative Law (Paris, France). Her interests cover comparative contract law, comparative tort law, global indicators and the relationship between law and numbers. She has been Visiting Professor at the University of Montreal (Canada), the Universidad de los Andes (Colombia), the European Business School (Germany), the Scuola Superiore Meridionale (Italy), the Université Catholique de Lille and the Fondation pour le droit continental (France). E-mail: minfantino@units.it.

Problematic Consequences of Personalisation of Advertisement: The Case of Insurance Contracts

Katarzyna Południak-Gierz

1 Introduction

The personalization of advertisement, understood as adjusting the communication presented to individuals[1] to *inter alias* their situation, traits, and preferences, is already common within e-commerce. The phenomenon has already attracted the

[1] Namysłowska and Jabłonowska (2020), point 2.1.

This chapter has been written within the framework of a Narodowe Centrum Nauki research project, (NCN) [The National Science Centre] in Poland, Grant Number 2018/29/B/HS5/01281. Parts of the analysis were presented during the 9th International Law and Economics Conference in Lucerne. Law and Economics of the Digital Transformation, 8-9.04.2022, Luzern, Switzerland and during the XIX International Scientific and Practical Conference of Young Scientists "Economic and social development of Ukraine in the twenty-first century: the national vision and challenges of globalization", 13-14.05.2022, WUNU in Ternopil, Ukraine and published in the post-conference volume of abstracts "Економічний і соціальний розвиток україни в ххі столітті: національна візія та виклики глобалізації" (2022) and the monograph "Law and Economics of the Digital Transformation" (2023).

K. Południak-Gierz (✉)
Jagiellonian University, Faculty of Law and Administration, Kraków, Poland
e-mail: katarzyna.poludniak@uj.edu.pl

C. Poncibò, P. Tereszkiewicz (eds.), *European Insurance Law within the Digital Age*, AIDA Europe Research Series on Insurance Law and Regulation 14,
https://doi.org/10.1007/978-3-031-96496-1_5

attention of legal scholars[2] and EU legislator,[3] giving rise to a vivid discussion. One of the key obstacles in this dialogue is the lack of a well-established terminology—the notion of personalization itself tends to be understood differently. It is a misnomer, and it may easily be misunderstood as tailoring the content to a specific, individual person based on the situation, characteristics, and preferences of that particular person only.[4] The fact is that various categories of data are used for content adjustment. Typically they include objective data on the person, data derived from the online activity of this person and/or others that have similar characteristics, data on one's social ties, and standardized data serving as a proxy to fill in the blanks.[5] Furthermore, content matching often does not require the identification of the person, as it is enough to specify the characteristics, situation, and preferences of an anonymous content addressee.[6]

Another issue is that frequently the online user will not know whether the communication presented to them is actually (directly) adjusted to their situation, traits, and preferences or only seems to be directly matched, but actually it is not, since the point of reference is not the data on that individual but proxies of various kinds (e.g.,

---

[2] For example see: Balkin (2018); to the Facebook platform: Pałka (2021), pp. 1213–1215; Namysłowska and Jabłonowska (2020), point 2.2; Article 29 Data Protection Working Party, Opinion 2/2010 on online behavioural advertising, URL: https://ec.europa.eu/justice/article-29/documentation/opinion-recommendation/files/2010/wp171_en.pdf (access date: 31.01.2023); Buczyński (2013), *passim*; Fourberg et al. (2021); Guidelines 8/2020 on the targeting of social media users. 2.0 URL: https://edpb.europa.eu/our-work-tools/our-documents/guidelines/guidelines-82020-targeting-social-media-users_en (access date: 31.03.2022); Helberger (2016); Klafkowska-Waśniowska (2012); Namysłowska and Jabłonowska (2020); Szymielewicz and Iwańska (2019); Południak-Gierz and Olechowski (2022); Tereszkiewicz and Południak-Gierz (2021); Zuiderveen Borgesius (2017).

[3] For example: Consumer market study on online market segmentation through personalized pricing/offers in the European Union. Request for Specific Services 2016 85 02 for the implementation of Framework Contract EAHC/2013/CP/04, Luxembourg 2018, p. 33; Commission Notice – Guidance on the interpretation and application of Directive 2005/29/EC of the European Parliament and of the Council concerning unfair business-to-consumer commercial practices in the internal market C/2021/9320, OJ C C 526 of 29/12/2021, pp. 86-103; Regulation (EU) 2022/2065 of the European Parliament and of the Council of 19 October 2022 on the digital single market and amending Directive 2000/31/EC (Digital Services Act) (OJ L 277, 27.10.2022, pp. 1-102) (rec. 88, 94, 69 in connection with art. 34 and 35, art. 26(3)); Directive 2011/83/EU of the European Parliament and of the Council of 25 October 2011 on consumer rights, amending Council Directive 93/13/EEC and Directive 1999/44/EC of the European Parliament and of the Council and repealing Council Directive 85/577/EEC and Directive 97/7/EC of the European Parliament and of the Council (art. 6(1)(ea)); Directive 2005/29/EC of the European Parliament and of the Council of 11 May 2005 concerning unfair business-to-consumer commercial practices in the internal market and amending Council Directive 84/450/EEC, Directives 97/7/EC, 98/27/EC and 2002/65/EC of the European Parliament and of the Council and Regulation (EC) No 2006/2004 of the European Parliament and of the Council ('Unfair Commercial Practices Directive'); Rott et al. (2022).

[4] Infantino (2022), pp. 618–619; Helberger et al. (2021), p. 104.

[5] Helberger et al. (2021), pp. 103–104.

[6] Pałka (2020), pp. 595, 616.

standard data on other users or the context in which the communication is being presented).

A good example is the personalization of advertisement: the ads may match one's situation, traits, and preferences based on context, behavioral, and segment targeting.[7] Context advertising matches the content of the website on which it is presented.[8] The advertisement is likely to be perceived as tailored to users' interests but, in fact, it merely aligns with the general theme of the website. For instance, advertisements for travel insurance products are displayed on an airline website. Data on individual users are not the point of reference in this scenario. In the case of such a method for the personalization of advertisements, the risk of a mistake on the client's side increases – the user is prone to assume that the product matches their individual situation whereas it only corresponds with the context in which it is displayed.

In the case of segment-based personalization, the advertisement is adjusted to traits characteristic of a group of addressees. Internet users are divided into groups based on criteria set by the entity using the personalization tool.[9] For example, the distributor of insurance may be targeting only members of given professions such as architects, doctors, or physiotherapists.[10] Here, the legal concerns will mainly be determined by the choice and number of criteria applied during segmentation. With their increase in number, the impact of the practice on its targets may also grow, in extreme instances even amounting to an undue influence.

Finally, in the case of behavioral personalization the advertisement presented to the user is a response to their individual behavior—e.g., if one visited a website with some information about car insurance, the advertisement of the said insurance product would appear on a website which this person opened shortly afterward. Frequently, however, the adjustment of content is not based only on a single action undertaken by that person but through the taking into consideration of their history of previous activities in general. The data generated while browsing the Internet enable the creation of a complex user profile and as a result, make an individualization of the presented content possible. Hence, the biases and weaknesses of an individual may be addressed and exploited. Consequently, this manner of personalization increases the risk of undue impact on consumer decision-making autonomy while causing serious concerns from the data protection law perspective.

What is more, these manners of targeting tend to be used together, insofar as online marketing strategies combine especially behavioral and contextual targeting.[11]

---

[7] Fourberg et al. (2021); Południak-Gierz and Olechowski (2022).

[8] Szymielewicz and Iwańska (2019); Południak-Gierz and Olechowski (2022).

[9] Article 29 Data Protection Working Party, Opinion 2/2010 on online behavioural advertising, URL: https://ec.europa.eu/justice/article-29/documentation/opinion-recommendation/files/2010/wp171_en.pdf; Guidelines 8/2020 on the targeting of social media users. 2.0 URL: https://edpb.europa.eu/our-work-tools/our-documents/guidelines/guidelines-82020-targeting-social-media-users_en.

[10] As an illustration see: https://iexpert.pl/.

[11] Fourberg et al. (2021), p. 20; on the effectiveness of such a mixed approach see: Lu et al. (2016).

In all these instances, in principle, the person to whom the advertisement is addressed might view it as adjusted to them individually. Due to the above, when discussing the personalization of advertisement, both situations are considered: those where technologies based on automated data processing are used to match the content presented to individuals to their situation, characteristics, and preferences taking into account their data and possibly additional information, and those where the matching is carried out in a different way, but may lead the person to whom it is applied to believe that the content has been selected especially for them, due to their particular situation, characteristics or preferences.[12]

The aim of this contribution is, while signaling some legal challenges identified in the EU legal literature, to present how the personalization of advertisements may influence the content of the contract in the insurance sector and what protection mechanisms may apply whenever advertisements are mispersonalized—meaning that they lead consumers to enter into contracts whose contents are not correctly adjusted to their situations, characteristics, and preferences. Establishing a link between personalization at the pre-contractual stage and the content of the contract turns out to be particularly important in the case of insurance contracts. This is because remedies, both stemming from general private law provisions as well as from consumer law, that weaken the content of contractual bonds, tend to be ill-suited for the protection of insurance client interests.[13] Hence, possibilities of correcting the irregularities of the content of insurance contracts caused by mispersonalization should be explored (Sect. 2). Here, both the mechanism provided by the Unfair Terms Directive and the legitimate consumer expectations standard come to mind. As the challenges and opportunities related to the application of the unfair terms framework in the case of personalization,[14] insurance,[15] and the personalization of insurance products[16] have already been noticed in the subject literature, this contribution will focus on whether the legitimate consumer expectations standard may also have an important role to play in mitigating any negative effects of mispersonalization in the advertising of insurance products (Sect. 3). As it will be shown (Sect. 4), the legitimate consumer expectations standard may be particularly useful in cases in which technologies based on automated data processing are used to match advertisements to the individually tailored situation, characteristics, and preferences of consumers.

---

[12] Południak-Gierz (2025), pp. 201–203.

[13] Południak-Gierz and Tereszkiewicz (2023), pp. 38–45.

[14] Esposito and Grochowski (2022), passim.

[15] From a general perspective see e.g.: Basedow et al. (2016), p. 140; Borselli (2011); Tarasiuk-Flodrowska (2014); from the national law perspective e.g.: Szczepańska, (2017), p. 30; in the context of insurance contracts with elements of an investment contract: Grochowski (2019); issue Niedozwolone postanowienia umowne w umowach ubezpieczenia of journal Wiadomości Ubezpieczeniowe 2013.

[16] Południak-Gierz (2025), pp. 212–213.

2 Mispersonalized Advertisements for Consumer Insurance Contracts: A Vast Portfolio of Generally Ill-suited Remedies

In case of the conclusion of an insurance contract under the impact of a mispersonalized advertisement, the portfolio of remedies that may be available to the insurance applicant include general private law instruments of individual protection (e.g., regulation of mistake, deceit, threat, unfair exploitation), consumer protection mechanisms (especially rules on unfair practices), supplemented by remedies foreseen in general contract law and in provisions governing this specific sector.

The personalization of advertising may lead to an unacceptable restriction on individuals' decision-making autonomy.[17] Hence, on the one hand, the national regulation on the vice of consent may be applicable[18] and, on the other, the admissibility of such a commercial practice may be examined in the light of provisions implementing Directive 2005/29/EC.[19]

National regulation on the defects of consent, such as mistake, deceit, threat, and exploitation may provide for different sanctions across Member States,[20] yet the principal remedy in the case of contracts that are concluded under the influence of factors that prevent there being valid consent, give rise to a right to avoidance.[21] In contrast, once a particular practice is considered unfair, the consumer harmed by it shall have access to proportionate and effective remedies, including compensation

[17] Namysłowska and Jabłonowska (2020), point 2.2.1.

[18] Południak-Gierz (2021a), pp. 128, 293–302.

[19] Directive 2005/29/EC of the European Parliament and of the Council of 11 May 2005 concerning unfair business-to-consumer commercial practices in the internal market (OJ L 149 11.6.2005, p. 22).) The personalization of advertisements makes it more problematic to assess whether a particular ad may be viewed as having the potential to cause a mistake. Obstacles arise also when verifying if a personalization of ads based on exploiting one's weaknesses constitutes an aggressive commercial practice under the Directive 2005/29/EC or unfair exploitation under the applicable national law. (Południak-Gierz 2019, passim) The assessment of the admissibility of personalized advertisement becomes especially complex if also the sector specific acts apply – as in the case of insurance products. For instance, according to Article 17(1) IDD insurance distributors shall always act honestly, fairly and professionally in accordance with the best interests of their customers. Furthermore, the marketing communications (clearly identifiable), addressed by the insurance distributor to customers or potential customers shall be fair, clear and not misleading.

[20] E.g. under Polish law they may give rise to contract avoidance (art. 84–88 of Polish Civil Code), and if the party concluded a contract because of the exploitation of a party's economic necessity or other, specified by law, circumstances: they may demand a reduction of its performance or an increase of the performance due to it or demand that the contract be declared null and void (art. 388 of the Polish Civil Code).

[21] Study Group on a European Civil Code, Research Group on EC Private Law (Acquis Group) Principles, Definitions and Model Rules of European Private Law Draft Common Frame of Reference (DCFR), Christian von Bar, Eric Clive and Hans Schulte-Nölke, Hugh Beale, Johnny Herre, Jérôme Huet, Matthias Storme, Stephen Swann, Paul Varul, Anna Veneziano, Fryderyk Zoll (eds), Extended version available at: http://www.transformacje.pl/wp-content/uploads/2012/12/european-private-law_en.pdf, pp. 480–481; 534–539.

for damage suffered by the consumer and, where relevant, a price reduction or the termination of the contract (art. 11a(1) Directive 2005/29/EC).[22]

Typically, personalization may also be related to the data protection law infringement—e.g., if the data subject did not consciously consent to the processing of their personal data for the purpose of personalizing such an advertisement (see also below, Sect. 4, scenario 2). If, in consequence, this person has suffered material or non-material damage, the right to compensation arises (art. 82 GDPR). Whether such an infringement shall give rise to any other private law remedies[23] or influence the existence of contractual relationships, e.g., leading to contract invalidity,[24] is still under discussion.

The mispersonalization of insurance products, possibly also at the early pre-contractual stage (the mispersonalization of advertisement), may give rise to the right to compensation under different provisions.[25] These may be specific provisions of national insurance law, contract law, tort law, or general civil law provisions (*culpa in contrahendo*). The adequacy of such protection will differ depending on the scope of eventual compensation claims, as the latter may vary substantially, from covering all the damage incurred within a causal relationship (in this instance—from the financial perspective—the consumer would be in a similar situation as if the insurance contract was correctly personalized) to including the negative interest only (then the consumer, in principle, would be in a situation as if the insurance contract had never been concluded).

Finally, some instances of the mispersonalization of insurance products may be corrected by the mechanism of unfair clauses control, provided for in the UCTD.[26] However, the mispersonalization of the advertisement of insurance products may

---

[22] E.g. under art. 12 sec. 1. of the Polish Act of 23.08.2007 on Counteracting Unfair Market Practices (consolidated version in Journal of Laws 2017, item 2070 with amendments), in the event of an unfair market practice, a consumer whose interest has been threatened or infringed may demand:

(1) abandoning this practice;

(2) removal of the effects of this practice;

(3) submitting a single or multiple statement of the appropriate content and in the appropriate form;

(3a) price reduction;

(4) compensation for the damage caused, based on general terms, in particular a request to cancel the contract with the obligation of a mutual return of benefits and reimbursement by the entrepreneur of the costs related to the purchase of the product;

(5) adjudication of an appropriate sum of money for a specific social purpose related to the promotion of Polish culture, the protection of national heritage or the protection of consumers.

[23] E.g. those specified in art. 11a Directive 2005/29/WE, see: Commission Notice – Guidance on the interpretation and application of Directive 2005/29/EC of the European Parliament and of the Council concerning unfair business-to-consumer commercial practices in the internal market (Text with EEA relevance), C/2021/9320, OJ C 526, 29.12.2021, pp. 1–129; Drazewski (2022)

[24] Walczak (2025), pp. 171–198.

[25] The right to damages under GDPR is without prejudice to any claims for damage deriving from the violation of other rules in Union or Member State law. (rec. 146 GDPR).

[26] Południak-Gierz (2025), p. 212.

trigger this legal response only exceptionally because under UCTD the provisions of a contract are the subject of control, and not the elements outside of the contract itself (such as marketing communication). That will be the case if users are targeted with an advertisement of certain products because their vulnerability reduces their ability to understand these contractual clauses, which cause an imbalance in the parties' rights and obligations arising under the contract, making such an offer clearly unattractive from the perspective of the average consumer. In principle, however, this mechanism designed to correct the content of B2C contracts is unlikely to cure the negative effects of the mispersonalization of advertisement in general.

This leads to the conclusion that the effects of mispersonalization on consumer insurance and non-insurance market are, in principle, remedied in three manners: the contractual bond formed under the influence of mispersonalization is weakened (typically by granting the consumer the right to challenge the contract, see e.g., art. 11a(1) Directive 2005/29/EC), compensation is awarded (see e.g., art. 82 GDPR) or the content of that bond is corrected (see: art. 6(1) Directive 1993/13/EEC; art. 11a(1) Directive 2005/29/EC).[27] The adequacy of the first and second group of remedies is questioned in the subject literature, mainly because it does not allow the consumer to achieve the purpose of the insurance contract (having a certain group of risks insured).[28] In contrast, the specific tool for the correction of the content of the contract provided for in Directive 2005/29/EC, namely the price reduction, may be effective in case of mispersonalization which leads to overpricing of insurance products but not when it caused the insurance cover to be inadequate.[29] Finally, the mechanism foreseen in Directive 1993/13/EEC in case of unfair terms—which could in principle be used not only in the context of mispersonalization of price but also when the other contractual provisions are concerned—has only a very limited scope of application when the mispersonalization of advertisement is concerned.

What tends to be overlooked is that the mechanism provided for under Directive 1993/13/EEC is not the only automatic tool for correcting the content of consumer contracts—the standard of legitimate consumer expectations has a similar function. The issue is that if that standard, which should be playing a predominant role when interpreting consumer contracts pursuant to *acquis communautaire*, was taken seriously, neither granting the possibility to challenge the contract, nor to claim compensation in cases of mispersonalization of insurance contract would be necessary.

---

[27] Południak-Gierz and Tereszkiewicz (2023) pp. 41–45.

[28] Południak-Gierz and Tereszkiewicz (2023) pp. 41–42; Cousy (2012) (but in the context of sanctioning shortcomings in information duties by insurance applicant).

[29] Południak-Gierz and Tereszkiewicz (2023), pp. 38–40.

3 How Adopting a General Consumer Law Standard May Help Insurance Law Rise to the Challenge Posed by the Personalization of Advertisement

From the perspective of the insurance applicant, the negative consequences caused by the mispersonalization of advertisement, as well as by the mispersonalization of the insurance product itself, may be remedied by interpreting the contract that was concluded in a manner reflecting the legitimate expectations of the consumer, including those formed based on the product advertisement.

In European contract law, the stages of forming a legal relationship merge into one process.[30] Consumers' reasonable expectations, ones that arise before the contract is entered into, begin to play a decisive role when determining the content of that contractual relationship. This is because the will of the parties is no longer seen as the sole cornerstone of the contract in *acquis communautaire*: the statements of the will of the parties cease to be the main elements forming the contractual bond; they are reduced to being one of the factors shaping "what can be reasonably expected from the customer in relation to her declaration",[31] and—consequently—what the contractual relationship resulting from the contract conclusion will look like. Consumer directives on sales, digital content, services, and package holidays[32] expressly recognize that the other element shaping the said relationship is the pre-contractual statements of the business party, including public statements about the product.[33] The same tendency appears in relation to other groups of contracts, giving rise to the general assumption that the business must be aware that marketing communication gives rise to reasonable expectations from its customers; and should assume responsibility for such pre-contractual statements when concluding the contract.[34]

From the perspective of an insurance contract, this will mean that the content of the agreement might adjust itself to the benchmark of legitimate consumer expectations.[35] To illustrate the above: if a consumer purchases a standardized insurance product that is distributed under a specific name on a given market, but according to

---

[30] Schulze and Zoll (2021), p. 42.

[31] Schulze and Zoll (2021), p. 42.

[32] Art. 6(5) CRD, Rec. 13, art. 7 SGD, Rec. 20-21, art. 8 DCD, art. 6(1) PTD; Schulze and Zoll (2021), p. 129.

[33] Rec. 21, 45, art. 8(1)(b) DCD; rec. 29, Art. 7(1)(d) SGD; rec. 26 and art. 6(1) and art. 5(1) PTD, Møgelvang-Hansen (Sellier 2007), pp. 169–179.

[34] Schulze and Zoll (2021), p. 143; Article 4:107 ACQP; II.–9:102 DCFR, Study Group on a European Civil Code, Research Group on EC Private Law (Acquis Group) Principles, Definitions and Model Rules of European Private Law Draft Common Frame of Reference (DCFR), Christian von Bar, Eric Clive and Hans Schulte-Nölke, Hugh Beale, Johnny Herre, Jérôme Huet, Matthias Storme, Stephen Swann, Paul Varul, Anna Veneziano, Fryderyk Zoll (eds), Extended version available at: http://www.transformacje.pl/wp-content/uploads/2012/12/european-private-law_en.pdf, pp. 612–613.

[35] Południak-Gierz and Tereszkiewicz (2023), pp. 43–44.

the black letters of the contract does not have all the standard features, then under the standard of legitimate consumer expectations the contract will be interpreted as if the parties had agreed on the insurance product having all of these typical characteristics.

The same mechanism could minimize the negative effects of typical cases of mispersonalization of insurance products, regardless of the stage of contract formation at which the mispersonalization appeared. If the personalized advertising mechanism may reasonably make the consumer believe that the insurance product corresponds with their individual needs and demands, then regardless of the declarations of the parties and standard terms, the contract should be interpreted as such. For instance, if the target addressee of the advertisement of a travel insurance product is a person who is comparing offers of ski holiday packages (the advertisement appears with search results when such offers are browsed or on the website where ski holiday packages offered by a travel agency can be purchased), then this person may reasonably expect these insurance products to cover typical risks associated with winter sports. Hence even if the latter were excluded pursuant to a standard contract signed by the parties, the contract should be interpreted as if the product covered such risks. If, instead, personalization appears later—the insurance product is tailor-made for an individual—miscalculation of price and/or ill-matching insurance cover may equally be corrected by an appropriate interpretation of that insurance contract.[36]

This approach, however, raises several challenges. One is obviously whether the circumstances of the case justify the consumer's expectation that the insurance contract they conclude is matching their traits, situation, and needs. In the offline context, such expectations might be triggered especially by the assurances of the insurance distributor. Online, they will typically arise either due to the information provided when consenting to data processing but may be also based on daily life observations (normally, the content displayed to the user in this context is well-tailored to their expectation, hence—despite the lack of explicit commitment on the side of the other party—the consumer assumes that they are supposed to receive well-matched content only[37]).

Another difficulty is finding a point of reference that would be functional and acceptable for the parties as well as from the perspective of protected values and principles. This point of reference would serve to verify the adequacy of personalization, and—provided that mispersonalization during contract formation occurred—establish a benchmark for contract adjustment.

Possible solutions to this problem include checking what insurance contract, under the same circumstances, would be normally advised by an insurance distributor. Here, the benchmark would be provided by empirical/ statistical analysis about what practices are common in the sector. Thus certain mistakes and inefficiency,

[36] Południak-Gierz and Tereszkiewicz (2023) p. 45.

[37] On consumers' bounded rationality e.g. Bălău (2018), and the tendency to develop unjustified expectations in the online environment: Południak-Gierz (2021b), pp. 271–272.

which would be seen as possible and normal despite the professional diligence of the insurance distributor in the offline sphere, would be acceptable.[38]

Alternatively, it could be verified what contract should have been advised in such a scenario by a professional (also here the desired outcome of tailoring the insurance contract to the situation of the individual by a natural person would constitute a point of reference, but there would be no room for the abovementioned typical mistakes and inefficiency). However, setting such a point of reference does not allow us to take into account the specificity of automated decision-making. The technology may be insensitive to some factors which would be intuitively and automatically considered by a human being,[39] but it also grants one new possibility—vast amounts of data may be processed to uncover the traits of the person which are unknown to that individual and to make highly accurate assessments as to the future events.

Consequently, instead of referring to the empirical or human-based standard, the examination should be what the optimal manner of the functioning of personalizing mechanism would be (what the consumer could reasonably expect as a result of a correct personalization).[40] This would require determining what the effect of the personalization of an insurance advertisement or product would be if the personalizing mechanism was not defective, its configuration was correct, the data processed was adequate and sufficient, and the aim of personalization was in line with the principle of contractual fairness.[41] Depending on the form of mispersonalization, the interpretation could lead to a re-tailoring of the cover of the insurance contract or a re-calculating of the insurer's premium.

Such a solution, apart from numerous practical difficulties,[42] may also raise more general questions. First, such a contract adjustment tool limits the autonomy of the parties—in the case of a lack of qualified consent, the content of the contract is influenced more by the data on the consumer and correlated risk evaluation than by the actual declarations of the parties. However, this argument loses its power once the contractual asymmetry between the parties is taken into account. The greater the disproportionality, the less influence the weaker party has over the content of the contract.[43] Yet, once the personalization of advertisements and then contracts are launched, a particular paradox emerges. The individual traits of the weaker party influence the final content of the contract from the advertisement phase itself; from

---

[38] Jungermann and Belting (2004).

[39] This matter is clearly visible in the context of self-driving cars which fail to recognize and avoid a threat that would be easily manageable by a human. See e.g.: Lee (8 November 2017); Yadron and Tynan (1 July 2016).

[40] Południak-Gierz (2021b), pp. 267, 270.

[41] Tereszkiewicz and Południak-Gierz (2021).

[42] How, in practice, this re-personalization should be performed is problematic to determine. Different solutions are possible, burdened with various flaws which reduce their practical usefulness and admissibility.

[43] Łętowska (1974), pp. 151–152.

this point of view, personalization could be seen as a modern form of negotiation.[44] However, even so, the consumer has virtually no possibility to negotiate the contractual provisions—the only difference is that these may no longer be standardized but individually tailored to the profile of that person by the toolset of the entrepreneur. Thus, even in instances where personalization means that the content of the contract is set individually for a particular consumer, it is nevertheless shaped unilaterally by the stronger party. As a result, the personalization mechanism, working to the benefit of the stronger party, in principle does not limit his power over the final wording of the contract. Thus, the interference with the content of the personalized contract by its adjustment to the above-described standard should not, in principle, be seen as endangering a consumer's decision-making autonomy or freedom of contract.[45]

Second, it should also be noticed that in some instances the personalization tool tailoring the insurance advertisement (and then the contract) is used by a different entity than the one which shall be obliged under that contract to cover certain risks. In this scenario, if it is the insurance cover that is being re-shaped during contract adjustment, then the scope of liability of the entity covering that risk will be increased as a result of reversing the effects of the mispersonalization performed by a different entity. Yet, if the mechanism is only adjusting the content of the contract to what the effect of proper personalization would be, then related costs should not be excessive or unexpected from the perspective of the insurer.

Provided that the mechanism is applied regardless of what type of result the mispersonalization has caused, it is crucial to determine the direction of its functioning, namely is it a unilateral tool of protection of the consumer or rather a general mechanism of correcting the content of the contract.[46] For instance, if mispersonalization leads to under-pricing of the insurance product and causes losses on the side of the entrepreneur, should that be corrected?

Given that consumer protection tools should be applied solely to consumer benefit and shall not lead to an increase in a consumer's contractual obligation, then if the legitimate expectation standard was qualified as such, the mispersonalization to the detriment of the entrepreneur could not be corrected. Consequently, the risks of mispersonalization are borne by the business party, pursuant to the fact that he ventured to harness new technologies for his business gain. Given that the re-personalized content of the contract would match what could be referred to as a fair personalization outcome, the application of the standard should not increase the scope of the liability of the business over the level that should have been expected in the first place.

---

[44] Południak-Gierz (2019), pp. 165–166.

[45] The fact that the contract clauses have not been individually negotiated (agreed) justifies a court's or legislative intervention as 'the lack of negotiations weakens the willingness to be bound by the contract'. Schulze and Zoll European Contract Law (2021), p. 57. The instruments limiting contractual autonomy of the parties, are, in principle, recommended in consumer turnover. Południak-Gierz (2021a), p. 192.

[46] Tereszkiewicz and Południak-Gierz (2021), p. 44; Południak-Gierz (2021a), pp. 34–35.

If, in contrast, the standard was seen as a general tool of interpretation, in the insurance contract scenario incorrect price could be either diminished or increased so that it matched the fair personalized insurer's premium. A similar result would be observed in the case of any mispersonalization of cover: insurance cover could be re-calibrated regardless of how it influences the consumer's situation. Under this approach, both the consumer and the insurer bear the risk of using the new technology by the professional party. This, however, clearly contradicts the objectives of consumer law: it may result in the consumer losing the cover he or she believed to have obtained under the insurance contract based on the black letter of the contract. For this reason, the standard of legitimate consumer expectation should be regarded as an asymmetrical correction tool, which cannot be invoked by the trader against the consumer.

4 The "Who and How": The Problematic Assessment of Whether Consumer Expectations are Justified

As mentioned before, the personalization of insurance advertisements may be carried out either by insurance distributors themselves or by other entities whose infrastructure and/or services insurance distributors use for that purpose. Depending on the national law, insurance law provisions regulating marketing communications, addressed by the insurance distributor to customers or potential customers, e.g., implementing art. 17 of Directive 2016/97, may not apply to such other entities.[47] Nevertheless, in principle, insurance distributors, regardless of whether they directly advertise to potential customers by themselves or use other entities in this process, are bound to meet the abovementioned insurance law requirements.[48] Hence, the identity of who actually distributed the ad should not influence if and how the application of the standard of legitimate consumer expectations standard shall transform the insurance contract formed with the use of personalization tools. What may, however, drastically diminish the scope of the application of the above mechanism is how this personalization is actually achieved.

In the online environment, there are three typical scenarios in which one is faced with personalized advertisements that might be distinguished.

(1) First, the user might be asked to consent to data processing for the purpose of the personalization of an advertisement of insurance products. This, *per se*, could give rise to the insurance distributor's duty to explore this client's insurance needs.[49]

[47] This is the case of e.g. Polish law, where the definition of an insurance distributor is narrow and covers solely insurance companies, insurance agents, and insurance brokers (art. 3 sec. 1 point 8 of ustawa z dnia 15 grudnia 2017 r. o dystrybucji ubezpieczeń [Act of 15 December 2017 on insurance distribution] (Journal of Laws 2022, item 905 with amendments). Południak-Gierz and Olechowski (2022), p. 708.

[48] Południak-Gierz and Olechowski (2022), p. 709.

[49] See e.g.: art. 20 Directive 2016/97.

However, if consent is granted to obtain personalized advertisement, then it may be viewed as requesting advice, consequently triggering the advice duty on the side of the insurance distributor.[50] Alternatively, the said consent may be seen as "paying" with personal data for an additional service, namely recommending a contract that is most appropriate from the perspective of the needs and situation of this individual client (that is providing advice as understood under art. 2(1) point 15 IDD).[51] This may reasonably give rise to consumers' expectations as to the adequacy of the advertised insurance product and be taken into account during contract interpretation, as is further discussed in Sect. 4 of this contribution).

(2) Second, the user may not be requested to consent to data processing but the content would nevertheless be matched to their situation, traits, and preferences because personal data processing requirements stemming from the current legal framework were not met (data processing was unlawful). In this instance, the user's behavior does not provide grounds for the distributor's duty to explore their needs or yet alone the duty to advise to arise. Nevertheless, the fact that the digital insurance distributor uses personalizing tools that can actually match the product that is advertised to clients' situations, traits, and preferences, may constitute exploring the client's situation and, under art. 20(1) in fine IDD, translates into distributors' obligation to display to this individual only an advertisement of insurance products that shall be consistent with the customer's insurance demands and needs (to display only ads of generally matching insurance products). Yet, it can hardly trigger advice duty on the distributor's side, namely the duty to display solely ads of insurance products that are personally recommendable, and not just roughly adequate. Only when "an insurance distributor starts offering personalized products, that is, products adjusted to the needs and the situation of a customer ("tailor-made" products), and not just grossly matching their profile, should this conduct be considered giving advice."[52]

Also, the client's expectations as to the adequacy of the advertised product are unlikely to be justified in this scenario (though, naturally, expectations in this regard may emerge if the client becomes accustomed to receiving only advertisements of products that match their characteristics, situation, and preferences[53]). The problem is that the unlawfulness of data processing in this instance allows the insurance distributor to avoid being burdened with insurance and contract law obligations that would follow if the consent was correctly obtained, though he may benefit from using personalization technology, that is tricking a user into concluding a contract, adjust the price to their willingness-to-pay, etc. Axiologically, it could be justified to burden the insurance distributor benefitting from personalization techniques with additional risk and/or costs. The tension between data protection law, contract law,

---

[50] Tereszkiewicz and Południak-Gierz (2021), p. 88; Korpalski (2020), p. 247.

[51] Elvy (2017), part II; Tereszkiewicz and Południak-Gierz (2021).

[52] Tereszkiewicz and Południak-Gierz (2021).

[53] Południak-Gierz and Olechowski (2022), pp. 699–702.

and insurance law grows as the legislator hobbles in the back, trying to catch up with the newest technologies.

(3) Finally, the user may not be requested to consent to data processing, the data protection framework may be respected but the content may, nevertheless, be matched to this user's situation, traits, and preferences. Technology adjusting the content may allow for matching communication to users' traits, situations, or preferences without individualizing them e.g., based on context or standardized data on "similar" users.[54] Such personalization may be as effective as the one fueled by personal data, and give rise to largely similar risks. Yet, GDPR is "blind to collective interests and completely toothless when data cannot be directly linked to an "identified or identifiable" person".[55] Also, the expectations of individual clients as to the adequacy of the advertised product are unlikely to be justified in this scenario, and consequently, may not be protected under the legitimate consumer expectations standard. The question is whether the same applies to insurance law. The main issue is whether processing non-personal, e.g. statistical or anonymous, data already constitutes exploring the demands and needs of the customer that art. 20 IDD refers to. The matter is that this provision seems to introduce exploration duty only once an individualized person is targeted and information from this individual customer can be obtained. Hence such personalization of an insurance products advertisement may trigger neither justified expectations as to the adequacy of such products nor obligations to explore the individual needs and demands of the individual that is targeted not to mention the obligation to advise.

5 Conclusions

Personalization techniques are highly granular: the process of matching the content may be designed differently, and the strength of their impact on the consumer towards whom they are used varies substantially. Their effectiveness is not solely determined by the type of data that fuels the mechanism but also by the trust and expectations the consumer bestows on it. For this reason, the notion of personalization should cover situations where technologies based on automated data processing are used to match the content presented to individuals to their situation, characteristics, and preferences taking into account their data and possibly additional information, as well as the situations where the matching is carried out in a different way, but may lead the person to whom it is applied to believe that the content has been selected especially for them, due to their particular situation, characteristics or preferences.

In instances where the content is incorrectly adjusted, the consumers have at their disposal a vast portfolio of private law remedies that may, theoretically,

[54] Pałka (2020), p. 595.

[55] Pałka (2020), p. 616.

mitigate the negative effects of the said mispersonalization. Yet, something that becomes especially evident in the case of insurance contracts, these remedies tend to be generally ill-suited for the protection of consumer interests. For this reason, it is advocated that mispersonalization needs to be cured by applying the standard of legitimate consumer expectations. The hypothetical effect of a correctly performed personalization should be the point of reference when determining what could be reasonably expected by the consumer.

Apart from the practical difficulties related to the re-personalization, especially how and by whom it should be performed, the main limitation to this approach is that the standard of legitimate consumer expectations cannot be applied once the personalization is carried out based solely on standardized information and the consumer is not informed that the content is being matched. Nonetheless, this lack of transparency in the online environment may be expected to be addressed by the EU legislator.[56]

References

Article 29 Data Protection Working Party, Opinion 2/2010 on online behavioral advertising. Available at: https://ec.europa.eu/justice/article-29/documentation/opinion-recommendation/files/2010/wp171_en.pdf

Bălău M (2018) The limited consumer rationality and the role of environmental cues. Int J Econ Behav 8(1):19–31

Balkin JM (2018) Fixing Social Media's Grand Bargain, Hoover Working Group on National Security, Technology, and Law, Aegis Series Paper No. 1814. Available at: https://papers.ssrn.com/sol3/papers.cfm?abstract_id=3266942

Basedow J et al (eds) (2016) Principles of European insurance contract law (PEICL). Köln

Borselli A (2011) Unfair terms in insurance contracts. Eur Insurance Law Rev 2:36–42

Buczyński SM (2013) Konsument wobec internetowej reklamy behawioralnej. In: Królikowska-Olczak M, Pachuca-Smulska B (eds) Ochrona konsumenta w prawie polskim i Unii Europejskiej. C.H. Beck, Warszawa

Commission Notice – Guidance on the interpretation and application of Directive 2005/29/EC of the European Parliament and of the Council concerning unfair business-to-consumer commercial practices in the internal market C/2021/9320, OJ C C 526 of 29/12/2021

Consumer market study on online market segmentation through personalized pricing/offers in the European Union. Request for Specific Services 2016 85 02 for the implementation of Framework Contract EAHC/2013/CP/04, Luxembourg 2018. https://op.europa.eu/en/publication-detail/-/publication/ed9ce056-c2cf-11e8-9424-01aa75ed71a1/language-en

Cousy H (2012) About sanctions and the hybrid nature of modern insurance contract law. Erasmus Law Rev 5(2):123–131

Directive (EU) 2016/97 of the European Parliament and of the Council of 20 January 2016 on insurance distribution (OJ L 26, 2.2.2016, pp. 19–59)

[56] The use of algorithms to adjust content in the online environment has already attracted the attention of the EU legislator and some norms aimed at assuring that it does not lead to results which are unacceptable from the perspective of the legal system have already been introduced. See e.g. art. 6(1)(ea) Directive 2011/83/EU; art. 25, 34 and 35 Regulation 2022/2065.

Directive 2005/29/EC of the European Parliament and of the Council of 11 May 2005 concerning unfair business-to-consumer commercial practices in the internal market (OJ L 149, 11.6.2005, pp. 22–39)

Directive 2011/83/EU of the European Parliament and of the Council of 25 October 2011 on consumer rights, amending Council Directive 93/13/EEC and Directive 1999/44/EC of the European Parliament and of the Council and repealing Council Directive 85/577/EEC and Directive 97/7/EC of the European Parliament and of the Council (OJ L 304, 22.11.2011, pp. 64–88)

Drazewski K (2022) EU Consumer Protection 2.0. Protecting fairness and consumer choice in a digital economy, BUEC. Available at: https://www.beuc.eu/sites/default/files/publications/beuc-x-2022-015_protecting_fairness_and_consumer_choice_in_a_digital_economy.pdf

Elvy S-A (2017) Paying for privacy and the personal data economy. Columbia Law Rev 117:1369–1459

Esposito F, Grochowski M (2022) The consumer benchmark, vulnerability, and the contract terms transparency: a plea for reconsideration. Eur Rev Contr Law 18(1). https://doi.org/10.1515/ercl-2022-2035

Економічний і соціальний розвиток україни в xxi столітті: національна візія та виклики глобалізації (2022) ЗУНУ, Тернопіль

Fourberg N, Taş S, Wiewiorra L, Godlovitch I, De Streel A, Jacquemin H, Hill J, Nunu M, Bourguigon C, Jacques F, Ledger M, Lognoul M (2021) Online advertising: the impact of targeted advertising on advertisers, market access and consumer choice. European Parliament

Grochowski M (2019) Postanowienia określające główne świadczenia stron (art. 385[1] § 1 KC) a umowa ubezpieczenia o funkcji inwestycyjnej, Monitor Prawniczy 7

Guidelines 8/2020 on the targeting of social media users. 2.0 Available at: https://edpb.europa.eu/our-work-tools/our-documents/guidelines/guidelines-82020-targeting-social-media-users_en

Helberger N (2016) Profiling and targeting consumers in the internet of things – a new challenge for consumer law. In: Schulze R, Staudenmayer D (eds) Digital revolution challenges for contract law in practice. Nomos, Baden-Baden

Helberger N, Lynskey O, Micklitz H-W, Rott P, Sax M, Strycharz J (2021) EU Consumer Protection 2.0. structural asymmetries in digital consumer markets, a joint report from research conducted under the EUCP2.0 project. BEUC, Brussels

Infantino M (2022) Big data analytics, insurtech and consumer contracts: a European appraisal. Eur Rev Priv Law 30(4):613–634

Jungermann H, Belting J (2004) Wir verstehen uns doch – nicht wahr! Psychologische Aspekte der Altersvorsorge und Anlageberatung, Kritische Vierteljahresschrift für Gesetzgebung und Rechtswissenschaft 87(3):325–344 DOI:https://doi.org/10.5771/2193-7869-2004-3-325

Klafkowska-Waśniowska K (2012) Internetowe reklamy behawioralne a ochrona prywatności. In: Namysłowska M (ed) Reklama. Aspekty prawne. LEX, Warszawa

Korpalski M (2020) Bankowe terminowe umowy walutowe. Wolters Kluwer, Warszawa

Lee D (8 November 2017) Self-driving shuttle bus in crash on first day, BBC News, Available at: https://www.bbc.com/news/technology-41923814

Łętowska E (1974) Problematyka ogólnych warunków i wzorów umów w świetle poglądów doktryny obcej, Studia Prawnicze 3

Lu X, Zhao X, Xue L (2016) Is combining contextual and behavioral targeting strategies effective in online advertising? ACM Transact Manage Inf Syst (TMIS) 7(1):1–20

Møgelvang-Hansen P (2007) The Binding Effects of Advertising. In: Schulze R (ed) New features in contract law. Sellier, pp 169–179

Namysłowska M, Jabłonowska A (2020) Personalizacja oparta na sztucznej inteligencji – nowe wyzwanie dla prawa konsumenckiego. In: Lai L, Świerczyński M (eds) Prawo sztucznej inteligencji. C.H. Beck, Warszawa

Niedozwolone postanowienia umowne w umowach ubezpieczenia, issue of journal Wiadomości Ubezpieczeniowe 2013

Pałka P (2020) Data management law for the 2020s: the lost origins and the new needs. Buff Law Rev 68:559–640

Pałka P (2021) World of fifty (interoperable) Facebooks. Seton Hall Law Rev 51(4):1193–1239

Południak-Gierz K (2019) Consequences of the use of personalization algorithms in shaping an offer – a private law perspective. Masaryk Univ J Law Technol 13(2):161–188

Południak-Gierz K (2021a) Defects of consent in consumer E-Commerce from the polish law perspective. V&R Unipress, Göttingen

Południak-Gierz K (2021b) Personalization of consumer contracts – should we personalize interpretation rules? In: Green MD, Mercedes Lopez Rodriguez A, Kubica M (eds) Legal challenges in the new digital age. Brill, Leiden

Południak-Gierz K (2025) Personalizacja w sektorze ubezpieczeń – perspektywa prywatnoprawna. In: Tereszkiewicz P, Południak-Gierz K (eds) Umowa ubezpieczenia. Nowe technologie i prawo konsumenckie. C.H. Beck, Warszawa.

Południak-Gierz K, Olechowski P (2022) Personalizacja reklam produktów ubezpieczeniowych : między teorią a praktyką. In: Namysłowska M (ed) Reklama. Aspekty prawne, vol II. Wolters Kluwer, Warszawa

Południak-Gierz K, Tereszkiewicz P (2023) Digitalization's big promise and peril: personalization of insurance contracts and its legal consequences. In: Mathis K, Tor A (eds) . Springer, Law and economics of the digital transformation

Regulation (EU) 2022/2065 of the European Parliament and of the Council of 19 October 2022 on the digital single market and amending Directive 2000/31/EC (Digital Services Act) (OJ L 277, 27.10.2022, pp. 1-102)

Rott P, Strycharz J, Alleweldt F (2022) Personalized pricing. Luxemburg, Available at: https://www.europarl.europa.eu/RegData/etudes/STUD/2022/734008/IPOL_STU(2022)734008_EN.pdf

Schulze R, Zoll F (2021) European contract law. C.H. Beck-Nomos-Hart

Study Group on a European Civil Code, Research Group on EC Private Law (Acquis Group) von Bar C, Clive E, Schulte-Nölke H, Beale H, Herre J, Huet J, Storme M, Swann S, Varul P, Veneziano A, Zoll F (eds), (2009) Principles, Definitions and Model Rules of European Private Law Draft Common Frame of Reference (DCFR). Extended version. Available at: http://www.transformacje.pl/wp-content/uploads/2012/12/european-private-law_en.pdf

Szczepańska M (2017) Abuzywność postanowień umownych w zakresie świadczeń oraz definiowania wypadku ubezpieczeniowego w treści umów ubezpieczenia na życie. Wiadomości Ubezpieczeniowe 2:27–40

Szymielewicz K, Iwańska K (2019) Śledzenie i profilowanie w sieci, Raport Fundacji Panoptykon

Tarasiuk-Flodrowska A (2014) Abusive clauses in consumer and insurance contracts - recent developments in Europe. Eur Ins Law Rev 31(1):21–40

Tereszkiewicz P, Południak-Gierz K (2021) Liability for incorrect client personalization in the distribution of consumer insurance. Risks 9(5):83. https://doi.org/10.3390/risks9050083

Ustawa z dnia 15 grudnia 2017 r. o dystrybucji ubezpieczeń [Act of 15 December 2017 on insurance distribution] (Journal of Laws 2022, item 905 with changes)

Walczak P (2025) Wpływ naruszenia RODO na etapie przedkontraktowym na ważność konsumenckiej umowy ubezpieczenia. In: Tereszkiewicz P, Południak-Gierz K (eds) Umowa ubezpieczenia. Nowe technologie i prawo konsumenckie. C.H. Beck, Warszawa.

Yadron D, Tynan D (1 July 2016), Tesla driver dies in first fatal crash while using autopilot mode, the Guardian. Available at: https://www.theguardian.com/technology/2016/jun/30/tesla-autopilot-death-self-driving-car-elon-musk

Zuiderveen Borgesius FJ, Poort JP (2017) Online price discrimination and EU data privacy law. J Consum Policy 40(3):347–366

Katarzyna Południak-Gierz PhD, Assistant Professor at the Civil Law Department, Faculty of Law and Administration, Jagiellonian University, Kraków, Poland.

The Impact of Technology on Information Asymmetry in Insurance. What Does It Mean for the Pre-contractual Duty of Disclosure?

Marta Ostrowska

1 Introduction

Contrary to the perfect competition theory, most markets are not perfectly competitive and insurance markets are no exception. The imperfectly competitive markets suffer different kinds of information problems, among which the problems of asymmetric information. Information asymmetry (IA) is particularly burdensome for insurance markets and therefore gives ground for regulation.

This chapter explores how technology being increasingly involved in all steps of the insurance value chain impacts the IA problem in insurance and the legal framework addressing IA. The author puts forward the thesis that the impact is such that it reverses the historical IA between insurers and (prospective) policyholders. This brings to the question of consequences of such a reversal, in particular for the legal framework. Does the reversal of IA deprive the legal framework addressing IA of the meaning? Should the reversal of IA drive the change in the legal framework? To these questions the author devotes this chapter.

The above questions are formulated based on the following assumptions:

The chapter continues the author's consideration on the topic in Ostrowska, M., Does new technology put an end to policyholder risk declaration? The impact of digitalization on insurance relationships, the Geneva Papers on Risk and Insurance - Issues and Practice, the Geneva Papers on Risk and Insurance - Issues and Practice, 2021, vol. 46(4), pp. 573–592.

M. Ostrowska (✉)
Universität Zürich, Zürich, Switzerland
e-mail: marta.ostrowska@ius.uzh.ch

C. Poncibò, P. Tereszkiewicz (eds.), *European Insurance Law within the Digital Age*, AIDA Europe Research Series on Insurance Law and Regulation 14,
https://doi.org/10.1007/978-3-031-96496-1_6

- There is commonly acknowledged causal relation between a market situation (cause), for instance IA, and a regulation (effect).[1] According to the public interest theory of regulation, which historically has been most often used to describe insurance, regulation is created to correct market imperfections.[2]
- The impact of the technology on the market (cause) is significant, but it is not yet fully reflected in or addressed by the regulation (effect).[3]
- Both market situations and regulations are dynamic. Typically, regulations evolve in accordance with economic and social changes.[4]

The above assumptions must be taken into account in questioning if the technology impacts the legal framework addressing IA. Besides, one must identify in what way regulation responses to the market situation or, more precisely, what exact elements of market situation are addressed by the regulation. To this end, the chapter begins with a brief presentation of the IA problem from purely economic and legal perspectives (Sect. 2). It will allow us to see what elements of the IA problem are essential for the legal order and to what extent the regulation responds to the market situation. Theoretically, if the elements stressed by the regulation turns out to be the same elements which are affected by the technology, the argument for a change of the regulation should sound more convincing. Section 3 then describes measures the regulation puts forward to address and mitigate the problem of IA. This is the object of a potential reform. It should be noted here that, in describing the measures, the chapter does not refer to any particular jurisdiction or legal system. Although the author does recognize that there are differences in how national jurisdictions address the IA, they all introduce some form of disclosure duty. Therefore, the chapter focuses on the *concept* of disclosure duty and, where necessary, it will refer to the

---

[1] For example, Zweifel et al. (2021), p. 391. More specifically for insurance, Siegelman argues that market failure, such as adverse selection, in insurance markets is often 'a decisive factor' in legal decision-making and in policy debates. Siegelman (2004), p. 1226.

[2] Brady et al. (1995), p. 28, Kwon (2012), p. 13.

[3] See for example Geneva Association, Big Data and Insurance: Implications for Innovation, Competition and Privacy, March 2018. The report provides an overview of what technology is implemented in insurance and what legal concerns it may rise. The pace of technology development is fast, and it is challenging for the regulation to keep up. Almost a decade has been spent by supervisors and regulators on understanding the technology and mapping potential supervisory risks resulting from the use of it. Only recently some developments of legislation attempting to control the use of data and technology is observed. In the European Union see for example General Data Protection Regulation (GDPR), Distance Marketing Directive for financial services (DMD) or proposal on Artificial Intelligence Act.

[4] Brady et al. (1995), p. 11 ("… regulation adjusts to events, such as changes in the economy, new products and services in the market, and new technology. For example, improvements and innovation in computer technology and telecommunications have significantly affected insurance regulation.").

Principles of European Insurance Contract Law (PEICL)[5] or the relevant EU law. Against this backdrop, Sect. 4 turns to demonstrate the core thesis of the chapter: the technology reverses the historical IA. The original "policyholder knows better" becomes "insurer knows better". This part will show what exact elements of IA are affected and will allow us to compare those elements with the elements stressed by the regulation. Finally, based on these findings, Sect. 5 attempts to address the main questions: Does the change in IA deprive the legal framework addressing IA of the meaning? Should the change in IA drive the reform of the legal framework?

2 Information Asymmetry in Insurance: Economic and Legal Perspective

The starting point for the economic literature on IA is usually the classical microeconomics' assumption of perfect market transparency where both consumers and producers know prices and qualities of the goods and services they deal with. Subsequently, it is explained that the assumption is however false where the marginal cost of acquiring information exceeds the expected return.[6] When this is the case, the perfect transparency is not attained, resulting in information being distributed asymmetrically and some market participants knowing more than others. In 1976, Rothschild and Stiglitz specified the problem for the insurance market and concluded that the market participant who knows more about the risk profile and risk affecting behaviour is a prospective policyholder and the one who suffers the lack of information is an insurer.[7] This is because the probability and severity of the loss depend, most of the time and at least in part, on the policyholder's behaviour. There are two harmful consequences of such an imbalance: moral hazard and adverse selection problem. The moral hazard occurs when the awareness of being insured allows the policyholder to act riskier (i.e. to reduce his effort at preventing a loss or mitigating its consequences) than if he had not been insured. This in turn changes the basis for calculating the premium and increases the overall cost of insurance. The adverse selection occurs when the insurer does not know the true risk profile of the prospective policyholder. For the policyholder, adverse selection allows him to purchase insurance based on his private knowledge about the likelihood that he will file a claim. Not knowing the private knowledge of the policyholder, to calculate the premium, the insurer must average the risk. Consequently, the cost of insurance is

[5] Principles of European Insurance Contract Law (PEICL) are an academic project intended to serve as a model for European insurance contract law. PEICL are modelled based on the national insurance contract laws and therefore reflect the standard concepts applied by the European jurisdiction. Hence, in the author's view, the PEICL serve best as a reference in a general discussion about the pre-contractual duty of disclosure where the reference to a specific jurisdiction is not required.

[6] See the classic paper of Akerloff (1970), pp. 488–500.

[7] Rothschild and Stiglitz (1976), pp. 629–649.

too high for low risk profile policyholders who are more willing to migrate to another insurer offering a contract better tailored to their risk profile.[8] This way, the insurer loses good quality (low) risks and is forced to increase the premiums to offset the rising loss payments. Meanwhile, more low risks are driven away to the competing insurers. The insurer runs into financial difficulties and the remaining high-risk profile policyholder must migrate to the competing insurers. Then, the adverse selection's 'death spiral' goes onto the next insurer. The consequences of adverse selection are considered broader, more far-reaching and thus more severe than those of moral hazard. This is the IA story told from the economists' perspective. We will now move to see how the same story looks through the lenses of the legal scholars.

The legal literature which pertains to the problem of IA in insurance contracts barely refers to the notion of IA. Rather, it talks about the IA under the label of 'the utmost good faith principle' (*uberrimae fidei*). The norm goes back to *Carter v Boehm* which, up to this day, has been widely regarded as having established the principle in insurance law. Lord Mansfield explains why insurance contract differs from other types of contracts which also require good faith and, therefore, why in insurance good faith should be elevated to *utmost* good faith:

> Insurance is a contract upon speculation. *The special facts, upon which the contingent chance is to be found, lie more commonly in the knowledge of the insured only*: the underwriter trusts to his representation, and proceeds upon confidence that he does not keep back any circumstance in his knowledge, to mislead the underwriter into a belief that the circumstance does not exist, and to induce him to estimate the risque as if it did not exist. The keeping back of such a circumstance is a fraud and therefore the policy is void. Although the suppression should happen through mistake, without fraudulent intention, yet still the underwriter is deceived, and the policy is void; because the risque run is really different from the risque understood and intended to be run at the time of the agreement.[9]

The case and further development of the case law[10] set early rules on a policyholder's duty of disclosure. The legal discourse revolves primarily around the scope of the duty (e.g. Should it be "broad" or "narrow"? How to determine if the information is material?) as well as the failure to comply with the duty (e.g. What constitutes the breach of the duty? What is the difference between the breach with and without fault? What consequences should follow if the policyholder breaches the duty fraudulently?). Although the duty of disclosure imposed *on the policyholder* is a central point of the principle of utmost good faith, in *Carter v Boehm,* Lord Mansfield underlines that the principle and thereby the duty of disclosure is of mutual nature. Namely, he says that neither the policyholder nor the insurer should withhold information privately within his knowledge in order to induce the other to enter into the insurance contract.[11] The duty of disclosure by the insurer has not however been defined in detail and failed to further develop.

---

[8] Pauly (1974), pp. 44–62.

[9] (1766) 3 Burr 1905; 97 ER 1162, pp. 1909, 1910.

[10] See detailed analysis of the development of utmost good faith principle for example in Hasson (1969), pp. 615–637.

[11] 3 Burr 1905, 1909-1910; 97 ER 1162, 1164.

The legal story has its continuum in regulations on the course of insurance business where it takes a different turn. While the utmost good faith concept positions the prospective policyholder (customer) at the "informational *advantage*" when it comes to the risk insured, the regulations on the course of insurance business portray him as at the "informational *disadvantage*" when it comes to the process of purchasing insurance. The "informational disadvantage" of the customer is primarily owed to the fact that, contrary to an insurance distributor (insurer, agent, broker), he does not have expert knowledge or experience necessary to make an informed decision about insurance and insurance products (i.e. how it works, how to evaluate coverage or insurer's business performance, etc.). Therefore, the decisions he must make to purchase an insurance product are, in most cases, unfamiliar and complex. Additionally, what may further deteriorate the customer's position is the insurer's desire to make a profit. As a more knowledgeable party, the insurer may be tempted to take advantage of the customer's lack of expertise and allow, or even lure, the customer to make unwise decisions. The consequence of such a disadvantaged position is the risk of purchasing 'an empty coverage'—a coverage that is not suited to the needs and demands of the customer. This risk becomes even more serious when we realise that, for the nature of insurance contracts, customers might not discover that a loss is not covered until after the loss occurs—leaving them to face the consequences that they believed to be covered by the insurance contract. To remedy the disadvantaged position of the customer, the regulations on the course of insurance business provide for a wide range of information duties of insurance distributors.

Having presented how the IA problem is seen from an economic and legal perspective, a few conclusions may be drawn. First, both stories talk about IA, however, the asymmetry is not always the same. The economic story and the part of the legal story where it talks about the information on the risk to be insured portrays the insurer as a disadvantaged party. Yet, it is the prospective policyholder who suffers the lack of information when it comes to the process of purchasing insurance. Second, the economic story focuses on two aspects of IA: (i) adverse selection (the insurer knowing less than the prospective policyholder about the policyholder's situation) and (ii) moral hazard (the propensity of the policyholder to alter its behaviour when risk is transferred to the insurer). The legal story, in turn, stresses three aspects of IA: the utmost good faith principle revolves around (i) adverse selection, whereas the regulations on the course of insurance business address (ii) the so-called 'lemons' problem (the insurance customer knowing less than the insurance distributor about insurance products) and (iii) the agency problem (the customer knowing less about its insurance distributor's actions and performance than the insurance distributor). Third, the legal discourse about the scope of the duty of disclosure (what information should be provided to the insurer by the prospective policyholder) is merely a legal parlance for adverse selection.[12] It translates into an

[12] Heiss and Mönnich refer to IA directly: "(…) the circumstances surrounding the risk are usually known to the policyholder, whereas it is only partially possible for the insurer to obtain this information (…). It is an almost archetypal case of information asymmetry." Heiss and Mönnich (2018), p. 388.

economic discussion about which of the contracting parties has 'superior access to information and is therefore the cheapest gatherer of information'[13]. That the economic story and the legal story talk virtually about the same adverse selection is also confirmed by Schoenbaum who argues that 'the rule of utmost good faith is grounded in *economic efficiency*.'[14] Fourth, whereas the economic story studies the effects of IA for the broader market, the legal story understandably narrows down the IA problem to its consequences for an individual insurance relationship. In particular, it looks in details into how the lack of a complete or truthful information create inequities in the relationship, what the consequences of these inequities are and how the equality in the relationship can be ensured and restored once it is imbalanced—these are the elements of IA problem which are of interest for the legal story. The focus on the scope of the duty of disclosure and the development of the discourse around the duty allows one to claim that the rationale of the duty is not limited to or concentrated on the protection of the insurer. Rather, its fundamental rationale is the need for a true and fair agreement between two contractual parties.[15] This claim is fostered by the mutuality of the duty.

3 The Disclosure

Having seen how the problem of IA is presented in economic and legal parlance, we will now take a closer look into measures the law takes to restore the information balance between the parties. In studying the measures, besides identifying how exactly the balance is restored, it is desirable to find out if the role of the measure is limited to restoring that balance only or if it serves other purposes as well.

An automatic response to information problems in any market is minimising or eliminating any information gap in business transactions. This is also the solution broadly introduced in the legal systems. In short, the law strives for equipping the disadvantaged party (the insurer or the (prospective) policyholder, depending on the perspective) with the information it lacks (information on the risk to be insured and information required to make an informed insurance decision, respectively), thereby to restore the information balance between the parties. Generally, it does so by imposing a duty to disclose on the party which is more knowledgeable. For instance, as mentioned earlier, in the regulation on the course of business, the EU law on insurance distribution requires the insurance distributors to disclose their corporate identity,[16] any potential conflicts of interest[17] and provide the customer with key

---

[13] Loacker (2015), p. 159. In a similar fashion: Heiss and Mönnich (2018), p. 388.

[14] Schoenbaum (1998), p. 3.

[15] Following Lowry (2011), p. 58 and the case law referred therein.

[16] Art. 18 of the Directive (EU) 2016/97 of the European Parliament and of the Council of 20 January 2016 on insurance distribution, OJ L 26, 2.2.2016, pp. 19–59.

[17] Art. 19 of the Directive (EU) 2016/97 of the European Parliament and of the Council of 20 January 2016 on insurance distribution, OJ L 26, 2.2.2016, pp. 19–59.

information about insurance products.[18] This information aims at helping the prospective policyholders to decide on what insurance product to purchase, how they may benefit from the product and to understand who the counterparty to the contract is. Further to the disclosures, a relatively new measure employed by the regulation is a duty to assist the prospective policyholder in choosing the right insurance product (this may include specifying the customers' demands and needs, providing advice or recommendation).[19] The assistance helps to understand what the information provided to the customers via the disclosures means specifically for them. However, the most common long-standing duty of disclosure pertains to the risk to be insured and is imposed on the prospective policyholder. Further considerations in this chapter will focus on the policyholder's pre-contractual duty to disclose the risk to be insured. Since insurance contract law differs among jurisdictions, for the purposes of a general presentation of the duty and for the sake of simplicity, if necessary, references will be made to the duty as it is recognized in the Principles of European Insurance Contract Law (PEICL).[20]

Insurance contract law imposes the duty of disclosure on the prospective policyholder. The duty arises at the inception of the contract (*and* at the moment where the adverse selection comes into play, which again connects the duty with adverse selection problem). In designing any legal measure, a law-making authority should specify (i) an objective that a measure advances, (ii) what amounts to an effective execution of the measure, (iii) potential ways of ineffective execution of the measure, (iv) consequences of ineffective execution and no execution of the measure (remedies). Accordingly, we will now attempt to draw the structure of the duty of disclosure by identifying these four elements.

As already mentioned, **the objective of the duty of disclosure** is to provide the insurer with the information on the risk which is required for the insurer to be able to assess the risk, decide whether or not to accept that risk and set an adequate price for accepting the risk. In other words, the disclosed information should enable the insurer to make an offer of insurance coverage that does not put the insurer's business at risk of becoming insolvent and for a price that reflects frequency and severity of the risk occurrence.

Generally, **the effective execution of the duty** would require the prospective policyholder to disclose all the circumstances relating to the risk to be insured before the contract is concluded. There are however a few issues arising around execution of the duty that the law considers avoiding putting too much of an

[18] Art. 20, 29 of the Directive (EU) 2016/97 of the European Parliament and of the Council of 20 January 2016 on insurance distribution, OJ L 26, 2.2.2016, pp. 19–59.

[19] See for example Art. 20 of the Directive (EU) 2016/97 of the European Parliament and of the Council of 20 January 2016 on insurance distribution, OJ L 26, 2.2.2016, pp. 19–59.

[20] Principles of European Insurance Contract Law (PEICL) are an academic project intended to serve as a model for European insurance contract law. PEICL are modelled based on the national insurance contract laws and therefore reflect the current status of insurance law in Europe. Hence, in the author's view, PEICL serves best as a reference in a general discussion about the pre-contractual duty of disclosure where the reference to specific jurisdiction is not required.

unnecessary burden on the prospective policyholder and thereby creating another form of imbalance between the parties. The first problem regards the information as such. Assuming that the information to be disclosed serves the insurer to assess the risk and calculate the premium, clearly it would be unreasonable to request all possible information on the risk. Moreover, if there is information that is already known to the insurer or may be presumed to be known by the insurer, the reason to request such information from the prospective policyholder no longer exists. Therefore, the law defines the scope of information required by putting quantitative and qualitative limits: the prospective policyholder is required to provide only the information *that is material to the risk* and *that is not known to the insurer.*

Nevertheless, the limitation does not solve the problem altogether and leaves the scope of the duty still relatively open. This is because the concept of 'materiality of information' is not entirely clear and there is no single formula that automatically determines what is material and what is not. Although there is a set of information that is by default considered material (e.g. policyholder's financial history in interruption insurance and property insurance, age in health insurance, vehicle's technical condition in motor insurance), in most cases, materiality of information will be decided case by case. The way national laws approach this problem differs, yet one solution applied is a test for determining materiality of any circumstance. For instance, in the UK, the Insurance Act 2015 provides that "A circumstance or representation is material if it would influence the judgement of a prudent insurer in determining whether to take the risk and, if so, on what terms."[21] Additionally, s.7(4) of the Insurance Act 2015 gives the following list of exemplary material circumstances: special or unusual facts relating to the risk, any particular concerns which led the insured to seek insurance cover for the risk, anything which those concerned with the class of insurance and field of activity in question would generally understand as being something that should be dealt with in a fair presentation of risks of the type in question. Although the test makes the meaning of materiality more precise, it does not remove all the uncertainty and the difficulty of defining "influence" or "prudent insurer" remains.

Besides materiality, typically, the scope of the duty is limited by indicating information which the prospective policyholder is *not required* to provide. This is information that is known to the insurer, that the insurer ought to know, that the insurer is presumed to know, that is waived by the insurer and information on any circumstance which diminishes the risk. As to the knowledge of the insurer, there are at least two reasons for excluding what is known to the insurer from the scope of the duty. First and foremost, the duty serves to provide the insurer with the required information because the insurer does not have that information and cannot receive it from elsewhere. Therefore, the duty serves to provide the insurer only with the information that is *private* to the policyholder. Second, it is explained that given his expertise, the insurer should not rely only on the policyholder's knowledge, and he

[21] Section 7(3) of the Insurance Act 2015.

should take an active part in investigating the risk himself.[22] This is another way in which the law tries to balance the positions of the contractual parties and to lighten the burden of the duty for the policyholder. In turn, the reason for why the policyholder does not have to inform the insurer about the circumstances which diminishes the risk is that the lack of that information does not affect the insurer negatively.[23]

For the difficulties in precise delimitation of the scope of the duty, some jurisdictions chose to design the duty based on a so-called "questionnaire model". In the questionnaire model, the prospective policyholder discloses the required information in response to questions posed by the insurer. The questionnaire model stands in opposition to a "voluntary disclosure model" where the policyholder must disclose the information on his own initiative. The questionnaire model is said to be more policyholder friendly as it shifts the burden of assessing the materiality of information from the policyholder to the insurer. This is considered justified given that it is the insurer who knows best what exact information he needs to assess the risk. This way, the problem of determining materiality of information by the policyholder is eliminated. Furthermore, it allows limiting unnecessary transaction costs and subsequent disputes.[24] For these reasons, the questionnaire model is usually applied in insurance practice even where the law sets out the voluntary disclosure model.[25]

The policyholder's knowledge poses yet another problem which is particularly important in the case of the breach of duty. Namely, the knowledge about risk may considerably differ among the policyholders. On the one hand, it is impossible to require the same level of knowledge from everybody, but on the other hand, the law must set a certain standard to prevent extreme cases where the policyholder's lack of knowledge results from his negligence. Therefore, typically, the law requires the policyholder to disclose information related to the risk *of which he is or ought to be aware.*[26]

As we see, the law strives for precision when it comes to determining the scope of the duty and the way it should be executed because a failure to effective execution may trigger harsh consequences for the policyholder. The consequences differ among jurisdictions, however, their common denominator is to provide for the system where consequences are proportional to the level of the policyholder's misbehaviour and, at the same time, they remedy harm the failure to effective execution of the duty by the policyholder caused to the insurer. Design of such a system is not an easy task as it must consider many factors, such as the reason of the failure, whether the policyholder responded to questions or the disclosure was voluntary, or whether the policyholder acted in bad or good faith. Accordingly, the law

[22] Lowry et al. (2011), p. 114.

[23] Lowry et al. (2011), p. 114.

[24] Basedow et al. (2016), p. 105.

[25] Basedow et al. (2016), p. 105.

[26] See Article 2:101 of the PEICL and the commentary to the Article.

recognizes different levels of the policyholder's misbehaviour (**ways of ineffective execution of the duty**): (i) deliberate concealment (which could be innocent, negligent or fraudulent), (ii) misrepresentation (which could be innocent, negligent or fraudulent) and (iii) innocent non-disclosure. Now, in principle, depending on the level of the misbehaviour (and sometimes also other circumstances, e.g. insurer's behaviour),[27] the law may provide the insurer with the following **remedies**: (i) the right to propose a reasonable variation of the contract,[28] (ii) the right to terminate the contract[29] and (iii) the right to avoid the contract.[30]

The above analysis of the legal design of the duty of disclosure shows that beside providing the insurer with the necessary information, scrupulous attention is constantly paid to maintain equality between the parties in terms of the burden of the duty they bear. The law recognizes that even though it is the insurer who is at an informational disadvantage, it is also the insurer who has the overall advantage over the policyholder (in terms of resources, knowledge, and expertise in insurance). For this reason, it would be unfair to place responsibility for providing information entirely on the policyholder. Hence, the efforts to limit the scope of the duty and to involve the insurer in active gathering of the risk-related information. Based on the analysis, it may be argued that the pre-contractual duty of disclosure serves two purposes. The first and the most important one is to provide the insurer with the information necessary to decide whether to accept the risk and, if so, what insurance premium to offer. This way the legal measure restores the informational balance between the parties. The secondary purpose, resulting from the first one, is to ensure fairness between the parties by easing the burden of the duty for the policyholder.

4 The Technology and the Reversal of IA

This section turns to the core thesis of the chapter: the technology implemented by insurers in the underwriting process (Big Data analytics) reverses IA such that the historical "policyholder knows better" becomes "insurer knows better". A look into what the technology *is* and *how* it improves the insurer's knowledge on the risk will back the thesis and, most importantly, it will allow us to see if the improved underwriting and more sophisticated knowledge of the insurer affect the elements stressed by the regulation.

[27] For instance, the insurer should not 'blindly' follow answers and statements of the policyholder. If the information provided by the policyholder is manifestly incorrect or incomplete, the insurer should recognize it and explain the error with the policyholder. If the contract is concluded anyways, the insurer will not be entitled to benefit from the legal remedies. See Article 2:103 of the PEICL and the commentary to the Article.

[28] See Articles 2:102 and 2:103 of the PEICL.

[29] See Articles 2:102 and 2:103 of the PEICL.

[30] See Article 2:104 of the PEICL.

Big data analytics is currently used across the entire insurance value chain. There is an impressive number of papers and reports produced by scholars and industry showing how technology is implemented by insurers and how it impacts their business.[31] It is impossible and not necessary to analyse them all here in detail. Rather, for the purposes of this chapter, it suffices to highlight a narrow part of the spectrum of the field - technology used specifically in the underwriting process. This includes (i) new sources of data, (ii) increased volume of data available, (iii) improved quality of data, and (iv) data analytics.

Traditionally, insurers used data that was largely *sourced directly from policyholders*. This information included, among others, demographic, medical, exposure, behavioural, and loss data. With the digitalization the scope of sources of information available to insurers has extended enormously. Today, not only do insurers collect the data directly from the policyholders (through the risk declaration), but also (or sometimes *primarily*) from *indirect sources such as mobile devices, sensors, satellite technology and the internet.*[32] EIOPA's report shows that traditional data sources are increasingly combined (*yet not replaced*) with new sources.[33]

Not only do new sources of data provide *more* data, but also *new types* of data. For example, the new types of data enabled by digitalization are: (i) geolocation data, speeding data, miles driven, harsh braking, time of day, road type, g-forces, the speed limit and type of street (in motor insurance via black boxes and mobile phones apps), (ii) life activity, steps walked in a day, calorie consumption, blood pressure (in health insurance via wearables and mobile phones apps), (iii) bank account and credit card data, shopping habits (via external sources, such as shopping stores), (iv) satellite pictures and geo data (in CAT and home insurance) or (v) third-party online media data.[34]

Easy access to this data is enabled by the Internet of Things which allows sensors and actuators embedded in physical objects to be linked through wired or wireless networks. Data collected from these connected sensors is then sent to the computers for analysis. Telematics is the most common example of the use of IoT in insurance. Another way to obtain new data is also an access to different kinds of data

---

[31] Among the most comprehensive analysis and overviews of new technology applied in the insurance value chain are Eling et al. (2022), pp. 205–241; IAIS (2020), IAIS (2022), OECD (2017); Geneva Association (2018).

[32] See a graphic presentation of non-exhaustive list of traditional and non-traditional data types and sources in insurance in Geneva Association (2018), p. 36.

[33] EIOPA (2019).

[34] "Some firms reportedly use the information provided by web analytics tools and social media listening tools for analysis of user behavior and for pricing and underwriting purposes." EIOPA (2019), pp. 13, 14; "[Derived data is] likely to include quantity and type of postings, topics written about and geolocation of where written from to indicate activities, social networks, time of day, income level, jobs held, minors in the household, are several factors that seem relevant to analyze, in addition to other factors that might combine with these." Wells and Weston (2020).

aggregators—platforms where personal data is stored from different institutions, such as government services and pension funds.[35]

The main result of the way new data is collected, its increased volume and improved quality is greater granularity (i.e. the level of detail in a data set) and frequency of information about policyholders' risk profiles.

As much as data itself is important, it does not always mean much without its proper processing (changing the form of data so that it is easier to view), understanding and analysis (deriving additional intelligence, useful insights from the data already available). Here as well innovation comes with help. Insurers increasingly adopt the use of algorithms and advanced predictive data analytics (process of exploring collected data to make appropriate decisions in the future by using valuable insights). The key feature of algorithms is that they can learn and improve as they are fueled with new data. The method used to train algorithms is machine learning. To put it simply, the algorithm is trained to find connections, patterns, structures between input and output variables of a data set.[36] As the algorithm learns from the data, it becomes increasingly accurate in determining the risk itself, the probability of its occurrence and therefore, in calculating the most adequate premium.

This section provides only a cursory summary of the improvements in the underwriting process and should be read together with the reports, surveys, and analyses referred to herein which explore this phenomenon in greater detail and demonstrate best the scale of it. The main finding is that the *trio* "more data, better data, and advanced data analytics" promises a considerable reduction of the uncertainty around the qualities of risk and its occurrence.[37] The vision of what the *trio* is and will be, given its continuous development, capable of delivering, initiated a discussion on the preventive role of insurance and insurers. The discussion suggests that the new technology would enable insurers to regularly inform policyholders on potentially risky behaviour and to incentivize them to modify that behaviour to lower the risk exposure. The information can be given in real time of changes to their risk profile.[38] Interestingly, the preventive role of insurance is more often mentioned also by policymakers. For instance, IAIS suggests that the insurers equipped in big data analytics may "assist customers by providing solutions to *help them better understand the size of their risk exposure*".[39] What is it if not an obvious acknowledgement of a reversal of the historical IA?

Furthermore, the core thesis that insurers know the policyholder's risk's qualities and probability of its occurrence much better than the policyholders and that the historical IA is therefore reversed is also supported, directly and indirectly, by other authors. According to Eling et al., the increased availability of detailed risk-relevant

---

[35] For example, MijnOverheid in the Netherlands, MyInfo system in Singapore.

[36] Eling et al. (2022), p. 213.

[37] IAIS (2020), p. 20.

[38] The Geneva Association (2021); IAIS (2020), p. 22.

[39] IAIS (2020), p. 22.

information about policyholders through historical and real-time data sets directly contributes to the reduction of adverse selection.[40] The same thesis is pursued by de Jong in his *Risk classification and the balance of information in insurance; an alternative interpretation of the evidence.*[41] He argues that since the risk classification is today "infinitely more refined" than at the time in which the theory of IA in insurance was formulated, it is plausible to say that "insurers know the accident probabilities of their policyholders better than the policyholders themselves".

To appreciate the value of Big Data and analytics in consideration of the subject matter of this chapter, it should be specified in more detail what new is it that Big Data and analytics give insurers. Based on the above, the obvious answer is new data and ability to extract insights valuable for the risk assessment. That together gives the insurer more sophisticated knowledge on risk itself and probability on its occurrence. However, bearing in mind the research questions of the chapter, it is more useful to notice that the new sources of data give insurers access to data that used to be *a private knowledge of the policyholder*. Furthermore, not only does the insurer know what used to be known only to the policyholder (or sometimes even more) but, having this knowledge, he is now also able to predict what will happen with the risk in the future. This, in turn, is unknown to the policyholder.

The insurer's access to the private knowledge of the policyholder is the connecting point between the market situation (IA and adverse selection) and regulation (pre-contractual duty of disclosure). Knowing how the use of technology affects the underwriting, we will now attempt to determine how it affects the design of the duty of disclosure described in Sect. 3. Already from the outset, we see that the use of technology has an impact on the scope of the duty. More specifically, it impacts the scope of information which is not subject to disclosure: information that is known to the insurer, that the insurer ought to know, that the insurer is presumed to know. As already mentioned, this exclusion is introduced to limit the scope of the duty to private knowledge of the policyholder that the insurer is unable to acquire from anywhere but the policyholder themself. However, because of the new sources of data and data processing, insurers are now able to acquire data which used to be private from sources other than the policyholder. Consequently, data received from smart devices seems to fall under the exclusion of "information that is known to the insurer, that the insurer ought to know, that the insurer is presumed to know", and thereby falls out of the scope of the duty. Furthermore, it is also possible to claim that the use of smart devices not only increases the knowledge of the insurer but also of the policyholder. Therefore, it may have an impact on the assessment of the ambit of what the policyholder knows and ought to know. That, in turn, may further affect the qualification of the level of the misbehaviour if a breach of the duty is considered.

---

[40] Eling et al. (2022), p. 225.

[41] De Jong (2021), pp. 445–461.

5 Discussion

So far, this chapter has demonstrated how the legal framework responds to the market situation (IA) by providing the legal measure addressing IA and aiming at restoring the informational imbalance, thereby mitigating the risk of adverse selection (Sect. 3). Section 4 gave foundation to the thesis that the new technology employed by the insurers reverses the historical IA in a sense that insurers know the risk better than policyholders. The results bring us to the main questions of the chapter: Does the reversal of IA deprive the duty of disclosure of the meaning? Should the reversal of IA trigger the reform of the duty of disclosure?

As mentioned earlier, the analysis of the duty of disclosure shows that it pursues two objectives: the primary one is to restore the informational balance and the secondary one is to ensure the fairness between the parties, i.e. that the burden of the imposed duty will not cause an unnecessary disadvantage to the duty holder. This alone might lead to a conclusion that the reversal of IA is enough to advocate a reform of the duty. However, this conclusion might be accused of being careless because it is made *in isolation* of the complex reality of the market situation, insurance business and, perhaps most importantly, in isolation of the full legal meaning behind the discussed duty. This section examines this complexity to illuminate that, despite the change in the market situation, which gave grounds for the regulation, the pre-contractual duty of disclosure *still is* a key element of the insurance contract and remains meaningful, although not unaffected by the reversal of IA.

There are three fundamental grounds for opposition to reforming the pre-contractual duty of disclosure: (i) related to the thesis on the reversal of IA as such, (ii) sociopolitical and (iii) related to the functional scope of the duty of disclosure.

The thesis on the reversal of IA does not prove true in all cases. There are several factors which effectively undermine the thesis. To start with, the use of new technology in underwriting differs between the insurers and between the lines of business.[42] Additionally, De Jong—supporter of the thesis—adds that it proves true only when there are "no impediments in gathering and using all the information that in [insurers'] view is relevant to assess the risk".[43] In verifying whether the claimed reversal of IA results in reduced adverse selection, he tests a number of scenarios where impediments, such as regulatory restrictions, time constraints, misrepresentation, influence of social programs or differences between companies, exist. His analysis shows that in some scenarios, the existence of impediment effectively prevents reduction of adverse selection, thereby, contradicts the thesis. More precisely, he finds out that a restrictive regulation, a large scale of undiscovered misrepresentation and existence of social programs may revert "insurer knows better" back to "policyholder knows better". In such a case, there is no reversal of IA and adverse selection persists. This is also confirmed by an empirical literature demonstrating that the incidence of adverse selection varies substantially across lines of insurance

[42] The Geneva Association (2021).

[43] De Jong (2021), p. 458.

and across markets.[44] Finally, there is also the problem of new risks. Where the insurer has no claims history and no technology to provide risk-relevant data, the policyholder again becomes the main source of information. These are effectively the reasons why insurers *combine* traditional data received from the policyholder with data received from new data sources, rather than replace it altogether.[45] To conclude, because the thesis is not universal and there are instances where the policyholder is or may be a fundamental source of information, the duty of disclosure, as it stands, is still indispensable.

The sociopolitical grounds pertain to a mix of arguments raised in a discussion about regulating the use of Big Data by insurers. Many regulatory concerns have been identified (issues around lack of explainability or transparency of algorithms, affordability, inclusion, exclusion of those who do not want to share personal data, and possibly unfair discrimination) and they are certainly not unwarranted.[46] As a result, there is a natural social and political pressure on securing new consumer risks emerging from the use of technology, rather than supporting development of new business models and innovations.[47] As demonstrated by De Jong, a restrictive regulation is one of the elements that prevent the reversal of IA and allows adverse selection to persist. A regulation is considered restrictive when it denies or hinders insurers access to and/or the use of risk factors which may deepen the asymmetry of information and cause a 'regulatory adverse selection'.[48] An example of such a regulation may be Belgian law imposing restrictions on the processing of lifestyle or health data collected by devices connected to the Internet in health insurance and life insurance.[49]

Finally, the legal argument against reforming the pre-contractual duty of disclosure might be that the function of the duty is not limited to addressing the IA and adverse selection. As mentioned in Sect 2 above, the fundamental rationale of the duty is not only the protection of the insurer but also the need to ensure a true and fair agreement between two contractual parties. This, on the one hand, is reflected in ensuring that both parties to the contract possess the same information about the subject of the contract and, on the other hand, in preventing that the duty does not place any unnecessary burden on the policyholder.

---

[44] See Siegelman and Cohen (2010), pp. 39–84.

[45] EIOPA (2019), p. 6.

[46] See for example a discussion on the perils resulting from the erroneous use of data by artificial intelligence in healthcare: Dueno (2020), pp. 337–358. The author demonstrates the correlation between data and algorithm and the possible scenarios where the algorithms produce wrong results. The conclusions are also applicable to insurance. In the same manner: Prince and Schwarcz (2020), pp. 1257–1318.

[47] See for example, BaFin (2018), EIOPA (2023).

[48] Regulation may increase or even create adverse selection. Cohen and Boardman (2011), p. 28. The term 'regulatory adverse selection" is coined by Hoy in Hoy (2006), pp. 245–269. For the supervisory approach see for example, EIOPA (2023).

[49] Art. 46(1), 46(2), 46(3) of Belgian Insurance law Act of 4 April 2014. The articles were introduced in December 2020. For the comment on these articles, see: Stroobants (2021), pp. 1930–1948.

From the economic perspective, imposing a duty of disclosure on the policyholder is only justified where the information can be obtained from him easily and cost-efficiently. The above shows that there are instances where the policyholder still is and will be the cheapest source of information. That, nevertheless, should not slow down the legal discourse around the need for adjustment of the legal constructs to the ever-changing market situation and insurance business. The adjustment does not have to be substantial. Yet, it is crucial that when interpreting the utmost good faith principle and executing or judging the execution of the duty of disclosure, one is aware that the use of Big Data in underwriting may reverse the IA and have impact on the execution of the duty.

For this purpose, the focus could be redirected from reforming the duty of disclosure to forming a modern understanding of the utmost good faith. Much has been already written about the obsolescence of the doctrine (which has been securing its future from 1766!). Suggestions about rethinking utmost good faith are based mostly on the socio-economic development[50] but it is also noticed that the advancement of technology in risk assessment may question the *raison d'être* of the policyholder's duty to disclose.[51] In the light of the remarks made so far, perhaps, another suggestion may be made. Namely, more stress could be placed on the mutuality of the utmost good faith. Insurers involving Big Data in their underwriting processes could be required to disclose how the use of Big Data influenced calculation of the premium (for instance, what data sources and what specific risk-related information were used, and how it was interpreted). This would address the privacy concerns around the use of Big Data and the problem of *asymmetrical use of data* (i.e. insurers having access to the data with which they can demonstrate the insured's fault in claim settlements process. The same access is not available to the insured.). The implementation of the idea may be, however, challenging. As rightly noticed by Soyer, the information materiality test that requires disclosing facts which have been actuarially shown to be objectively relevant to the level of the risk may allow insurers who use non-causal risk proxies (such as social media posts or shopping habits) to not disclose them.[52] Furthermore, it should be ensured that the information provided by the insurer is of use to the insured (i.e. the insured can access the information, is able to understand and correctly interpret it and, finally, use it). Here, the classic problem of ineffectiveness of disclosures arises.[53] Nevertheless, these obstacles should not be seen as making the suggestion impractical. Rather, they show that the potential implementation should carefully consider issues surrounding information disclosure in general.

The reasons discussed in this section show that the pre-contractual duty of disclosure is still a central part of the insurance contract, and it is needless to reform it, at least at the moment. To determine what a prospective policyholder knows about

---

[50] For arguments for rethinking the utmost good faith see Han (2018), pp. 447–469.

[51] Ibidem, p. 468.

[52] Soyer (2022), p. 172.

[53] On the ineffectiveness of disclosures see Ben-Shahar and Schneider (2014).

the risk is and will be important. It may also become essential for other, new, reasons. If not for providing insurers with risk-relevant information, it may be essential to educate the policyholder on how to mitigate the risk occurrence, in particular, if the primary function of insurance will shift to prevention. It is beyond the author's writ to propose any specific guidelines for future policies. But that the legal framework will need an adjustment becomes more and more evident.

References

Akerloff G (1970) The market for "Lemons": quality, uncertainty and the market mechanism. Quart J Econ 84(3):488–500

BaFin, Big data meets artificial intelligence. Challenges and implications for the supervision and regulation of financial services, 2018. https://www.bafin.de/SharedDocs/Downloads/EN/dl_bdai_studie_en.html. Accessed 22 Oct 2024

Basedow J, Birds J, Clarke M, Cousy H, Heiss H, Loacker L (eds) (2016) Principles of European insurance contract law (PEICL), 2nd edn. Otto Schmidt

Ben-Shahar O, Schneider CE (2014) More than you wanted to know: the failure of mandated disclosure. Princeton University Press

Brady JL, Mellinger JH, Scoles KN (1995) The regulation of insurance, 1st edn. Insurance Institute of America

Cohen LR, Boardman ME (2011) Methodology: applying economics to insurance law – an introduction. In: Burling J, Lazarus K (eds) Research handbook on international insurance law and regulation. Edward Elgar Publishing

De Jong CH (2021) Risk classification and the balance of information in insurance; an alternative interpretation of the evidence. Risk Manage Insur Rev 24:445–461

Dueno T (2020) Racist Robots and the lack of legal remedies in the use of artificial intelligence in healthcare. Connecticut Insur Law J 27:337–358

EIOPA (2019) Big data analytics in motor and health insurance: a thematic review

EIOPA (2023) Supervisory statement on differential pricing practices in non-life insurance lines of business, EIOPA-BoS-23/076, 22 February 2023

Eling M, Nuessle D, Staubli J (2022) The impact of artificial intelligence along the insurance value chain and on the insurability of risks. Geneva Pap Risk Insur Iss Pract 27:205–241

Han YQ (2018) Conclusions: (utmost) good faith and pre-contractual duties globally in the twenty-first century. In: Han YQ, Pynt G (eds.) Carter v Boehm and pre-contractual duties in insurance law. A global perspective after 250 years. Hart Publishing pp 447–469

Hasson RA (1969) The Doctrine of Uberrima fides in insurance law – a critical evaluation. Mod Law Rev 32(1):615–637

Heiss H, Mönnich U (2018) Precontractual duties in European insurance contract law. In: Han YQ, Pynt G (eds) Carter v Boehm and Pre-contractual duties in insurance law. A global perspective after 250 years. Hart Publishing

Hoy M (2006) Risk classification and social welfare. Geneva Pap 31:245–269

IAIS (2020) Issues Paper on the Use of Big Data Analytics in Insurance, February 2020

IAIS (2022) Report on FinTech developments in insurance sector, December 2022

Kwon WJ (2012) Economic rationale for insurance regulation. In: Insurance regulation: reflections for a post-crisis world. Geneva Association, January 2012

Loacker LD (2015) Informed insurance choice? The insurer's pre-contractual information duties in general consumer insurance. Edward Elgar Publishing

Lowry J (2011) Pre-contractual information duties: The insured's pre-contractual duty of disclosure – convergence across the jurisdictional divide. In: Burling J, Lazarus K (eds) Research handbook on international insurance law and regulation. Edward Elgar Publishing
Lowry J, Rawlings P, Merkin R (2011) Insurance law. Doctrines and principles, 3rd edn. Hart Publishing
OECD (2017) Technology and innovation in insurance sector
Pauly MV (1974) Overinsurance and public provision of insurance: the role of moral hazard and adverse selection. Quart J Econ 88(1):44–62
Prince AER, Schwarcz D (2020) Proxy discrimination in the age of artificial intelligence and big data. Iowa Law Rev 105(3)
Rothschild M, Stiglitz J (1976) Equilibrium in competitive insurance markets: an essay on the economics of imperfect information. Quart J Econ 90(4):629–649
Schoenbaum TJ (1998) The duty of utmost good faith in marine insurance law: a comparative analysis of American and English law. J Maritime Law Commer 29(1)
Siegelman P (2004) Adverse selection in insurance markets: an exaggerated threat. The yale law journal 113:1223.
Siegelman P, Cohen A (2010) Testing for adverse selection in insurance markets. J Risks Insur 77(1):39–84
Soyer B (2022) Use of big data analytics and sensor technology in consumer insurance context: legal and practical challenges. Cambridge Law J 81(1):165–194
Stroobants N (2021) Het gebruik van persoonsgegevens inzake levensstijl of gezondheid verzameld door met het internet verbonden apparaten in individuele levensverzekeringen en ziekteverzekeringen: het segmentatiebeleid van private verzekeraars verder aan banden gelegd. Tijdschrift voor Belgisch Handelsrecht / Revue de Droit Commercial Belge 9:1930–1948
The Geneva Association, Big Data and Insurance: Implications for Innovation, Competition and Privacy, March 2018
The Geneva Association, From Risk Transfer to Risk Prevention. How the Internet of Things is reshaping business models in insurance, May 2021
Wells B, Weston H (2020) Social media as factor in personal injury underwriting: risk, rate and regulation. J Insur Regul 39(1):1–20
Zweifel P et al (2021) Insurance economics, 2nd edn. Springer

Marta Ostrowska is a lecturer in Insurance Law and Policy at the University of Zurich and Secretary General of the Project Group 'Principles of Reinsurance Contract Law'. Before joining the University of Zurich in 2019 Marta lectured on Insurance Law at the University of Warsaw and practised with the law firm Hogan Lovells LLP in Warsaw. Her research explores insurance law, supervision and regulation using insights from economics, psychology and sociology Her current research topics include the principle of proportionality, effects of digitalization on insurance contract, the preventive value of insurance and soft law instruments She frequently speaks on insurance related topics at scientific conferences and industry events Her scholarship has been published in a wide range of leading law reviews and journals, including the Geneva Papers on Risk and Insurance Marta is a member of AIDA and the European Law Institute.

Automating Compliance Assessment of Insurance Contracts Using AI: Promises and Challenges

Agnieszka Jabłonowska, Francesca Lagioia, Rūta Liepiņa, Hans-Wolfgang Micklitz, and Giovanni Sartor

1 Introduction: Assessing Legal Documents Through AI

With the increasing availability of data and computing power, artificial intelligence (AI) technologies are becoming more advanced and accessible, leading to a proliferation of applications across different domains, including legal services.[1] One of

[1] Ashley (2017).

A. Jabłonowska (✉)
Institute of Private Law, Leiden University, Leiden, Netherlands
e-mail: a.a.jablonowska@law.leidenuniv.nl

F. Lagioia
CIRSFID-Alma AI, University of Bologna, Bologna, BO, Italy

Robert Schuman Centre for Advanced Studies, European University Institute, Rimini, Italy
e-mail: francesca.lagioia@unibo.it

R. Liepiņa
CIRSFID-Alma AI, University of Bologna, Bologna, BO, Italy
e-mail: ruta.liepina@unibo.it

H.-W. Micklitz
Robert Schuman Centre for Advanced Studies, European University Institute, Rimini, Italy

Law Department, European University Institute, Rimini, Italy
e-mail: Hans.Micklitz@eui.eu

G. Sartor
CIRSFID-Alma AI, University of Bologna, Bologna, BO, Italy

Robert Schuman Centre for Advanced Studies, European University Institute, Rimini, Italy

Law Department, European University Institute, Rimini, Italy
e-mail: giovanni.sartor@unibo.it

C. Poncibò, P. Tereszkiewicz (eds.), *European Insurance Law within the Digital Age*, AIDA Europe Research Series on Insurance Law and Regulation 14,
https://doi.org/10.1007/978-3-031-96496-1_7

the most notable impacts is in the field of legal research, where AI-powered tools allow legal professionals to quickly and accurately find relevant case law and other legal information. The overall trend in law is broader than that and includes using AI to automate routine legal tasks, such as document drafting and e-discovery, freeing up lawyers to focus on more complex and strategic work. However, the use of AI by companies may contribute to exacerbating power imbalances. While advanced systems are increasingly used by companies to provide efficient services, there is very little consumer-facing AI available on the market.[2] Some of the few examples of public interest AI include Polisis/Pribot,[3] Claudette,[4] and various topic-specific chatbot tools (e.g. Resolver[5] and Vera[6]).

Similar trends can be observed in the field of insurance law. Companies use AI systems for automated risk assessment, fraud detection, and other task automation[7] while there is little to no availability of tools for policyholders. In particular, policyholders may find it difficult to navigate through the legalese of insurance contracts and may not fully understand their rights and options. This pressing issue motivated us to explore whether a custom-made AI system can automatically detect problematic clauses in insurance contracts. As part of the Scudo project (Semantic Clauses Understanding and Detection),[8] we set up an experiment with insurance contracts from several European markets to achieve this goal. In doing so, we built upon the Claudette project methodology and a machine learning system developed in that context.

The chapter is organised as follows. In Sect. 2, the methodology and results of the Claudette project are introduced. This project, focusing on consumer protection in digital transactions, provides the groundwork for the present study. Sections 3 and 4 detail the preliminaries of extending Claudette's methodology to insurance law and creating a multi-jurisdictional data set in this field. Section 5 explores the legal challenges of designing a unified framework for analysing the rights and obligations of the parties in insurance contracts. It discusses the fragmented approach taken in Europe and how it leads to uncertainty in the protection of individuals. Section 6 includes a proposal of a new common benchmark for AI-supported protection of policyholders—the so-called "maximisation approach". Section 7 presents how the maximisation approach is implemented into text annotation guidelines, which are used to create a training set for the machine learning system. We conclude the chapter by presenting preliminary results (Sect. 8), summarising the findings and discussing future work (Sect. 9).

---

[2] Lippi et al. (2020).

[3] Harkous et al. (2018). Polisis is a visualisation tool identifying problematic passages in online privacy policies. Pribot is a question-answering system that allows users to ask specific questions and tries to return relevant passages from the website's privacy policy.

[4] Claudette (2017).

[5] Resolver (2013).

[6] Vera (2018).

[7] Eling et al. (2022).

[8] Scudo (2021).

2 The Claudette System

Claudette is an innovative legal analytics project that uses machine learning and natural language processing (NLP) techniques to automatically analyse online terms of service (ToS) and privacy policies (PP).[9] The project aims to address the overwhelming amount of information consumers need to process when entering into online agreements. Studies show that users do not read service agreements and even if they wished to do so, it would take them several days.[10] Moreover, the language used in the agreements is often too complex to comprehend for the average consumer. To support consumers in their decision-making and to protect their rights, Claudette provides online tools that analyse ToS and PPs for them. It identifies potentially unfair clauses based on EU legislation.[11]

Claudette uses a supervised machine learning approach. This means that to train Claudette to identify the unfair clauses, it is necessary to provide the system with examples of both fair and (potentially) unfair clauses. In other words, the system is provided with annotated documents signalling the category to which a clause belongs and whether the clause is fair or (potentially) unfair. Based on this training, the system performs two tasks—first, it needs to recognise whether the sentence is fair or unfair (the detection task), and then, whether the sentence belongs to categories of interest, e.g., termination, arbitration, applicable law, and jurisdiction (the classification task). The Claudette training set includes 140 ToS and 100 PPs, which have been tagged by legal experts. Once the system has been trained, it can recognise the relevant clauses and their (un)fairness in new documents, not included in the training set.

Claudette also provides users with confidence scores (a probability score that measures the certainty of a particular prediction or output) and explanations of why a given sentence was considered unfair. The latter functionality was achieved by relying on memory networks to provide legally relevant reasons why certain clauses are unfair.[12] It enables users to better understand and interpret the results of the system and provides additional transparency metrics.

Figure 1 presents the results of the Claudette analysis. A clause is identified as unfair under two categories—unilateral termination and unilateral change. In addition to the fairness score, the system also produces rationales as to why the clause has been considered unfair. Each rationale is accompanied by a confidence score.

The Claudette methodology can be applied to different domains (such as online contracts in the areas of finance, health and travel), as shown by our comparative analysis.[13]

---

[9] Lippi et al. (2019).

[10] Milne et al. (2006). Obar and Oeldorf-Hirsch (2020). Elshout et al. (2020).

[11] Unfair Contract Terms Directive 93/13/EEC for consumer contracts and General Data Protection Regulation 2016/679 for privacy policies.

[12] Ruggeri et al. (2022).

[13] Jabłonowska et al. (2021).

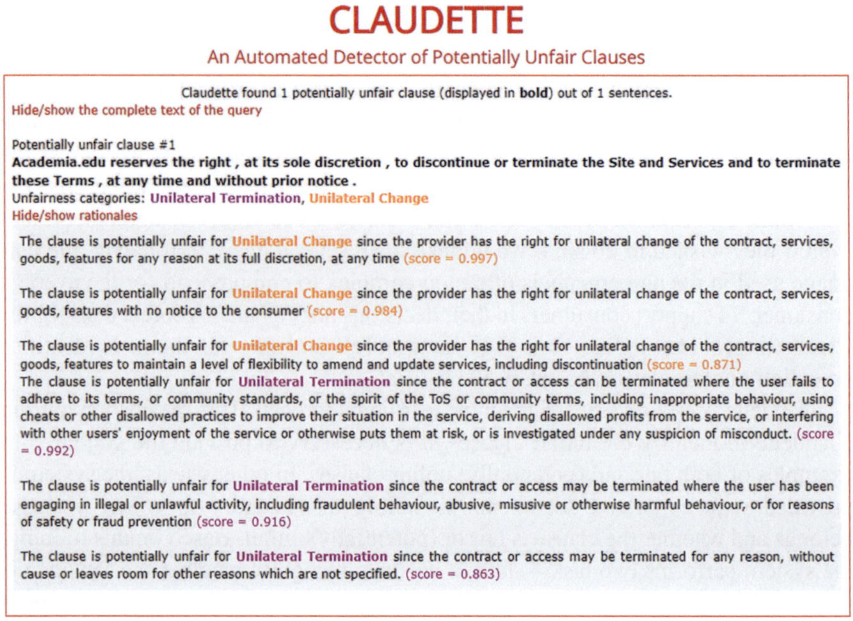

Fig. 1 Claudette system output for a sample clause

3 A New Domain: Insurance Sector and the Scudo Project

While the prevalence of standard terms has substantially increased in the digital economy, pre-formulated contracts have also shaped economic relations before the advent of digitalisation. A prominent case in point is the insurance sector. Considering the nature of insurance as a "legal product,"[14] contracts assume a fundamental role in this domain and tend to be extensive. Accordingly, a system such as Claudette could bring significant value to the parties involved in insurance contracting. Developing the prototype of such a system has been the key objective of the Scudo project.

To develop a system for the automated assessment of contracts using supervised learning, it is important to collect a sufficient number of documents. Therefore, as a first step, it is necessary to better understand the market for which the envisaged system is to be developed. Insurance contracts may differ depending on three main factors: (i) the subject matter covered, (ii) the status of the insurer's counterparty and (iii) the distribution channel. As regards the former, insurance can cover either persons or properties.[15] Typical examples include, on the one hand, life and health insurance and, on the one hand, buildings and contents insurance. Cover for differ-

[14] See e.g. Reiff (2020), p. 2163.

[15] Clarke (2012), pp. 3–4.

ent risks, e.g. damage to property and liability to third parties, may also be combined and offered in one package. Moreover, the increasingly popular "all-risk policies" specify their scope by listing what is excluded rather than what is covered.

As for the status of the insurer's counterparties, a line can be drawn between, on the one hand, business-to-consumer contracts (B2C) and, on the other hand, business-to-business (B2B) contracts. Within B2B contracts, a distinction is made depending on whether the policyholder is a small and medium-sized enterprise (SME) or a large enterprise. In both B2C contracts and B2B contracts involving SMEs the terms are typically standardised, while in B2B contracts with large enterprises they are often negotiated. Finally, concerning distribution channels, a distinction can be made between (i) contracts marketed on the Internet, for which the price is a central factor and the coverage is more limited, (ii) contracts marketed by independent insurance brokers who can compare various offers, and (iii) contracts marketed exclusively through agents engaged by the insurer, whereby the price is typically higher and the number of exclusions smaller.

Given the above, a decision was reached in the Scudo project to focus on the contracts between insurers and SMEs, marketed online and via brokers. Contracts of this kind are generally standardised and tend to cover similar types of risks, most notably relating to business property and liability. Even though Scudo does not focus on consumer contracts, its overarching goal remains to support weaker parties, in line with Claudette's approach.

4 The Scudo Data Set

We collected 50 contracts, in the English language, in the following domains: (i) property insurance, including all risk, (ii) professional indemnity, and (iii) breakdown coverage for motor vehicles.

The collection and selection of insurance contracts was more challenging than the similar exercise performed in the Claudette project. Firstly, unlike ToS for digital services, insurance contracts tend to differ depending on relevant jurisdictions. Thus, it is not possible to identify a single reference version, applicable to multiple markets and available in multiple languages. Drawing from experience, the choice was made to start with contracts in English, for which the available NLP tools are already well-established. A potential extension of the system to other languages may be considered at later stages of the project.[16] At the same time, it was important to ensure that a sufficient variety of contracts, drafted according to the requirements of different legal systems, was represented in the corpus. Accordingly, our data set includes not only documents aimed directly at English-speaking markets but also English translations of contracts originally drafted in other languages, for other geographical markets.

[16] For a possible approach to developing a multilingual system, see Drazewski et al. (2021) and Galassi et al. (2024).

Secondly, insurance contracts tend to be composed of several documents. In particular, such contracts usually include a policy schedule that contains information about the parties to the contract, its specific object and duration, the sum insured and the premium. The parties may further agree on the application of deductibles and various special clauses which are optionally listed in the standard terms. Only the combination of these documents provides a full picture of the contractual relationship between the insurer and the policyholder. However, policy schedules are generally available only to the contracting parties as well as potentially to intermediaries.

Against this background, we set out to collect our sample of insurance contracts focusing on the terms used by major insurance companies active in different markets, including Italy, Germany, Poland and the United Kingdom. Documents aimed directly at English-speaking markets were retrieved from openly available websites of insurers (addressed either directly at potential customers or at insurance brokers). Translated documents in use in other geographical markets were obtained thanks to collaborations with insurance brokers. The availability of English versions of the documents used in non-English speaking markets suggests that insurers are open to the possibility of concluding contracts with parties from other jurisdictions.

The majority of documents collected were standard terms. In 9 out of 50 cases, the standard terms were also accompanied by policy schedules. While the data set does not fully reflect the landscape of insurance contracting, we believe that it provides a solid basis for testing the feasibility of the envisaged system and identifying some of the associated promises and challenges.

5 Beyond EU Law: A Comparative Analysis

5.1 Preliminary Remarks

To establish the legal benchmark against which insurance contracts are to be assessed, existing legislation and case law need to be examined. The relevant analysis provides pivotal input to the annotation guidelines, on which the legal experts involved in the creation of the training set can later rely (see Sect. 7). Building upon Claudette experience and after a preliminary assessment of the structure of insurance contracts, five categories of clauses were considered most relevant to the Scudo project: (i) applicable law, (ii) jurisdiction, (iii) limitation of liability, (iv) contract modification, and (v) termination. The legal analysis we performed was therefore focused on these five categories.

Following the approach of Claudette, European Union law provided the starting point for our study. Indeed, the EU engages with the insurance sector on several levels. Most notably, insurance contracts are the subject of common provisions of private international law, laid down in Regulation 593/2008 on the law applicable to contractual obligations (Rome I) and Regulation 1215/2012 on jurisdiction and the recognition and enforcement of judgments in civil and commercial matters (Brussels I recast). However, beyond this important domain, the situation is more complicated. Admittedly, Directives 2009/138/EC and 2016/97 extensively regulate the business of insurance and reinsurance as well as insurance distribution,[17] but they do not focus on contractual relationships between insurers and policyholders. While there have been attempts to develop a set of common principles on insurance contracts in the form of the Principles of European Insurance Contract Law (PEICL), these principles are mostly academic.[18] Moreover, unlike in the case of B2C relationships, to which Directive 93/13/EEC applies, the rules on unfair terms in B2B contracts have not been horizontally harmonised.

Therefore, except for applicable law and jurisdiction, to determine the legal benchmark for assessing insurance contracts, attention must turn to national laws. Due to the lack of harmonisation of the general "unfairness" standard, we decided to avoid this notion. Instead, we adopted a more neutral language of "defectiveness", alluding to the nature of insurance as a legal product.

5.2 *Applicable Law and Jurisdiction*

As far as the provisions of private international law are concerned, both Rome I and Brussels I recast Regulations contain provisions protective of policyholders. Specifically, Article 7 of Rome I Regulation provides the parties to insurance contracts with varying degrees of flexibility in their choice of law, depending on the size and location of risk. The most protective rules apply to contracts covering risks other than large risks[19] situated inside the territory of the Member States. In this group of cases, the parties in principle may only choose the laws stipulated in Article 7(3) of the Regulation.[20] This also applies to active policyholders requesting foreign insurance products, which some scholars have described as potentially counterproductive.[21] The fact remains that the freedom to choose the law applicable to insurance contracts is severely constrained with a view to protecting policyholders as the weaker parties.[22]

Matters relating to insurance are also the subject of a dedicated section in Brussels I recast Regulation. The competence of courts to hear relevant disputes depends on the contractual role of the defendant, i.e., on whether a claim is brought against the insurer or the policyholder. In both cases, strong emphasis is placed on the protection of the latter. On the one hand, the policyholder may choose to sue the insurer domiciled in a Member State in the courts for the place where the claimant,

[17] See generally Everson (2015), p. 409; Looschelders and Michael (2020), p. 793. Marano and Noussia (2021).

[18] Basedow et al. (2016). Heiss et al. (2012), p. 603 et seq.

[19] Cf. Article 13(27) of Solvency II Directive.

[20] Such laws include, among others, the law of Member States where the risk is situated and the law of the country where the policyholder has his or her habitual residence.

[21] Heiss (2009), pp. 271–272.

[22] Kowalewski and Bzdyń (2012), p. 75. See also: Fuchs and Jagielska (2011).

i.e., the policyholder, is domiciled.[23] On the other hand, in principle, the insurer may bring proceedings only in the courts of the Member State in which the defendant is domiciled, irrespective of whether the latter is the policyholder, the insured or a beneficiary.[24] Jurisdiction agreements departing from the above are bound to strict requirements which are generally meant to favour the policyholder.[25] An exception applies to contracts covering specific types of (typically large) risks, where the insurer is not necessarily the stronger party.

Translating the above-mentioned provisions into the annotation guidelines was not significantly more complex than in the case of the Claudette project. The methodology adopted in this context is discussed in more detail in Sect. 7 below.

5.3 Limitation of Liability, Contract Modification and Termination

For the clauses on limitation of liability, contract modification and termination, a common EU benchmark is not available. Based on the preliminary analysis of the PEICL, and taking into account the expertise available in the project team, three national legal orders were selected for comparative analysis: Italian, German and Polish. The analysis revealed that insurance contracts are regulated to a significant degree in each of these jurisdictions. More specifically, in Germany, they are the subject of a dedicated legal act (*Versicherungsvertragsgesetz*, VVG), while in Italy and Poland, dedicated rules in the respective Civil Codes exist.[26] The German Civil Code lays down horizontal rules on the fairness control of standard terms in B2B relationships.[27] Conversely, the Polish provisions on fairness control in B2C relations apply *mutatis mutandis* to B2B insurance contracts, where the policyholder is an individual who enters into a contract directly related to his or her business or professional activity.[28] All this underscores the importance attached to the protection of the weaker party, namely the policyholder, in the insurance sector.

For each of the three categories of clauses, the comparative analysis began with a survey of relevant legislation. The most extensive rules were generally found in Germany, where insurance contracts are closely regulated.[29] However, even where the relevant Italian and Polish rules were not as detailed, the specific issues addressed by them were broadly similar to those governed by German law. For instance, all of

[23] Article 11(1)(b) of Brussels I recast Regulation.

[24] Article 14(1) of Brussels I recast Regulation.

[25] Article 15 of Brussels I recast Regulation.

[26] Article 805 et seq. of the Polish Civil Code (*Kodeks cywilny*) and Libro Quarto –Delle obbligazioni–Titolo III–Dei singoli contratti–Capo XX Dell'Assicurazione, Articles 1882–1903 of the Italian Civil Code (*Codice civile*).

[27] §305 et seq. of the German Civil Code (*Bürgerliches Gesetzbuch*).

[28] Article 805 § 4 of the Polish Civil Code. The approach adopted by the Polish lawmaker has been criticised as overly restrictive. See: Gnela (2011).

[29] For a detailed analysis see: Wandt (2016). Bruns (2015).

the analysed regimes address the problem of terminating the insurance contract after the change (especially aggravation) of risk.[30] Other prominent specifications of termination clauses include the policyholder's failure to disclose risk factors before contract conclusion,[31] to pay the insurance premium on time,[32] or to take precautionary measures.[33]

Similar circumstances are also prominent with respect to liability limitation and contract modification, both in the analysed jurisdictions[34] and in the PEICL.[35] In these cases, the law typically lays down specific conditions, e.g. related to the policyholder's degree of fault or to applicable time limits, under which the insurer—or in some cases the policyholder—is authorised to take relevant actions. Thus, differently from the case of Claudette, a decision was reached to consider all clauses granting to one or both parties the right to terminate and/or modify the contract. Moreover, also the right of withdrawal was included in the analysis and considered together with contract termination.

The analysis of applicable legislation was complemented with an examination of the relevant case law. A notable observation in this regard concerns potential differences between judicial rulings on B2B and B2C relations. The distinction does not appear to play a major role in German jurisprudence, where the courts tend to refer more generally to the policyholder as the weaker party.[36] In Poland, by contrast, a significant number of cases concern consumer contracts. This, however, seems to be linked primarily to the differences in the enforcement frameworks, and a significant number of cases initiated in Poland by the consumer protection authority. At the level of material law, as was said, Polish provisions on fairness control in B2C contracting apply *mutatis mutandis* to at least some of the B2B insurance contracts. Accordingly, Polish judgments involving B2C relations were not excluded from the scope of analysis, but provided a reference point for the B2B domain, particularly as far as SMEs are concerned.

To illustrate the above, consider the Polish case law concerning the economic implications of terminating the contract by the policyholder. Under Article 813(1) of the Polish Civil Code, the premium is calculated for the duration of the insurer's liability. A number of insurers nevertheless provided in their contracts that no refunds would be made for premiums advanced for the periods which, after termination, were no longer covered. This may be the case, e.g., where the insured event occurred during the insurance period and indemnity was paid or the insurer was obliged to pay it. Clauses of this kind were repeatedly found to be unfair by the

---

[30] Cf. § 24 VVG, Article 1898 of the Italian Civil Code, Article 816 of the Polish Civil Code. See also: Article 4:203 PEICL.

[31] Cf. §19 VVG, Articles 1892 and 1893 of the Italian Civil Code. See also: Articles 2:102 and 2:104 PEICL.

[32] Cf. § 37 and § 38 VVG, Article 814 of the Polish Civil Code. See also: Article 5:103 PEICL.

[33] Cf. § 28 VVG. See also: Article 4:102.

[34] Cf. § 19, 25, 26 and 82 VVG, Article 1897 of the Italian Civil Code, Articles 814–816 and 826 of the Polish Civil Code.

[35] See e.g. Articles 2:102, 4:202, 4:203, 4:301, 5:102.

[36] Looschelders and Michael (2020), pp. 826–827.

national courts and eliminated from standard terms in B2C relations.[37] In 2007, Article 813(1) of the Civil Code was amended to stress that in the case of early termination, the policyholder is entitled to the reimbursement of the premium for the unused coverage. Thus, it has been clarified that the judicial reading in consumer cases applies to all policyholders.

Another notable insight concerns the possibility of subjecting the liability limitation clauses to fairness control. This controversial issue affects the B2C and B2B domains alike. Indeed, pursuant to Article 4(2) of the Unfair Contract Terms Directive, assessment of the unfair nature of the terms shall relate neither to the definition of the main subject matter of the contract nor to the adequacy of the price and remuneration. This applies when the price or remuneration is provided against the services or goods supplied in exchange and the relevant terms are expressed in plain intelligible language. Recital 19 explicitly mentions insurance contracts, clarifying that "the terms which clearly define or circumscribe the insured risk and the insurer's liability shall not be subject to [fairness] assessment since these restrictions are taken into account in calculating the premium paid by the consumer". It has thus been debated whether the clauses limiting the insurer's liability should be excluded from fairness analysis and if so, which ones. In both Germany and Poland the dominant view is that the scope of core terms in insurance contracts (those terms specifying covered risks and limiting liability) excluded from fairness review is very narrow.[38] Still, considering the controversial nature of this problem, our analysis of the limitation of liability clauses is primarily based on the applicable legislation and does not engage with cases requiring careful balancing.

In sum, based on the comparative analysis we decided to focus on the following specifications of each of the three categories, as illustrated in Table 1 below.

6 Finding a Common Benchmark: The Maximisation Approach

The level of detail of national provisions devoted to the matters listed in Table 1 may differ. This legal fragmentation leads to uncertainty in the protection of individuals and poses a practical challenge to the development of the envisaged AI system. In the following, we present our approach to address this issue.

From a practical perspective, the main purpose of the legal analysis summarised above was to develop the annotation guidelines, on which legal experts can rely

[37] See e.g. judgement of the District Court in Warsaw of 30 October 2007, XVII AmC 86/06; judgement of the District Court in Warsaw of 11 October 2007, XVII AmC 68/06; judgement of the Court of Appeal in Warsaw of 6 February 2009, XVII AmC 83/06; judgement of the District Court in Warsaw of 30 December 2009, XVII AmC 960/09; judgement of the Polish Supreme Court of 9 October 2015, III SK 40/14. A similar conclusion was also reached with regard to the clauses requiring the policyholder to additionally request to have the premium reimbursed, see: judgement of the Polish Supreme Court of 27 October 2006, I CSK 173/06.

[38] For a more detailed analysis, see: Schmidt (2016), p. 1882 et seq. Looschelders and Michael (2020), pp. 846–847. Reiff (2020), p. 2162 et seq. Nawracała (2013), p. 66.

Table 1 Specifications of the limitation of liability, contract modification and contract termination categories derived from comparative analysis

Limitation of liability	• occurrence of the insured event before contract conclusion and insured events stemming from pre-existing risks • damage caused by the policyholder • failure of the policyholder to disclose relevant risk factors before contract conclusion • failure of the policyholder to take precautionary measures • failure of the policyholder to take required measures after the insured event (e.g. notify the event, minimize the damage) • failure of the policyholder to pay the premium • change of risk after contract conclusion • possibility of claiming other compensation (e.g. from other insurers) • acknowledgement of third-party claims • actions or failure to act by the insurer or its representatives • existence of underinsurance
Contract modification	• change of risk after contract conclusion • existence of overinsurance • failure of the policyholder to disclose relevant risk factors before contract conclusion • other important reasons • request of the policyholder
Contract termination	• termination by any party without mentioning reasons • termination by any party for one of the specified reasons (e.g. change of risk after contract conclusion or failure of the policyholder to pay the premium) • refund of pre-paid premiums following contract termination • policyholder's right to withdraw from the contract during the cooling-off period

when creating the training set (see Sect. 7). As said above, harmonised provisions of private international law offered a clear and common benchmark which could be translated directly into guidelines. The situation was different for the remaining three categories of contract terms, i.e., limitation of liability, contract termination and modification.

To find a common benchmark for the latter categories, the level of protection afforded to policyholders under relevant national laws was compared. If a certain issue was only addressed in one jurisdiction, the relevant norms were treated as the common benchmark.

The problem of gaps in coverage needs to be distinguished from the more complex instances of conflict between the level of protection afforded in different jurisdictions. To illustrate the latter situation, consider the relevant legislation and case law on the termination of the contract after the insured event occurred. The German Act on insurance contracts explicitly confers to both parties the right to terminate the contract when the insured event occurs, in property and liability insurance. It also specifies that termination of a property insurance contract is only permissible within one month after the conclusion of negotiations in respect of the compensation and that the insurer termination will be effective after one month's notice (see § 92(1) VVG). Similar provisions, applicable to liability insurance, are found in § 111 VVG.

Unlike in Germany, the possibility of terminating the contract, following the occurrence of the insured event, is not explicitly regulated in Poland. However, there are several judgments stating that clauses, according to which the insurer can terminate the contract if an insured event occurred, are unfair.[39] The courts found that even if the right of termination is granted to both parties it does not affect them in the same way, but rather serves, for the most part, the insurer's interest. In particular, the clause may lead the policyholder to refrain from claiming compensation for small amounts, for fear of being deprived of further coverage and having to sustain the costs and inconvenience of concluding a new contract.

To account for this conflict, we adopted an innovative solution termed "the maximisation approach". Accordingly, clauses reflecting rules most protective for the policyholder were considered to be best practices and thus "fair". In the example above, this is the case for clauses according to which the insurer does not have the right to terminate the contract after the insured event occurred. In the case of a conflict between provisions of different jurisdictions, clauses less protective for the policyholder (in our example, those reflecting the conditions stated in German law) were considered as having a "minor defect". Finally, clauses less protective than the least protective rules in studied jurisdictions were considered to be "defective". For a more detailed explanation of the applied annotation methodology, including the levels of defectiveness, see Sect. 7 below.

The adopted maximisation approach provides useful insights to insurers who seek to operate across borders. This is directly connected to the unified EU rules on private international law, which for the most part are also favourable to the policyholder, including in B2B relations. As we sketched out before, the EU Regulations in principle authorise the policyholder to bring proceedings in the country in which he or she is domiciled and apply the law of the country where the policyholder has his or her habitual residence. Thus, information about the more protective rules in other jurisdictions is also relevant to the insurers contracting with policyholders from different EU countries.

7 The Annotation Guidelines

To recall, we identified five different categories of (potentially) defective clauses concerning: (i) the law governing the contract, (ii) jurisdiction for disputes, (iii) the insurer's limitation of liability, (iv) the conditions under which the parties can modify the contract terms and (v) terminate the contract. It is worth noting that not all collected contracts contain the clauses belonging to all categories.

Based on the analysis of EU law and selected national laws we defined a set of guidelines, establishing, for each category, a set of rules and criteria to evaluate the (potential) defectiveness of a clause and to annotate the corpus. For each type, we

[39] See e.g. judgement of the District Court in Warsaw of 11 October 2007, XVII AmC 68/06; judgement of the Court of Appeal in Warsaw of 10 December 2007, XVII AmC 42/06.

established a corresponding xml tag. Nested tags were used to annotate text segments relevant to more than one type of clause. We also defined mandatory and optional attributes and their possible values, as reported in the following. Attributes are aimed at describing some legally relevant properties. They are intended to capture different aspects of the rules applicable to each category, so as to assess the (potential) defectiveness of clauses.

If an attribute's value is composed of multiple items, each item is separated by the vertical bar (|).[40] The annotation was done at the sentence level by three experts in the legal domain, using periods, semicolons, and line breaks as delimiters. Both the definition of the guidelines and the labelling process included several revisions. Corrections were also suggested by an analysis of the annotation agreement. All annotations have been checked, controversial instances have been discussed in a reconciliation phase by two or more expert annotators.

Mandatory Attributes We identified three mandatory attributes, as reported in Table 2. In particular, each clause is denoted through a unique Identifier (ID), whose value is constructed by joining the abbreviation of the category to which the clause belongs (e.g. *T* for termination clauses) with a progressive number, which distinguishes the single clause within the document (e.g., *T1*, *T2*, T_n). Depending on the category of the clause, we distinguish different types (Type) of specifications, i.e., circumstances under which a certain rule should be applied. For instance, with regard to the right to terminate the contract, we identified three main types, aimed at capturing the different circumstances under which this right can be exercised. In particular such hypotheses concern: (i) the specific reasons (Type="Reason") that can justify the contract termination (e.g., the policyholder's failure to pay the insurance premium on time or to take the required precautionary measures to prevent the damage), (ii) the policyholder's right to withdraw if the contract is concluded for more than 6 months and within a certain time limit (Type="PhWithdraw"), and (iii) the policyholder's right, following contract termination, to only pay part of the premium for the coverage period or his or her right to be refunded if the premium has been paid in full (Type="Refund").

As a further example, consider the applicable law category. In this case, we differentiated between insurance (Type="Ins") contracts—regulated by Article 7(2) to (4) of the Rome I Regulation—and re-insurance (Type="ReIns") contracts, which are excluded from those special provisions as per Article 7(1). Finally, the Level attribute (L) denotes the degrees of defectiveness of a clause, with a value equal to 1 meaning clearly fair, 2—affected by minor defect, and 3—clearly defective.

Optional Attributes The optional attributes may vary depending on the considered category of the clause, as reported in Table 3. To illustrate, consider the SubType attribute (SubType), which follows the Type attribute in several cases, e.g.

[40] Note that in the xml DTD format, the separator (|) is used to denote an alternative. Conversely, in our usage, within the inverted commas enclosing the values for an attribute, it denotes the sequence of such values.

Table 2 Annotation scheme—mandatory attributes

Category of clause and Tag	Mandatory Attributes		
	Name	Value	Tag
Applicable Law <law>	Unique Identifier	Law1, Law2, Law*n*	ID="Law*n*"
	Type	Ins (insurance contract) ReIns (reinsurance contract)	Type="Ins" Type="ReIns"
	Level	1 2 3	L="1" L="2" L="3"
Jurisdiction <j>	Unique Identifier	J1, J2, J*n*	D="J*n*"
	Type	/	/
	Level	1 2 3	L="1" L="2" L="3"
Limitation of Liability <ltd>	Unique Identifier	Ltd1, Ltd2, Ltdn	
	Type	PreEx (pre-existing insurance event or risk) PhDamage (damage caused by the policyholder (Ph)) PhBreach (duty violation by the policyholder before or after contract conclusion) RiskCh (increased risk) OtherComp (multiple insurance for the same object against the same risk) TPClaim (third-party claim) InsRep (actions or omissions by the insurer or its representatives) UnderIns (underinsurance)	Type="PreEx" Type="PhDamage" Type="PhBreach" Type="RiskCh" Type="OtherComp" Type="TPClaim" Type="InsRep" Type="UnderIns"
	Level	1 2 3	L="1" L="2" L="3"
Contract Modification <ch>	Unique Identifier	Ch1, Ch2, Ch*n*	ID="Ch*n*"
	Type	RiskCh (increased or decreased risk) OverIns (overinsurance) NoDiscRisk (non-disclosure of risk factor(s)) Imp (important reasons) PhRequest (request of change by the policyholder)	Type="RiskCh" Type="OverIns" Type="NoDiscRisk" Type="Imp" Type="PhRequest"
	Level	1 2 3	L="1" L="2" L="3"
Contract Termination <ter>	Unique Identifier	T1, T2, T*n*	ID="T*n*"
	Type	Reason PhWithdraw (policyholder's right to withdraw) Refund (policyholder's right to not pay the entire premium or to be refunded)	Type="Reason" Type="PhWithdraw" Type="Refund"
	Level	1 2 3	L="1" L="2" L="3"

Table 3 Annotation scheme—optional attributes

Category of clause and Type		Optional Attributes: Name	Value	Tag
Applicable law <law>	Insurance Contract Type="Ins"	Risk Size	Large NoLarge	RiskS="Large" RiskS="NoLarge"
		Risk Location	EU (European Union) TC (Third Country) Miss (Unspecified)	RiskL="EU" RiskL="TC" RiskL="Miss"
		Reference	Law1, Law2, Law*n*	Ref="Law*n*"
	Re-insurance Contract Type="ReIns"	Reference	Law1, Law2, Law*n*	Ref="Law*n*"
Jurisdiction <j>	/	Risk Size	NoSpecial NoLarge Miss (Unspecified)	RiskS="NoSpecial" RiskS="NoLarge" RiskS="Miss"
		Defendant	Ins (Insurer) Ph (Policyholder) Ben (Beneficiary) Insd (Insured) Miss (Unspecified)	Def="Ins" Def="Ph" Def="Ben" Def="Insd" Def="Miss"
		Place	InsDom (Insurer Domicile) PhDom (Policyholder Domicile) InsdDom (Insured Domicile) BenDom (Beneficiary Domicile)	P="InsDom" P="PhDom" P="InsdDom" P="BenDom"
		Reference	J1, J2, J*n*	Ref="J*n*"

(continued)

Table 3 (continued)

Category of clause and Type		Optional Attributes		
		Name	Value	Tag
Limitation of liability <ltd>	Pre-existing insurance event or risk Type="PreEx"	Fault	Int (Intention) GNeg (Gross Negligence) ONeg (Ordinary Negligence) Miss (Unspecified) No	F="Int" F="GNeg" F="ONeg" F="Miss" F="No"
		Reference	Ltd1, Ltd2, Ltd*n*	Ref="Ltd*n*"
	Damage caused by the policyholder Type="PhDamage"	Fault	Int (Intention) GNeg (Gross Negligence) ONeg (Ordinary Negligence) Miss (Unspecified) No	F="Int" F="GNeg" F="ONeg" F="Miss" F="No"
		Causal link between the action and the event	Yes Multi (Multiple causes occurring simultaneously) Miss No	F="Yes" F="Multi" F="Miss" F="No"
		Reference	Ltd1, Ltd2, Ltd*n*	Ref="Ltd*n*"
	Violation of precaution duties by the policyholder before the conclusion of the contract Type="PhBreach"	SubType	NoDiscRisk NoPrecaution PostDamage NoPay	SubType="NoDiscRisk" SubType="NoPrecaution" SubType="PostDamage" SubType="NoPay"
		Fault	Int (Intention) GNeg (Gross Negligence) ONeg (Ordinary Negligence) Miss (Unspecified) No	F="Int" F="GNeg" F="ONeg" F="Miss" F="No"
		Causal link between the action and the event	Yes Multi (Multiple causes occurring simultaneously) Miss No	F="Yes" F="Multi" F="Miss" F="No"
		Reference	Ltd1, Ltd2, Ltd*n*	Ref="Ltd*n*"

	Change of the insured risk(s) after the conclusion of the contract Type="RiskCh"	Fault	Int (intention) GNeg (Gross Negligence) ONeg (Ordinary Negligence) Miss (Unspecified) No	F="Int" F="GNeg" F="ONeg" F="Miss" F="No"
		Causal link between the action and the event	Yes Multi (Multiple causes occurring simultaneously) Miss No	F="Yes" F="Multi" F="Miss" F="No"
		Reference	Ltd1, Ltd2, Ltd*n*	Ref="Ltd*n*"
	Possibility of claiming other compensation (e.g., from other insurers) Type="OtherComp"	Reference	Ltd1, Ltd2, Ltd*n*	Ref="Ltd*n*"
	Acknowledgement of third-party claim(s) Type="TPClaim"	Reference	Ltd1, Ltd2, Ltd*n*	Ref="Ltd*n*"
	Actions of failure to act by the insurer or its representatives Type="InsRep"	Causal link between the action and the event	Yes Miss No	F="Yes" F="Miss" F="No"
	Underinsurance Type="UnderIns"	Reference	Ltd1, Ltd2, Ltd*n*	Ref="Ltd*n*"

(continued)

Table 3 (continued)

Category of clause and Type		Optional Attributes		
		Name	Value	Tag
Contract modification <ch>	Change of risk after the conclusion of the contract Type="RiskCh"	Subject	Ins Ph	S="Ins" S="Ph"
		Object	MinusCover (Exclusion or reduction of coverage) MinusPremium (Premium reduced) PlusPremium (Premium increased)	O="MinusCover" O="MinusPremium" O="PlusPremium"
		Effect	PlusCh (After the risk change) PlusChFromIP (After the risk change and not earlier than from the beginning of the current insurance premium) Miss (Unspecified) MinusCh (Before the risk change)	E="PlusCh" E="PlusChFromIP" E="Miss" E="MinusCh"
		Reference	Ch1, Ch2, Ch*n*	Ref="Ch*n*"
	Over Insurance Type="OverIns"	Subject	Ins Ph	S="Ins" S="Ph"
		Object	MinusPremium (Premium reduced) NoMinusPremium (No right to Premium reduced) Miss (Unspecified)	O="MinusPremium" O="NoMinusPremium" O="Miss"
		Effect	Imm (Immediate) Miss (Unspecified) NoImm (Not Immediate)	E="Imm" E="Miss" E="NoImm"
		Reference	Ch1, Ch2, Ch*n*	Ref="Ch*n*"
	Non-disclosure of risk(s) Type="NoDiscRisk"	Subject	Ins	S="Ins"
		Object	ChCond (Change of contract conditions)	O="ChCond"
		Effect	StartIP (From the beginning of the current insurance period) Miss (Unspecified) Ret (Retroactive) MinusIP (Before the current insurance period)	E="StartIP" E="Miss" E="Ret" E="MinusIP"

		Fault	Int (Intention) GNeg (Gross Negligence) ONeg (Ordinary Negligence) Miss (Unspecified) No	F="Int" F="GNeg" F="ONeg" F="Miss" F="No"
		Reference	Ch1, Ch2, Ch*n*	Ref="Ch*n*"
	Important Reasons Type="Imp"	Subject	Ins	S="Ins"
		Object	ChCond (Change of contract conditions)	O="ChCond"
		Effect	Yes Miss	E="Yes" E="Miss"
		Reference	Ch1, Ch2, Ch*n*	Ref="Ch*n*"
	Request by the Policyholder Type="PhRequest"	Subject	Ins	S="Ins"
		Object	ChCond (Change of contract conditions)	O="ChCond"
		Reference	Ch1, Ch2, Ch*n*	Ref="Ch*n*"

(continued)

Table 3 (continued)

Category of clause and Type		Optional Attributes		
		Name	Value	Tag
Contract termination <ter>	Reason(s) of Termination Type="Reason"	SubType	AnyReason (Any reason) Imp (Specified important reasons) Law (Termination under national laws) RiskCh (Change of risk after the conclusion of the contract) NoPay (Failure of the policyholder to pay the premium) NoDiscRisk (Non-disclosure of risk(s)) NoDiscOther (Non-disclosure of information specified in the contract) NoPrecaution (Failure of the policyholder to take the required precautionary measures) OccurredEvent (Occurrence of the insured event) ChCond (Change of contract conditions) OtherComp (Multiple insurances for the same object against the same risk(s))	SubType="AnyReason" SubType="Imp" SubType="Law" SubType="RiskCh" SubType="NoPay" SubType="NoDiscRisk" SubType="NoDiscOther" SubType="NoPrecaution" SubType="OccurredEvent" SubType="ChCond" SubType="OtherCom"
		Duration of the contract	Unl (Unlimited) / (Not Applicable)	D="Unl"
		Subject	Ins Ph	S="Ins" S="Ph"
		Notice	R1M3M (Notice range 1-3 month(s)) In3M (within 3 months) Miss (Unspecified) Plus3M (After more than 3 months) Minus3M (In less than 3 months) Diff (Different for the two parties, i.e., the insurer and the policyholder) In14D (In 14 days) Minus14D (In less than 14 days) Plus14D (More than 1 month) In1M (In 1 month) Plus1M (Later than 1 month)	N="In3M" N="Miss" N="Plus3M" N="Minus3M" N="Diff" N="In14D" N="Minus14D" N="Plus14D" N="In1M" N="Plus1M" N="Minus1M" N="R14DMinus1M" N="Miss" /

			Minus1M (in less than 1 month) R14DMinus1M (Range between 14 days and less than 1 month) Miss (Unspecified) / (Not Applicable)	
		Effect	EndIP (From the end of the current insurance period) EndIPPlus2Y (From the end of the insurance period plus max 2 years) End3Y (From the end of the third year) Plus3Y (More than 3 years) PlusEndIP (After the end of the current insurance period) Miss (Unspecified) Imm (Immediate) PlusImm (More than immediately) NoRet (Not retroactive) Ret (Retroactive)	E="EndIP" E="EndIPPlus2Y" E="End3Y" E="Plus3Y" E="PlusEndIP" E="Miss" E="Imm" E="PlusImm" E="NoRet" E="Ret"
		Fault	Int (Intention) ONeg (Ordinary Negligence) GNeg (Gross Negligence) Miss (Unspecified) No (No Fault) \Not Applicable	F="Int" F="ONeg" F="GNeg" F="Miss" F="No" \
		Reference	Ter1, Ter2, Ter*n*	Ref="Ter*n*"
	Policyholder's right to withdraw from the contract during the cooling-off period Type="PhWithdraw"	Duration of the contract	Plus6M (More than 6 months) Miss (Unspecified) Lim (Limited)	D="Plus6M" D="Miss" D="Lim"
		Subject	Ph	S="Ph"
		Notice	In7D (In 7 days) Plus7D (More than 6 days) Minus7D (in less than 7 days) Miss (Unspecified)	N="In7D" N="Plus7D" N="Minus7D" N="Miss"
		Reference	Ter1, Ter2, Ter*n*	Ref="Ter*n*"
	Refund of pre-paid premiums following contract termination Type="Refund"	Subject	Ins Ph	S="Ins" S="Ph"
		Reference	Ter1, Ter2, Ter*n*	Ref="Ter*n*"

when the clause limits the insurer's liability due to the policyholder's breach of contractual or pre-contractual obligations (Type="PhBreach"). In the above scenario, the following behaviours of policyholders were identified: (i) failure to disclose risk factors before the contract conclusion (SubType="NoDiscRisk"), (ii) failure to pay the insurance premium on time (SubType="NoPay"), (iii) failure to take the necessary precautionary measures before the occurrence of the insured event (SubType="NoPrecaution"), and (iv) non-compliance with a duty after the insured event occurred (SubType="PostDamage"), such as the duty to promptly inform the insurer about the occurrence of the event or to attempt to save the insured object.

Another illustration is provided by the optional attribute Subject (S), which identifies the party who can exercise a certain action, e.g. terminate the contract. Depending on the context, this can be either the insurer (S="Ins"), the policyholder (S="Ph") or both (S="Ins|Ph"). Note that this attribute is only relevant for certain categories of clauses, i.e., contract modification and termination clauses.

Rules and Examples As noted, for each category, we designed a set of rules to assess the potential defectiveness of a clause. As an illustration, consider the contract termination category and, in particular, the case of non-payment of the insurance premium (SubType="NoPay") as a reason (Type="Reason") for termination.

Rule 1. Fair – Level 1
IF

the insurer has the right to terminate the contract with no

notice

AND

the effect of termination is immediate

GIVEN THAT

the policyholder did not pay on time a subsequent premium

AND

the insurer has set a deadline of at least 2 weeks

AND

the policyholder still did not pay

AND

the policyholder is responsible for the delay.

Rule 1. Minor defect – Level 2
IF

the insurer has the right to terminate the contract

GIVEN THAT

the policyholder did not pay on time a subsequent premium

AND

one of the following information is missing:

the deadline after which the termination right arises

OR

whether the policyholder is responsible for the delay

OR

when the termination becomes effective.

Rule 1. Defective – Level 3
IF

the insurer has the right to terminate the contract

GIVEN THAT

the policyholder did not pay on time a subsequent premium

AND

one of the following conditions apply:

the termination right can be exercised with no time limit

OR

the insurer has set a deadline of less than 2 weeks

OR

the insurer has set a deadline of at least 2 weeks

AND

the policyholder did not pay

AND

the policyholder is not responsible for the delay

OR

the policyholder has paid within 1 month from the

termination or from the deadline expiration

AND

the termination continues to be effective

OR

the termination becomes effective retroactively.

As an example, consider the following clause:
<ter ID="T1" Type="Reason" SubType="NoPay" S="Ins" N="Minus2W" F="Miss" L="3">If the premium is not paid as set out above, this Policy may be cancelled by the Insurer by giving the Insured 10 (ten) days written notice.</ter> (Source: Nardac All Risks)

This is a termination clause (<ter>), characterised by a unique identifier (ID="T1"). It concerns the possible reasons for terminating the contract (Type="Reason") and, more specifically, a termination due to non-payment of the insurance premium (SubType="NoPay"). Note that the clause has been classified as defective (Level="3") since the notification period is shorter than the one provided by the law (i.e. two weeks, N="Minus2W"). In addition, it is not specified whether the policyholder is responsible for non-payment (F="Miss").

8 Experiments and Preliminary Results

Building upon the previous experience in Claudette, we modelled the problem as (i) a detection task and (ii) a sentence classification task. In our preliminary experiments, we dealt with the first task, i.e., the detection task, which is aimed at predicting whether a given sentence contains a (potentially) defective clause. Moreover, we focused on three out of five categories of clauses, i.e., termination, jurisdiction and applicable law. In particular, we considered the detection problem as a binary classification task, where model evaluation is defined as a standard 10-fold cross-validation.

As for the features represented to encode sentences, we decided to opt for traditional features for text categorization, leaving possibly more sophisticated, handcrafted features for future experiments. One of the most classic, yet still widely used, set of features for text categorization, is the well-known bag-of-words (BoW) model. In such a model, one feature is associated with each word in the vocabulary: the value of such a feature is either zero, if the word does not appear in the sentence, or other than zero, if it does. Such a value is usually computed as the TF-IDF score, that is the number of occurrences of the word in the sentence (Term Frequency, TF) multiplied by a term that amplifies the weight of infrequent words (Inverse Document

Frequency, IDF).[41] The BoW model can be extended to also consider n-grams, i.e., consecutive word combinations, rather than simple words, so as to exploit, at least locally, the ordering of words in the sentences. Grammatical information can be included as well, by constructing a bag of part-of-speech tags, i.e., word categories such as nouns, verbs, etc.

We address the problem of detecting (potentially) defective clauses as a sentence classification task. Such a task could be tackled by treating sentences independently of one another (sentence-wide classification). This is the most standard and classic approach in machine learning. To this end, we compared two traditional methods, i.e., Support Vector Machines (SVM) and Random Forest.

To quantitatively evaluate the different tested classifiers, we computed precision (P) as the fraction of positive predictions, which are actually labelled as positive, recall (R) as the fraction of positive examples that are correctly detected, and finally $F1$ as the harmonic mean between precision and recall ($F1 = 2P\,R$). The best performance was obtained by using an ensemble of three classifiers based on SVM (i) with bigrams weighted with tf-dif; (ii) with bigrams weighted only with binary features; and (iii) with trigrams weighted with tf-idf. In particular, the classifier achieved a micro-F1 on the 10-fold cross-validation equal to 0.68, as a result of a precision equal to 71% and a recall equal to 65%.

9 Conclusions

The chapter presented our experience with developing an AI system seeking to automate the identification and classification of (potentially) defective clauses in standardised B2B insurance contracts. We chose the insurance sector as the application area due to the prominent role of contracts in this field. The envisaged system, signalling the existence of (potentially) defective clauses, could therefore bring significant value to the parties involved in insurance contracting.

In designing the system we relied on our previous work carried out as part of the Claudette project. Numerous insights from that project could be directly transferred to the insurance sector. The types of clauses addressed in the two projects overlap to some extent, as do the annotation and machine learning methods applied in the two projects.

Differently from Claudette, the focus of the Scudo project has been on contracts between insurers and small and medium-sized enterprises. Even though consumer contracts were no longer in the spotlight, the overarching goal of the system, namely to support weaker parties, remained in line with Claudette. Such a protective vision is also a distinctive feature of the insurance contract law.

An important practical challenge experienced by the project team concerned the access to insurance contracts. Drawing from experience, we chose to start with

[41] Sebastiani (2002), Lippi et al. (2019).

English documents. Ultimately, a corpus of 50 contracts was created, consisting mostly of the standard terms. Overall, we believe that the corpus, despite its limitations, provides a solid basis for testing the feasibility of the envisaged system and identifying some of the associated promises and challenges.

The second major difficulty was related to the identification of the legal benchmark to assess insurance contracts with the help of AI. Firstly, insurance contracts are quite extensively regulated, but mostly at the national level. Secondly, different from B2C contracting, the rules on unfair terms in B2B contracts have not been horizontally harmonised in the EU. This legal fragmentation leads to uncertainty in the protection of individuals and poses a practical challenge to the development of AI systems, supporting weaker parties across multiple jurisdictions.

The challenge of legal fragmentation was addressed in the Scudo project by what we have termed a "maximisation approach". The choices made when addressing this problem were directly connected with the envisaged goal of our system, that is primarily to support weaker parties. Naturally, a different approach may be taken in the context of other projects (e.g. AI systems developed by insurers for their internal use).

To account for the level of detail of the legal rules forming the benchmark of assessment, more complex annotation guidelines were adopted in the Scudo project, compared to our earlier work on consumer contracts. This more complex methodology, however, did not have a major impact on the performance of the system. Indeed, the first experimental results are quite encouraging, showing that the machine learning experience from the Claudette project can successfully be transferred to other domains.

The research presented in this chapter was performed during the early stages of the Scudo project. For the time being, we only evaluated the performance of the detection task focusing on three categories. Looking forward, we intend to extend the scope of experiments and also include the classification task as well as the remaining two categories of clauses, i.e., limitation of liability and contract modification. In addition, attempts can be made to refine the system, e.g. by expanding the data set and experimenting with new machine learning methods. Extensive work carried out during the annotation process can also make it possible to generate new insights about the market practice in the insurance sector.

Acknowledgements This research has been supported by the European Research Council (ERC) Project "CompuLaw" (Grant Agreement No 833647) under the European Union's Horizon 2020 research and innovation programme, and by the SCUDO project, within the POR-FESR 2014-2020 programme of Regione Toscana.

Appendix

Act on Insurance Contracts (Versicherungsvertragsgesetz) of 23 November 2007, BGBl. I S. 2631 as amended.

Civil Code (Bürgerliches Gesetzbuch) in the version promulgated on 2 January 2002, BGBl. I S. 42, 2909; 2003 I S. 738, as amended.
Civil Code (Kodeks cywilny) of 23 April 1964, Dz.U. 1964 nr 16 poz. 93, as amended.
Civil Code (Codice Civile) of 16 March 1942, n. 262, Gazzetta Ufficiale n.79 del 4-4-1942, as amended.
Council Directive 93/13/EEC of 5 April 1993 on unfair terms in consumer contracts [1993] OJ L 95/29.
Directive 2009/138/EC of the European Parliament and of the Council of 25 November 2009 on the taking-up and pursuit of the business of Insurance and Reinsurance (Solvency II) (recast) [2009] OJ L 335/1.
Directive (EU) 2016/97 of the European Parliament and of the Council of 20 January 2016 on insurance distribution (recast) [2016] OJ L 26/19.
Regulation (EC) No 593/2008 of the European Parliament and of the Council of 17 June 2008 on the law applicable to contractual obligations (Rome I) [2008] OJ L 177/6.
Regulation (EU) No 1215/2012 of the European Parliament and of the Council of 12 December 2012 on jurisdiction and the recognition and enforcement of judgments in civil and commercial matters (recast) [2012] OJ L 351/1.
Regulation (EU) 2016/679 of the European Parliament and of the Council of 27 April 2016 on the protection of natural persons with regard to the processing of personal data and on the free movement of such data, and repealing Directive 95/46/EC (General Data Protection Regulation) [2016] OJ L 119/1.

References

Ashley KD (2017) Artificial intelligence and legal analytics: new tools for law practice in the digital age. Cambridge University Press
Basedow J, Birds J, Clarke M, Cousy H, Heiss H, Loacker L (eds) (2016) Principles of European insurance contract law (PEICL). Otto Schmidt
Bruns A (2015) Privatversicherungsrecht. C.H. Beck
Clarke M (2012) An introduction to insurance contract law. In: Burling J, Lazarus K (eds) Research handbook on international insurance law and regulation. Edward Elgar Publishing
Claudette (2017) An automated detector of potentially unfair clauses. http://claudette.eui.eu/demo/. Last visited February 22, 2023
Drazewski K, Galassi A, Jabłonowska A, Lagioia F, Lippi M, Micklitz H-W, Sartor G, Tagiuri G, Torroni P (2021) A corpus for multilingual analysis of online terms of service. In: Aletras N, Androutsopoulos I, Barrett L, Goanta C, Preotiuc-Pietro D (eds) Proceedings of the natural legal language processing workshop 2021. Association for Computational Linguistics
Eling M, Nuessle D, Staubli J (2022) The impact of artificial intelligence along the insurance value chain and on the insurability of risks. Geneva Pap Risk Insur Issues Pract 47:205
Elshout M, Elsen M, Leenheer J, Loos M, Luzak J (2020) Study on consumers' attitudes towards terms and conditions (T&Cs): final report. https://op.europa.eu/s/zKBy. Last visited February 22, 2023
Everson M (2015) Regulating the insurance sector. In: Moloney N, Ferran E, Payne J (eds) The Oxford handbook of financial regulation. Oxford University Press

Fuchs B, Jagielska M (2011) Kolizyjnoprawna ochrona strony słabszej stosunku ubezpieczenia. In
Galassi A, Lagioia F, Jabłonowska A, Lippi M (2024) Unfair clause detection in terms of service across multiple languages. Artif Intell Law https://doi.org/10.1007/s10506-024-09398-7. Last visited June 11, 2024
Gnela B (2011) Problem kwalifikacji stron umowy ubezpieczenia ze szczególnym uwzględnieniem ubezpieczającego. In: Gnela B (ed) Ubezpieczenia gospodarcze. Wybrane zagadnienia prawne, Wolters Kluwer
Harkous H, Fawaz K, Lebret R, Schaub F, Shin KG, Aberer K (2018) Polisis: automated analysis and presentation of privacy policies using deep learning. In: Proceedings of the 27th USENIX Security Symposium
Heiss H (2009) Insurance contracts in Rome I: another recent failure of the European legislature. In: Bonomi A, Volken P (eds) Yearbook of private international law. Volume X – 2008. Sellier
Heiss H, Clarke M, Lakhan M (2012) Europe: towards a harmonised European insurance contract law – the PEICL. In: Burling J, Lazarus K (eds) Research handbook on international insurance law and regulation. Edward Elgar Publishing
Jabłonowska LF, Lippi M, Micklitz H-W, Sartor G, Tagiuri G (2021) Assessing the cross-market generalization capability of the Claudette system. In: Schweighofer E (ed) Legal knowledge and information systems. JURIX 2021: the thirty-fourth annual conference, Vilnius, Lithuania, 8–10 December 2021. IOS Press
Kowalewski E, Bzdyń A (2012) Prawo właściwe dla umów ubezpieczenia w świetle prawa polskiego na tle regulacji europejskich. Wiad Ub 1:67
Lippi M, Pałka P, Contissa G, Lagioia F, Micklitz H-W, Sartor G, Torroni P (2019) Claudette: an automated detector of potentially unfair clauses in online terms of service. Artif Intell Law 27:117
Lippi M, Contissa G, Jabłonowska A, Lagioia F, Micklitz H-W, Pałka P, Sartor G, Torroni P (2020) The force awakens: artificial intelligence for consumer law. J Artif Intell Res 67:169
Looschelders D, Michael L (2020) Europäisches Versicherungsrecht. In: Ruffert M (ed) Europäisches sektorales Wirtschaftsrecht. Nomos
Marano P, Noussia K (eds) (2021) Insurance distribution directive: a legal analysis. Springer
Milne GR, Culnan MJ, Greene H (2006) A longitudinal assessment of online privacy notice readability. J Public Policy Mark 25:238
Nawracała J (2013) Ograniczenie odpowiedzialności ubezpieczyciela z tytułu ryzyk, które wystąpiły przed zawarciem umowy ubezpieczenia (na przykładzie klauzuli wpisanej do rejestru niedozwolonych postanowień pod nr 3456). Wiad Ub 1:57
Obar JA, Oeldorf-Hirsch A (2020) The biggest lie on the internet: ignoring the privacy policies and terms of service policies of social networking services. Inf Commun Soc 23:128
Reiff P (2020) Versicherungsbedingungen (AVB). In: Lindacher WF, Pfeiffer T (eds) AGB-Recht. C.H. Beck
Resolver (2013) A chat-bot tool supporting consumer complaint resolution in the UK and Ireland. www.resolver.co.uk. Last visited February 22, 2023
Ruggeri F, Lagioia F, Lippi M, Torroni P (2022) Detecting and explaining unfairness in consumer contracts through memory networks. Artif Intell Law 30:59
Schmidt H (2016) Versicherungsbedingungen (AVB). In: Ulmer P, Brandner HE, Hensen HD (eds) AGB-Recht. Otto Schmidt
Scudo (2021) Semantic clauses understanding and detection. www.eui.eu/research-hub?id=scudo-semantic-clauses-understanding-and-detection-1. Last visited February 22, 2023
Sebastiani F (2002) Machine learning in automated text categorization. ACM Comput Surv 34:1
Vera (2018) A chat-bot tool supporting consumers in submitting online complaints against a company in the Netherlands. www.vera.com. Last visited February 22, 2023
Wandt M (2016) Versicherungsrecht. Vahlen

Agnieszka Jabłonowska is affiliated with the Institute of Private Law, Leiden University as part of the project 'These Shoes Don't Fit! - How can consumer interests be protected when consumer identities are increasingly diffuse?' (project number VI.C.211.012) financed by the Dutch Research Council (NWO). Prior to that, she held post-doctoral positions at the European University Institute and at the Institute of Law Studies, Polish Academy of Sciences. Her academic interests lie at the intersection of law and technology, with a focus on consumer protection. She is also interested in the connection between protecting weaker parties and fostering sustainability.

Francesca Lagioia is Senior Assistant Professor in Legal Informatics, AI and Law and Ethics for AI, at the University of Bologna and Part-time Professor at the European University Institute, Florence. In November 2020 she obtained the Italian National Scientific Qualification as Associate Professor, scientific sector 12H3 IUS/20. She has been Max Weber Postdoctoral Fellow and Senior Research Fellow at the EUI. In March 2016, she earned her Ph.D. in Law Science and Technology from the University of Bologna. She has participated in many National, European and International Projects. Currently she is the Principal Investigator for the PRIN 2022 project EQUAL, EQUitable Algorithms—Promoting Fairness and Countering Algorithmic Discrimination through Norms and AI. Her research interests include: artificial intelligence and law, computer law and internet law, in particular privacy and data protection law, consumer law; Artificial Intelligence and Democracy, algorithmic fairness and transparency, AI explainability, computable law, legal theory, law and automation in socio-technical systems, with a specific focus on normative and deliberative agents, and the liability issues arising in connection with the use of autonomous systems. She has published widely on these topics and developed a number of AI Legal Technologies.

Rūta Liepiņa is a research fellow at the ALMA-AI, University of Bologna interdisciplinary research centre for AI and Law (since 2022). She obtained a PhD from the European University Institute (2020) on work about logic models of causality and evidence in law. She was an Assistant Professor in Digital Legal Studies at Maastricht University (2019–2022). Her work focuses on the application of AI methods for legal analytics and formal models of legal reasoning.

Hans-Wolfgang Micklitz , Part-Time Professor of Economic Law at the European University Institute, Florence Italy, main research interests national, European, international Private and Economic Law, AI and Law, Legal Theory.

Giovanni Sartor is professor in Legal Informatics at the University of Bologna and professor in Legal informatics and Legal Theory at the European University Institute of Florence. He holds an ERC-advanced grant for the project CompuLaw. He is co-director of Summer Schools on "Artificial Intelligence and Law" e on "Law and Logic", and hold courses at the University Boccani (Milan), the university Catolica (Lisbon) and Surrey (London).

He is past-president of the AI & law Association, co-editor-in-chief of the Artificial Intelligence and Law Journal, co-editor of the Ratio Juris Journal, and member of the ERC Scientific Council. He participates in the executive board of the Italian Society for the Ethics of AI. He has published widely in legal theory, computational logic, computer law, and AI & law. He is co-editor-in-chief of the Artificial Intelligence and Law Journal and co-editor of the Ratio Juris Journal. His research interests include legal theory, early modern legal philosophy, logic, argumentation theory, modal and deontic logics, logic programming, multiagent systems, computer and Internet law, data protection, e-commerce, law and technology.

Data Protection Rights and Automated Decision-Making in the Field of Insurance

Jonas Knetsch

1 Introduction

Automated decision-making is generally understood as the process of making a decision without any human involvement. The insurance market has always been an economic sector in which decision management plays a key role in the success of the stakeholders. Controlling data sources, information flow and the decision-making process is critical to allow insurance companies to operate efficiently and manage their resources better. Information technology (IT) thus has a central role to play in the insurance sector, and the rapid development of innovative IT tools has steadily increased insurers' dependence on algorithms designed to facilitate or even automate the underwriting of insurance contracts and the processing of claims. It has been a commonplace to observe that, in the current decade, automation solutions, some of them based on artificial intelligence, has extended to almost every domain in the insurance industry.[1]

At first sight, automated decision-making, implemented by the integration of reliable data sources in the insurer's IT system, may appear to be a cost-effective solution to avoid misguided decisions made solely or mainly on the basis of human experience. However, experts in the insurance sector often strike a different tone, emphasising that it is crucial to keep a human perspective in automated decision-making.[2] Indeed, the enormous potential of algorithms in the insurance

[1] See for example Armbrüster and Prill (2020), p. 110; Sood et al. (2022).

[2] Keast (2021).

J. Knetsch (✉)
University of Paris 1 Panthéon-Sorbonne (École de droit de la Sorbonne), Paris, France
e-mail: jonas.knetsch@univ-paris1.fr

C. Poncibò, P. Tereszkiewicz (eds.), *European Insurance Law within the Digital Age*, AIDA Europe Research Series on Insurance Law and Regulation 14,
https://doi.org/10.1007/978-3-031-96496-1_8

sector also carries risks. An insurance company might be tempted to develop automated 'scoring systems' that use vast data sets to identify cases that pose a higher risk, in order to exclude low-profit clients from insurance coverage or to delineate the category of insurable incidents in too restrictive a way.

Given the traditional importance of personal data for insurers, the issue of data protection has long been a Cinderella subject for the insurance business.[3] For a long time, collecting and processing sensitive personal data was considered a necessary and normal operation, with the consent of the insured party being at best assumed and hardly ever explicitly requested. Insurance contracts have rarely been studied under the light of data protection, as there has been a general feeling that insurance companies are the 'natural' operators of personal data and that it is necessary for them to assess that data to provide a reliable picture of the insured risk.

The introduction of the General Data Protection Regulation (GDPR) has had a major impact on the insurance industry, as this new legal framework imposed new obligations and stricter requirements on every kind of organisation involved in the processing of personal data.[4] Despite intense lobbying efforts, the Regulation does not contain a specific basis for processing personal data for insurance purposes, which means that, since 25 May 2018, insurance companies have been subject to the general provisions of the GDPR.

As a contribution to the debate on data protection in the field of insurance business, this paper will focus on the individual data protection rights regarding automated decision-making. In article 22(1), the GDPR provides for a right for a data subject 'not to be subject to a decision based solely on automated processing, including profiling, which produces legal effects concerning him or her or similarly significantly affects him or her'. Articles 13(2)(f), 14(2)(g), and 15(1)(h) GDPR implement a right for individuals to be informed about the 'existence of automated decision-making, including profiling' and to get access to 'meaningful information about the logic involved' in 'automated decision-making, including profiling' based on personal data.

These provisions create difficulties for the insurance industry: on the one hand, the protection of individuals against the excesses of a 'black box society' collides with the right of commercial companies to optimise their business with the assistance of new technologies; on the other hand, the requirement of transparency arising from the GDPR seems incompatible with the confidentiality interests of the insurance companies, since the way in which personal data are processed is widely seen as strategic and critical information that should be protected as a business secret.[5]

The aim of this paper is not only to assess the feasibility of applying the underlying rationale of data protection law to insurance businesses, but also to investigate

---

[3] Things are changing gradually. See KPMG (2018); McGurk (2019), pp. 176–199; Spittka (2019); Binon (2021); Čertický (2021); Béguin-Faynel (2022). See also the pioneering work of Dhont (2000).

[4] Günthner and Krohm (2020).

[5] Armbrüster (2017); Amankwah and Stroobants (2022).

the litigation risks arising from articles 13 to 15 and 22 GDPR and to present the current state of case law in the European Union. The simplest way to do this is first to address the implementation of the prohibition on fully automated decision-making laid out in article 22 GDPR (part 2), and then to consider the application of the specific right to information about the existence of automated decision-making and the logic involved, under articles 13 to 15 GDPR (part 3), before making some brief conclusive remarks (part 4).

2 The Strict Control of Fully Automated Decision-Making (Art 22 GDPR)

The GDPR has, at the level of the European Union, introduced a set of new provisions regarding decision-making 'based solely on automated processing, including profiling' that has legal effects or similarly significantly affects the data subject. The legal term 'profiling' is referred to in article 4 GDPR and is defined as 'any form of automated processing of personal data consisting of the use of personal data to evaluate certain personal aspects relating to a natural person, in particular to analyse or predict aspects concerning that natural person's performance at work, economic situation, health, personal preferences, interests, reliability, behaviour, location or movements'.[6] However, there is no legal definition of automated decision-making, since this does not necessarily rely on profiling.

In the field of insurance, automated decision-making and profiling have always been part of modern contract management processes.[7] During the phase of application for coverage, it is common practice, especially in a B2C context, to use algorithms designed in such a way that the applicant's responses to a questionnaire lead directly to a decision on whether or not to accept the applicant's proposal.[8] A specific field of algorithmic risk assessment and tariffication is health insurance.[9] Another topical example would be the termination of a contract, for example after the occurrence of an insured event, depending on the profile of the insured person.[10] It is common for insurance companies to perform an automatic calculation of an individual cost-benefit ratio for each policyholder, based on the insurance premiums collected and the proceeds paid out, allowing them to terminate the contracts of low-profit clients for reasons of cost effectiveness.

---

[6] See also Article 29 Data Protection Working Party (2018), p. 7: 'Broadly speaking, profiling means gathering information about an individual (or group of individuals) and evaluating their characteristics or behaviour patterns in order to place them into a certain category or group (…).'

[7] For a list of examples, see Hänold (2017), pp. 7–19.

[8] See, for example, Biddle et al. (2018), pp. 13–15.

[9] Pnevmatikakis et al. (2022); Hänold (2017), pp. 12, 15.

[10] Another application of profiling is the automated detection of insurance fraud. See Hänold (2017), p. 17.

If an insurer's decision is based on automated decision-making, article 22(1) GDPR gives the individual a right 'not to be subject to a decision based solely on automated processing'. In order to understand the practical implications of this provision for insurance purposes, it is necessary to identify the underlying rationale of this prohibition (A) before addressing the relevant exceptions laid out in article 22(2) GDPR (B) and assessing the litigation risks in insurance matters (C).

2.1 *The Rationale for the Prohibition*

The 2012 European Commission proposal for the GDPR explicitly refers to the Council of Europe's work on profiling. The Council of Europe had been particularly active in the field of data protection and the automated processing of personal data, as it had become clear that an effective protection of the right to privacy, laid out in article 8 of the European Convention on Human Rights, requires more specific legal tools, especially in the light of the development of IT.[11] This led to the drafting of the 1981 Convention for the Protection of Individuals with regard to Automatic Processing of Personal Data, better known as 'Convention no 108', and the establishment of a specific Consultative Committee, the so-called 'T-PD'.[12]

In 2010, the Council of Europe published a recommendation on the protection of individuals with regard to the automatic processing of their personal data in the context of profiling, which was a major source of inspiration for article 22 GDPR. In this recommendation, it is stated that 'the profiling technique is capable of having an impact on the people concerned by placing them in predetermined categories, very often without their knowledge',[13] and that 'the lack of transparency, or even "invisibility", of profiling and the lack of accuracy that may derive from the automatic application of pre-established rules of inference can pose significant risks for the individual's rights and freedoms'.[14] Despite the advantages of profiling and automated decision-making for both the professional and the customer, the recommendation stresses the fact that 'profiling an individual may unjustifiably deprive her or him of access to certain goods or services and thereby violate the principle of non-discrimination'.[15]

[11] On the historic development of the European data protection laws and the role of the Council of Europe, see González Fuster (2014), pp. 75–107.

[12] The legislative origins of article 22 GDPR reach back to the French 1978 Data Protection Act. For a more detailed assessment, see Bygrave (2020), p. 529.

[13] Council of Europe (2010), p. 6.

[14] Council of Europe (2010), p. 6.

[15] Council of Europe (2010), p. 6.

The drafters of the GDPR therefore considered that it was necessary to enhance the protection of individuals beyond the level of the 1995 Data Protection Directive.[16] The overall objective of article 22 GDPR is to prohibit the delegation of individual decision-making to an algorithm in circumstances in which no room is left for the 'human element' of judgment.[17] This explains why the provision only applies to decisions 'based *solely* on automated processing, including profiling'. According to the provision's rationale and in the light of the guidelines set down by the Article 29 Data Protection Working Party, the controller has to ensure that there is effective human oversight of the decision-making so that someone who has the authority and competence to do so may change the decision suggested by the IT system. In other words, 'if someone routinely applies automatically generated profiles to individuals without any actual influence on the result, this would still be a decision based solely on automated processing'.[18] The importance of human oversight has also been stressed in the Guiding Principles for Automated-Decision Making in the EU, elaborated by the European Law Institute,[19] as well as in the Draft Artificial Intelligence Act, as amended by the European Parliament on 14 June 2023.[20]

In practice however, the delineation of the scope of application of article 22 GDPR leaves room for interpretation. In the field of insurance, it will not be easy for an applicant or a policyholder to establish that the decision to refuse an application or to terminate a contract was 'solely based' on an algorithm and not the result of a human intervention or at least human supervision. In any particular case, it will be difficult to distinguish between an IT-based decision-support system, which does not fall under the scope of article 22 GDPR, and a 'decision based solely on automated processing'.

The GDPR drafters also wanted to limit the prohibition on automated decision-making to those decisions which have 'legal effects concerning' data subjects or

[16] According to article 15(1) of the Data Protection Directive, 'Member States shall grant the right to every person not to be subject to a decision which produces legal effects concerning him or significantly affects him and which is based solely on automated processing of data intended to evaluate certain personal aspects relating to him, such as his performance at work, creditworthiness, reliability, conduct, etc.'. For commentary on this text, see, for example, Bainbridge (1997), Bygrave (2001).

[17] See, for example, Bygrave (2020), pp. 526–527.

[18] Working Group Guidelines, p. 21.

[19] European Law Institute (2022), p. 22.

[20] According to article 14(2), 'Human oversight shall aim at preventing or minimising the risks to health, safety, fundamental rights or environment that may emerge when a high-risk AI system is used in accordance with its intended purpose or under conditions of reasonably foreseeable misuse, in particular (…) where decisions based solely on automated processing by AI systems produce legal or otherwise significant effects on the persons or groups of persons on which the system is to be used' (ref. P9_TA(2023)0236). In the final version of the EU Artificial Intelligence Act however, article 14(2) does not refer to automated decision-making as a particular example of the importance of human oversight.

'similarly significantly affect' them.[21] A legal effect means a modification of the legal status of the data subject. A typical example would be the termination of a contract or even the decision of an insurer to bring a legal action on the basis of an existing right.[22] As for a decision that similarly significantly affects the data subject, one could think of the refusal to accept an application for insurance coverage made by a claimant. The example of the 'automatic refusal of an online credit application', referred to in recital 71 of the GDPR, may thus be easily transposed to the insurance business.

2.2 *Provisos and National Margin of Appreciation*

To legitimise the use of automated decision-making, article 22(2) GDPR lays down a series of provisos, the extent of which is, however, still unclear. According to this text, a controller should not undertake the automated processing of personal data unless the decision is '(a) necessary for the performance of or entering into a contract; (b) authorised by Union or Member State law to which the controller is subject and which also lays down suitable measures to safeguard the data subject's rights and freedoms and legitimate interests; or (c) based on the data subject's explicit consent'.[23]

At first sight, the most relevant proviso in an insurance law context seems to be the reference to automated decision-making for contractual purposes. The guidelines set out by the Article 29 Data Protection Working Party give the example of the establishment of a shortlist of possible candidates for a job vacancy when the employer receives an exceptionally high volume of applications.[24]

An insurance company could argue that the number of applications and the sheer quantity of data to be processed make it necessary to sift out unattractive clients via an algorithm, in order to deliver decisions within a shorter time frame and improve the efficiency of operational procedures. However, it is questionable whether the example from labour law cited in the guidelines can be transposed to the application for, or the termination of, an insurance contract. According to article 22 GDPR, in order for the automated decision-making to be compliant, the controller must establish that this type of processing is 'necessary', meaning that no other less privacy-intrusive method exists to achieve the same goal.

---

[21] On this requirement, see Abel (2018), p. 306; Bygrave (2020), pp. 534–535; Helfrich (2022), nos 47–52; Hladjik (2018), nos 9–10; Martini (2021), nos 25–28. For a critical assessment, see Glatzner (2020), pp. 313–314.

[22] Martini (2021), no 26.

[23] For commentary on this provision, see, for example, Bygrave (2020) pp. 536–538; Martini (2021), nos 30–41e.

[24] Article 29 Data Protection Working Party (2018), p. 23. For a critical assessment of those guidelines, see Veale and Edwards (2018).

The range of the exception laid down in article 22(2)(a) thus depends on the interpretation of what is 'necessary' to deliver decisions relevant for the performance of or the application for an insurance contract in a timely and efficient manner. So far, the Court of Justice of the European Union (the CJEU) has not had an opportunity to address this issue.[25] Taking into account the reality of current practices, it is likely that automated decision-making will be allowed for contractual purposes on the sole basis that it improves the efficiency of operational procedures. It cannot be ruled out, however, that the Court will interpret this text restrictively, allowing automated decision-making without human intervention only in those cases in which the supervision of the algorithm is virtually impossible.

The second proviso that appears to be relevant in an insurance context relates to 'explicit consent' given by the data subject. The GDPR refers here to the same standard as is required under article 9(2) for the processing of especially sensitive personal data. There is no legal definition in the GDPR of what is meant by the 'explicit' character of the consent. Practitioners may refer to the guidelines set out by the Article 29 Data Protection Working Party, followed by the European Data Protection Board, on consent under the GDPR.[26] While the GDPR prescribes, in article 4, that a 'statement' or a 'clear affirmative act' is a prerequisite for *regular* consent, clarification is needed as to what an insurance company (or a distributor of insurance products) should do in order to obtain '*explicit* consent'. According to the guidelines, the term 'explicit' refers to the way consent is expressed, meaning that the data subject must give an express statement of consent, for example in a written and signed statement.[27]

In view of these requirements, it is not realistic to assume that, in the field of insurance contracts, the 'explicit consent' of a policyholder or an applicant may provide a legal basis for automated decision-making. In particular, in the case of the refusal of an application for an insurance contract, it is hard to see how the insurance company (or its distributor) may legitimately ask for the applicant's consent precisely when there is no pre-existing legal relationship between the two parties.

This leaves the third and last proviso, laid out in article 22(2) GDPR. According to this text, automated decision-making is exempted from the prohibition of article 22(1) if it is carried out in accordance with 'Union or Member State law'.[28] In order to explain this provision, recital 71 of the GDPR gives the example of 'fraud and tax-evasion monitoring and prevention purposes conducted in accordance with the regulations, standards and recommendations of Union institutions or national oversight bodies'. One could also cite section 57 of the Irish Data Protection Act 2018, which authorises automated decision-making when 'the effect of that decision is to grant a request of the data subject'.[29]

---

[25] Bygrave (2020), p. 536; Martini (2021), nos 31–32. See also Tambou (2020), pp. 215–216.

[26] Article 29 Data Protection Working Party (2017); European Data Protection Board (2020).

[27] See, for example, Article 29 Data Protection Working Party (2017), pp. 18–19.

[28] Bygrave (2020), p. 537; Martini (2021), nos 33–37.

[29] See Malgieri (2019), pp. 10–11. See also Castets-Renard (2019), pp. 126–135.

More interesting are the cases in which the lawmakers of a Member State have decided to use the margin of appreciation granted by the GDPR to allow automated decision-making in a specific area and, in particular, in an insurance context.[30] To the best of the author's knowledge, this is only the case in Germany. Section 37 of the Federal Data Protection Act (*Bundesdatenschutzgesetz*) contains an exemption from the prohibition if a decision 'based solely on automated processing' is made 'within the context of performing (*Leistungserbringung*) an insurance contract', provided that the decision is in favour of the person concerned or solely concerns the 'application of binding fee arrangements for health expenses'.[31] It is noteworthy that the *travaux préparatoires* of the Act of 30 June 2017 on the Amendment of Data Protection Law Rules to Implement the GDPR state that this exception was provided for in order to take into account 'specific concerns of the insurance industry'.[32] German insurance companies argued that a legal basis for automated claims management in the field of motor vehicle and health insurance would be a significant asset for Germany as a centre for the insurance industry.

2.3 *Potential for Litigation in the Field of Insurance*

Because of its unwieldy wording ('a right not to be subject to'),[33] article 22(1) GDPR can be interpreted in two different ways: either as the legal basis of a general prohibition on automated decision-making, or as a norm conferring on data subjects a right to object to a decision 'solely based on automated processing, including profiling'.[34] The potential for litigation depends strongly on the interpretation of the provision, as the different interpretations offer different protections and guarantees.

From its initial words ('the data subject shall have the right') and its position in chapter 3, which is entitled 'Rights of the data subject', one could argue that the protection offered by article 22(1) GDPR requires a positive action and needs the data subject to invoke his or her right by way of action.[35] With this interpretation, it is likely that insurance companies and other professionals will rely on the reluctance of their clients to invoke their right to object or even, in most cases, on their sheer ignorance regarding their data protection rights.

In order to guarantee the effectiveness of the legislative choices, the majority of legal commentators interpret article 22 GDPR as a general prohibition that allows

[30] On this sectorial approach, which is specific to Germany, see Malgieri (2019), pp. 20–21.

[31] For commentary on this provision, see Paschke and Scheurer (2022); Helfrich (2020); Taeger and Gabel (2022). See also Castets-Renard (2019), pp. 130–131.

[32] Deutscher Bundestag (2017), p. 106.

[33] Bygrave (2022), p. 180 ('intricate, complex and clumsily structured').

[34] For a detailed assessment of this controversy, see Bygrave (2020), pp 530–532.

[35] See Tosoni (2021).

automated decision-making only in limited cases.[36] Besides arguments arising from the drafting history, it is stated that a prohibition would be the only way to ensure the effective protection of personality rights and even human dignity. In other words, article 22(1) GDPR should be interpreted as a prohibition on a decision based on automated processing without any human intervention, even when the person concerned does not assert his or her 'right not to be subject to it'.[37]

Potential litigation under article 22 GDPR also depends on the capacity of the data subject to prove that the contested decision was made on the sole basis of automated processing, especially in the field of insurance contracts. As seen previously, it is quite easy for an insurance company to 'fabricate' human involvement in the decision-making process, for example with a scanned signature on a (paper or electronic) document suggesting that a manager has approved the decision made by the IT system.[38] It is therefore only in specific scenarios, for example when an insurer implicitly or explicitly admits having used profiling software or an automated process, that policyholders or applicants may realise that their personal data were processed in a way that falls under article 22 GDPR. Even though articles 13 and 14 GDPR impose a duty to inform data subjects of the existence of automated decision-making, the concrete circumstances of automated data processing will often prevent data subjects from claiming damages for the unlawful processing of their personal data and from notifying the national supervisory authority of a violation of article 22 GDPR.

If the automated decision-making is covered by one of the exceptions listed in article 22(2) GDPR or in a provision of national law, the controller has to respect certain guarantees. According to article 22(3) GDPR, 'the data controller shall implement suitable measures to safeguard the data subject's rights and freedoms and legitimate interests, at least the right to obtain human intervention on the part of the controller, to express his or her point of view and to contest the decision'.[39] In the case of a refusal to implement such measures, a data subject might assert their rights by way of action and claim damages, at least for the moral harm caused by the unlawful automated processing of their personal data.[40]

Furthermore, insurance companies will have to be aware of an even more increased potential for litigation due to the current efforts to implement specific liability rules for damage caused by artificial intelligence[41] and to revise the 1985 product liability directive.[42] Even though both proposals do not mention the use of

---

[36] Bygrave (2020), p. 531; Martini (2021), nos 29–29b.

[37] Bygrave (2019); Bygrave (2022), pp. 180–181 ('there is widespread perception that it is essentially a prohibition masquerading as a right').

[38] Article 29 Data Protection Working Party (2018), pp. 20–21.

[39] Or the controller must respect similar guarantees laid out in national provisions.

[40] On this issue, see below under Sect. 3.2.

[41] Proposal for a Directive of the European Parliament and of the Council on adapting non-contractual liability rules to artificial intelligence (AI Liability Directive), ref 2022/0303 (COD).

[42] Proposal for a Directive of the European Parliament and of the Council on liability for defective products, ref COM/2022/495 final.

AI-based software in an insurance context, it is highly likely that claimants will seize the opportunity of new liability rules to claim compensation on alternative legal grounds. In particular, the proposal to broaden the scope of the product liability directive by including software[43] shall make it possible for clients to sue insurance companies insofar as they qualify as the manufacturer of software used for automated decision-making.

3 The Right to Information and Access in the Context of Automated Decision-Making (Articles 13–15 GDPR)

The prohibition laid out in article 22 GDPR comes with a series of information rights regarding the transparency and comprehensibility of automated decision-making. During the preparatory work on the GDPR, it was argued that recognising a right to explanation would serve the broader objective of enhancing the accountability of economic players using algorithms, artificial intelligence, robotics and other automated systems.[44]

Articles 13(2)(f) and 14(2)(g) GDPR require data controllers to provide information to data subjects about 'the existence of automated decision-making, including profiling, referred to in Article 22(1) and (4) and, at least in those cases, meaningful information about the logic involved, as well as the significance and the envisaged consequences of such processing for the data subject'. In addition, article 15 GDPR grants data subjects the right of access to information on those same elements, even after the decision-making process has been undertaken or concluded. Finally, according to article 22(4) GDPR, the data controller must, if the automated decision-making is based on explicit consent or allowed for contractual purposes, implement 'suitable measures to safeguard the data subject's rights and freedoms and legitimate interests, at least the right to obtain human intervention on the part of the controller, to express his or her point of view and to contest the decision'.[45]

It is understandable that this complex set of provisions, creating different rights to information and access, gives rise to questions and uncertainties, especially as to their exact scope and effectiveness.[46] The legal debate on the exact interpretation of articles 13 to 15 GDPR is of particular interest for the insurance sector, as the algorithms used in contract management often represent core intellectual property of the

[43] Article 4(1) of the Proposal.

[44] For a study of the practice of responding to GDPR information requests related to automated decision-making, see Dexe et al. (2022).

[45] Recital 71 explains that such suitable safeguards 'should include specific information to the data subject and the right to obtain human intervention, to express his or her point of view, to obtain an explanation of the decision reached after such assessment and to challenge the decision'. There is a controversy as to the exact legal value of recitals in European regulations and directives. See, for example, Klimas and Vaiciukaite (2008).

[46] Malgieri and Comandé (2017), p. 243; Wachter et al. (2017), p. 74.

insurance companies that cannot easily be made public. While the drafters of the GDPR were aware of the need to find an appropriate balance between the right to access and the protection of trade secrets and intellectual property, national courts and the CJEU face serious difficulties in adopting a sound approach to this issue.[47]

3.1 The Right to Explanation of Insurance-related Automated Decision-Making

The exact scope of the right to explanation in the field of automated decision-making, and therefore the potential of articles 13 to 15 GDPR to become crucial in insurance litigation, depends in particular on the interpretation of the words 'at least in those cases', which is used in all three provisions. While the right to know 'the existence' of automated decision-making is applicable in all cases,[48] the right to receive 'meaningful information' about the logic, significance and consequences is applicable 'at least' in the cases of profiling referred to in articles 22(1) and (4).[49] The use of the term 'at least' can be described, at best, as ambiguous, and at worst as the clumsy expression of an unreachable compromise. Applied literally, the provision means that all data controllers performing automated decision-making that is not included in the definition of articles 22(1) and (4) *can* provide meaningful information about the logic, significance and consequences of the algorithmic process, but that only data controllers performing decision-making falling under the definition of articles 22(1) and (4) *must* provide such information.

In other words, while there is no doubt that the text enshrines a right to an explanation of automated decision-making, the exact range of the coverage is strongly dependent on what constitutes 'a decision based solely on automated processing, including profiling, which produces legal effects concerning him or her or similarly significantly affects him or her'. The provisions on the right to an explanation are intertwined with those on the prohibition of automated decision-making, so that the interpretation of the latter has necessarily an impact on the interpretation of the former.

The final say in the interpretation of both sets of rules rests with the CJEU, and it is very likely that the Court will decide in the near future how to apply the GDPR rules regarding insurance-related automated decision-making, especially in the light of the recent case-law on the compliance of credit scoring practices. In two cases, one brought by a German and the other by an Austrian administrative court, the

---

[47] Bayamlıoğlu (2022), p. 1069.

[48] See also European Law Institute (2022), p. 16 ('Guiding Principle 4: Disclosure that the decision-making is automated'); Article 16(6) of the Digital Services Act ('where [providers of hosting services] use automated means for that processing or decision-making, they shall include information on such use in the notification referred to in paragraph 5').

[49] Sesing (2021), p. 289.

Court was asked to deliver a preliminary ruling on the interpretation of articles 15 and 22 GDPR.[50]

In the first case, the German administrative court (*Verwaltungsgericht*) asked whether the automated creation of a credit score value by a private company (better known as *Schufa*) is an automated decision within the meaning of article 22 GDPR and, if so, whether a national provision allowing the automated calculation of credit score values under certain conditions[51] is compatible with the requirements laid out in article 22(1) GDPR.

In the second case, a private person requested access to information about the logic involved in an instance of automated decision-making by a company specialising in credit assessments (*Dan & Bradstreet*). In an earlier ruling,[52] the Austrian Federal Administrative Court (*Bundesverwaltungsgericht*) had held that the company had infringed the data subject's right to access their data related to an automated decision, since it had not provided meaningful information on the logic involved in the decision. Trying to enforce this judgment, the claimant met with a refusal on the part of the Vienna local administration, which led to a new case before the regional administrative court (*Landesverwaltungsgericht*) of Vienna. The court decided to submit to the CJEU a substantial number of questions related to the interpretation of article 15 GDPR. The central issue was whether information on the functioning of the automated credit assessment must be disclosed to the data subject, where such information is protected by trade secrets under Directive (EU) 2016/943.

In its much-awaited Schufa ruling of 2023, the CJEU decided to reassess the issue completely in the light of the policy considerations underlying the current European data protection law.[53] The judgment has made an undeniable contribution to a better understanding of article 22 GDPR on at least two points.

At first, the Schufa ruling made it clear that the concept of 'decision' under article 22(1) GDPR has to be interpreted in a broader sense, holding that a credit score may qualify as a decision, even though it is only a preparatory step towards the final decision of a bank. For the Court, even if the score were to be subject to a human review by the bank, this does not bar the application of article 22(1), as the bank's decisions 'draw strongly' from the score.[54]

---

[50] Administrative Court Wiesbaden, 1 October 2021, ref 6 K 788/20.WI (the request for a preliminary ruling was published in OJEU 24 January 2022, C 37/14 under case number C-634/21); Regional Administrative Court Wien, 11 February 2022, ref VGW 101/042/791/2020-44 (the request for a preliminary ruling was published in OJEU 7 June 2022, C 222/18 under case number C-203/22).

[51] § 31 of the German Federal Data Protection Act regulates the use of 'probability value(s) concerning the ability of a data subject to service a loan in the future'.

[52] Bundesverwaltungsgericht, 23 October 2019, ref Zl. W256 2217011-1/11E.

[53] CJEU, 7 December 2023, ref C-634/21. On this judgment, see the case notes of Aza (2024); Huttner (2024a); Palmiotto (2024); Paal and Aliprandi (2023); Genicot (2023). See also Huttner (2024b); Genicot (2025).

[54] CJEU, 7 December 2023, nos 48–49.

Second, the score itself has to be considered as a decision in order to avoid a 'lacuna in legal protection' regarding informational rights. Under the GDPR, data subjects are entitled to receive 'meaningful information about the logic involved [in the automated decision], as well as the significance and the envisaged consequences of such processing for the data subject'. In a context of an automated decision-making with multiple steps, it is necessary to entitle data subjects to informational rights against the scoring company, as the bank will not be able to provide information about the underlying algorithm. The CJEU emphasizes thus its commitment to the efficiency of the right of information under article 15(1) GDPR, as confirms the Dun & Bradstreet ruling of 2025 in the second case.[55]

However, commentators of the Schufa ruling have observed that it is not entirely clear whether the final decision of the bank can be qualified as an automated decision under article 22(1) GDPR, given that it must be 'based solely on automated processing'.[56] Even though the bank's actions are strongly influenced by the scoring result, it can not be excluded that the final decision on a credit falls outside the scope of article 22 GDPR because of the proof of human intervention. The CJEU does not, however, establish any clear criteria to clarify what is meant by 'based solely on automated processing'.

One can readily see that the scoring cases are of the utmost importance for the insurance industry. As mentioned previously, insurance companies are increasingly reliant on automated decision-making processes, whether in the form of profiling or of scoring or algorithmic claims management. Both cases, however, do not provide sufficient clarity as for the compliance requirements of insurance-related scoring practices, which are mostly operated internally and not by external service providers such as Schufa. It is to be hoped that forthcoming CJEU judgments will determine whether those practices, rarely disclosed by the insurance industry for image reasons, can be kept in operation or need to be updated or partially replaced. In this debate, much also depends on the sanctions which can be imposed if automated decision-making amounts to a violation of the GDPR.

3.2 *What Are the Sanctions in Cases of Non-compliance with Those Rights?*

The GDPR provides the national data protection authorities with the possibility of imposing a comprehensive set of sanctions if an infringement is reported by a data subject according to article 77[57] or established by the authority itself. Administrative

---

[55] CJEU, 27 February 2025, ref C-203/22.

[56] See in particular Huttner (2024a), nos 15–18. See also Aza (2024), pp. 849–850.

[57] Under this article, 'every data subject shall have the right to lodge a complaint with a supervisory authority, (…) if the data subject considers that the processing of personal data relating to him or her infringes this Regulation'.

fines are crucial for the enforcement of the Regulation, even though the national authorities have various other instruments allowing them to impose other sanctions on non-compliant data processors and data controllers, such as warnings, reprimands, bans, withdrawals of certification or even suspensions.[58] The public enforcement of the GDPR also includes criminal prosecutions for particularly severe violations of data protection rules.

The second pillar of the enforcement regime of the GDPR is the right to compensation, which is granted to data subjects under article 82(1).[59] According to this article, 'any person who has suffered material or non-material damage as a result of an infringement of this Regulation shall have the right to receive compensation from the controller or processor for the damage suffered'. There is broad agreement among policy-makers and legal academics that private enforcement can substantially improve the effectiveness of data protection rules, because compliance with those rules does not just depend on the efficiency of public prosecutors and administrative bodies.

In order to be awarded civil damages, a claimant is required to establish an 'infringement' of the GDPR, or in other words a violation of, or non-compliance with, the provisions of the Regulation. While recital 146 indicates that the term 'infringement' refers to the 'processing' of personal data that is not in compliance with the data protection rules laid out in the GDPR, some national courts, mostly in Germany and Austria, have held that the mere failure to provide relevant information related to the processing of personal data may give rise to liability for the controller. It was up to the CJEU, to which several preliminary questions had been referred, to decide whether a wide or a restrictive vision of a cause of action under article 82 GDPR is in line with the underlying political goals and the wording of the Regulation.

It goes without saying that the case law has a direct impact on the efficacy of individual rights in the field of profiling and automated decision-making. As we have seen, the data subject's right to information under article 13 GDPR is independent of any data processing, so arises, for example, in cases in which an insurance company suspected of applying automated decision-making processes rejects applications arising from specific groups of applicants.[60]

In this context, a clarification of the requirements regarding the proof of 'material or non-material damage' was crucial. Can non-material damage to data subjects be inferred from the mere breach of the data protection rules, or is their subjective discomfort not sufficient for compensation, which would mean that claimants would have to establish a 'non-pecuniary loss' that exceeds a certain threshold? If so, how can the level of gravity that has to be reached by the claimant's personal situation be determined? In other words, one must ask if the mere violation of the GDPR data protection rules can give rise to a claim for compensation even if the infringement

---

[58] See the list established in article 58(2) GDPR.

[59] On this text and its potential for privacy litigation cases, see, among others, Knetsch (2022).

[60] On the practice of discrimination in the case of algorithmic insurance, see Kuschke (2022).

has not had any serious impact on the everyday life of the claimant: for example, if they are able without too much trouble to find another insurance company after the rejection of their application or the termination of their contract.

In its judgment issued on 4 May 2023 in the case Österreichische Post AG (also known as the 'Austrian Post Case'),[61] the EUCJ tried to find a middle ground between a wide interpretation of article 82(1) GDPR, which would have provided an important stimulus to private enforcement, and the restrictive vision arising, at least in symbolic terms, from the enshrinement of a *de minimis rule*.

The Court states in its judgment that 'it cannot be held that any "infringement" of the provisions of the GDPR, by itself, confers (a) right to compensation (…) such an interpretation would run counter to the wording of Article 82(1) GDPR'.[62] However, the Court also decides that 'making compensation for non-material damage subject to a certain threshold of seriousness would risk undermining the coherence of the rules established by the GDPR, since the graduation of such a threshold, on which the possibility or otherwise of obtaining that compensation would depend, would be liable to fluctuate according to the assessment of the courts seized'.[63]

This means in substance that claimants have to establish the existence of a 'non-material harm' and of a causal link between the unlawful data processing and that loss. National courts will have to assess the alleged loss regardless of any criteria of seriousness, which might exist under domestic tort law. However, the Court of Justice also made it clear that 'national courts must apply the domestic rules of each Member State relating to the extent of financial compensation, provided that the principles of equivalence and effectiveness of EU law are complied with'.[64]

To put it mildly, with these statements (largely reiterated in subsequent cases),[65] which may seem commonplace, it is likely that the judges in the EU Member States are not smarter than before.[66]

In this regard, the Österreichische Post ruling as well as the subsequent judgments on article 82(1) GDPR are rather disappointing, as the central issue (what exactly means 'non-material harm'?) has still not been addressed by the Court's judges. Bound by the wording of the regulation, they did not have the fortitude to lay the groundwork for a European understanding of non-pecuniary loss, leaving it to the national courts to scramble for solutions in an area where legal uncertainty is now greater than ever before. The contradictory reactions provoked by the judgment (while some consumer protection groups saw a 'turn of an era', business

[61] CJEU, 4 May 2023, ref C-300/21.

[62] CJEU, 4 May 2023, no. 33.

[63] CJEU, 4 May 2023, no. 49.

[64] CJEU, 4 May 2023, no. 59.

[65] CJEU, 14 December 2023, ref C-340/21 and C-456/22; 21 December 2023, ref C-667/21; 25 January 2024, ref C-687/21. For a commentary on those judgments, see Knetsch (2024). See also CJEU, 20 June 2024, ref C-182/22 and C-189/22; 4 October 2024, ref C-200/23 and C-507/23.

[66] See also Janeček and Teixeira Santos (2024), pp. 538–543; Salziger (2024), pp. 327–329; Douville (2023), pp. 536–539. For a comprehensive assessment of the requirement of 'non-material damage', see Stegemann (2024), pp. 69–194.

representatives were relieved that the Court of Justice has removed the legal basis of a significant part of the claims) speak for themselves.[67]

As in other data-protection relevant areas, the insurance sector will be subject to GDPR infringement litigation and it is now up to the national courts and, eventually, the CJEU to determine to what extent data protection rules may apply to profiling practices that used to pass under the radar.

4 Conclusion

This brief study describes one of the highly interesting issues related to the interplay of insurance law and data protection law. The drafters of the GDPR have laid the foundations of a stricter control framework on profiling practices and other forms of automated decision-making based on personal data. However, subtle ambiguities in the language used makes it difficult to predict the specific outcome of the confrontation between the data protection rules and the overall philosophy of insurance business, which cannot be conceived to operate without the processing of information related to the risk to be covered.

Regulatory Guidance, Legislation and Case Law

1981 Convention for the Protection of Individuals with regard to Automatic Processing of Personal Data. Council of Europe

Article 29 Data Protection Working Party (2018) Guidelines on Automated individual decision-making and Profiling for the purposes of Regulation 2016/679, ref 17 EN WP251rev.01. https://ec.europa.eu/newsroom/article29/items/612053

Article 29 Data Protection Working Party (2017) Guidelines on Consent under Regulation 2016/679, ref 17/EN WP259. https://ec.europa.eu/newsroom/article29/items/623051/

Council of Europe (2010) The protection of individuals with regard to automatic processing of personal data in the context of profiling. Recommendation CM/Rec(2010)13 and explanatory memorandum. https://rm.coe.int/16807096c3

Court of Justice of the European Union, 4 May 2023, ref C-300/21 https://eur-lex.europa.eu/legal-content/en/TXT/?uri=CELEX:62021CJ0300

Court of Justice of the European Union, 7 December 2023, ref C-634/21 https://eur-lex.europa.eu/legal-content/en/TXT/?uri=CELEX:62021CJ0634

Court of Justice of the European Union, 14 December 2023, ref C-340/21 https://eur-lex.europa.eu/legal-content/en/TXT/?uri=CELEX:62021CJ0340

[67] On the critical reception of the 'Austrian Post' case by the stakeholders, see Knetsch (2023).

Court of Justice of the European Union, 14 December 2023, ref C-456/22 https://eur-lex.europa.eu/legal-content/en/TXT/?uri=CELEX:62022CJ0456

Court of Justice of the European Union, 21 December 2023, ref C-667/21 https://eur-lex.europa.eu/legal-content/en/TXT/?uri=CELEX:62021CJ0667

Court of Justice of the European Union, 25 January 2024, ref C-687/21 https://eur--lex.europa.eu/legal-content/en/TXT/?uri=CELEX:62021CJ0687

Court of Justice of the European Union, 20 June 2024, ref C-182/22 and C-189/22 https://eur-lex.europa.eu/legal-content/en/TXT/?uri=CELEX:62022CJ0182

Court of Justice of the European Union, 4 October 2024, ref C-200/23 https://eur--lex.europa.eu/legal-content/en/TXT/?uri=CELEX:62023CJ0200

Court of Justice of the European Union, 4 October 2024, ref C-507/23 https://eur--lex.europa.eu/legal-content/en/TXT/?uri=CELEX:62023CJ0507

Court of Justice of the European Union, 27 February 2025, ref C-203/22 https://eur-lex.europa.eu/legal-content/en/TXT/?uri=CELEX:62022CJ0203

Deutscher Bundestag (2017) Gesetzentwurf der Bundesregierung: Entwurf eines Gesetzes zur Anpassung des Datenschutzrechts an die Verordnung (EU) 2016/679 und zur Umsetzung der Richtlinie (EU) 2016/680 (Datenschutz-Anpassungs- und -Umsetzungsgesetz EU – DSAnpUG-EU), ref Drucksache 18/11325, 24 February 2017. https://dserver.bundestag.de/btd/18/113/1811325.pdf

European Data Protection Board (2020) Guidelines 05/2020 on Consent under Regulation 2016/679. https://edpb.europa.eu/sites/default/files/files/file1/edpb_guidelines_202005_consent_en.pdf

Administrative Court (*Verwaltungsgericht*) Wiesbaden, 1 October 2021, ref 6 K 788/20.WI. https://dejure.org/dienste/vernetzung/rechtsprechung?Gericht=VG Wiesbaden&Datum=01.10.2021&Aktenzeichen=6%20K%20788%2F20

Federal Administrative Court (*Bundesverwaltungsgericht*) of Austria, 23 October 2019, ref Zl. W256 2217011-1/11E https://rdb.manz.at/document/ris.bvwg.BVWGT_20191023_W256_2217011_1_00

Regional Administrative Court (*Landesverwaltungsgericht*) Vienna, 11 February 2022, ref VGW 101/042/791/2020-44. https://www.ris.bka.gv.at/Dokumente/Lvwg/LVWGT_WI_20220211_VGW_101_042_791_2020_44_00/LVWGT_WI_20220211_VGW_101_042_791_2020_44_00.html

References

Articles, Documents, Textbooks

Abel RB (2018) Automatisierte Entscheidungen im Einzelfall gem. Art. 22 DS-GVO: Anwendungsbereich und Grenzen im nicht-öffentlichen Bereich. Zeitschrift für Datenschutz 8:304–307

Amankwah J, Stroobants N (2022) GDPR and the processing of health data in insurance contracts: opening a can of worms? In: Lima Rego M, Kuschke B (dir.), Insurance and human rights. AIDA Europe research series on insurance law and regulation, Vol 5. Springer, Cham, pp 173–227

Armbrüster C (2017) Auskunftsansprüche des Versicherungsnehmers und Geheimhaltungsinteressen des Versicherers. In: Looschelders D, Michael L (eds) Düsseldorfer Vorträge zum Versicherungsrechts 2016. Düsseldorfer Schriften zum Versicherungsrecht, Vol 33. Karlsruhe, Verlag Versicherungswissenschaft, pp 15–38

Armbrüster C, Prill J (2020) Künstliche Intelligenz im Versicherungssektor – rechtliche Herausforderungen. Zeitschrift für Versicherungswesen 71(4):110–113

Aza A (2024) Scores as decisions? Article 22 GDPR and the judgment of the CJEU in SCHUFA Holding (scoring) in the labour context. Ind Law J 53(4):840–858

Bainbridge DI (1997) Processing personal data and the data protection directive. Info Commun Technol Law 6(1):17–40

Bayamlıoğlu E (2022) The right to contest automated decisions under the General Data Protection Regulation: Beyond the so-called "right to explanation". Regul Gov 16:1058–1078

Béguin-Faynel C (2022) Clarification des principes de protection des données personnelles en matière d'assurance. Responsabilité civile et assurances 35(2):7–11

Biddle R, Liu S, Tilocca P, Xu G (2018) Automated underwriting in life insurance: predictions and optimisation. In: Wang J, Cong G, Chen J, Qi J (eds) Databases theory and applications: 29th Australasian database conference, ADC 2018, Gold Coast, QLD, Australia, May 24-27, 2018, Proceedings. Lecture Notes in Computer Science. Springer, Cham, pp 135–146

Binon JM (2021) Assurances de personnes et protection des données personnelles: un mariage tumultueux à l'ombre du RGPD. Revue de droit commercial belge 31(9):1949–1971

Bygrave LA (2001) Minding the machine: Article 15 of the EC data protection directive and automated profiling. Comp Law Secur Rev 17(1):17–24

Bygrave LA (2019) Minding the Machine v2.0: The EU general data protection regulation and automated decision-making. In: Yeung K, Lodge M (eds) Algorithmic regulation. OUP, Oxford, pp 246–260

Bygrave LA (2020) Article 22 Automated individual decision-making, including profiling. In: Kuner C, Bygrave LA, Docksey C, Drechsler L (eds) The EU general data protection regulation (GDPR): a commentary. OUP, Oxford, pp 522–542

Bygrave LA (2022) Machine learning, cognitive sovereignty and data protection rights with respect to automated decisions. In: Ienca M, Pollicino O, Liguori L, Stefanini E, Andorno R (eds) The Cambridge handbook of information technology, life sciences and human rights. Cambridge law handbooks. CUP, Cambridge, pp 165–188

Castets-Renard C (2019) Accountability of algorithms in the GDPR and beyond: a European legal framework on automated decision-making. Fordham Intell Prop Media Ent Law J 30:91–137

Čertický M (2021) Certain issues of innovations affecting the insurance business in the light of the GDPR and Hungarian insurance law. Acta Univ Sapientiae: Legal Stud 10(1):35–53

Dexe J, Franke U, Söderlund K, van Berkel N, Hagensby Jensen R, Lepinkäinen N, Vaiste J (2022) Explaining automated decision-making: a multinational study of the GDPR right to meaningful information. Geneva Pap Risk Insur Iss Pract 47:667–697

Dhont J (2000) Le traitement des données à caractère personnel dans le secteur d'assurances: la légalité des banques de données. Revue de droit de l'ULB 21(1):289–334

Douville T (2023) Des fonctions de la responsabilité civile des responsables de traitement de données à caractère personnel. Revue des affaires européennes 28(2):535–542

European Law Institute (2022) Guiding principles for automated decision-making in the EU. Vienna, European Law Institute. https://www.europeanlawinstitute.eu/fileadmin/user_upload/p_eli/Publications/ELI_Innovation_Paper_on_Guiding_Principles_for_ADM_in_the_EU.pdf

Genicot N (2023) To score is to decide. About the SCHUFA case. Verfassungsblog.de, 14 December 2023. https://verfassungsblog.de/to-score-is-to-decide/

Genicot N (2025) Scoring the European citizen in the AI era. Computer Law & Security Review 57(7):106130

Glatzner F (2020) Profilbildung und algorithmenbasierte Entscheidungen. Datenschutz und Datensicherheit 44:312–315

González Fuster G (2014) The emergence of personal data protection as a fundamental right of the EU. Law, governance and technology, Vol 16. Springer, Cham
Günthner C, Krohm N (2020) Datenschutz. In: Bürkle J (ed) Compliance in Versicherungsunternehmen: rechtliche Anforderungen und praktische Umsetzung, 3rd edn. Munich, CH Beck, pp 535–570
Hänold S (2017) Profiling und Automatisierte Einzelentscheidungen im Versicherungsbereich. Hannover, Gottfried-Wilhelm-Leibniz-Universität. https://www.repo.uni-hannover.de/handle/123456789/5167
Helfrich M (2020) BDSG § 37. In: Sydow G (ed) Bundesdatenschutzgesetz. Nomos Kommentar. Nomos, Baden-Baden, pp 425–433
Helfrich M (2022) DS GVO Art 22. In: Sydow G, Marsch N (eds), DS-GVO BDSG, 3rd edn. Nomos Kommentar. CH Beck, Munich, pp 554–570
Hladjik J (2018) DS-GVO Art 22. In: Ehmann E, Selmayr M (eds) Datenschutz-Grundverordnung, 2nd edn. Beck'sche Kurz-Kommentare. CH Beck, Munich, pp 460–465
Huttner L (2024a) Décisions automatisées: Le réveil d'un géant endormi? Communication Commerce électronique 25(2):7–11
Huttner L (2024b) La décision de l'algorithme: Étude de droit privé sur les relations entre l'humain et la machine. LGDJ, Paris
Janeček V, Teixeira Santos C (2024) The autonomous concept of "damage" according to the GDPR and its unfortunate implications: Österreichische Post. CML Rev 61(2):531–544
Keast G (2021) Why Keeping a Human Perspective is Essential in Automated Decision-Making, Forbes.com 13 October 2021. https://www.forbes.com/sites/forbestechcouncil/2021/10/13/why-keeping-a-human-perspective-is-essential-in-automated-decision-making/
Klimas T, Vaiciukaite J (2008) The law of recitals in European community legislation. ILSA J Int Comp Law 15(1):61–93
Knetsch J (2022) The compensation of non-pecuniary loss in GDPR infringement cases. JETL 13(2):132–153
Knetsch J (2023) GDPR's right to compensation and the 'Österreichische Post' case (C-300/21): major breakthrough or much ado about nothing? EU Law Live, 31 mai 2023. https://eulawlive.com/op-ed-gdprs-right-to-compensation-and-the-osterreichische-post-case-c-300-21-major-breakthrough-or-much-ado-about-nothing-by-jonas-knetsch/
Knetsch J (2024) Le contentieux de la réparation des dommages causés par la violation du RGPD: les tiraillements de la CJUE. Revue des contrats 22(2):32–38
KPMG (2018) The GDPR and key challenges faced by the Insurance industry. KPMG Creative Services. https://assets.kpmg/content/dam/kpmg/ie/pdf/2018/03/ie-gdpr-for-insurance-industry.pdf
Kuschke B (2022) Discrimination in the context of parametric insurance. In: Lima Rego M, Kuschke B (eds) Insurance and human rights. AIDA Europe research series on insurance law and regulation, vol 5. Springer, Cham, pp 27–51
Malgieri G (2019) Automated decision-making in the EU Member States: The right to explanation and other 'suitable safeguards' in the national legislations. Comp Law Secur Rev 35(5):105327
Malgieri G, Comandé G (2017) Why a right to legibility of automated decision-making exists in the general data protection regulation. Int Data Priv Law 7(4):243–265
Martini M (2021) DS-GVO Art 22. In: Paal BP, Pauly DA (eds) Datenschutz-Grundverordnung Bundesdatenschutzgesetz, 3rd edn. Beck'sche Kompakt-Kommentare. CH Beck, Munich, pp 335–368
McGurk B (2019) Data profiling and insurance law. Hart, Oxford
Paal B, Aliprandi C (2023) Immaterieller Schadensersatz bei Datenschutzverstößen vor dem EuGH. Neue Juristische Wochenschrift 77(27):1914–1917
Palmiotto F (2024) When is a decision automated? A taxonomy for a fundamental rights analysis. German Law J 25:210–236
Paschke A, Scheurer M (2022) BDSG § 37. In: Gola P, Heckmann D (eds) Datenschutz-Grundverordnung – Bundesdatenschutzgesetz, 3rd edn. Munich, CH Beck, pp 1265–1291

Pnevmatikakis A, Kanavos S, Perikleous A, Kyriazakos S (2022) Risk assessment for personalized health insurance products. In: Soldatos J, Kyriazis D (eds) Big data and artificial intelligence in digital finance. Springer, Cham, pp 281–294

Salziger S (2024) Between data protection and AI: civil liability for non-material damage in Article 82 GDPR. Eur Data Prot Law Rev 10(4):324–335

Sesing A (2021) Grenzen systemischer Transparenz bei automatisierter Datenverarbeitung: Umfang und Grenzen der Pflicht zur Bereitstellung aussagekräftiger Informationenüber die involvierte Logik. Multimedia und Recht 24:288–292

Sood K, Dhanaraj RK, Balusamy B, Grima S, Maheshwari RU (2022) Big data: a game changer for insurance industry. Emerald studies in finance, insurance, and risk management, Vol 6. Emerald Publishing, Bingley

Spittka J (2019) Datenschutz in der Privatversicherung. In: Specht L, Mantz R (eds) Handbuch europäisches und deutsches Datenschutzrecht. CH Beck, Munich, pp 336–364

Stegemann L (2024) Der immaterielle Schadensersatz bei Datenschutzverstößen. Frankfurter Studien zum Datenschutz, vol 70. Nomos, Baden-Baden

Taeger J, Gabel D (2022) DSGVO – BDSG – TTDSG (4th edn) Kommunikation und Recht. Frankfurt, Fachmedien Recht und Wirtschaft

Tambou O (2020) Manuel de droit européen de la protection des données à caractère personnel. Droit administratif/Administrative Law, Manuels, Vol 28. Bruxelles, Bruylant

Tosoni L (2021) The right to object to automated individual decisions: resolving the ambiguity of Article 22(1) of the general data protection regulation. Int Data Priv Law 11(2):145–162

Veale M, Edwards L (2018) Clarity, surprises, and further questions in the Article 29 Working Party draft guidance on automated decision-making and profiling. Comp Law Secur Rev 34(2):398–404

Wachter S, Mittelstadt B, Floridi L (2017) Why a right to explanation of automated decision-making does not exist in the general data protection regulation. Int Data Priv Law 7(2):76–99

Jonas Knetsch is a professor of private law at the Sorbonne Law School (University Paris 1 Panthéon-Sorbonne). He is also the director of the Paris Institute of Insurance Law (IAP Paris-Sorbonne) and the co-director of the Department "Law of Contract, Tort Law and Insurance Law" at the Sorbonne Institute for Legal Research (IRJS). His research interests include tort law and insurance law, both from a domestic and comparative perspective.

How Do Consumers Inform Themselves About Insurance Products in the Digital Age? Analysing the Results of a Consumer Survey

Ewa Cichowicz and Piotr Tereszkiewicz

1 Introduction

Despite the insurance sector being relatively slow in accepting new technologies compared to other areas of the financial system,[1] digitalisation is gaining increasing recognition in the insurance sector. Changes in the virtual space, which also affect insurance, take place at a faster pace, reinforced by favourable external conditions, translating into a specific increase in pressure to use technological progress.[2] The dynamic growth and diversity of artificial intelligence applications is an important element of the insurance sector's technological transformation.[3] Moreover, no reasonable premises have emerged so far that would indicate a slowdown in

[1] See Beltratti and Corvino (2008), Werth et al. (2020).

[2] More about digitalisation as a major driving force in the contemporary economy and society in: Matt et al. (2023).

[3] See Gupta et al. (2022), Ceylan (2022).

Some aspects of the research project discussed in this chapter are presented in: Piotr Tereszkiewicz, Ewa Cichowicz (2024), Findings from the Polish InsurTech market as a roadmap for regulators, Computer Law & Security Review, vol. 52. https://doi.org/10.1016/j.clsr.2024.105948.
This chapter has been written within the framework of a research project supported by the National Science Centre (NCN) in Poland, grant number 2018/29/B/HS5/01281.

E. Cichowicz
SGH Warsaw School of Economics, Warsaw, Poland
e-mail: ecicho1@sgh.waw.pl

P. Tereszkiewicz (✉)
Private Law Department, Jagiellonian University, Krakow, Poland
e-mail: piotr.tereszkiewicz@uj.edu.pl

C. Poncibò, P. Tereszkiewicz (eds.), *European Insurance Law within the Digital Age*, AIDA Europe Research Series on Insurance Law and Regulation 14,
https://doi.org/10.1007/978-3-031-96496-1_9

technological development in the coming years. This is all the more so since digitalisation allows for meeting the requirements of a customer-centric model, greater individualisation (personalisation) of insurance cover, and the calculation of an adequate insurance premium.[4] Additionally, digitalisation stimulates changes towards self-service insurance processes based on the appropriate involvement of consumers in the digital reality.[5] On the other hand, modern technologies allow for improving customer experience and a faster adaptation of subsequent stages of the insurance relationship to the circumstances in which the buying process takes place.[6]

The needs and wishes of insurance consumers are essential factors in implementing technological solutions within the insurance sector. Specifically, consumer expectations regarding access to modern technologies have been further strengthened by the consequences of the COVID-19 pandemic, which contributed to the transfer of significant parts of private and professional activities to digital channels.[7] The end of the pandemic did not lead to the return of habits from before the outbreak of COVID-19; habits related to the use of new technologies, including communicating via remote tools, which emerged along with the need to limit direct interpersonal contacts, have remained and have even consolidated themselves. Consumers not only notice the benefits of digital tools but increasingly perceive the availability of such tools as a factual condition for entering into a relationship with financial services providers, including insurance companies. Consumers expect non-stop access, new functionalities, and highly personalised products and services, making the adoption of a new approach to the communication between the parties to insurance contracts inevitable.

At the same time, business models of insurance companies have been evolving.[8] On the one hand, they are adapting to consumer expectations, while, on the other, they aim at finding competitive advantages and ensuring stable expansion of these companies in the long term within the new environment.[9] In this context, one should pay attention to the specific nature of the industry in which insurance intermediaries have traditionally played an important role. Digitalisation processes have influenced the functioning of the agency network, including the perception of intermediaries' importance and their actual role in it.[10] The emergence of previously unprecedented market strategies is expected to become increasingly visible. Thanks to operations based on modern technologies, insurance companies can strengthen their direct sales and compete for consumers with a network of intermediaries. On the other hand, intermediaries with an established market position may ultimately become

[4] See Małek et al. (2022), Eckert and Osterrieder (2020).

[5] See Południak-Gierz and Tereszkiewicz (2023).

[6] See Eling and Lehmann (2018).

[7] See Pauch and Bera (2022), Volosovych et al. (2021).

[8] See Nicoletti (2021), Cappiello (2018).

[9] See Chojan et al. (2022).

[10] See Marano (2019), Stricker et al. (2023).

the organisers of insurance services as creators of ecosystems.[11] In the case of multi-agents, an increasingly common approach allows the client to analyse offers with tools based on modern technologies, and then complete the purchase process themselves. Some intermediaries use their own IT systems, in which they place only some processes, e.g., the presentation of quotes, so that consumers can compare the offers of different insurance companies. By contrast, other processes (e.g., sales) are already performed within the insurance company's digital infrastructure (i.e., a website, a mobile app) whose offer was chosen. Intermediaries can also create multi-sales portals, which—thanks to application programming interfaces (API)—are integrated with the transaction systems of many insurers, but with all functionalities available to the intermediary and all processes unified within the multi-agency system. At the same time, a third option is relatively popular: the use of digital solutions by insurance companies that protect the interests of intermediaries and focus on ensuring the satisfaction of comprehensive (including digital) consumer requirements. In order to guarantee consumer satisfaction, it is necessary to properly match products with the buyer's needs, conditioned by a prior comparison of offers.

Another significant trend in insurance distribution is the omnichannel approach,[12] within which consumers can choose from various distribution channels (including digital) that best suit their needs. From the perspective of insurance companies, however, it is not primarily a matter of the chosen channel for establishing and maintaining relationships but rather creating purchasing opportunities so that access to information, product availability and process optimisation meet consumer expectations and are consistent with one another at every level, regardless of the communication channel.

In the case of digitalisation, another aspect that merits attention is the method of concluding the contract. Consumers can now purchase insurance products in-store or via remote channels. In the first case, the approach of "online research and offline purchase" is gaining importance: from the clients' perspective, an essential element of the pre-contractual stage is acquiring information about the offer and comparing individual variants (also offered by different insurers). In the second case, an increasingly popular solution is to conclude a distance contract, with the entire process taking place online. The role of consumer awareness and knowledge then increases, as consumers should be able to compare and choose an appropriate variant of the insurance product and sign the contract in full knowledge, knowing what scope of protection they will be receiving in exchange for the premium paid.

The above, in turn, creates the need to gradually redefine the process of using services offered in the insurance sector, with an essential element being that consumers can obtain information about insurance products. One should note, however, that this issue should be viewed from a broader perspective than just the fact of familiarisation with a given product. Consumers' motives when choosing an offer,

[11] See the chapter by Antti Talonen in this book.

[12] See Eckert et al. (2022).

how they obtain information, awareness of the consequences of providing additional data and their willingness to provide it, as well as openness to modern technologies, knowledge of them, and the degree of use, are all important. Another critical issue in this regard is comparing individual offers and understanding the content of insurance contracts and their annexes.[13] When a consumer signs a contract remotely, final information about the purchased insurance product is provided remotely, and the awareness of specific information to be found in the contractual documents becomes particularly relevant. Separate but equally significant problems are the legal conditions related to the pre-contractual process and the conclusion of insurance contracts. Consumers, insurance companies and insurance intermediaries operate within specific regulatory frameworks that should respond to the needs and protect the interests of individual parties, provided that the most vulnerable of them, requiring the greatest protection, is the insurance consumer.[14]

2 Methodology and the Research Results

To examine consumers' attitudes and expectations on the insurance market in the era of dynamic digitalisation, a representative survey was conducted in November 2021. The survey included 2136 Polish citizens who had concluded an insurance contract at least once in their lives. Performed using the CAWI (Computer Assisted Web Interview) method, 31 research questions were asked, divided into three thematic blocks.[15] The first group of questions concerned respondents' experiences in the insurance field, the second group included questions related to the insurance selection process, and the third group of questions was devoted to new technologies used in insurance.

57% of women and 42.6% of men participated in the study, with the largest group (25.8%) being those aged 26–35. Almost one in five respondents (19.2%) were between 36 and 45 years old, and the smallest group (11.7%) was made up of those aged between 56 and 65 years old. 42.3% of respondents had secondary education, while 33.2% had higher education (of which 8.2% were individuals with a higher economics education, while 25% had a higher education without a background in economics). 32% of respondents were rural residents, and 68% lived in cities, including 14% of the total sample in cities with over 500,000 inhabitants. Slightly more than half of the respondents (53.4%) formed households of at least two persons, which included at least one child. About one-third of the respondents (34.1%) were in a household of at least two persons without children.

Analysing the respondents' experience in concluding insurance contracts, one should note that most often, at least once in their adult life, they concluded a

[13] This model is assumed by legislation, see Locker (2015).

[14] See Ratowska-Dziobak (2023), Malinowska (2014).

[15] Most survey questions are available at www.insurance-survey.net

contract regarding compulsory third-party liability insurance for the owner of a motor vehicle or a life insurance contract (about 65% of respondents) or a home insurance contract (60% of respondents). Other types of insurance were concluded in less than 50% of responses. In turn, during the 12 months before the survey date, most respondents (approx. 90%) concluded or had concluded between 1 and 5 insurance contracts, while 9.2% of respondents had not concluded any contract during that time. 48.1% of the survey participants had been through a claims settlement process at least once, while 6.4% could not indicate whether a payout had ever been made under their insurance policy. It is also worth adding that 40.7% of respondents answered that they most often concluded insurance contracts to protect against risk and its negative consequences. In comparison, 29.2% did so out of necessity, i.e., compulsory insurance and another 5% did so due to a necessity arising from another contract. 13.2% of respondents had never thought about it; they just believed it to be necessary. Only 1.5% of those participating in the study most often conclude contracts having been convinced by an insurance company advertisement, or an offer proposed by an agent/multi-agent/broker. In turn, price was in 67.6% of cases the factor with the most significant impact on the choice of a given insurance company (respondents could indicate a maximum of three answers). For 42.2% of respondents, the most important aspect when deciding was the scope of the cover and the insurance amount. 38% indicated an individually tailored offer as a critical factor when purchasing an insurance product. Interestingly, only 4.5% of respondents considered purchasing a product via the Internet or telephone as a consideration in choosing a product.

Respondents were asked where they most often looked for information about the insurance they wanted to purchase. The results are presented in Table 1.

According to the respondents, insurers or insurance intermediaries are still the most common source of information about the offer. What is interesting, however, is that almost half of the people participating in the study (46.7%) most often look for such information on the Internet, meaning that every second consumer learned about the insurance on their own, which is assumed to have been to a large extent

Table 1 Primary sources of the information about the insurance offer to be concluded

The main source of the information about the insurance offer	Frequency	Percentage
Individual insurers' websites	408	19.1%
Websites about insurance (e.g., special services)	194	9.1%
Internet forums or blogs	92	4.3%
Comparison websites	303	14.2%
The insurers or insurance agents/multi-agents/brokers	599	28.0%
Family or friends	272	12.7%
More than one of the abovementioned sources of information	89	4.2%
Other sources	23	1.1%
Nowhere, I just sign the contract	156	7.3%
Total	2136	100%

Source: results of own research

without obtaining feedback from a professional. When using comparison websites or just content on websites, they cannot discuss any potential doubts with an advisor or ask additional questions, which is where the appropriate awareness and knowledge of those seeking insurance protection becomes essential. Equally relevant is that the information provided via remote channels is correct, truthful and formulated using clear and understandable language. Important information should be easy to find or presented in a way that is intended to confuse the consumer or go unnoticed. It is also worth noting that as many as 7.3% of respondents did not check any offers at all but signed the documents when concluding a contract, which can lead to a dubious situation in which the consumer is not aware of the protection they will obtain and under what conditions.

Analysing the sources from which consumers obtain information about insurance products in more detail, it can be concluded that the men participating in the study used the Internet more often than did the women. Moreover, statistically, the men used each Internet source more often in the general research sample. For example, in the case of comparison websites as a source of information, this was 16.5% of male respondents vs. 12.5% of female respondents. On the other hand, the women look for information about insurance products at insurers' branches or intermediaries slightly more often than did the men (also slightly more often than all the study participants combined). However, a significant difference is visible in the case of indications regarding family and friends as a source of information, with this being the most important source for 16.5% of women, while the corresponding indication for men is 7.6%.

Further, the survey inquired into where respondents in particular age groups most often looked for information about the insurance offer to be purchased (see Fig. 1). In the case of the youngest group of study participants, the main source of

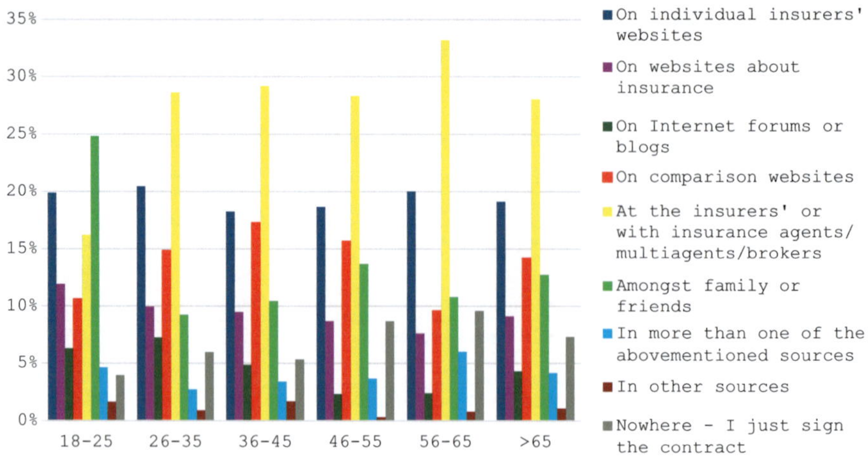

Fig. 1 Primary sources of information about the insurance offer to be concluded, divided into age groups (in %). Source: results of own research

information (for one in four respondents) was family or friends, while for other age groups, the share of this source was in the range of 9–14% of respondents. In turn, respondents from all other groups indicated branches of insurers or insurance intermediaries as the most important source of information, with as many as 33% of respondents aged 56–65 pointed to this source, while the share of those aged 26–55 and over 65 was very similar, amounting to 28–29%. For respondents aged 18 to 25, the corresponding number of indications reached 16%. With regard to comparison websites as the primary source of information for respondents, it can be seen that they are most popular among respondents aged 36–45 (17% of responses), while least often indicated as the primary source of information by respondents aged 56–65 (10% of responses). What may come as a surprise is that comparison websites received only 11% of responses in the 18–25 age group, which was the second lowest result among all the age groups. Regarding all the listed Internet sources together, it can be seen that they are the most important source of obtaining information about the insurance products to be purchased for people aged 26 to 35 (52% of responses), and mentioned least often by respondents from the 56–65 age group (40% of responses).

Another consideration criterion was the respondents' education, analysed within the context of the main source of obtaining information about insurance products. For respondents from all education groups, insurers' branches or intermediaries were the most frequently indicated source of information. Additionally, among consumers with primary and basic vocational education, 16% of respondents considered family or friends to be the most important source, which was the highest share of this answer among all the education groups (3 to 5 percentage points higher than the answers of people with both secondary and higher education). Similarly, respondents with primary and basic vocational education tend not to seek information about insurance products anywhere and sign a contract without prior knowledge of the topic (9% vs. 6–7% of respondents from other education groups). On the other hand, people with primary and basic vocational education were the least likely to consider online comparison websites as the most important source from which they obtain information, constituting 11% of their indications. In turn, such a source was indicated by 14% of people with secondary education and 17% of people with higher education (irrespective of an academic background in economics or other fields).

When analysing the sources of information in the context of the level of respondents' gross monthly income, three interesting relationships stand out. First, as income increases (five income groups were distinguished), the importance of using online comparison websites as the primary source of information increases. In the lowest income group, only one in ten respondents (10%) did so, with the percentage among the highest earners reaching 21%. Second, the higher the respondents' income group, the importance of family or friends as the source of information decreases: for respondents from the lowest income group, the percentage was 18%. By contrast, the score was ten percentage points lower for the wealthiest respondents. Third, one in ten respondents (10%) from the lowest income group only looked for information about the insurance after concluding the contract. The percentage of such indications decreased with increasing wealth, dropping to just 4% in the highest income group.

Further conclusions are provided by grouping respondents' answers according to their place of residence. A general tendency can be noticed that as the population residential numbers increase, the importance of online sources for obtaining information regarding the insurance contract to be concluded increases for respondents. In the case of rural residents, this answer was chosen by 40% of respondents, while in the case of respondents residing in large cities, this value reached the level of 52–55%. For 11% of respondents living in settlements with up to 50,000 inhabitants, as well as for 13% of rural residents, the primary source of information was comparison websites. In contrast, in the largest cities, this percentage was 17%. However, the most exciting comparison in this aspect seems to be the one relating to the branches of insurers and intermediaries, which was the primary source of information for 35% of respondents from rural areas but for only 16% of residents of cities with over 500,000 inhabitants. Moreover, respondents from large cities most often looked for information on the websites of particular insurers (21% of respondents did so), while the second most frequently mentioned were the comparison websites. It can, therefore, be assumed that due to technical possibilities, as well as access to and the spread of technology in various spheres of life, residents of large cities are much more likely to choose remote forms of contact with insurers, including in the pre-contractual period. This may be surprising because modern technologies in the finance sector are often indicated as a factor favouring financial inclusion (e.g., due to the lack of geographical access to local insurance branches).[16] On the other hand, one should remember the digital exclusion occurring in Poland (especially in less urbanised areas), which undoubtedly contributes to consumers' lower use of digital tools, including in the insurance sector.

Furthermore, the survey examined which sources of information about the product offers consumers indicated as the most important factors in choosing an insurance product. Where the price was such a factor, 29.5% of respondents usually looked for information at insurer's branches or intermediaries, while only 15.5% of respondents used comparison websites for this purpose. Where this factor was the possibility of purchasing it via the Internet or by telephone, one in three respondents most often looked for information on comparison websites, with only 11.5% contacting insurers or insurance intermediaries. However, it should be noted that the subsample of people for whom the possibility of concluding a contract via remote channels was crucial when choosing an offer was small (approx. 100 people). Respondents for whom the most important factor when choosing an offer was the scope of insurance cover and those for whom it was not a critical statistical factor equally often chose a comparison website as the main source of information about the offer (approximately 14% of respondents each). A similar lack of differences and level of indications occurred in the case of respondents for whom the priority in choosing an offer was that it be tailored to individual needs. Respondents who did

[16] See Nayak et al. (2019), Flückiger and Duygun (2022).

not consider the scope of cover the most important factors were twice as likely not to look for information about products anywhere else (9.6% vs. 4.2% of responses).

The respondents were also asked about their experiences using comparison websites. 82.5% of them compared offers before purchasing insurance, with approximately half of them always or almost always doing so and the other half doing so only sometimes. 46% of the men surveyed always or almost always compared offers (39% did sometimes), while in the case of women, similar answers were given by 39% and 42%, respectively. Men compare insurers' offers before purchasing insurance more often than women. For 14.2% of the entire sample, this is also the main source of information about the insurance offer they are interested in purchasing. However, comparison websites are not the only instrument for selecting the best offer, and therefore, the discrepancies revealed suggest that respondents usually prefer other ways of obtaining product information. Notably, only 4.4% of the study participants have yet to compare offers. The respondents were also asked to assess the usefulness of comparison websites that compare the insurance offered by various insurers. The vast majority found these tools helpful, with one in four giving them the highest rating on the usefulness scale and only 5.4% strongly emphasising the lack of such usefulness.

Additionally, the survey inquired into how respondents assessed the ease of comparing offers from different insurers for the same insurance (one should note that the question was not about using comparison websites but about comparing products regardless of the tool used). Taking into account the answers obtained, only 3.7% of respondents found it very difficult to compare products offered by different insurers. In comparison, just over half (51.6%) considered the comparison to be very easy, choosing one of the two highest marks for the ease of comparison on a multi-level scale. However, the question remains as to what extent this is just the respondents' belief and to what extent this view accurately reflects the similarities and differences among the offers.

To deepen the analysis, the survey inquired about the respondents' approach to providing additional information about themselves at the pre-contractual stage and understanding the effects of such actions. As many as 25.9% of the survey participants believed that providing additional data about themselves (e.g., regarding their health condition when purchasing life insurance) and giving consent to the processing of personal data can only have a positive impact on the presented offer, e.g., lowering the price of the insurance. On the other hand, 10.5% of respondents believed that this could only have a negative impact and would result, for example, in a price increase. 36.7% answered that providing additional information may have both a positive and negative impact, of which 36% clarified that this impact is more often unfavourable and 64% that it is more often beneficial. It follows from the above that almost two-thirds of the respondents, each of whom had concluded an insurance contract at least once, actually did not know the outcome of providing information about themselves and giving consent to the processing of personal data. It is also worth indicating why respondents would be most willing to share their additional data. Regardless of whether this data was to be provided online or directly to an insurance company employee or insurance intermediary, the most significant incentive would be to get broader insurance cover for the same premium. Slightly over 70% of respondents would then provide such data rather willingly or very willingly. At the same time, about 60% of respondents would do so if it resulted in receiving an offer better suited to their expectations and needs, and slightly fewer if it resulted in a reduction in the price of the insurance itself, and if it gave them access to a "premium" offer. In both cases, however, respondents would be even less willing to provide information if they had to do so online.

In broadening the analytical perspective on the issue of consumers obtaining information about insurance products, the survey focused on whether consumers are familiar with the content of the insurance contract and its appendixes and whether their content is understandable. It seems essential to consider whether the consumers had information about the product they were purchasing at the last stage of the contract conclusion process before the contract was signed. The respondents were therefore asked whether they had read the content of the insurance contract (or some of its parts), the General Terms and Conditions of Insurance (GTC) and the Insurance Product Information Document (IPID)[17] and marketing materials. It was decided that these three types of documents should be separated for the purpose of the survey, because they differ in the information they contain and the difficulty of the wording employed.

According to the survey participants, 40.3% read everything, while another 19.8% read the contract without any attachments. One in four respondents did not read the documents or only read the Insurance Product Information Document and verified the correctness of their personal data. In this context, respondents may be inclined to make optimistic rather than truthful declarations; they indicate that they have read the contract even though they had only skimmed through it. If this means that 25% of all respondents indicate a lack of knowledge of the documents related to the concluded contract, then this would be particularly high and disturbing. All the more so that nowadays, more and more contracts are concluded remotely, with the process of concluding them becoming more and more simplified, which—even though in line with consumer expectations—raises the risk of a lack of awareness of the fact and the moment of concluding the contract. This issue becomes even more pronounced when considering situations in which consumers have not previously obtained information about a given product or conducted a comparative analysis of offers in order for the purchased product to fully meet their needs.

It is important to remember that simply reading documents differs from an understanding of them. Therefore, respondents were asked to indicate whether the contents of the contract, the General Terms and Conditions of Insurance and the Insurance Product Information Document, and marketing materials, were understandable to them. The answer "always or almost always" was chosen by 46.2% of respondents concerning insurance contracts, 42.3% for the General Terms and Conditions, and 33.9% for insurance product key documents and marketing

[17] About information obligations of insurers see Ostrowska (2021), Południak-Gierz and Tereszkiewicz (2023).

materials. On the other hand, the answers indicating that each of these documents was not understandable (usually or always) were chosen by 9.5%, 10.3% and 13.7% of respondents, respectively, with the rest of the respondents providing intermediate answers. Taking into account the fact that these are only declarative indications, showing the respondents' view of their understanding of the documents signed when concluding an insurance contract and the existence of a clear tendency for individuals to overestimate their financial knowledge,[18] these results are rather disturbing. They suggest that fewer than half of the respondents think that they understand the content of the documents they sign and are aware of what rights and obligations they acquire by concluding an insurance contract in order to provide the policyholder with specific protection in the event of the occurrence of specific random events. On the other hand, this is not the case for one in ten respondents; for example, one in ten respondents does not actually have information about the product purchased. These issues are of particular importance, specifically when consumers purchase cover that does not correspond to their needs or expectations. This aspect was highlighted in the answers given by respondents to the question regarding their dissatisfaction with the claims settlement process when the actual reason for the said was the previous failure to read or understand the provisions of the insurance contract (or annexes). Only 32.4% of respondents never or almost never experienced dissatisfaction with claims settlement due to a lack of reading or understanding of the contents of the documents, or the claims settlement process was always satisfactory. In turn, for 24.2% of respondents, this was a reason for dissatisfaction sometimes, always or almost always (always or almost always only for 6.6%). The indications regarding the Insurance Product Information Document and marketing materials are also noteworthy, as they show that either the respondents do not know what an IPID is or its comprehensibility is lower than that of an insurance contract or the General Terms and Conditions of Insurance attached to it. The second possibility appears more likely because while they may not identify the term "Insurance Product Information Document", the phrase "marketing materials" used as the second element in the question is certainly common knowledge. As a result of the above, the case could be that the document attached in concluding an insurance contract, which was supposed to provide a better understanding of the product, does not fulfil in fact its role. This is a very disturbing phenomenon, therefore it is advisable to deepen the analysis in this area and find an answer to the question of how to improve the content of the Insurance Product Information Document so that it can perform the task assigned to it.[19]

When analysing the process of obtaining information about insurance products by consumers and placing it in the context of concluding insurance contracts, it is important to consider the questions relating to modern technologies, i.e., their use, consumers' approach and expectations towards them and their understandability.

[18] See Lusardi and Mitchell (2014), Kicia (2015), Anderson et al. (2017), Contreras and Bendix (2021).

[19] For a survey of different national approaches to implementing the Insurance Distribution Directive see Marano and Noussia (2021).

The issues related to the digitalisation of the insurance sector mentioned in the introduction are increasingly reflected in consumers' opportunities to obtain information in the virtual space but also reveal new problems and resulting risks.

In the survey, 72% of respondents agreed with the statement that the use of modern technologies in insurance allowed the process of concluding contracts to be speeded up, 70% expressed the opinion that it enabled a simplification of this process, 63.9% indicated that technologies enabled the implementation of new solutions and contributed to expanding the offer, and 62.9% believed that they allowed the offer to be better tailored to the consumers' needs. Less than half of the survey participants (47.8%) believed that the use of modern technologies reduced the possibility of misleading or persuading the consumer to conclude a less advantageous contract, by an insurer or an intermediary (e.g., an agent). On the other hand, for 35.5% of respondents, technologies are too complicated, and it is easier to make a mistake when concluding a contract remotely. For 40.6% of respondents, technologies are problematic because they require additional activities, such as installing smartphone apps, software, and access to the Internet. 47.1% agreed that the use of modern technologies in insurance is associated with the need to provide excessively large amounts of customer data. When interpreting the results presented in this paragraph, it should be noted that the respondents were asked to express their opinion about the technology by indicating whether they agreed with the presented statements, with the following three answers to choose from: "yes or rather yes", "no or rather no", and "I do not know or I cannot say". Given the above, it can be concluded that despite the dynamic development and dissemination of modern technologies, consumers in the insurance market are not entirely comfortable using them in connection with searching for the best offer or concluding insurance contracts. This means that, along with the inevitably progressing process of digitalisation of insurance, it is necessary to ensure financial education in the field of insurance, contributing to an increase in insurance literacy and ensuring an appropriate level of protection for the most vulnerable market participants.[20]

The respondents also answered several questions about specific tools based on modern technologies, including: Internet offer comparison websites (or offer comparison apps) and chatbots/voicebots/robo-advisors. For 74.8% of respondents, the concept of an offer comparison website was known and understandable (16.7% knew this term but did not understand it, while the remaining respondents did not even know of this term). In the case of chatbots/voicebots/robo-advisors this was 49.5%, respectively, while 28.6% were not familiar with these concepts. It should be added that a glossary with all the terms accompanied the survey questionnaire so the respondents were familiar with what they meant. Therefore, if they answered "I don't know" in the case of a given term, it should be assumed that they had never heard of this tool. In turn, 56.4% of respondents had used an offer comparison website at least once, while only 13.3% had contact with chatbots/voicebots/robo-advisors. When asked to indicate on a five-point scale how willing they would be to

[20] See Fornero and Lo Prete (2023), Xiao and Porto (2019), Baranauskas and Raišienė (2021).

use such tools, in the case of an insurance comparison website the two highest values (meaning the highest level of interest) were chosen by 39.1% of respondents, while in the case of chatbots/voicebots/robo-advisors it was 27.9%. It should be added that the largest number of indications regarding the comparison tool (42%) were for the middle value on the scale. At the same time, the responses regarding chatbots/voicebots/robo-advisors gravitated more towards lower values (less interest in using them). In analysing the above results in the context of obtaining information about the offer of insurance products, one should observe that the knowledge of comparison websites among respondents is quite common. However, this tool is not as popular as one could expect. In turn, the use of chatbots/voicebots/robo-advisors as a source of information remained relatively low. This can be only partly explained by low familiarity with these concepts and may have several reasons, the most important being the imperfection of this type of tool, the high complexity of insurance products, and a possible lack of trust in this form of communication with insurance companies.

3 Conclusion

The collected data demonstrate that the importance of modern technologies in insurance has increased in recent years, manifesting itself in many aspects, including methods of searching for information about insurance products or the use of online tools for comparing offers. However, depending on demographic and social factors, motives for concluding insurance and their determinants, attitudes towards modern technologies in insurance, and insurance literacy, the use of opportunities related to digitalisation varies. The analysis of survey results on a representative sample of Polish society has shown this. However, since activities related to insurance contracts are being increasingly transferred to the virtual space at all stages of concluding and implementing these contracts, a tailored and predictable legal framework should be continually developed to ensure a satisfying level of consumer protection.

References

Anderson A, Baker F, Robinson D (2017) Precautionary savings, retirement planning and misperceptions of financial literacy. J Financ Econ 126(2):383–398. https://doi.org/10.1016/j.jfineco.2017.07.008

Baranauskas G, Raišienė AG (2021) Reflections on the customer decision-making process in the digital insurance platforms: an empirical study of the Baltic market. Appl Sci 11:8524. https://doi.org/10.3390/app11188524

Beltratti A, Corvino G (2008) Why are insurance companies different? The limits of convergence among financial institutions. Geneva Pap Risk Insur Iss Pract 33:363–388. https://doi.org/10.1057/gpp.2008.13

Cappiello A (2018) Technology and the insurance industry. Re-configuring the competitive landscape. Palgrave Macmillan

Ceylan IE (2022) The effects of artificial intelligence on the insurance sector: emergence, applications, challenges, and opportunities. In: Bozkuş Kahyaoğlu S (ed) The impact of artificial intelligence on governance, economics and finance, Vol 2. Springer

Chojan A, Lisowski J, Manikowski P (2022) Digitalisation trends in insurance and their impact on the functioning of the insurance market entities. Insurance Review 1/2022. https://doi.org/10.33995/wu2022.1.1

Contreras O, Bendix J (2021) Financial literacy in the United States, Milken Institute. https://milkeninstitute.org/sites/default/files/2021-08/Financial%20Literacy%20in%20the%20United%20States.pdf. Accessed 15 Dec 2023

Eckert C, Osterrieder K (2020) How digitalisation affects insurance companies: overview and use cases of digital technologies. Zeitschrift für die gesamte Versicherungswissenschaft 109(5):333–360. https://doi.org/10.1007/s12297-020-00475-9

Eckert C, Neunsinger C, Osterrieder K (2022) Managing customer satisfaction: digital applications for insurance companies. Geneva Papers on Risk Insurance – Issues and Practice 47. https://doi.org/10.1057/s41288-021-00257-z

Eling M, Lehmann M (2018) The Impact of Digitalization on the Insurance Value Chain and the Insurability of Risks. Geneva Pap Risk Insur Iss Pract 43 https://doi.org/10.1057/s41288-017-0073-0

Flückiger I, Duygun M (2022) New technologies and data in insurance. Geneva Pap Risk Insur Iss Pract 47:495–498. https://doi.org/10.1057/s41288-022-00274-6

Fornero E, Lo Prete A (2023) Financial education: from better personal finance to improved citizenship. J Financ Liter Wellbeing 1(1):12–27. https://doi.org/10.1017/flw.2023.7

Gupta S, Ghardallou W, Pandey DK, Sahu GP (2022) Artificial intelligence adoption in the insurance industry: evidence using the technology–organisation–environment framework. Res Int Bus Financ 63:101757. https://doi.org/10.1016/j.ribaf.2022.101757

Kicia M (2015) Między mitem eksperta a nadmierną pewnością siebie—o decyzjach finansowych w warunkach naturalnego eksperymentu. Annales Universitatis Mariae Curie-Skłodowska, sectio H – Oeconomia 49(4). https://doi.org/10.17951/h.2015.49.4.215

Locker LD (2015) Informed insurance choice?: The insurer's pre-contractual information duties in general consumer insurance. Edward Elgar Publishing

Lusardi A, Mitchell OS (2014) The economic importance of financial literacy: theory and evidence. J Econ Lit 52(1):5–44. https://doi.org/10.1257/jel.52.1.5

Małek A, Monkiewicz J, Monkiewicz M (2022) Ubezpieczenia w świecie cyfrowym: nowe uwarunkowania i wyzwania. In: Ubezpieczenia cyfrowe. Możliwości, oczekiwania, wyzwania, Monkiewicz J, Gąsiorkiewicz L., Gołąb P, Monkiewicz M (eds) Wydawnictwo Naukowe PWN

Malinowska K (2014) Consumer protection in e-insurance in European Union law. Insur Rev 4:39–56

Marano P (2019) Navigating InsurTech: the digital intermediaries of insurance products and customer protection in the EU. Maastricht J Eur Comp Law 26(2):294–315. https://doi.org/10.1177/1023263X19830345

Marano P, Noussia K (2021) Insurance distribution directive. A legal analysis. Springer. https://doi.org/10.1007/978-3-030-52738-9

Matt DT, Pedrini G, Bonfanti A, Orzes G (2023) Industrial digitalization. A systematic literature review and research agenda. Eur Manag J 41(1):47–78. https://doi.org/10.1016/j.emj.2022.01.001

Nayak B, Bhattacharyya SS, Krishnamoorthy B (2019) Democratising health insurance services; accelerating social inclusion through technology policy of health insurance firms. Bus Strategy Dev 2(3):242–252. https://doi.org/10.1002/bsd2.59

Nicoletti B (2021) Insurance 4.0. Benefits and challenges of digital transformation. Palgrave MacMillan

Ostrowska M (2021) Information duties stemming from the insurance distribution directive as an example of faulty application of the principle of proportionality. In: Marano P, Noussia K (eds) Insurance distribution directive. A legal analysis. Springer. https://doi.org/10.1007/978-3-030-52738-9_2

Pauch D, Bera A (2022) Digitization in the insurance sector—challenges in the face of the Covid-19 pandemic. Proc Comput Sci 207(30):1677–1684. https://doi.org/10.1016/j.procs.2022.09.225

Południak-Gierz K, Tereszkiewicz P (2023) Digitalization's big promise and peril: the personalization of insurance contracts and its legal consequences. In: Mathis K, Tor A (eds) Law and economics of the digital transformation. Springer

Ratowska-Dziobak E (2023) Protection of the consumer rights on the polish insurance market. Ekonomia i Prawo Econ Law 22(1):177–189. https://doi.org/10.12775/EiP.2023.010

Stricker L, Wagner J, Zeier Röschmann A (2023) The future of insurance intermediation in the age of the digital platform economy. J Risk Financ Manage 16(9):381. https://doi.org/10.3390/jrfm16090381

Volosovych S, Zelenitsa I, Kondratenko D, Szymla W, Mamchur R (2021) Transformation of insurance technologies in the context of a pandemic. Insur Mark Comp 12(1):1–13. https://doi.org/10.21511/ins.12(1).2021.01

Werth O, Schwarzbach C, Rodríguez Cardona D, Breitner MH, Graf von der Schulenburg J-M (2020) Influencing factors for the digital transformation in the financial services sector. Zeitschrift für die gesamte Versicherungswissenschaft 109(2–4):155–179. https://doi.org/10.1007/s12297-020-00486-6

Xiao JJ, Porto N (2019) Financial education and insurance advice seeking. Geneva Papers on Risk Insurance – Issues and Practice 44 https://doi.org/10.1057/s41288-018-0108-1

Ewa Cichowicz is an assistant professor at SGH—Warsaw School of Economics, PhD in Economics, triple master's degree in Economics (Finance and Banking, Informatics and Econometrics, International Relations). A participant with papers or panellist/moderator at almost eighty academic conferences (also international). A participant on seventeen research teams (in four of them as a leader) and head of fourteen individual research studies. The author and co-author of several dozen publications on economic and financial topics, including banking and new technology in banking, financial exclusion, financial education, efficiency in the public sector, CSR, social policy, and social insurance.

Piotr Tereszkiewicz Ph.D. (Jagiellonian University in Kraków), M.Jur (Oxford) is a professor at the Jagiellonian's University Private Law Department, and a senior affiliated researcher at the University of Leuven (KU Leuven). His research interests include private law, law and economics, insurance law and financial services in a comparative and international perspective. He was Deputy Chair of the Scientific Advisory Committee at the Financial Ombudsman in Poland (2019–2021).

Supervisory Authorities as Value Creators in the Age of Digitalisation: Towards an Ecosystem View of the Insurance Industry

Antti Talonen

1 Introduction

The insurance industry is a context defined by the dynamic relationship between various actors and individuals at different levels of society. These include regulators, supervisors, insurance companies, as well as end-users as individual policyholder companies and households. Regulators and supervisory bodies can be seen as representations of public values, ideas, and norms (often politically negotiated) on how the insurance industry, services and related contracts should be defined, organised, and developed.[1] Within these frames, insurance companies provide services to end users in collaboration with an extensive network of other actors that together form the insurance value chain.[2] Moreover, consumers' attitudes, skills, and background significantly influence the way insurance services and related contracts are perceived and adopted.[3] In sum, the insurance industry can be characterised by the dynamic interaction of actors that take decisions independently but are clearly dependent on and impacted by each other's decisions.

Existing research is limited in its description of the above-mentioned nature of the insurance industry. Scholars have extensively studied regulation and supervision,[4]

[1] See Marano (2017), pp. 5–29; Veljanovski (2010); Tereszkiewicz (2023), pp. 1–21.

[2] E.g. Eling and Lehmann (2018), pp. 359–396; Eling et al. (2021), pp. 1–37; Van Rossum et al. (2002), pp. 89–101.

[3] E.g. Talonen et al. (2021a).

[4] E.g. Tereszkiewicz (2019), pp. 127–146; Marano and Noussia (2021).

A. Talonen (✉)
UEF Business School, University of Eastern Finland, Kuopio, Finland
e-mail: antti.talonen@uef.fi

C. Poncibò, P. Tereszkiewicz (eds.), *European Insurance Law within the Digital Age*, AIDA Europe Research Series on Insurance Law and Regulation 14,
https://doi.org/10.1007/978-3-031-96496-1_10

insurance companies,[5] as well as consumers.[6] Further, the government-company[7] and insurer-consumer relationship[8] as well as the insurance value chain[9] have been topics of interest. What is largely lacking from the literature, however, is a systematic evaluation of the interaction between actors at different levels. Furthermore, the way actors' roles are perceived can be incomplete. For example, supervisory bodies are often seen as 'police' monitoring insurance companies and ensuring that they do not act to the detriment of their policyholders. This mindset implicitly presumes that insurance companies and supervisors might have differing interests. Nonetheless, what remains unclear in this thinking is that the common end goal of the industry—eventually—is to create value for the end-users of services and smoothen the contracting between consumers and insurance companies.

It is important to consider that consumers would probably decrease the level and number of policies if supervisory bodies did not exist. This is, at least partly, due to individual consumers' relatively low level of financial literacy regarding rather complicated insurance products and their logic.[10] Thus, without supervisory bodies creating an additional layer of trust, consumers would perceive the transaction costs of making contracts with insurance undertakings to be much higher.[11,12] In more practical terms, consumers would be less certain of the benefits and value for money offered by insurance policies. As previously mentioned, insurance services and products are rather complicated for consumers to understand, and thus the existence of supervisory bodies creates an additional layer of trust between the consumers and companies and thus lowers transaction costs.[13] Here, trust-related transaction costs decrease the policyholder's level of perceived value gained from insurance. Consequently, supervisory bodies (as creators of additional trust) indeed play an important role in value-creation processes, which benefits insurance companies as well. Viewed in this manner, supervisory bodies should be considered part of the value-creating ecosystem of the insurance industry. Furthermore, this emphasises a mindset where the interests of supervisory bodies and companies are seen as aligned rather than conflicting. This also echoes the definition of a value-creating ecosystem proposed by Kapoor[14] as "encompassing a set of actors that contribute to the focal offer's user value proposition". However, earlier research has not systematically examined the connection between supervisory actions and consumer perceptions.

[5] E.g. Johne and Davies (2000), pp. 6–14; Myers and Read (2001), pp. 545–580; Talonen et al. (2022b).

[6] E.g. Talonen et al. (2022a), pp. 1–13.

[7] E.g. Baker and Shortland (2022).

[8] E.g. Maas and Rüfenacht (2018), pp. 1010–1014.

[9] E.g. Eling and Lehmann (2018), pp. 359–396.

[10] e.g. Pitthan and De Witte (2021).

[11] See Schmeiser and Wagner (2016), pp. 277–294.

[12] Mukherjee and Nath (2003).

[13] Hägg (1998).

[14] Kapoor (2018), p. 2.

From these premises, this chapter aims to describe the thematic connection between supervisory actions and multidimensional consumer perceptions in the context of insurance. To achieve this, the chapter juxtaposes consumer perceptions from earlier research[15] with examples of supervisory actions identified through an internet search. The supervisor-consumer relationship can be seen as an illustrative case for examining wider interaction relationships where the actors concerned do not necessarily interact directly with each other. As a novel contribution, the study illustrates the activities and actions of financial supervisory authorities as part of a value-creating insurance ecosystem in the age of digitalization. Accordingly, the chapter creates a new intellectual framework for considering and developing ecosystem thinking in the context of the insurance industry. In addition, the chapter provides interesting avenues for future research in contexts that combine characteristics of the public and private sector.

The remaining part of the chapter is structured as follows. It begins by offering definitions and some key literature related to ecosystems and value as well as the way these two concepts align. From there, the chapter continues by describing the interface and interaction between supervisory actions and consumer perceptions from the perspective of multidimensional value. The study ends with a summary and concluding remarks offering avenues for future research and implications for managers and policy.

2 European System of Insurance Supervision and Its Actors

This chapter is limited to an examination of the European system of insurance supervision, which comprises the European Insurance and Occupational Pensions Authority (EIOPA), at the European level, and national supervisory bodies. EIOPA was founded in 2011, and its tasks are defined as (a) helping to maintain the stability of the financial system, (b) ensuring the transparency of markets and financial products, and (c) helping to protect insurance policyholders, pension scheme members and beneficiaries.[16] In addition to these functions, EIOPA provides advice to the European Commission, the European Parliament and the Council of the European Union in developing the insurance industry. Furthermore, EIOPA plays a role in identifying, monitoring, and addressing potentially developing (insurance-service-related) protection gaps among individual consumers. Accordingly, the tasks and role of EIOPA clearly emphasise the benefits to insurance consumers, which are naturally connected with consumers' perception of the value of insurance services.

The second level of the supervision system consists of national supervisory bodies. In Finland, for example, the tasks of the insurance supervisor (Finanssivalvonnan

---

[15] Talonen et al. (2021a).

[16] https://european-union.europa.eu/institutions-law-budget/institutions-and-bodies/search-all-eu-institutions-and-bodies/eiopa_en.

vakuutusvalvonta) are to supervise (a) companies' solvency and financial position, (b) internal governance and risk management procedures, (c) underwriting risks, and (d) investment risks.[17] In the European Union, there has been a tendency to harmonise several areas of financial supervision and regulation. Consequently, national supervisory bodies collaborate closely with EIOPA and other national supervisory bodies.

This chapter concentrates on examining the supervisory activities of EIOPA at the European level. On one hand, this focus is justified since many supervisory activities are pan-European and based on the work of EIOPA (such as the principles for ethical AI in insurance). Furthermore, national supervisory bodies may exhibit certain differences in the nature of their operations, which might be challenging to consider in this chapter. On the other hand, the nature of interaction with industry stakeholders (companies, consumers, etc.) might differ according to whether the supervisory body operates at the national or European level. This could create challenges for the validity of the scientific analysis in this chapter.

3 Value Creation in Ecosystems

Value can be seen as a definitive concept in whether a contract is made between an insurance company and a consumer. In other words, consumers purchase a service if they perceive they will gain value from it. Gaining value refers to a situation where a customer perceives more benefits than disadvantages from a transaction or service experience. Value is a multidimensional construct and can exist in various forms. This chapter builds on the framework created by Rintamäki, Kuusela & Mitronen,[18] who identify economic, functional, emotional, and symbolic (social and identity-related) value dimensions. Moving on to value creation, scholars have recently begun to emphasise an ecosystem view where value is created not only in company-customer interactions, but also in interactions involving various other actors and social norms and values.[19]

The term ecosystem has become a metaphor for describing the logic of business environments and industries as "dynamic, interactive, and self-sustaining ecological systems".[20] This metaphor has been borrowed from the natural sciences, where different parts of nature influence each other. In the context of business and societies, the ecosystem view differs from that of networks in terms of actors' level of independence. While networks are characterised by a central leading organisation, ecosystems grow and develop in dynamic interaction between different participants.[21]

---

[17] https://www.finanssivalvonta.fi/en/insurance/.

[18] Rintamäki et al. (2007).

[19] Vargo and Lusch (2016), pp. 5–23; Vargo et al. (2017), pp. 117–124.

[20] Osborne et al. (2022), p. 637.

[21] E.g. Kinder et al. (2022), pp. 8–33.

In the ecosystem view, the notion of value creation processes cannot be limited to understanding the actions and activities of an individual company or business; instead, it must also include the way key actors in the industry operate and the impact of societal values, rules and culture on these actors.[22]

When investigating these complex interaction relationships, some scholars have even claimed that organisations cannot solely be considered part of one specific industry; rather, they are present in much wider ecosystems comprising various industries. While this notion is partly true, the logic of an ecosystem also works well in the context of a specific industry when the aim is to describe the nature of the interaction between different industry actors.

In the context of the insurance industry, Pütz et al.[23] adopt an ecosystem approach to the study of automated vehicles and insurance. Their article's focus is more on the organisational meso-level, exploring traditional insurance companies and potential newcomers in the industry as auto manufacturers. In addition, their article describes the insurance industry as a context where cooperation between specific actors is led by a 'central company'. In this regard, the methodology of Pütz et al. is closer to a network approach than one of ecosystems, which are defined through direct or indirect interaction between independent actors. While the network approach is useful for analysing the insurance value chain and its development, it makes it challenging to illustrate the interaction and role of other actors and/or societal dimensions. Such roles and dimensions can be, for example, societal values and culture, and regulations and supervisory bodies that impact the ways insurance services and the industry should be defined, organised, and developed.[24] In addition, the development of insurance services is impacted by consumers and their attitudes, skills and capabilities to use insurance services. In sum, the insurance industry cannot be seen as a centrally guided or led context. Rather, its nature and development are defined through the interaction of several different independent actors whose decisions are nevertheless interdependent. Thus, the insurance industry as a context can be described as an ecosystem. This chapter approaches ecosystem thinking in insurance by illustrating the thematic connection between supervisory activities and consumer perceptions.

Conceptually, the chapter is informed and inspired by the ecosystem framework introduced by Osborne, Powell, Cui & Strokosch.[25] In their approach, ecosystem thinking also considers public sector organisations and politics and thus provides a good basis for analysing the insurance industry. Osborne et al.'s framework contains various levels. At the macro level, ecosystems are influenced by public policies, which are in several ways impacted by and defined by public values and culture. As the insurance industry is one of the most regulated industries, the macro-level is a defining part of it. In turn, the meso level refers to the organisations in the industry,

---

[22] Vargo and Lusch (2016), pp. 5–23; Vargo et al. (2017), pp. 117–124.

[23] Pütz et al. (2019).

[24] Marano (2017), pp. 5–29; Veljanovski (2010); Tereszkiewicz (2023), pp. 1–21.

[25] Osborne et al. (2022), pp. 634–645.

as public sector supervisory bodies (partly representations of public values and policies) or private insurance companies. Finally, the micro level describes the behaviour of individuals, as consumers or people in organisations. This level is further complemented by a sub-micro level that describes individual beliefs and values.

4 Juxtaposing Consumer Perceptions and Supervisory Actions

The next section elaborates and discusses supervisory actions and consumers' perceived sacrifices along different dimensions of value—economic, functional, emotional, and symbolic. Consumer perceptions are based on an article by Talonen et al. (2021a),[26] which examines and frames insurance consumers' perceived value sacrifices multidimensionally and comprehensively. That article considered new behavioural-tracking-based insurance applications and consumers' negative perceptions related to them. The central idea of these applications is to provide policyholders with cheaper premiums when they behave in the desired manner. In turn, the examples of practical supervisory actions analysed here were identified through an internet search. This identification process was performed by studying public material on the Internet regarding EIOPA's operations and reflecting on them with the above-mentioned framework of consumer perception. This analysis process allows for a description of the multidimensional nature of the thematic connection between supervisory actions and consumer perceptions.

4.1 Economic Value

Economic value refers to monetary benefits and rewards gained by the consumer. As Chandon et al.[27] describe, these benefits can come in the form of, for example, discounts or gaining more for the same price. Behaviour-tracking-based applications in insurance have been developed around these economic rewards: the healthier the living habits that policyholders exhibit, the lower the insurance premiums they must pay. However, consumers may not always perceive these applications in this way; rather, they might attach economic sacrifices to them. According to Talonen et al.,[28] perceived sacrifices related to economic value can be divided into risks related to customer-company interaction and challenging processes for obtaining rewards (see Table 1). This chapter now proceeds to elaborate and reflect on these issues in detail in relation to supervisory and legal actions.

[26] Talonen et al. (2021a).

[27] Chandon et al. (2000), pp. 65–81.

[28] Talonen et al. (2021a).

Table 1 The economic dimension of value (reproduced from Talonen et al. 2021a[a])

Economic value		
Concepts (2nd order)	Themes (1st order)	Illustrative quotes
The risks related to customer–company interaction	The insurance company's economic aims cannot be trusted	"Insurance companies have only one goal: to increase their own profits. They are not making objective decisions but using all means possible to increase the level of premiums".
	Exercising control is expensive	"If you don't accept the insurance company's decision, often the only way to change it is via the courts."
The challenging process for obtaining rewards	'Little things' reduce the bonus	"When tracking is used, minor factors may decrease the amount of the bonus."
	Monetary rewards are not within reach for normal people	"Premiums can be lowered only by the behaviour of a professional athlete."

[a] Talonen et al. (2021a)

First, consumers may categorically perceive that insurance companies only take their own economic interests into account. While this perception does not relate to behavioural tracking applications alone,[29,30,31] it is indeed present in this context as well. Accordingly, behavioural tracking technology and the promised opportunity to gain lower insurance premiums are perceived by consumers solely as a new tool to increase overall premiums and thus earnings for the benefit of the insurance company. Moreover, consumers may perceive that it is challenging to gain the potential rewards and lower premiums since such rewards are either reduced by minor factors or are achievable only via unrealistically 'good' behaviour.[32] The question here is how the insurance industry as an ecosystem can strengthen consumer trust in the aims of insurance companies when establishing new behavioural tracking applications.[33] Closely related to this, the European Insurance and Occupational Pensions Authority (EIOPA) recently began to investigate how the value for money of unit-linked products could be guaranteed.[34,35] This initiative is one example of how a supervisory body may contribute to ensuring that economic value is delivered to consumers. Similarly, such an initiative could be established in relation to new digital insurance applications as well. In addition, to influence consumer perceptions, it

[29] Bieck and Tjioe (2015).

[30] Armstrong et al. (2012), p. 381.

[31] Pukała et al. (2017), pp. 28–40.

[32] See Guillen et al. (2021), pp. 569–589.

[33] See Iglesias et al. (2020), pp. 151–166.

[34] https://www.eiopa.europa.eu/media/news/eiopa-issues-its-methodology-assessing-value-money-unit-linked-market_en.

[35] https://www.eiopa.europa.eu/content/eiopa-sets-out-framework-delivering-better-value-money-consumer-centric-way_en.

is important to communicate the results of such activity to consumers successfully. Moreover, EIOPA has paid attention to poor consumer advice provided by the insurance company representatives.[36] Poor advice can relate to commissions-based selling creating conflicts of interest between the sales staff and customers. Consequential mis-selling of insurance products can lead to decreased economic value from the customer's perspective.

Second, some consumers may perceive the difficulty in disagreeing with insurance companies' decisions. In fact, attempts to change specific decisions can be perceived as expensive processes. This sense of powerlessness[37,38] is due to consumers' uneven position and relative lack of agency compared to the legal departments of insurance companies. Some insurance companies have considered it important to increase customer trust in this regard and have voluntarily established redress possibilities for their customers. For example, the Swedish insurance company Folksam has a specific officer, 'a customer ombudsman', whose task and responsibility is to help customers redress potentially erroneous decisions made by the company and offer an impartial view on those decisions.[39] Moving on to the context of digitalization, the European Commission's high-level expert group on artificial intelligence[40,41] has emphasised the importance of easy and convenient redress procedures. In this context (company) decisions are made by digital tools such as artificial intelligence systems. Here, it is seen as important to provide consumers with convenient opportunities to change the decisions made by digital systems. In all, creating ethical principles for digitalization or concrete recommendations to develop redress processes (as with the customer ombudsman) are examples of how supervisory bodies and legislators can participate in the boosting of customer trust.

4.2 Functional Value

Functional value refers to the utilitarian benefits that consumers perceive they gain by using a product or service.[42] In concrete terms, this can mean that a person finds a specific product or service more convenient than others to use, or that using it helps that person accomplish tasks more easily.[43,44] In the context of interactive

[36] https://www.eiopa.europa.eu/system/files/2023-01/eiopa-consumer-trends-report-2022.pdf.

[37] See Bunker and Ball (2009), pp. 268–283.

[38] See Cao et al. (2022), pp. 129–142.

[39] See, e.g., Talonen et al. (2021b).

[40] https://digital-strategy.ec.europa.eu/en/policies/expert-group-ai.

[41] https://digital-strategy.ec.europa.eu/en/library/ethics-guidelines-trustworthy-ai.

[42] E.g. Rintamäki et al. (2007).

[43] E.g. Cheung and Vogel (2013), pp. 160–175.

[44] E.g. Bhattacherjee and Sanford (2006), pp. 805–825.

insurance applications, this can be understood as, for example, enabling health tracking in a convenient way or offering means to gain inclusive insurance cover. However, consumers may not always perceive these utilitarian benefits but may focus more on the sacrifices related to interactive insurance applications.[45] As shown by Talonen et al.,[46] these sacrifices can come in the form of the perceived complexity of the logic of the application or its lack of usefulness.

First, the complexity of the insurance application may relate to one's health as a challenging target to control or to complicated policy terms.[47,48] In part, these concerns have existed for a long time (specifically, complicated contract terms) but they are of ever greater significance in an age when behavioural tracking is gaining traction (how to control and influence one's health). From the supervisory perspective, EIOPA has stressed the importance of clear and understandable contract terms[49] as well as customer-centric disclosures that fit the digital age.[50] Opaque and complicated terms can even lead to so-called expectation gaps, where individual policyholders may think they are covered in a certain situation although they are not.[51,52,53] Thus, supervisory actions that aim to 'smooth' company-policyholder interaction in terms of contract terms may potentially play a significant value-creation role (Table 2).

Second, consumers may perceive that the interactive insurance application is not useful to them. For example, some may consider that this new way of insuring fails to increase their opportunities for acquiring insurance cover. This perception can be deemed to be in direct conflict with the central idea of interactive insurance applications: providing individuals with greater opportunities to demonstrate via their own 'good' behaviour that they are an 'insurable risk'.[54,55,56] In line with this, EIOPA and its consultative expert group on digital ethics have stressed the importance of ensuring the inclusiveness of artificial intelligence-based insurance applications. Here, a specific focus is assigned to the explainability and transparency of AI systems in

---

[45] See Gebert-Persson et al. (2019), pp. 579–594.

[46] Talonen et al. (2021a).

[47] Peverelli and de Feniks (2010).

[48] See Weedige et al. (2019).

[49] https://www.eiopa.europa.eu/document-library/consultation/consultation-supervisory-statement-exclusions-insurance-products_en.

[50] https://www.eiopa.europa.eu/eiopa-publishes-advice-retail-investor-protection-2022-04-29_en.

[51] For expectation gaps, see also: https://www.eiopa.europa.eu/system/files/2022-09/supervisory_statement_on_exclusions_related_to_risks_arising_from_systemic_events.pdf.

[52] https://www.eiopa.europa.eu/publications/addressing-protection-gap-challenges-and-opportunities-reinsurers_en.

[53] https://www.eiopa.europa.eu/system/files/2023-01/eiopa-consumer-trends-report-2022.pdf.

[54] See Eling and Kraft (2020), pp. 77–109.

[55] See Kraft and Drerup (2023), pp. 277–293.

[56] See Guillen et al. (2021), pp. 569–589.

Table 2 The function-related dimension of value (reproduced from Talonen et al. 2021a[a])

Functional value		
Concepts (2nd order)	Themes (1st order)	Illustrative quotes
The excessively complex logic behind smart life insurance	Health is a challenging target of control and influence	"Driving behaviour is dependent on the individual. Getting old or sick cannot be influenced. … The 'genetically handicapped' are the outcasts of tomorrow, not appreciated in society even if they eat carrots and run marathons."
	The insurance terms are complicated	"From an individual's point of view, the terms of the insurance contract easily become too complicated."
The application not being perceived as useful	Interactive health/life insurance doesn't increase access to insurance services	"As far as I understand it, my age prevents me from purchasing life insurance. At least the previous [insurance plans] have stopped."
	Interactive health/life insurance doesn't make it more convenient to track one's health	"Today's technology and medical centres provide good possibilities [for tracking one's health]."

[a] Talonen et al. (2021a)

guaranteeing fair treatment for every policyholder.[57] This initiative represents an apt example of how supervisory actions can be directed towards fostering the inclusivity of the digital insurance market and supporting consumers' positive perceptions of it. Furthermore, one of EIOPA's tasks is to monitor existing or developing protection gaps. Accordingly, if protection gaps evolve, it is important to address them in an adequate way to ensure that individual consumers will not be unfairly excluded from insurance cover. Ultimately, full participation in society is predicated on access to several insurance products, which can thus be viewed as basic needs that should be ensured for every citizen.

In addition to exclusivity, consumers may understand interactive insurance applications solely as one more tool to track their health. If this occurs, the insurance application competes directly with other means and providers of health tracking. Here, the key question is how to communicate and make visible the importance of the protection dimension (insurance) as well. EIOPA, as the industry's supervisory body, can be seen to play a natural role in this context, since one of its tasks is to monitor protection gaps and contribute to addressing them. Further, one component of that task is to make consumers aware of those gaps that relate to them. Fostering the financial literacy skills of individual policyholders and consumers is thus critical in helping them understand the importance of including the protection (insurance dimension) dimension in health tracking—to avoid individual-level protection gaps.

[57] https://www.eiopa.europa.eu/media/speeches-presentations/contribution/ai-governance-ensuring-trusted-and-financially-inclusive_en.

4.3 Emotional Value

Emotional value refers to the capability of a product or service to "arouse feelings or affective states".[58] These emotions can be linked to, for example, aesthetics and pleasure,[59] entertainment and playfulness,[60] and/or exploration.[61] The idea of interactive insurance and behavioural tracking can generate *negative* feelings and emotions among consumers as well, which can further hinder the adoption of the related applications. As identified by Talonen et al. (2021a),[62] concrete example themes include lack of trust in insurance companies in affective terms and unpleasant emotions related to behavioural tracking and the policyholder's own role in this process.

As illustrated in Table 3, the first two themes relate to perceptions that insurers and their digital applications possess the supreme right to draw their own conclusions on premiums and claims without even taking changing life situations into account.[63,64] Juxtaposing these emotional sacrifices with exemplary supervisory actions, EIOPA's expert group on digital ethics (also discussed above) has explicitly emphasised the importance of the explainability of digital (and AI) tools in making insurance decisions.[65] More specifically, this group's report states that it is important to "reduce potential discriminatory biases from the trained models" (p. 58). The required explainability combined with adequate and convenient redress procedures[66] for consumers can potentially create an additional layer of positive emotions towards insurance companies and their established digital applications.

Losing a sense of control can also relate to consumers' perception of how their personal data is governed. This can concern the insurer's potential opportunity to resell the data, loss of control of the data while changing insurance providers, or the possibility that the insurance company's staff misuses their position in governing the data.[67,68] EIOPA's expert group on digital ethics states that there are clear ethical questions if an insurance company commodities and re-sells the personal data gathered from its policyholders. This development of the safe governance of sensitive data is particularly important in the context of health-data-related applications and can be seen as a potentially value-creating mechanism for consumers. In addition, a possible supporting initiative could be to foster policyholders' ownership of their

---

[58] Sheth et al. (1991), p. 161.

[59] Jung Choo et al. (2012), pp. 81–101.

[60] Mathwick et al. (2001), pp. 39–56

[61] Rintamäki et al. (2006), pp. 6–24.

[62] Talonen et al. (2021a).

[63] See Gidaris (2019), pp. 132–138.

[64] See Ledger and McCaffrey (2014).

[65] https://www.eiopa.europa.eu/sites/default/files/publications/reports/eiopa-ai-governance-principles-june-2021.pdf.

[66] See https://digital-strategy.ec.europa.eu/en/library/ethics-guidelines-trustworthy-ai.

[67] See Langley (2014).

[68] See Crawford et al. (2015), pp. 479–496.

personal data, which could enable them to withdraw that data from their former insurance provider and transfer it to the new one. Furthermore, as the above-mentioned group's report states, it is important for companies to "identify all the roles and responsibilities of the staff involved in the design and implementation of the AI models as well as their training needs" (p. 59). This requirement is obviously directed towards minimising the misuse of data among staff members. On a more general level, EIOPA has put forward (in cooperation with other European supervisory authorities) suggestions on how to improve legislation related to ICT risk management requirements[69] as well as coherent cyber resilience testing framework.[70] Among monitoring cyber risks among European insurance undertakings, the above-mentioned joint declarations are solid examples of how to support digital resilience within the insurance industry. These initiatives are furthered by EIOPA's supervisory role regarding the EU's Digital Operational Resilience Act (DORA) as well the Proposal for Regulation on a Framework for Financial Data Access (FiDA).[71,72,73]

Moving towards policyholders' own role in the tracking process, the application's logic might be perceived as laborious, complicated, and/or onerous.[74,75] Clearly, this can potentially cause negative and even stressful emotions for policyholders. One possible supervisory action linked to this is to support consumers in developing their financial literacy skills. By becoming ever more aware of the importance of insurance as a risk management tool, consumers may experience greater willingness or even excitement to adopt new digital insurance applications.

4.4 *Symbolic Value*

The symbolic dimension moves the discussion towards the social side of consumption. Accordingly, consumers' interaction with a product or service aids in the development and maintenance of their identity and supports its expression to others.[76] While new technological and digital tools as well as fitness devices and health tracking can help individuals in building and maintaining their self-identity,[77,78] they

---

[69] See https://www.eiopa.europa.eu/system/files/2019-04/jc_2019_26_joint_esas_advice_on_ict_legislative_improvements.pdf.

[70] See https://www.eiopa.europa.eu/system/files/2019-04/jc_2019_25_joint_esas_advice_on_a_coherent_cyber_resilience_testing_framework.pdf.

[71] https://www.eiopa.europa.eu/publications/digital-operational-resilience-addressing-risks-digital-transformation_en.

[72] https://www.digital-operational-resilience-act.com.

[73] https://www.ipe.com/eiopa-lays-down-strategic-priorities-for-2024/10069348.article.

[74] E.g. Similä et al. (2018), pp. 499–505.

[75] E.g. Lupton (2016), pp. 101–122.

[76] Rintamäki et al. (2006), pp. 6–24.

[77] Carter and Grover (2015), pp. 931–958.

[78] Giddens et al. (2016).

Table 3 Emotional value (reproduced from Talonen et al. 2021a[a])

Emotional value		
Concepts (2nd order)	Themes (1st order)	Illustrative quotes
Lack of trust in insurance companies	Insurance companies can draw their own conclusions related to premiums and claims	"The insurance company has a supreme right and ability to reach their own conclusions."
	Insurance companies don't care about changes in a customer's life situation	"When I purchased the insurance, my activity may have been at a good level. However, there are many [times of] challenges and hardship in life when taking care of one's health may not get that much attention. This may, in turn, lead to a situation the insurance company interprets as me having not fulfilled the insurance contract in terms of my activity."
	An insurance company may sell the data to outsiders	"The data will be sold on to third parties at a later stage."
	Control of the data is lost upon switching insurer	"If I change insurance providers often, my data will be in everybody's hands. Not good!"
	An insurance company's staff could abuse their position	"Courts are handling cases in which civil servants have intruded to look at information related to other people. When this reaches court, the damage and harm has already occurred and rumours about people have been set in motion. Therefore, it doesn't help to go to court anymore."
Unpleasant emotions related to tracking	Tracking is perceived as laborious and complicated	"[Tracking] feels so laborious and complicated."
	Tracking is perceived as a responsibility	"What does this application obligate me to do? How and how often will health be checked?"

[a] Talonen et al. (2021a)

might also exert the opposite effect. As Talonen et al. (2021a)[79] describe, there are several examples of how interactive insurance applications may hinder individuals in this regard, thus hampering the adoption of such applications (Table 4).

When considering supervisory actions in this regard, the approach comes rather close to the one discussed in conjunction with consumers' perception of insurance companies drawing their own conclusions about individuals' behaviour. Accordingly, the supervisory body should monitor and assess that the level of explainability of

[79] Talonen et al. (2021a).

Table 4 Symbolic value (Retrieved from Talonen et al. 2021a[a])

Symbolic value		
Concepts (2nd order)	Themes (1st order)	Illustrative quotes
The app not assisting in development of self-identity	Use of the application restricts freedom of choice	"Smoking cigarettes is, of course, unhealthy, but one needs to have the freedom to make stupid decisions."
	Use of the application detracts from self-acceptance	"As a young woman, you already face so much pressure related to your living habits and looks. It feels disturbing that you would be penalised for gaining a few extra kilos or not exercising enough. There are many individuals who can't do anything about their health."
The app not aiding in maintaining continuity of self-identity	The company's interpretation of the behaviour conflicts with the sense of identity built by using the application	"Whatever information is gained can be interpreted in a way that serves the insurance company's own purposes. [Let me] exaggerate: one who follows healthy living habits can be made to look like an orthorexic, who can be further categorised as a mental-health patient."
	Use of the application stands in contradiction to the self-identity developed	"My problem with the application is the definition of healthy living habits. If the insurance company agrees with me, I would be interested in using the application. If they define healthy living habits according to the official view, we don't agree. For example, [what makes a] healthy diet is one thing on which our views probably do not match. So I would get to pay more for my insurance even though I'm living a healthy life and don't get sick. Merely because my view of a healthy life differs from the official one. This little fact destroys the incentives on my part."
	Encouragement may support or be detrimental to the self-identity developed, depending on one's life situation	"When I purchased the insurance, my activity may have been at a good level. However, there are many [times of] challenges and hardship in life when taking care of one's health may not get that much attention. This may, in turn, lead to a situation the insurance company interprets as me having not fulfilled the insurance contract in terms of my activity."

[a] Talonen et al. (2021a)

digital (AI) tools is adequate and that redress procedures exist.[80] This maximises the possibility that policyholders will perceive the decisions as justified, understandable, and acceptable. Otherwise, conclusions may be interpreted wrongly by policyholders as penalising them without reason or as constituting a threat to their identity.

[80] https://www.eiopa.europa.eu/sites/default/files/publications/reports/eiopa-ai-governance-principles-june-2021.pdf.

However, when individual policyholders receive a well-justified decision, they may well consider it aligned with their identity.

5 Summary and Conclusions

This chapter illustrates the thematic connection between supervisory actions and consumer perceptions. As a concrete case, the chapter juxtaposed examples of practical supervisory activities with consumers' perceived value sacrifices. The relationship between supervisory bodies and consumers can be seen as an illustrative case for examining wide interaction relationships where the actors concerned do not necessarily interact directly with each other. As the chapter demonstrates, the role and activities of the supervisory authority (EIOPA) connect thematically with consumers' value-creation processes. Thus, utilising ecosystem thinking offers a fruitful intellectual approach for better understanding the dynamics, nature and development of the insurance industry. As a novel contribution, the study takes into account the activities and actions of financial supervisory bodies in creating value and potentially boosting consumers' willingness to sign insurance contracts in the age of digitalization (the adoption of new technology and digital applications in insurance) (Table 5).

While the chapter illustrates the thematic connection between supervisory actions and consumer perceptions, it cannot model or describe the clear interaction process between the parties involved. From the perspective of future studies, one interesting question is how consumers perceive the value-creating role of supervisory bodies in practice. Are the actions of these bodies visible to consumers or do they merely become apparent indirectly via companies' activities? On the other hand, what would be the effect on consumer perceptions if supervisory bodies adopted a more public role, interacting with policyholders directly? Furthermore, do adequate means exist for such direct interaction, or, alternatively, what kind of tools should be developed? In addition, it would be beneficial to extend the analysis to other forms and types of insurance and to cover the actions and nature of national-level supervisory bodies.

Linking these ideas to a more theoretical discussion, scholars should strive to understand and elaborate the nature of the interaction between the different levels and actors in the insurance ecosystem. Specific interest could be directed to understanding how macro-level values and public policy as well as meso-level supervisory activities influence consumer perceptions at the micro-level. In sum, the insurance industry offers a truly interesting context in which to study ecosystems at the *intersection of public and private sectors and organisations*. As a highly regulated industry, it provides fruitful lessons on the way public values and policy (regulation) influence the private sector and private consumers. As earlier research on ecosystems is more focused on either private markets or the public sector, scholars should be encouraged to consider ecosystems characterised by a combination of, and dynamic relationship between, these sectors (such as the insurance industry).

Table 5 Summarising the thematic areas of supervisory actions in a value-creating insurance ecosystem

Dimension of value	Themes (2nd order)	Concepts (1st order)	Illustrative supervisory actions as part of a value-creating ecosystem
Economic value	The risks related to customer-company interaction	The insurance company's economic aims cannot be trusted	Assessing, monitoring and communicating value for money in economic terms Assessing and monitoring the quality of customer advice provided by the undertakings Assessing and monitoring trigger to conflict of interests between the undertakings and the customers (as commissions-based selling)
		Exercising control is expensive	Supporting creation, development and communication of easy and convenient redress procedures
	A challenging process for obtaining rewards	'Little things' reduce the bonus	Assessing, monitoring and communicating value for money in economic terms
		True monetary rewards are not within reach for normal people	Assessing, monitoring and communicating value for money in economic terms
Functional value	Excessively complex logic behind smart life insurance	Health is a challenging target of control and influence	'Smoothing' company-policyholder interaction by stressing and fostering the development of clear contracts and related terms (such as how the company interprets controlling health)
		The insurance terms are complicated	
	The application not being perceived as useful	Interactive health/life insurance does not increase access to insurance services	Ensuring that digital (AI) tools and algorithms do not treat the policyholder unfairly Monitoring and addressing potentially developing protection gaps caused by new digital tools and applications
		Interactive health/life insurance does not increase the convenience of tracking one's health	Monitoring and fostering individual consumers' financial literacy regarding their personal protection gaps, and the importance of integrating the insurance dimension into health tracking

(continued)

Table 5 (continued)

Dimension of value	Themes (2nd order)	Concepts (1st order)	Illustrative supervisory actions as part of a value-creating ecosystem
Emotional value	Lack of trust in insurance companies	Insurance companies can draw their own conclusions related to premiums and claims	Monitor and assess the explainability (and potential biases) of the companies' algorithms. Supporting creation, development and communication of easy and convenient redress procedures
		Insurance companies do not care about changes in a customer's life situation	
		An insurance company may sell the data to outsiders	Addressing and monitoring good data governance mechanisms and denying companies the opportunity to resell policyholders' personal data Supporting consumers' ability to own their personal data and delete this data from the former insurance provider when switching insurer
		Control of the data is lost upon switching insurer	
		An insurance company's staff could abuse their position	Monitoring and requiring identification of the staff dealing with consumer data as well as the staff's education needs Supporting undertakings in developing resilient ICT and cyber risk management
	Unpleasant emotions related to tracking	Tracking is perceived as laborious and complicated	Monitoring and fostering individual consumers' financial literacy
		Tracking is perceived as a responsibility	
Symbolic value	The app not assisting in development of self-identity	Use of the application restricts freedom of choice	Monitoring and assessing the explainability (and potential biases) of the companies' algorithms to provide well-justified decisions and interpretations. Supporting creation, development, and communication of easy and convenient redress procedures to ensure fair handling of the insurer's decisions and interpretations
		Use of the application detracts from self-acceptance	
	The app not aiding in maintaining continuity of self-identity	The company's interpretation of the behaviour conflicts with the sense of identity built by using the application	
		Use of the application stands in contradiction to the self-identity developed	
		Encouragement may support or be detrimental to the self-identity developed, depending on one's life situation	

Moreover, one interesting characteristic of the insurance industry, that private companies possess the right to sell statutory products (such as motor vehicle liability), may potentially have important theoretical implications at a more general level as well. Furthermore, a set of comparative studies could prove fruitful since European, American and, for example, Chinese environments differ in terms of ethical discussions regarding digitalization. Finally, as new players such as Big Tech or car manufacturers are considering offering insurance services, it will be interesting to assess how their decisions or potential future decisions influence the insurance ecosystem as a whole.

From a managerial and policy perspective, the chapter provides an additional tool for evaluating the role of supervisory bodies as actors in a value-creating ecosystem. This approach adopts a wider perspective on the role of such bodies than a mere focus on their own activities related to the monitoring and control of insurance companies. Thus, it is vital to understand and even evaluate the activities of supervisory bodies as part of a wider ecosystem where they contribute together with insurance companies to the creation of value for insurance consumers.

Acknowledgements This chapter has been produced as part of the Academy of Finland funded research project “Shaping, fixing and making markets via IPR: regulating sustainable innovation ecosystems” (SHARE)(332326).

This chapter is an extended version of a Finnish language article: Talonen, A. P. (2023). Valvojat osana arvoa luovaa vakuutusekosysteemiä. In *Yritys, kirjanpito, kestävyys-Juhlajulkaisu Jukka Mähönen* (pp. 539–553). Alma Talent.

Other Online Resources

EIOPA (2022) EIOPA issues its methodology for assessing value for money in the unit-linked market. https://www.eiopa.europa.eu/media/news/eiopa-issues-its-methodology-assessing-value-money-unit-linked-market_en. Accessed 1 May 2023.

European Union. European Insurance and Occupational Pension Authority. https://european-union.europa.eu/institutions-law-budget/institutions-and-bodies/search-all-eu-institutions-and-bodies/eiopa_en. Accessed 1 May 2023.

EIOPA (2021) EIOPA sets out a framework for delivering better value for money in a consumer-centoric way. https://www.eiopa.europa.eu/content/eiopa-sets-out-framework-delivering-better-value-money-consumer-centric-way_en. Accessed January 2023.

EIOPA (2022) Consumer trends report 2022. https://www.eiopa.europa.eu/system/files/2023-01/eiopa-consumer-trends-report-2022.pdf. Accessed January 2023.

EIOPA (2022) Consultation on the supervisory statement on exclusions in insurance products related to risks arising from systemic events. https://www.eiopa.europa.eu/document-library/consultation/consultation-supervisory-statement-exclusions-insurance-products_en. Accessed February 2023.

EIOPA (2022) Consultation on the supervisory statement on exclusions in insurance products related to risks arising from systemic events. https://www.eiopa.europa.eu/system/files/2022-09/supervisory_statement_on_exclusions_related_to_risks_arising_from_systemic_events.pdf. Accessed February 2023.

EIOPA (2022) Addressing the protection gap: challenges and opportunities for (re) insurers. https://www.eiopa.europa.eu/publications/addressing-protection-gap-challenges-and-opportunities-reinsurers_en. Accessed March 2023.

EIOPA (2022) AI governance: Ensuring a trusted and financially inclusive insurance sector. https://www.eiopa.europa.eu/media/speeches-presentations/contribution/ai-governance-ensuring-trusted-and-financially-inclusive_en. Accessed January 2023.

EIOPA (2021) Artificial Intelligence governance principles: Towards ethical and trustworthy artificial intelligence in the European insurance sector. https://www.eiopa.europa.eu/system/files/2021-06/eiopa-ai-governance-principles-june-2021.pdf . Accessed December 2022.

EIOPA (2019) Joint Advice of the European Supervisory Authorities on the need for legislative improvements relating to ICT risk management requirements in the EU financial sector. https://www.eiopa.europa.eu/system/files/2019-04/jc_2019_26_joint_esas_advice_on_ict_legislative_improvements.pdf. Accessed December 2022.

EIOPA (2019) Joint Advice of the European Supervisory Authorities on the costs and benefits of the developing a coherent cyber resilience testing framework for significant market participants and infrastructures within the whole EU financial sector. https://www.eiopa.europa.eu/system/files/2019-04/jc_2019_25_joint_esas_advice_on_a_coherent_cyber_resilience_testing_framework.pdf. Accessed December 2022.

EIOPA (2021). Digital operational resilience: Addressing risks of the digital transformation. https://www.eiopa.europa.eu/publications/digital-operational-resilience-addressing-risks-digital-transformation_en. Accessed December 2022.

Cyber Risk Gmbh. Digital operational resilience act. https://www.digital-operational-resilience-act.com. Accessed April 2023.

Ipe.com (2023) EIOPA lays down strategic priorities for2024. https://www.ipe.com/eiopa-lays-down-strategic-priorities-for-2024/10069348.article. Accessed January 2024.

European Union (2019) High-level expert group on artificial intelligence. https://digital-strategy.ec.europa.eu/en/policies/expert-group-ai. Accessed December 2022.

European Union (2019) Ethics guidelines for trustworthy AI. https://digital-strategy.ec.europa.eu/en/library/ethics-guidelines-trustworthy-ai. Accessed December 2022.

Finanssivalvonta. Financial market participants: Insurance supervision. https://www.finanssivalvonta.fi/en/insurance/. Accessed April 2023.

References

Books, Book Chapters, and Articles

Armstrong K, Putt M, Halbert CH, Grande D, Schwartz, JS, Liao K, Shea J (2012) The influence of health care policies and health care system distrust on willingness to undergo genetic testing. Med Care 50(5):381

Baker T, Shortland A (2022) The government behind insurance governance: lessons for ransomware. Regulation & Governance

Bhattacherjee A, Sanford C (2006) Influence processes for information technology acceptance: an elaboration likelihood model. MIS Q 30(4):805–825

Bieck C, Tjioe L (2015) Capturing hearts, minds and market share – how connected insurers are improving customer retention. www.ibm.com/downloads/cas/VWVGDELZ. Accessed 29 July 2023

Bunker M, Ball AD (2009) Consequences of customer powerlessness: secondary control. J Consum Behav: Int Res Rev 8(5):268–283

Cao Z, Xiao Q, Zhuang W, Wang L (2022) An empirical analysis of self-service technologies: mediating role of customer powerlessness. J Serv Market 36(2):129–142

Carter M, Grover V (2015) Me, Myself, and I(T): conceptualizing information technology identity and its implications, MIS Q 39(4):931–958

Chandon P, Wansink B, Laurent G (2000) A benefit congruency framework of sales promotion effectiveness. J Market 64(4):65–81

Cheung R, Vogel D (2013) Predicting user acceptance of collaborative technologies: an extension of the technology acceptance model for e-learning. Comput Educ 63:160–175

Crawford K, Lingel J, Karppi T (2015) Our metrics, ourselves: a hundred years of self-tracking from the weight scale to the wrist wearable device. Eur J Cult Stud 18(4–5):479–496

Eling M, Kraft M (2020) The impact of telematics on the insurability of risks. J Risk Finance 21(2):77–109

Eling M, Lehmann M (2018) The impact of digitalization on the insurance value chain and the insurability of risks. Geneva Pap Risk Insur-Issues Pract 43:359–396

Eling M, Nuessle D, Staubli J (2021) The impact of artificial intelligence along the insurance value chain and on the insurability of risks. Geneva Pap Risk Insur-Issues Pract 47:205–241

Gebert-Persson S, Gidhagen M, Sallis JE, Lundberg H (2019) Online insurance claims: when more than trust matters. Int J Bank Market 37(2):579–594

Gidaris C (2019) Surveillance capitalism, datafication, and unwaged labour: the rise of wearable fitness devices and interactive life insurance. Surveill Soc 17(1/2):132–138

Giddens L, Gonzalez E, Leidner D (2016) I track, therefore I am: exploring the impact of wearable fitness devices on employee identity and well-being, paper presented at the Americas Conference on Information Systems, 11–14 August, San Diego, CA

Guillen M, Nielsen JP, Pérez-Marín AM (2021) Near-miss telematics in motor insurance. J Risk Insur 88(3):569–589

Hägg PGT (1998) An Institutional Analysis of Insurance Regulation-The Case of Sweden (Doctoral dissertation, Lund University)

Iglesias O, Markovic S, Bagherzadeh M, Singh JJ (2020) Co-creation: a key link between corporate social responsibility, customer trust, and customer loyalty. J Bus Ethics 163:151–166

Johne A, Davies R (2000) Innovation in medium-sized insurance companies: how marketing adds value. Int J Bank Market 18(1):6–14

Jung Choo H, Moon H, Kim H, Yoon N (2012) Luxury customer value. J Fashion Market Manag: Int J 16(1):81–101

Kapoor R (2018) Ecosystems: broadening the locus of value creation. J Organ Design 7(1):1–16

Kinder T, Six F, Stenvall J, Memon A (2022) Governance-as-legitimacy: are ecosystems replacing networks? Public Manag Rev 24(1):8–33

Kraft M, Drerup B (2023) Digitalization of controlling in insurance companies: along the limits of insurability in theory and practice. In: The digitalization of management accounting: use cases from theory and practice. Springer Fachmedien Wiesbaden, Wiesbaden, pp 277–293
Langley MR (2014) Hide your health: addressing the new privacy problem of consumer wearables. Geo Law J 103:1641
Ledger D, McCaffrey D (2014) Inside wearables: how the science of human behavior change offers the secret to long-term engagement. Endeavour Partners
Lupton D (2016) The diverse domains of quantified selves: self-tracking modes and dataveillance. Econ Soc 45(1):101–122
Maas P, Rüfenacht M (2018) Creating customer value in insurance markets–research perspectives and managerial relevance. Int J Bank Market 36(6):1010–1014
Marano P (2017) Sources and tools of the insurance regulation in the European Union. In: Marano P, Siri M (eds) Insurance regulation in the European Union: Solvency II and beyond, 1st edn. Palgrave Macmillan, pp 5–29
Marano P, Noussia K (2021) Transparency in insurance regulation and supervisory law. Springer International Publishing
Mathwick C, Malhotra N, Rigdon E (2001) Experiential value: conceptualization, measurement and application in the catalog and internet shopping environment. J Retail 77(1):39–56
Mukherjee A, Nath P (2003) A model of trust in online relationship banking. Int J Bank Market 21(1):5–15
Myers SC, Read Jr JA (2001) Capital allocation for insurance companies. J Risk Insur 68(4):545–580
Osborne SP, Powell M, Cui T, Strokosch K (2022) Value creation in the public service ecosystem: an integrative framework. Public Adm Rev 82(4):634–645
Peverelli R, de Feniks R (2010) Reinventing financial services: what consumers expect from future banks and insurers. Pearson Education
Pitthan F, De Witte K (2021) Puzzles of insurance demand and its biases: a survey on the role of behavioural biases and financial literacy on insurance demand. J Behav Exp Finance 30:100471
Pukała R, Vnukova N, Achkasova S (2017) Identification of the priority instruments affecting regulations on the development of insurance in the framework of international requirements. J Insur Financ Markets Consumer Prot 23(1):28–40
Pütz F, Murphy F, Mullins M, O'Malley L (2019) Connected automated vehicles and insurance: analysing future market-structure from a business ecosystem perspective. Technol Soc 59:101182
Rintamäki T, Kanto A, Kuusela H, Spence MT (2006) Decomposing the value of department store shopping into utilitarian, hedonic and social dimensions. Int J Retail Distrib Manag 34(1):6–24
Rintamäki T, Kuusela H, Mitronen L (2007) Identifying competitive customer value propositions in retailing. Manag Serv Qual: Int J 17(6):621–634
Schmeiser H, Wagner J (2016) What transaction costs are acceptable in life insurance products from the policyholders' viewpoint? J Risk Finance 17(3):277–294
Sheth JN, Newman BI, Gross BL (1991) Why we buy what we buy: a theory of consumption values. J Bus Res 22(2):159–170
Similä H, Immonen M, Toska-Tervola J, Enwald H, Keränen N, Kangas M, Jämsä T, Korpelainen R (2018) Feasibility of mobile mental wellness training for older adults. Geriatr Nurs 39(5):499–505
Talonen A, Mähönen J, Koskinen, L, Kuoppakangas P (2021a) Analysis of consumers' negative perceptions of health tracking in insurance–a value sacrifice approach. J Inf Commun Ethics Soc 19(4):463–479
Talonen H, Talonen AP, Stenvall J, Prakash P (2021b) Disclosing functional value of customer ownership: analysis of mutual insurers' annual reports. Int J Manag Pract 16(4):515–533
Talonen A, Koskinen L, Voutilainen R, Talonen H (2022a) Adoption of incentive-based insurance applications: the perspective of psychological ownership. J Financ Serv Market 28(4):1–13
Talonen A, Mähönen J, Kwon WJ (2022b) Examining the investment operations as a derived core function of mutual insurance companies: research agenda and guide. J Co-op Organ Manag 10(1):100168

Tereszkiewicz P (2020) Digitalisation of insurance contract law: preliminary thoughts with special regard to insurer's duty to advise. In: InsurTech: a legal and regulatory view. Springer International Publishing, Cham, pp 127–146

Tereszkiewicz P (2023) Introduction: financial consumers, complex contractual products, and dispute resolution–setting the scene. In: Protecting financial consumers in Europe. Brill Nijhoff, pp 1–21

Van Rossum A, De Castries H, Mendelsohn R (2002) The debate on the insurance value chain. Geneva Pap Risk Insur Issues Pract 27(1):89–101

Vargo SL, Lusch RF (2016) Institutions and axioms: an extension and update of service-dominant logic. J Acad Market Sci 44:5–23

Vargo SL, Akaka MA, Vaughan CM (2017) Conceptualizing value: a service-ecosystem view. J Creat Value 3(2):117–124

Veljanovski C (2010) Strategic use of regulation. In: Baldwin R, Cave M, Lodge M (eds) Oxford handbook of regulation. Oxford University Press, Oxford

Weedige SS, Ouyang H, Gao Y, Liu Y (2019) Decision making in personal insurance: impact of insurance literacy. Sustainability 11(23):6795

Antti Talonen is an Associate Professor of Management at the University of Eastern Finland. He obtained his Ph.D. in insurance science from Tampere University in 2018. Talonen has served as a member of EIOPA's Insurance and Reinsurance Stakeholder Group from 2020 onwards. In addition, he was a member of EIOPA's expert group in digital ethics in insurance. Talonen is the Editor-in-Chief of the Journal of Co-operative Organization and Management (Elsevier). He serves as a Visiting Professor at the University of Zagreb and holds an Adjunct Professor (Dosentti) title in administrative science at the University of Tampere.

Specific Applications of Digitalisation in the Insurance Sector

Smart Contracts in Insurance Law

Andrea Durovic Simikic

1 Introduction and Methodology

Smart contracts, as one of the major technical innovations in Contract Law, are unquestionably among the most prominent current topics in the entire legal world.

Although there are a lot of unknown factors arising with the use of blockchain and smart contracts, it is certain that when properly used, new technologies have great potential to completely change the course of various industries and the insurance industry is not an exception. The use of new technology such as the blockchain in insurance can also: automate a sizable portion of the claims-handling process (which limits the room for disagreement between parties), reduce settlement times and the cost of claims-handling, store events related to claims, and potentially disable fraud by facilitating better collaboration between insurers.[1]

This article begins with the examination of smart contracts, their definition and their features. Furthermore, the potential of smart contracts in insurance will be analysed, followed by the identification of the challenges that arise and finally highlighting the smart contracts use case as well as mentioning some of the current blockchain products in insurance.

In order to write this Article, a qualitative research approach was employed, combining a thorough literature review, in-depth case studies, and expert insights. The primary objective was to scrutinise the adoption of blockchain and smart

[1] EIOPA. "Discussion paper on blockchain and smart contracts in insurance" (2021). Available at: https://www.eiopa.europa.eu/sites/default/files/publications/consultations/eiopa-discussion-paper-on-blockchain-29-04-2021.pdf (Accessed 12 Oct 2022).

A. Durovic Simikic (✉)
University of Belgrade Faculty of Law, Business Law, Belgrade, Serbia
e-mail: andrea.djurovic@hotmail.com

C. Poncibò, P. Tereszkiewicz (eds.), *European Insurance Law within the Digital Age*, AIDA Europe Research Series on Insurance Law and Regulation 14,
https://doi.org/10.1007/978-3-031-96496-1_11

contracts within the insurance industry, focusing on their impact on insurance processes, data management, and customer experiences. The research drew from diverse data sources, encompassing relevant literature, real-world case studies, and insights from industry experts. Qualitative analysis techniques were applied to identify overarching themes and address associated challenges.

Additionally, a comparative analysis was conducted, contrasting Etherisc's decentralised model with Fizzy's centralised approach, allowing for a comprehensive assessment. Throughout the research, regulatory complexities were acknowledged. This comprehensive exploration underscores the considerable potential benefits of blockchain and smart contracts in the insurance domain, while recognizing the intricate regulatory landscape that must be navigated.

2 Definition and Features of Smart Contracts

2.1 Definition

Smart contracts can be explained as computer programs based on blockchain technology, as opposed to merely digitally signed contracts, where the terms of the agreement are managed by code.[2] An agreement with automatic execution known as a "smart contract" is frequently carried out by a computer running code that converts legal terms into an executable program.[3] Once they are in place, smart contracts cannot be altered or stopped and are created to guarantee performance without turning to the courts.[4] When a smart contract is drawn up, it is stored on the blockchain as a block of data, and when the requirements are satisfied, the terms are carried out (in the case of a purchase agreement, once the agreed-upon product is delivered, the payment is released automatically).[5] It is a digital agreement written in computer code that is "understandable" to a computer**.** Therefore, they are written onto an immutable blockchain (Ethereum) in an "if-X-then-Y" language. Smart contracts are most efficient for contracts that can be reduced to simple "if-then" statements, as their terms are easy to convert to computer code and can be executed automatically.[6]

Secure data (input) from outside the ledger is frequently required to check whether the conditions for a smart contract's performance have been met- the

[2] Forbes, "Smart Contracts And The Law: What You Need To Know" (2022). Available at: https://www.forbes.com/sites/forbesbusinesscouncil/2022/03/17/smart-contracts-and-the-law-what-you-need-to-know/?sh=1054aeda3d03 (Accessed Sep 2022).

[3] Raskin (2017), p. 309.

[4] Ibidem, p. 310.

[5] Forbes, "Smart Contracts And The Law: What You Need To Know" (2022). Available at: https://www.forbes.com/sites/forbesbusinesscouncil/2022/03/17/smart-contracts-and-the-law-what-you-need-to-know/?sh=1054aeda3d03 (Accessed Sep 2022).

[6] Cohn et al. (2017), pp. 273–304.

so-called "oracles" provide this data.[7] A third-party service called an oracle or data feed provider is generally created for use in smart contracts on a distributed ledger; they locate and validate real-world events, typically using external databases, and send this data to a blockchain so that smart contracts can utilise it (e.g. flight delay database or weather database).[8] The agreement of the parties to the smart contract regarding the oracle's identity is crucial (these sources of information must be reliable and secure against hacking in order for the parties to use them).[9]

These contracts are designed to meet common contractual terms (such as payment terms, confidentiality, and enforcement, etc.), minimise exceptions, reduce the need for reliable intermediaries (banks or agents), having in mind the economic objectives as well (reducing potential losses in the event of fraud, enforcement costs, administrative and other transaction costs, etc).

One of the first countries to give a definition is Italy with its "*Decreto Semplificazioni*", stating in Article 8-ter(2): **"Smart contracts are *computer programs that operate on distributed registers-based technologies and whose execution automatically binds two or more parties according to the effects predefined by said parties*".**

Furthermore, they can be applied in numerous areas, and are considered to have significant potential, particularly in the field of insurance. Smart contracts are currently used in a wide range of sectors, including supply chains, real estate, insurance, banking, and decentralised finance.

2.1.1 Smart Contract and a Street Vending Machine

One of the best-known examples of smart contracts is the simple street vending machine. Provided that the machine is operating properly, and money is inserted into the machine, then a contract for sale will be executed automatically, which is similar to how a smart contract works.[10] Like a street vending machine, a smart contract has three functions,

1. **It follows** the rules,
2. **It verifies compliance with the rules** (whether the customer has entered the correct amount),
3. It is **able to implement the rules** independently, i.e., fulfil the act (throws out the can and returns the change).

Certainly, unlike a street vending machine, a smart contract relies on software instead of mechanics. Furthermore, this contract poses no legal problems if the

---

[7] EIOPA, "Discussion paper on blockchain and smart contracts in insurance" (2021). Available at: https://www.eiopa.europa.eu/sites/default/files/publications/consultations/eiopa-discussion-paper-on-blockchain-29-04-2021.pdf (Accessed 12 Oct 2022).

[8] Ibidem.

[9] Ibidem.

[10] Raskin (2017).

machine were to dispense candies or soda, but legal questions arise if the machine instead dispenses heroin, posing a question of whether laws should be passed to ban vending machines because they can be used to further illegal ends?[11]

2.2 Smart Contract Features

What is considered to be a flaw but at the same time an advantage is that one of the main characteristics is their immutability. Once set, a smart contract cannot be modified. Obviously, that can be quite challenging. So, to make any change, the entire contract must be cancelled and redrawn since, since once in force, it cannot be modified.[12] Due to their nature and to the fact that for the smart contract "the code is law," there can be no legal disputes over the terms of the agreement.[13] There is no longer a need to have trust in the other party once the parties have entered into a contract, it is impossible to make changes to the agreement or to change one's mind as well. Additionally, if the code is the law, lawyers are no longer necessary.[14] However, due to the fact that traditional contract law is flexible, whereas smart contracts are inherently firm and fixed (since smart contracts do not interpret anything; instead, they solely use binary logic) more complex legal matters could not be carried out without legal professionals. Also, due to its firmness, simply put, smart contracts cannot be created if the specifics of any potential dangers or the precise nature of the loss are unknown.

Furthermore, it operates on a decentralised blockchain, meaning it is autonomous from third parties and from the contractors themselves open to everyone, with a global reach. Therefore, one of the reasons why they are so interesting is their capability to exclude the interference of third parties. Thanks to its traits, the smart contract executes without human interference, and although that is one of the advantages, it is important to note that human involvement is still necessary at the development stage of the smart contract. However, despite the decentralised nature of blockchain, third parties like blockchain developers and nodes are inevitable, nonetheless. Thanks to its automatic execution (without human intervention) the possible abuses may be eliminated, and can be settled entirely on the blockchain, providing full transparency.

One of the main matters is whether these contracts are legally enforceable. Although some concerns about their enforceability exist, the answer is yes,

---

[11] Raskin (2017).

[12] Forbes, "Smart Contracts And The Law: What You Need To Know" (2022). Available at: https://www.forbes.com/sites/forbesbusinesscouncil/2022/03/17/smart-contracts-and-the-law-what-you-need-to-know/?sh=1054aeda3d03 (Accessed Sep 2022).

[13] Bitlaw, "Smart Contracts And The Law". Available at: https://www.bitlaw.com/blockchain/smart-contracts.html (Accessed 12 Oct 2022).

[14] Ibidem.

provided they comply with Contract Law principles and its basic contractual elements, which include the following:[15]

1. *Offer* (one or both parties offer the terms of the agreement), *Acceptance* (both parties accept the terms as offered), *Consideration* (there is something of value being offered to each party),
2. If the *terms are legally permissible*,
3. If it is *legal to sign electronically*.

So, to be enforceable, a smart contract needs to be legally eligible for electronic signatures, unlike some types of agreements that cannot be signed electronically (wills and other estate paperwork, court orders, health and safety-related product recall warnings, paperwork needed to transport hazardous materials, notices of utility service cancellation, and eviction notices are just a few examples of the paperwork that may be necessary).[16] Still, the main problem is that their application is still in the experimental phase so many questions remain to be answered.

2.3 Regulation of Smart Contracts

It is challenging to determine where and how smart contracts fit under the regulatory frameworks of conventional contract law because of the distinctiveness and complexity inherent in them.[17] Moreover, integrating smart contracts into a regulatory framework is quite difficult since courts and legislators have not yet fully considered their possibilities; no court has yet offered recommendations about the enforceability of smart contracts, and there is no smart contract market with specified procedures in place, so conflicting opinions about the enforceability of smart contracts are brought on by the absence of authority and guidance.[18] At the supranational level, the European Union has established directives governing various electronic money transactions, such as Directive 2015/2366/EU on Payment Services in the Internal Market, Directive 2014/65/EU on Markets in Financial Instruments, and Regulation EU 600/2014 on Markets in Financial Instruments primarily address electronic transactions but do not specifically regulate conflicts of law in smart contract usage.[19] Instead, general contract regulations handle issues arising from smart contracts, such as sale and purchase agreements or leases.[20]

---

[15] Forbes, "Smart Contracts And The Law: What You Need To Know", (2022). Available at: https://www.forbes.com/sites/forbesbusinesscouncil/2022/03/17/smart-contracts-and-the-law-what-you-need-to-know/?sh=1054aeda3d03 (Accessed Sep 2022).

[16] Ibidem.

[17] Kiviat (2015), pp. 569–608.

[18] Temte (2019), pp. 87–117.

[19] Volos (2020), pp. 563–568.

[20] Ibidem.

Governments worldwide have embraced a variety of approaches to address the intricate regulatory challenges posed by smart contracts, underscoring the fragmentation of regulatory frameworks across different regions. These challenges arise due to the rapid evolution of smart contracts that often outpaces the development of suitable regulatory frameworks, thereby presenting a daunting task for governments aiming to stay current. Additionally, the complexity intensifies with cross-border smart contracts, raising intricate issues related to jurisdiction, enforceability, and liability that necessitate careful consideration within the global regulatory landscape.[21] Nonetheless, governments employ a spectrum of regulatory strategies to tackle these challenges:[22]

- Observation and evaluation: Some governments choose to closely monitor technological advancements without hastily implementing regulatory actions, focusing on accumulating knowledge and understanding potential impacts;
- Issuance of directives: Governments offer explicit legal clarifications and guidance within existing legal frameworks, asserting that smart contracts can adhere to customary contract law, thereby enhancing legal certainty;
- Customising regulatory structures: Governments introduce precise legal provisions designed to recognize smart contracts and bestow legal standing upon them within the existing legal system;
- Regulatory sandbox environments: Controlled environments are established to enable innovators to test smart contracts and other innovative technologies under regulatory supervision, fostering innovation while managing potential risks;
- Conventional regulatory tools: Governments engage in collaboration initiatives and international partnerships with other nations to address challenges that span national borders, aiming to promote the advancement of smart contracts globally.

Therefore, countries employ an array of regulatory strategies to navigate the complex landscape of smart contracts, reflecting the multifaceted challenges posed by these emerging technologies. A concise depiction of the diverse regulatory responses to these issues is offered by illustrating selected governmental approaches:

- **Wait and see:** In many instances, governments have chosen a "wait and see" strategy, as exemplified by the European Commission's active monitoring of Distributed Ledger Technologies (DLTs) and the establishment of the EU Blockchain Observatory and Forum in 2018, which provides guidance for policymakers on addressing smart contract regulatory challenges, and in 2019, the European Commission formed the International Association of Trusted Blockchain Applications (INATBA) to promote collaboration across different countries and sectors in advancing Distributed Ledger Technologies (DLTs).[23]

[21] Amaral, "Blockchain and smart contracts: regulatory challenges and regulatory approaches" OECD Publishing (2021). Available at: https://doi.org/10.1787/fbf2ebe9-en (Accessed 2 Oct 2022).

[22] Ibidem.

[23] EU Blockhain Observatory and Forum (2020), "2018-2020 Conclusions and Reflections". https://blockchain-observatory.ec.europa.eu/document/download/2df0bb3c-61fd-4ac6-921b-

- **Issuing guidance** (entails governments providing clear and authoritative instructions within current legal systems to clarify the legal status and operation of smart contracts under conventional contract law, enhancing legal certainty and providing valuable information and interpretation guidelines):

  UK Ministry of Justice: In the United Kingdom, the Lord Chancellor initiated smart legal contract research inclusion in the Law Reform Program.[24] In November 2019, the UK Jurisdiction Taskforce (UKJT) provided a legal opinion on cryptocurrencies and smart contracts, recognizing their potential for legally binding obligations enforceable as per their provisions.[25] Following this, the Ministry of Justice initiated a thorough examination of current legal aspects related to smart legal contracts, with a focus on identifying ambiguities, gaps, and potential legislative needs, both immediate and future.[26] The conclusion affirms that statutory law reform is unwarranted, as the current legal framework in England and Wales effectively accommodates smart legal contracts, leveraging the adaptability of common law to provide an optimal environment for commerce and innovation, despite potential challenges posed by certain types of smart legal contracts;[27]

  Dutch Ministry of Justice and Security: In the Netherlands, the Research and Documentation Centre examined DLTs and smart contracts, confirming the applicability of Dutch contract law.[28] They emphasised the importance of external conditions when interpreting contract clauses.

  Swiss Federal Council: Switzerland's Federal Council issued a report in 2019, recognizing the unique features of smart contracts and refraining from premature legislation.[29]

- **Adapting regulatory frameworks** (involves the implementation of specific legal provisions tailored to accommodate smart contracts, granting them legal recognition within the existing legal framework. This approach aims to provide legal certainty and support the effective operation of smart contracts):

  Italy: In 2019, the Italian Parliament introduced a law that defines distributed ledger technologies and smart contracts in the legal framework. This law provides legal recognition to smart contracts;

ff50fc32aeb9_en?filename=report_conclusion_book_v1.0.pdf (Accessed 11 Oct 2022).

[24] Law Commission, "Smart contracts" (2021). Available at: https://www.lawcom.gov.uk/project/smart-contracts (Accessed 20 Dec 2022).

[25] Law Commission, "Smart contracts" (2021). Available at: https://www.lawcom.gov.uk/project/smart-contracts (Accessed 20 Dec 2022).

[26] Ibidem.

[27] Ibidem.

[28] Amaral (2021).

[29] Catalini and Gans (2016).

US Federal States: Several US states, including Arizona, Delaware, Florida, Ohio, Nevada, Tennessee, Wyoming, and New York, have passed specific laws to clarify the legal status and enforceability of smart contracts.

The evolution and integration of smart contracts into our legal and regulatory frameworks are met with various challenges and complexities. The distinctiveness and complexity inherent in smart contracts make it difficult to categorise them within the existing conventional contract law.[30] The regulatory landscape for smart contracts is marked by significant challenges for governments, encompassing issues of jurisdiction, enforceability, and liability. However, governments have responded with diverse regulatory approaches, reflecting both the rapid evolution of smart contracts and the complexities introduced by their borderless nature. International collaboration emerges as a pivotal factor in addressing transnational challenges and ensuring the effective integration of smart contracts into legal and business frameworks. As smart contracts continue to reshape our socioeconomic systems, adaptability and cooperation among governments and stakeholders remain essential for successful regulatory endeavours in this dynamic domain.

3 Smart Contracts in Insurance Law

3.1 Insurance Industry Overview

The insurance market is huge, but the rapport between parties and stakeholders is absent. Furthermore, the lack of trust is considered to be one of the biggest issues causing poor customer engagement as well as the occurrence of fraud. All of this costs the industry millions. Also, insurance companies bear the administrative costs of even the simplest contracts, which are often passed on to consumers of insurance services in the form of increased premiums. In addition, with the constant development of the insurance sector, new problems such as inefficiency, the possibility of human error and cybercrime are created.

The regulatory framework of the insurance industry provides a degree of consistency in the market while allowing individual insurance companies to tailor their products to the specific needs of their customers and their characteristics are:[31]

- **Complexity and Specialization of the Insurance Industry**: the parties involved in an insurance contract often possess varying levels of understanding regarding insurance principles. Despite the statutory requirement that all parties in an insurance contract must act with utmost good faith, practical considerations often favour policyholders over insurers. This tendency arises from the fact that

[30] Amaral (2021).

[31] Tsung-Chih et al. (2023).

the general insured population may not fully comprehend the content, theories, and principles of insurance;

- **Unique Nature of Insurance Contracts**: Insurance contracts exhibit distinct features, including the uncertainty of fully determining the rights and obligations of both parties upon contract signing. These rights and obligations may fluctuate depending on the occurrence of insured accidents, rendering insurance contracts aleatory in nature. Consequently, the rights and obligations of the involved parties hinge on the event of insured accidents, with no equivalent exchange of value;
- **Social Aspects of the Insurance Industry:** Within the insurance industry, contracts often take the form of "adhesion contracts," signifying an unequal relationship between insurers and the insured. Insurance contracts are standard agreements created and tailored in advance by insurers, granting policyholders the simple choice of either "agreeing" or "disagreeing", which results in an unequal distribution of bargaining power (additionally, policyholders frequently encounter difficulties in assessing the reasonableness of insurance premiums due to their limited knowledge).

What can transform the entire industry are smart contracts in insurance instead of inconvenient paper agreements. Transparency, service automation, and a decrease in administrative costs can all be guaranteed by digitising current operations and utilising cutting-edge technologies to offer new solutions.

Furthermore, new kinds of insurance policies can be developed to satisfy various consumer needs by overcoming potential obstacles. Moreover, they could increase the possibility to re-establish lost trust and to eliminate the manipulation on both sides. In addition to their apparent significance for the banking industry, new technical advancements have a lot of potential for the insurance industry as well.

3.2 The Advantages and Potential of Smart Contracts in Insurance

Smart contracts, facilitated by blockchain technology offer a framework through which both policyholders and insurers can effectively oversee claim management in a manner characterised by transparency, responsiveness, and indisputability: contracts and claims can be registered on a blockchain ledger and subsequently verified by the decentralised network, thereby guaranteeing the disbursement of funds exclusively for substantiated claims.[32] To illustrate, the blockchain ledger would unequivocally dismiss multiple claims associated with a singular accident, as the network maintains a record of a previously filed claim.[33]

---

[32] Deloitte, "Blockchain applications in insurance", Available at: https://www2.deloitte.com/content/dam/Deloitte/ch/Documents/innovation/ch-en-innovation-deloitte-blockchain-app-in-insurance.pdf (Accessed 11 Oct 2022).

[33] Ibidem.

Undoubtedly, the application of blockchain in insurance will change the entire insurance industry, introducing new products and services, I improving fraud detection and leading to cost reductions that would affect the development of insurance companies. Blockchain can be used in various ways in insurance, and one of the ways of application is in the aspect of smart contracts.[34] As an example, Etherisc, an insurtech startup, aims to speed up insurance claims processing with blockchain and smart contracts, using third-party data providers to verify payment terms, promptly notifying insurers for immediate assessment, greatly enhancing efficiency.[35]

Several advantages associated with the integration of smart contracts within the insurance sector encompass:

- *Automation of the insurance process and lower costs:* The application of smart contracts in combination with blockchain technology can lead to the automation of the insurance process: from the verification of claims to the payment of compensation in favour of the insured, because smart contracts and blockchain allow insurance companies to automate the stage of handling claims by eliminating manual processes and simplifying work processes (given that the intervention of a third party would not be needed) and, accordingly, to reducing the associated costs and improving efficiency.[36] Lower costs could lead to a steady reduction in premiums charged, allowing insurers to increase their market share by offering more competitive premiums and policies, and those most likely to be impacted by smart contracts and blockchain are those associated with short-term risks, such as policies insurance aimed at compensating air travellers due to flight delays or adverse weather conditions.[37]
- *Blockchain's transparency and trust can enhance underwriting efficiency:* Because of the inherent trust and openness in blockchain, using it in the underwriting process may increase efficiency and save costs, especially when combined with automated information gathering and assimilation procedures (e.g., external data can be included to decrease risk and provide semi-automatic pricing).[38]
- *Automated claims handling, event storage and reduced fraud:* The use of blockchain in insurance can also automate a sizable portion of the claims-handling process (which limits the room for disagreement between parties), reduce settlement times and the cost of claims-handling, store events related to claims, potentially disable fraud (any attempt to manipulate or falsify data within a smart

[34] Tomić (2018), p. 136.

[35] AIMultiple, "7 blockchain case studies from different industries in 2023", (2023). Available at: https://research.aimultiple.com/blockchain-case-studies/ (Accessed: October 12, 2023).

[36] Durovic and Janssen (2019), p. 6.

[37] Ibidem, p. 7.

[38] IBM, "Three areas in the insurance industry to use blockchain." (2018). Available at: https://www.ibm.com/blogs/blockchain/2018/03/three-areas-in-the-insurance-industry-to-use-blockchain (Accessed 10 Oct 2022).

contract is detectable and traceable) by facilitating better collaboration between insurers.[39]

- *Smart contracts ensure precise execution of insurance terms, promoting transparency and security:* Smart contracts can simplify the process by enabling automated sharing of the necessary information between all parties involved and streamlining payment transfers. This approach is often time-consuming and prone to errors. Traditional contracts involve future performance by putting one or more parties under obligation.[40] Due to the fact that neither party is legally required to take any action after the smart contract is formed, it does not result in any future obligations, for instance, neither party is obligated to take action after the establishment of a smart contract requiring an airline to pay out to a client if the airline delays or cancels the customer's flight (the smart contract will self-execute and payout to the customer).[41] The feature of smart contracts in insurance is that the contracting parties are required to precisely define the terms of the insurance policy so that the entered terms can be executed using a digital protocol, thus eliminating potential errors while ensuring transparency and security for consumers. Consequently, large insurance companies concentrate primarily on blockchain among the new technologies since it gives them the opportunity to build automated insurance systems through the Internet without intermediaries, based on smart contracts. Using smart contracts, or autonomous programs that, once launched, autonomously carry out predetermined terms and conditions by registering in the blockchain without requiring human intervention, it is possible to automate the provision of services.

The use of modern technology in insurance has the potential to significantly improve the effectiveness of health insurance, reinsurance, property and casualty insurance, and fraud detection. It is evident that, despite any potential difficulties, using modern technology lowers costs, expedites the decision-making process, and helps to increase customers' levels of satisfaction and trust in insurance services.

Smart contracts are currently in a trial phase, and various problems of a technical and legal nature appear, but new technologies have great potential in insurance, especially for the following:[42]

- **Indemnification claims** (in case of death of the user, a Smart Contract would automatically check whether the deceased was covered by insurance, and pay the insured amount to policyholders),
- **Efficient claims processing** can be achieved through the use of smart contracts that represent insurance policies. For instance, let us consider the scenario of a

---

[39] EIOPA, "Discussion paper on blockchain and smart contracts in insurance" (2021). Available at: https://www.eiopa.europa.eu/sites/default/files/publications/consultations/eiopa-discussion-paper-on-blockchain-29-04-2021.pdf (Accessed 12 Oct 2022).

[40] Kolber (2018), p. 221.

[41] Ibidem.

[42] Tomić (2018).

car accident involving two drivers:[43] • If one driver submits a claim to the insurer for compensation, the company investigates the case to recover the losses from the other driver's insurer. • Meanwhile, the second company also receives the claim for the same accident submitted by the other participant,
- **Fraud** (new technology allows insurance fraud to be recognized and prevents risk between unreliable parties, eliminating errors, detecting, and preventing fraud)—smart contracts can play a crucial role in enhancing fraud detection and prevention in the insurance market. By providing insurers with access to more complete and accurate data, these technologies can help mitigate the risks of fraudulent activity, which has long plagued the industry.[44] Furthermore, by leveraging the inherent immutability of blockchain, insurance claims can be made tamper-proof, making it challenging for fraudsters to manipulate. Additionally, since the ledger is accessible to multiple insurers, there is improved coordination between them, which facilitates the identification of any fraudulent activity,[45]
- **Travel Insurance** (a product that covers damage caused by flight delays)—The steps to be followed to obtain flight delay protection and submit a claim are:[46]

  1. Register the flight approximately 24 h before departure;
  2. Connect digital wallet to pay for coverage;
  3. If the flight is delayed for at least 45 min, it becomes eligible for a claim;
  4. Upon landing, compensation will be automatically disbursed. The insurance provider utilises a decentralised network that monitors your flight status and disburses compensation when a claim is eligible (this decentralised network is enabled by multiple nodes using the Ethereum and Chainlink framework, which enables instant payments and reduces the risk of monitoring or payment failure. The use of multiple nodes also eliminates the need for follow-up inquiries from the traveller),[47]

- **Reinsurance** (recording the details of claims, which is not variable so that costs can be accurately distributed between insurers and reinsurers) – allows for the streamlining of processes and information flows, which is advantageous for both reinsurers and insurers. Particularly, blockchain technology and smart contracts offer a promising solution to streamline data and payment processing, reducing the burden on insurers and reinsurers alike: by leveraging distributed ledger technology and smart contracts, all participants involved in the reinsurance process

---

[43] Itexus, "Smart contracts development for insurance companies" (2023). Available at: https://itexus.com/smart-contracts-development-for-insurance-companies (Accessed 9 Oct 2023).

[44] Ibidem.

[45] Ibidem.

[46] Forbes, "Will you purchase Blockchain Flight Delay Insurance?" (2022). Available at: https://www.forbes.com/sites/geoffwhitmore/2022/01/21/will-you-purchase-blockchain-flight-delay-insurance/?sh=5c5a79316dca (Accessed 13 Oct 2023).

[47] Forbes, "Will you purchase Blockchain Flight Delay Insurance?" (2022). Available at: https://www.forbes.com/sites/geoffwhitmore/2022/01/21/will-you-purchase-blockchain-flight-delay-insurance/?sh=5c5a79316dca (Accessed 13 Oct 2023).

can concurrently access all the pertinent data related to losses, bonuses, fees, and policies.[48]

In insurance, a smart contract is a blockchain-based insurance contract that pays out when specific, predetermined conditions are met. Since smart contracts have developed over the past ten years, they are now transparent and data-driven and can be compared to parametric insurance contracts.[49] Today, smart contracts can provide a safe environment for storing sensitive information and data on customers and their policies.

In general, blockchain ledgers cannot be manipulated or corrupted because they are encrypted and the data is timestamped, providing a transparent record of actions that can also serve as evidence of potential tampering, should it occur.[50]

As an example of an "if-then" statement in the contract, a life insurance contract can be coded to specify that if the policyholder dies, then payment to the beneficiaries commences.[51]

In an environment where risks appear to be more volatile due to climate change and health crisis events, the need to develop products that provide quick payouts has become critical. Smart contracts are still a relatively new technology, and because the insurance industry was initially slow to adopt digital innovations (which were then accelerated by the pandemic), they have yet to become a mainstream option.[52] As a less expensive alternative to conventional contracts, they do not require the interference of a third party, which brings down administrative costs and insurance premiums.[53] Similar to traditional contracts, smart contracts establish clear parameters between two parties, and in contrast to conventional contracts, track insurance claims and hold both parties responsible.[54]

The European Commission (with the support of the European Parliament) launched the European Union Blockchain Observatory and Forum on February 1, 2018, with the goal of accelerating the implementation of blockchain technology, innovation, and development of the blockchain ecosystem. In this regard, European institutions have recently started to consider the necessity of intervention at the legislative level in order to identify the principles applicable to the new

[48] Itexus, "Smart contracts development for insurance companies" (2023). Available at: https://itexus.com/smart-contracts-development-for-insurance-companies (Accessed 9 Oct 2023).

[49] Beinsure, "How Blockchain and Smart Contracts Transform Insurance and InsurTech?" (2022). Available at: https://beinsure.com/how-blockchain-smart-contracts-transforms-insurance (Accessed 30 Nov 2022).

[50] Beinsure, "How Blockchain and Smart Contracts Transform Insurance and InsurTech?" (2022). Available at: https://beinsure.com/how-blockchain-smart-contracts-transforms-insurance (Accessed 30 Nov 2022).

[51] Cohn et al. (2017).

[52] Beinsure, "How Blockchain and Smart Contracts Transform Insurance and InsurTech?" (2022). Available at: https://beinsure.com/how-blockchain-smart-contracts-transforms-insurance (Accessed 30 Nov 2022).

[53] Ibidem.

[54] Ibidem.

technology.[55] The observatory's goals include taking note of blockchain initiatives taking place in Europe, building a comprehensive database of information about the technology, setting up a public platform for the discussion of ideas, and offering advice for the EU's potential involvement in the blockchain industry.[56] Then, in October 2018, the European Parliament passed a resolution referring to smart contracts as potentially one of the most significant and innovative uses of blockchain. It also noted that the Commission must assess the potential and legal entanglements of blockchain, taking into account, among other things, the risks associated with the authority and legal security of the digital cryptographic signature.

3.3 Blockchain and Smart Contracts Use Cases in Insurance

In the domain of insurance, blockchain technology offers a diverse array of applications that have the potential to address a multitude of concerns and improve various facets of the industry:[57]

- **Better data storage and exchange**—A blockchain could replace the traditional insurance company's databases since it can store, update, and monitor a wide variety of transactions and data (all previously distributed stored data centrally, securely, immutably, and visible to all network participants with the appropriate authorization), avoiding, errors, wasteful spending, and delays associated with the verification, reconciliation, and synchronisation of various databases. The implementation of secure and transparent real-time access to insurance-related information reduces redundancy, enhances data accuracy, and streamlines data sharing, benefiting all involved parties;
- **Improving customer experience and management**—As an example, home insurance claims management is now time-consuming and difficult due to the requirement to involve numerous parties. The customer must file a claim by providing all the necessary documentation for payout, for example, if a flood damages the insured person's home.[58] This could be challenging because many records might be lost, depending on how badly the harm was done. However, a settlement procedure that can take months or even years begins even if the customer files all required paperwork[59]). Smart contracts offer a transformative potential in insurance, with key benefits including efficient claims processing, enhanced transparency, reduced administrative burden, personalised policies,

---

[55] Durovic (2020), pp. 305–317.

[56] Ibidem.

[57] Friehoff (2020), pp. 305–321.

[58] PWC, "Blockchain, a catalyst for new approaches in insurance" (2017). Available at: https://www.pwc.ch/en/publications/2017/Xlos_Etude_Blockchain_UK_2017_Web.pdf (Accessed 22 Sep 2022).

[59] Ibidem.

instant policy updates, cost reduction, fraud prevention, data security, and improved customer engagement. These advancements aim to significantly enhance the overall customer experience and management within the insurance sector.

- **The introduction of new insurance products**—Additionally, the use of blockchain technology and smart contracts may enable insurance to diversify their clientele. For instance, over the past few years, the sharing economy has grown. Through on-demand or just-in-time insurance, smart contracts have the potential to hasten the development of accompanying insurance coverage.[60]
- **The introduction of a new way of insurance based on a peer-to-peer system**—Peer-to-peer insurance gives interested persons the opportunity to organise into groups to offer each other insurance coverage under the (insurance) terms established by the group.[61] Additionally, peer-to-peer insurance platforms already exist, and some of them work to allay the common mistrust that policyholders have for traditional insurance companies due to the occasionally onerous process of enforcing an insurance claim and the challenging calculations of the insurance requirements.[62]

Blockchain products in insurance

Smart contracts are proving to be extremely beneficial in parametric insurance since they offer a simpler, more transparent solution to coverage than claim variables and are already being used to develop new products and services, these are some examples from the world:[63]

- *IBM*—providing a variety of smart contract solutions to the insurance industry, particularly those related to claims and underwriting, that have resulted in fewer fraud incidents, faster completion times, and increased customer trust;
- *Ryskex*—through its blockchain-based platform, Ryskex, an insurtech startup, enables insurers to more easily assess and manage risks;[64]
- *Fidentiax*—a blockchain marketplace for trading insurance policies, introduced its digital ledger product (ISLEY) for insurance policies in 2018 (users may store, view, and get notifications for their insurance portfolios using this tool that can be shared with specific loved ones via the ledger to support beneficiary distributions after death, the portfolios);[65]

---

60 Ibidem.

61 BaFin, "Big data meets artificial intelligence" (2018). Available at: https://www.bafin.de/SharedDocs/Downloads/EN/dl_bdai_studie_en.pdf?__blob=publicationFile&v=9 (Accessed 1 Oct 2022).

62 Ibidem.

63 Beinsure, "How Blockchain and Smart Contracts Transform Insurance and InsurTech?" (2022). Available at: https://beinsure.com/how-blockchain-smart-contracts-transforms-insurance (Accessed 30 Nov 2022).

64 Imaginovation, "Top 7 Use Cases of Blockchain in the Insurance Industry" (2022). Available at: https://imaginovation.net/blog/blockchain-insurance-industry-examples (Accessed 11 Nov 2022).

65 Ibidem.

- *Lemonade*—one of the fastest-growing insurers in the US, uses ledger and AI technology to offer smart contracts to consumers looking for homeowner and rental cover (the solution is economical and effective, with monthly policy premiums as little as $5–25 USD) and there is a set monthly charge that includes a portion for possible claim submissions (if a claim is lodged, Lemonade's blockchain-based contract can instantly determine loss and guarantee that payments are promptly provided to the customer)*;*
- *Nationwide Insurance*—the first insurer to use the blockchain for smart contracts, which let clients submit claims by validating their damages through police records and resulting in prompt payments;
- *Reask*—a climate-risk-focused technology insurtech startup that provides parametric cover for customers at risk of flood damage (when they take out the cover, a parameter for flood levels is pre-set and if that level is met, payments are automatically triggered).

3.4 A Comparative Case Study of Fizzy and Etherisc

The principal objective of this study is to assess and compare Etherisc and Fizzy, two divergent models within the insurance sector, investigating their strategies, challenges, and potential prospects. Also, the study examines how blockchain experts can assist traditional insurers in adopting blockchain technology.

In the evolving landscape of insurance, two distinct approaches to employing smart contracts have emerged. Etherisc, a pioneer in the field, prioritises decentralisation and seeks to reduce dependence on conventional insurers, while Fizzy, developed in-house, restricts access to its smart contracts exclusively to Axa, an established insurance company.[66] Blockchain expedites insurance claims processing: Etherisc is on a mission to streamline the often-lengthy process of settling insurance claims, a conventional process that typically spans several weeks.[67] It is worth emphasising that the speed and efficiency of claims processing are pivotal considerations for approximately 90% of policyholders when choosing an insurance provider.[68]

In the forthcoming discussion, we will delve into a thorough examination of both models:

- Etherisc

Founded in November 2017 by Stephan Karpischek, Christoph Mussenbrock, and Renat Khasanshyn, Etherisc operates on the Ethereum blockchain to establish a

[66] Hoffmann (2021), pp. 69–87.

[67] AIMultiple, "7 blockchain case studies from different industries in 2023" (2023). Available at: https://research.aimultiple.com/blockchain-case-studies/ (Accessed: October 12, 2023).

[68] Ibidem.

platform for decentralised insurance applications[69] Etherisc is a collaborative ecosystem that offers the tools and templates for individuals to create their insurance products. Its objectives encompass the provision of on-chain insurance, cost reduction, and the democratisation of reinsurance access via blockchain automation, consequently enhancing claims processing efficiency and security measures.[70] Etherisc utilises blockchain technology to streamline claims processing, offering a more efficient and cost-effective alternative through its "parametric insurance" structure that guarantees immediate predefined payouts based on specific weather conditions, making insurance more accessible and financially viable for beneficiaries.[71]

Since its inception, Etherisc has employed its platform to licence Crop Insurance and Flight Delay Insurance, both of which are decentralised with automated, nearly instantaneous payouts activated based on reported flood or drought events for Crop Insurance and reported flight cancellations or delays for Flight Delay Insurance.[72] Additionally, Etherisc is in the process of developing a prototype for Social Insurance, aimed at offering protection against the risks of death or illness among community members with immediate emergency payments to assist policyholders during critical periods.[73]

Etherisc operates on a "Decentralised Insurance Protocol" (DIP) token system, involving community members who contribute assets.[74] The DIP token, offers a permission-less and versatile method to assess, manage, and transfer various types of risks through a network of independent service providers, reducing the dependence on centralised entities (DIP encompasses the Decentralised Insurance Protocol and the Decentralised Insurance Platform).[75] The Protocol provides a framework for managing risks in a decentralised manner, and the system relies on DIP Tokens, with a total supply limited to 1 billion.[76] Users can engage with the Decentralised Insurance Platform by using DIP tokens, which they can stake to ensure proper performance, demonstrate their expertise, and generate income by offering services or skills within the system.[77] These DIP tokens offer three primary utilities: staking in risk pools, staking for quality and reputation, and staking for

[69] The Defiant, "What is Ethersic?" (2023). Available at: https://thedefiant.io/what-is-ethersic (Accessed 10 Oct 2023).

[70] Ibidem.

[71] The Defiant, "What is Ethersic?" (2023). Available at: https://thedefiant.io/what-is-ethersic (Accessed 10 Oct 2023).

[72] Etherisc, "Products built by the ETHERISC Community" Available at: https://etherisc.com (Accessed 13 Oct 2023).

[73] Etherisc, "Products built by the ETHERISC Community" Available at: https://etherisc.com (Accessed 13 Oct 2023).

[74] ITIJ, "ETHERISC launches Automated Blockchain Travel Insurance" (2022). Available at: http://www.itij.com/latest/news/etherisc-launches-automated-blockchain-travel-insurance (Accessed 24 Oct 2023).

[75] Etherisc, "Products built by the ETHERISC Community" Available at: https://etherisc.com (Accessed 13 Oct 2023).

[76] Ibidem.

[77] Ibidem.

governance, resembling lending Apps such as Aave or Compound, enabling DIP token holders to use them as collateral in risk pools to provide liquidity for insurance claims and receive rewards in accordance with the Etherisc staking model.[78] Etherisc token holders create insurance risk pools, similar to depositing money for loans on Aave, but instead, people can use Etherisc to automate flight delay coverage with smart contracts i.e. users sign up for policies online, and oracle networks track real-world conditions, like flight data, to trigger payouts if a flight is delayed for more than 45 min.[79] Specifically, Etherisc's application, FlightDelay, offers policies for global passenger flights and employs blockchain payments through Gnosis Chain.[80] FlightDelay simplifies the process, allowing policyholders to secure their flights, and if delayed for over 45 min, receive a payment directly to their wallet.[81] It combines Ethereum blockchain security with Chainlink's decentralised oracle framework, ensuring the security and reliability of flight insurance policies.[82] Built on Ethereum's decentralised security and supported by Chainlink's decentralised oracle framework, FlightDelay provides a transparent and secure flight insurance solution for policyholders. Collaborating with Chainlink's oracles and leveraging numerous premium data sources and a decentralised network of Chainlink nodes, Etherisc significantly mitigates the risk of single oracle failures and inaccurate data reporting, thereby ensuring a reliable claims process.

Some of the benefits that Etherisc enable are:[83]

- Facilitation of decentralised insurance applications.
- Enhancement of insurance transparency and fairness.
- Reduction of operational costs.
- Improved efficiency in buying and selling insurance.
- Provision of a common infrastructure, product templates, and insurance licence-as-a-service for creating custom insurance products.
- Fair distribution of value to independent workers and risk capital providers.

3.4.1 Challenges for Etherisc

- Absence of customer segmentation,
- Uncertain early-stage growth.

---

[78] The Defiant, "What is Ethersic?" (2023). Available at: https://thedefiant.io/what-is-ethersic (Accessed 10 Oct 2023).

[79] Ibidem.

[80] ITIJ, "ETHERISC launches Automated Blockchain Travel Insurance" (2022). Available at: http://www.itij.com/latest/news/etherisc-launches-automated-blockchain-travel-insurance (Accessed 24 Oct 2023).

[81] Ibidem.

[82] Ibidem.

[83] Knowledge for policy, "Competence Centre on Foresight" (2020). Available at: https://knowledge4policy.ec.europa.eu/foresight/tool/dlt4good/etherisc_en (Accessed 11 Oct 2023).

Etherisc's model faces challenges, as it lacks the tailored customer segmentation advantages of traditional insurers and requires substantial development time to establish a new token ecosystem, ensure platform security, and enhance resilience against moral hazards, resulting in an uncertain path toward achieving full functionality and a substantial customer base in its early stages.[84]

- Fizzy

One of the best examples of the use of a smart contract in insurance, launched in 2017, is the European company Axa. It introduced "Fizzy", a smart contract policy, which enables the policyholder to receive compensation automatically in the event of delay or cancellation of flight. A user could get flight insurance through a website up to five days before the flight after purchasing an airline ticket and the price of the insurance was calculated by a website's algorithm.[85] To detect when a flight has ended, the smart contract employed an external yet reputable flight status database as its oracle (smart contracts frequently use data sources and software that resides outside of the blockchain as their oracle) and specified that money should be provided to the consumer if the flight was cancelled or delayed by more than two hours.[86] Some of the challenges that AXA faced were:[87] One of the primary challenges was constructing a business case that could accurately forecast revenue and cost efficiencies, which were highly uncertain; Navigating the regulatory framework was another significant challenge that AXA encountered while launching Fizzy. It required extensive coordination within the organisation to determine which entity had the requisite licence to sell Fizzy and provide reinsurance. Regulatory complexity arose from the need to ensure that Fizzy's operation did not endanger the airline and insurance industries; Achieving complete automation in Fizzy's processes was a technical challenge due to the existing legacy technology. Unfortunately, after only two years, Fizzy was shut down due to inability to reach commercial targets therefore making it an unprofitable business for Axa.[88]

3.4.2 Challenges for Fizzy

- Ambitious financial goals.
- Early blockchain hurdles, partnership gaps, and marketing issues.
- Payout delays in blockchain.
- Significant blockchain expertise costs.

---

[84] Hoffmann (2021).

[85] Bitlaw, "Smart Contracts And The Law". Available at: https://www.bitlaw.com/blockchain/smart-contracts.html (Accessed 12 Oct 2022).

[86] Ibidem.

[87] Ibidem.

[88] Hoffmann (2021), p. 73.

Fizzy, developed in-house, faced the above-mentioned challenges leading to its discontinuation, primarily due to unrealistically high initial financial targets, despite its success in selling numerous contracts within a year, as the early stage of blockchain adoption in the insurance sector and the absence of strategic partnerships with third-party entities for sales expansion, along with suboptimal marketing efforts, presented notable shortcomings.[89]

Moreover, Fizzy's payout structure inefficiencies, causing delays in blockchain-based payments, coupled with the costly and inefficient acquisition of necessary blockchain expertise, established substantial entry barriers for smaller insurers venturing into blockchain technology adoption.[90]

3.4.3 Opportunity

- Blockchain specialists assist insurers.
- Valuable for established insurers.
- Leverages trust and industry success.

Etherisc leverages blockchain technology to automate claims processing by employing smart contracts, which enforce agreements upon meeting specific contract-defined conditions. This innovative approach includes third-party data providers responsible for validating compliance with the designated payment terms.[91] As a result, Etherisc swiftly notifies the insurance provider, leading to immediate evaluations of the initial claim investigation and policy validation procedures, significantly enhancing the efficiency of claims processing. In conclusion, through the implementation of blockchain technology in insurance claims processing, particularly within the framework of Etherisc, the time needed for claims settlement is diminished, and automated investigations into potentially fraudulent activities are conducted by leveraging data from third-party sources.[92]

Consequently, there seems to be an opportunity in the insurance market for a technology company specialising in blockchain expertise to assist in establishing blockchain-based insurance products for traditional insurers, offering substantial value to established insurance companies seeking blockchain adoption without the complexities of in-house development and leveraging the reputable brands of incumbent insurers to effectively address trust-related concerns and establish a successful presence in the industry.[93]

---

[89] Ibidem.

[90] Ibidem.

[91] AIMultiple, "7 blockchain case studies from different industries in 2023" (2023). Available at: https://research.aimultiple.com/blockchain-case-studies/ (Accessed: October 12, 2023).

[92] AIMultiple, "7 blockchain case studies from different industries in 2023" (2023). Available at: https://research.aimultiple.com/blockchain-case-studies/ (Accessed: October 12, 2023).

[93] Hoffmann (2021).

3.4.4 Conclusion

Finally, the summary of the comparative case study is as follows:

- Access and business model: Fizzy was an in-house creation by Axa, exclusively accessible to Axa's customers, while Etherisc is a decentralised platform accessible to diverse entities, fostering decentralisation in insurance, aiming to provide tools for a broader audience.
- Blockchain integration: Fizzy employed blockchain for flight insurance and relied on external oracles for data and Etherisc operates on the Ethereum blockchain, utilising blockchain for streamlined claims processing and is not limited to flight insurance.
- Challenges: Fizzy faced issues with ambitious financial goals, early blockchain complexities, partnership gaps, and payout delays, ultimately ceasing operation, on the other hand, Etherisc deals with challenges related to customer segmentation and early-stage growth but is actively developing its platform.
- Prospects: Fizzy was discontinued due to profitability challenges, while Etherisc continues to develop and expand its platform, addressing obstacles and seeking to grow its user base.

This comparative case study looks at two different paths in the insurance industry: Etherisc and Fizzy and suggests an opportunity for blockchain experts to assist established insurance companies in adopting blockchain-based insurance products. This approach leverages the trust and track record of established insurers while avoiding the complexity of in-house development, creating a strong foundation for success in the industry. Consequently, this opportunity could significantly impact the insurance industry, fostering innovation, efficiency, and security by offering advantages to both the insurance industry and consumers.

3.5 *Parametric Insurance and Smart Contracts*

A smart contract acts similarly to traditional parametric insurance (that uses triggers/indexes rather than claims to pay and offers pre-specified payouts upon a trigger event). The payouts are carried out after a clearly defined event takes place (a flood, an earthquake, or a flight delay).

However, a legal counsel should be consulted when deciding whether to use a smart contract to distribute a parametric policy to help ensure the policy complies with regulatory requirements in the relevant jurisdiction and that the parametric offering will be viewed by relevant regulatory authorities as an insurance product that can be properly underwritten and issued by the insurer.[94]

[94] Cassels, "The One Where Insurance Meets Blockchain and Parametrics" (2022). Available at: https://cassels.com/insights/the-one-where-insurance-meets-blockchain-and-parametrics (Accessed 12 Oct 2022).

In future, it is expected that smart contracts will replace insurance documents, blockchain "oracles" will replace claim adjusters, and decentralised autonomous organisations (DAOs) will take over traditional insurance carriers; millions of poor farmers in Africa and Asia will now be eligible for crop insurance coverage, whereas previously they were too poor and dispersed to justify the cost of underwriting.[95]

According to the United Nations, subsistence farming, in which families basically live off what they grow and almost nothing is left over, accounts for up to two-thirds of the developing world's three billion rural people who rarely qualify for insurance (and, if they did, they probably wouldn't know what to do with it), and also, insurance is difficult to obtain in underprivileged countries for a variety of reasons (for example, it cannot be easily distributed because there are not many local insurance agents or brokers).[96] Furthermore, insurance claims cannot be validated without significant expense because there are usually no claims adjusters on the scene to assess damage and by automating many traditional insurance processes, parametric insurance models have the potential to reduce producer costs, making it profitable to underwrite those previously deemed uninsurable.[97] These models, also known as "index insurance," insure a policyholder against a specific event by paying a fixed amount based on the magnitude of the event rather than the losses incurred (for example, if rain hasn't fallen in a predetermined region of Kenya for three weeks, a blockchain "oracle"—which could be a local weather station—sends a message to a smart contract, which remotely triggers a payout to the policyholder's smartphone and completely avoids the claims adjustment process)—meaning that it makes no difference whether a single farmer's field is harmed, all policyholders in the area have been compensated.[98]

Crop insurance is a good application for parametric models because many of the forces that can harm crops can be measured objectively, such as rainfall, wind speeds, temperatures, and others.

According to Sid Jha, founder, and CEO of Arbol, a parametric insurance provider, self-executing smart contracts also means that compensation for weather disasters and the like is nearly immediate, which is crucial in developing countries where many farmers live on the edge.[99]

To summarise, while blockchain-enabled smart contracts can ensure that impoverished farmers receive payouts almost immediately during disasters, and parametric insurance models may allow insurance underwriters to pool risks, making it profitable to insure the previously uninsurable, much work remains to be donc to

---

[95] Cointelegraph, "Smart contract-enabled insurance holds promise, but can it be scaled?" (2022). Available at: https://cointelegraph.com/news/smart-contract-enabled-insurance-holds-promise-but-can-it-be-scaled (Accessed 1 Nov 2022).

[96] Cointelegraph, "Smart contract-enabled insurance holds promise, but can it be scaled?" (2022). Available at: https://cointelegraph.com/news/smart-contract-enabled-insurance-holds-promise-but-can-it-be-scaled (Accessed 1 Nov 2022).

[97] Ibidem.

[98] Ibidem.

[99] Ibidem.

persuade farmers to sign up for such programs. The concept of parametric insurance is not brand-new, it has been around for a while, however, its use cases are still primarily, if not entirely, in the pilot stage, however, state agencies might need to get involved because technology alone will not solve the problem.

A forecast is that the application of smart contracts in insurance will change the entire insurance industry by introducing new products and services. So far, various countries have begun to use blockchain and smart contracts, in the following are some examples:[100]

- Italy—parametric policies for travel/holidays insurance or for coverage of damages to crops in the agri-food industry, blockchain has been tested for dispute resolution;
- The Netherlands—pension funds (value transfer and personal information sharing between pension fund and the Ministry of the Interior Relations);
- Portugal—Aliança Portuguesa de Blockchain—developing a new insurance product based on smart contracts for sports events;
- Hungary—ski insurance automatically compensates for the damage due to bad weather conditions or the technical fault of the lifts (users are allowed to customise the conditions of their travel insurance and the contract is recorded as a smart contract in a public blockchain and if the requirements are satisfied, the consumer will automatically get the compensation without a claim process);
- Insurwave—international project—"launched in 2018 – the idea to connect all stakeholders in the insurance value chain with the same risk information (the platform uses blockchain to support marine hull insurance).

3.6 *Challenges of Smart Contracts in Insurance Law*

So far, we have witnessed that the use of smart contracts in insurance law has been accompanied by various challenges. The implementation of the new technology may present new risks to insurance companies, supervisors, and customers even while it has the potential to improve business operations' efficiency and reduce some existing dangers. Moreover, having in mind the very early stages of blockchain and smart contract development and implementation, as well as the lack of prior experience, it is challenging to predict both the potential risks of blockchain and smart contracts as well as their benefits.[101] However, some of the challenges that have already been noted are:

[100] EIOPA, "Discussion paper on blockchain and smart contracts in insurance" (2021). Available at: https://www.eiopa.europa.eu/sites/default/files/publications/consultations/eiopa-discussion-paper-on-blockchain-29-04-2021.pdf (Accessed 12 Oct 2022).

[101] EIOPA, "Discussion paper on blockchain and smart contracts in insurance" (2021). Available at: https://www.eiopa.europa.eu/sites/default/files/publications/consultations/eiopa-discussion-paper-on-blockchain-29-04-2021.pdf (Accessed 12 Oct 2022).

- *Legal and Regulatory Uncertainty:* Smart contracts, being a relatively new technology, have brought about significant legal and regulatory uncertainty. One of the biggest debates in the legal literature is whether or not a smart contract qualifies as a contract in the legal sense, and the majority of the legal literature appears to disagree, claiming that a smart contract can only execute the parties' contractual rights automatically and cannot, in and of itself, contain their rights.[102] Following that line of reasoning, a court could rule that a smart contract is not a legally binding contract if an insurer wishes to utilise it exclusively as an insurance contract without a separate agreement, so an insurance undertaking may run the risk of being subject to regulatory remedies if it introduces a blockchain application where the legal observance of applicable regulations is in question because such a situation would most likely be detrimental to the interests of an insured person.[103] While smart contracts are designed to be self-executing and automate the process of contract execution, their legal enforceability remains untested in many jurisdictions. Therefore, there is an urgent need to align these contracts with existing legal frameworks and regulations to ensure their compliance, especially keeping in mind the specifics of the insurance sector.

Some challenges are generally connected to their status as an emerging technology and the blockchain's decentralised structure that may introduce vulnerabilities not present in conventional centralised solutions.[104] Although automation and the lack of intermediaries undoubtedly lower costs associated with the phase of fulfilling obligations and storing information, they also lower the risk of potential errors and fraud (improving, concurrently, the speed of transactions and, most importantly, encouraging the establishment of reliable relationships among all blockchain participants). Considering the growing interest in the potential benefits of smart contracts, legal experts and researchers have recently published a paper in which they propose a framework for analysing the legal issues that may arise from the use of smart contracts.

- *Limited flexibility:* Smart contracts, being self-executing digital contracts with pre-coded terms, may not be able to incorporate the complexity of certain insurance claims that involve human judgement or interpretation. These types of claims may require an insurance adjuster to assess the situation and use their expertise to determine the appropriate course of action. In contrast, smart contracts are unable to account for such human factors and may therefore be limited in their application. To specify, the insurer is the one who decides on the amount of compensation based on special circumstances that differ in each insurance contract, however, a smart contract cannot automatically repeat this action.

[102] Friehoff (2020), p. 311.

[103] Ibidem.

[104] EIOPA, "Discussion paper on blockchain and smart contracts in insurance" (2021). Available at: https://www.eiopa.europa.eu/sites/default/files/publications/consultations/eiopa-discussion-paper-on-blockchain-29-04-2021.pdf (Accessed 12 Oct 2022).

Therefore, although it is evident that smart contracts contribute to legal certainty in general, their character trait, irreversibility, is at the same time a shortcoming.

- *Programming complexity and lack of knowledge:* Creating smart contracts demands specific programming skills, especially on blockchain platforms like Ethereum. This complexity can make it challenging for widespread adoption, as insurers may need specialised expertise to handle these contracts. Not only that, but there is a general lack of knowledge on blockchain. Consequently, insurer often rely heavily on external platforms and IT suppliers. Moreover, the so-called bugs in code pose a significant problem since if at least one vital piece is missing, the contract will not run. Then, their scope is limited due to the difficulty of translating into code some parts of the contract. The presence of programming errors or vulnerabilities within the code of a smart contract can give rise to substantial ramifications. A minor oversight or omission in the code can render the entire contract non-functional, potentially culminating in substantial financial losses and contentious legal disputes.
- *Data privacy and security:* Smart contracts involve the collection and storage of sensitive data (information concerning policyholders, beneficiaries, and the specifics of insurance contracts), a matter of increasing significance due to the escalating cybersecurity risks. This, in turn, gives rise to legal and privacy concerns, as it involves accumulating substantial data and the potential for its indirect use, which may not comply with legal regulations. Developers of smart contracts and insurance providers must implement robust data protection measures to safeguard this information from unauthorised access.
- *Absence of amicable termination*: The absence of an amicable termination can be a limitation in situations where insurance parties need to adapt to changing circumstances, modify the terms of the contract, or negotiate claims since insurance contracts often involve complex and evolving scenarios, such as adjusting coverage, revising terms, or accommodating unforeseen developments. With smart contracts, these adjustments are not easily achievable, as the contracts are self-executing and immutable. This could be portrayed as a significant challenge, as there may be scenarios where parties need to mutually agree to terminate or amend a contract due to changing risk profiles, policyholders requests, or other unforeseen circumstances. Finally, the parties involved may need to resort to legal remedies or create additional contracts to address these situations, potentially increasing administrative burdens and costs.
- *Incompatibility with existing legal Rules:* One of the primary obstacles in the application of a smart contract is the inconsistency of legal rules with technological innovations. The successful creation of an adequate legal framework with the integration of technology is crucial for the automation of insurance contracts. However, that can be very challenging since the legal landscape varies significantly from one jurisdiction to another.
- *Reinsurance complexities:* In reinsurance, given that the reinsurer decides on the amount of compensation based on special circumstances that differ in each contract, no smart contract can automatically repeat such an action. The (re)insurer that paid the claim now owns all of the claimant's rights in relation to the

indemnified event, including potential future recovery and subrogation (the insured's legal right to seek recovery from a third party), none of which are contained in the smart contract.[105]

To conclude, it is certain that smart contracts in insurance law raise a variety of ethical and practical challenges although they can completely transform the entire industry. Despite the fact that automation and the lack of intermediaries undoubtedly lower costs associated with the phase of fulfilling obligations and storing information, they also lower the risk of potential errors and fraud (improving, concurrently, the speed of transactions and, most importantly, encouraging the establishment of reliable relationships among all blockchain participants). In light of the growing interest in the potential benefits of smart contracts, legal experts and researchers have recently published a paper in which they propose a framework for analysing the legal issues that may arise from the use of smart contracts.[106]

4 Conclusion

Finally, the aforementioned cases of potential and current blockchain applications in insurance demonstrate how the insurance sector could significantly benefit gain a lot from the technology. It can also assist established insurance companies in addressing issues including low client engagement, slow growth in the mature markets, and ongoing digitalization trends. Additionally, there is a possibility that previously uninsured people could be offered new insurance models using blockchain—and smart contract-based insurance concepts. Despite all of this potential, a project needs to take the regulatory framework into account when assessing the introduction of blockchain applications.

While the technology for the execution of smart contracts is available, the development of blockchain-based insurance products is still in its early stages. Thus, there are only a few products available at this moment. Notably, much work remains to be done regarding smart contracts and their implementation, keeping in mind that the smart contract space has an enormous potential for adoption, growth, and expansion.

The conclusion is that the digitisation process in insurance can significantly improve business relations, trust and secure exchange of data and information, while also reducing costs. Also, to enhance insurance services, it is significant to note that, in the future, smart contracts could have an important impact on the handling of claims and payments. Therefore, to enable smart contracts to reach their full potential, it is necessary to create an adequate regulatory framework, especially considering the current discrepancy of legal rules with technological innovations.

---

[105] Ledgerinsights, "Can blockchain smart contracts replace (re)insurance contracts?" (2019). Available at: https://www.ledgerinsights.com/blockchain-smart-contracts-insurance (Accessed 11 Nov 2022).

[106] Durovic and Janssen (2019).

References

Books, Book Chapters, and Articles

Cohn A, West T, Parker C (2017) Smart after all: blockchain, smart contracts, parametric insurance, and smart energy grids. Georgetown Law Technol Rev 1(2):273–304. https://doi.org/10.2139/ssrn.3023676

Durovic A (2020) Smart contracts as an innovation in insurance law. Pravo i Privreda 58:305–317

Durovic M, Janssen A (2019) The formation of smart contracts and beyond: shaking the fundamentals of contract law? In: Smart contracts and blockchain technology: role of contract law. Cambridge University Press, Cambridge

Friehoff L (2020) Blockchain in the insurance industry: implications and legal boundaries. Leg Revol - E-J Bus Law Digit 305–321

Hoffmann CH (2021) A double design-science perspective of entrepreneurship – the example of smart contracts in the insurance market. J Work-Appl Manag 13(1):69–87

Kiviat TI (2015) Beyond Bitcoin: issues in regulating blockchain transactions. Duke Law J 65:569–608. https://scholarship.law.duke.edu/dlj/vol65/iss3/4

Kolber AJ (2018) Not-so-smart blockchain contracts and artificial responsibility. Stanford Technol Law Rev 21(2):198–234

Raskin M (2017) The law and legality of smart contracts. Georgetown Law Technol Rev 305–341 1:304. https://ssrn.com/abstract=2959166 or https://doi.org/10.2139/ssrn.2842258

Temte MN (2019) Blockchain challenges traditional contract law: just how smart are smart contracts? Wyoming Law Rev 19:87–117

Tomić K (2018) Blockchain tehnologija, pametni ugovori i njihova implementacija u industriji osiguranja. In: Insurance law and practice - challenges, new technologies, and corporate governance. Association of Serbian Insurers and Association for Insurance Law of Serbia, p 136

Tsung-Chih H, Hsieh N-K, Chang C-Y, Chen T-L (2023) Research on the application of smart contracts in travel insurance claims. Heliyon. Posted: Jun 28, 2023 [Preprint]. Available at SSRN: https://ssrn.com/abstract=4480435

Other Resources

Adam-Kalfon P, El Moutaouakil S (2017) Blockchain, a catalyst for new approaches in insurance. PWC. https://www.pwc.ch/en/publications/2017/Xlos_Etude_Blockchain_UK_2017_Web.pdf. Accessed 22 Sep 2022

Amaral M (2021) Blockchain and smart contracts: regulatory challenges and regulatory approaches. OECD Publishing. https://doi.org/10.1787/fbf2ebe9-en. Accessed 2 Oct 2022

BaFin (2018) Big data meets artificial intelligence. https://www.bafin.de/SharedDocs/Downloads/EN/dl_bdai_studie_en.pdf?__blob=publicationFile&v=9. Accessed 1 Oct 2022

Benichou L (2018) Ep. 22 – Fizzy, AXA's blockchain case study. Insureblocks. https://insureblocks.com/?p=2833. Accessed 10 Oct 2023

Catalini C, Gans J (2016) Some simple economics of the blockchain. National Bureau of Economic Research, Cambridge. https://doi.org/10.3386/w22952. Accessed 11 Oct 2022

Competence Centre on Foresight (2020) Etherisc. Knowledge for policy. https://knowledge4policy.ec.europa.eu/foresight/tool/dlt4good/etherisc_en. Accessed 11 Oct 2023

Cuenca O (2022) ETHERISC launches automated blockchain travel insurance. ITIJ. http://www.itij.com/latest/news/etherisc-launches-automated-blockchain-travel-insurance. Accessed 24 Oct 2023

Da Costa R, Goodman G (2022) The one where insurance meets blockchain and parametrics. Cassels. https://cassels.com/insights/the-one-where-insurance-meets-blockchain-and-parametrics. Accessed 12 Oct 2022

Derebail A (2018) Three areas in the insurance industry to use blockchain. IBM. https://www.ibm.com/blogs/blockchain/2018/03/three-areas-in-the-insurance-industry-to-use-blockchain. Accessed 10 Oct 2022
Dilmegani C (2023) 7 blockchain case studies from different industries in 2023. AIMultiple. Available at: https://research.aimultiple.com/blockchain-case-studies/. Accessed 12 Oct 2023
Edmonds C (2019) Can blockchain smart contracts replace (re)insurance contracts? Ledger Insights. https://www.ledgerinsights.com/blockchain-smart-contracts-insurance. Accessed 11 Nov 2022
EIOPA (2021) Discussion paper on blockchain and smart contracts in insurance. https://www.eiopa.europa.eu/sites/default/files/publications/consultations/eiopa-discussion-paper-on-blockchain-29-04-2021.pdf. Accessed 12 Oct 2022
England J (2022) How blockchain and smart contracts transform insurance and InsurTech? Beinsure. https://beinsure.com/how-blockchain-smart-contracts-transforms-insurance. Accessed 30 Nov 2022
EU Blockchain Observatory and Forum (2020) 2018-2020 Conclusions and Reflections. https://blockchain-observatory.ec.europa.eu/document/download/2df0bb3c-61fd-4ac6-921b-ff50fc32aeb9_en?filename=report_conclusion_book_v1.0.pdf. Accessed 11 Oct 2022
Georgiou M (2022) Top 7 use cases of blockchain in the insurance industry. Imaginovation. https://imaginovation.net/blog/blockchain-insurance-industry-examples. Accessed 11 Nov 2022
Herpy J (2022) Smart contracts and the law: what you need to know. Forbes. https://www.forbes.com/sites/forbesbusinesscouncil/2022/03/17/smart-contracts-and-the-law-what-you-need-to-know/?sh=1054aeda3d03. Accessed Sep 2022
Kemp L Blockchain applications in insurance. Deloitte. https://www2.deloitte.com/content/dam/Deloitte/ch/Documents/innovation/ch-en-innovation-deloitte-blockchain-app-in-insurance.pdf. Accessed 11 Oct 2023
Nambiampurath R (2023) What is Ethersic? The Defiant. https://thedefiant.io/what-is-ethersic. Accessed 10 Oct 2023
Products built by the ETHERISC Community. Etherisc. https://etherisc.com. Accessed 13 Oct 2023
Singer A (2022) Smart contract-enabled insurance holds promise, but can it be scaled? Cointelegraph. https://cointelegraph.com/news/smart-contract-enabled-insurance-holds-promise-but-can-it-be-scaled. Accessed 1 Nov 2022
Smart contracts (2021) Law Commission. https://www.lawcom.gov.uk/project/smart-contracts. Accessed 20 Dec 2022
Team I (2023) Smart contracts development for insurance companies. Itexus. https://itexus.com/smart-contracts-development-for-insurance-companies. Accessed 9 Oct 2023
Tysver D Smart contracts and the law. Bitlaw. https://www.bitlaw.com/blockchain/smart-contracts.html. Accessed 12 Oct 2022
Volos A (2020) The technology of blockchain and smart contract and their regulation under the conflict of laws of the European Union. Advances in Economics, Business and Management Research (2nd International Scientific and Practical Conference on Digital Economy (ISCDE 2020)) 156:563–568
Whitmore G (2022) Will you purchase blockchain flight delay insurance? Forbes. https://www.forbes.com/sites/geoffwhitmore/2022/01/21/will-you-purchase-blockchain-flight-delay-insurance/?sh=5c5a79316dca. Accessed 13 Oct 2023

Andrea Durovic Simikic is currently pursuing a Doctor of Laws degree in Insurance Law focusing on Innovations in Insurance Law at the Faculty of Law, University of Belgrade in Serbia. She holds a Master of Laws from the same institution and a Master of International Business from Università Cattolica del Sacro Cuore in Milan, Italy. Andrea works as a Legal Counsel for an international IT company, specialising in contract drafting, IP management, legal research, GDPR compliance, and international legal matters. Beyond her corporate role, Andrea is a prolific author, contributing several insightful articles on topics such as the impact of smart contracts on insurance law and the adoption of regulatory directives in the insurance sector. She actively participates in seminars and conferences across Europe, enriching her understanding of global legal dynamics.

Smart Contracts and the "Oracle Problem" in the Context of InsurTech

Eliza Mik

1 Introduction

Smart contracts are associated with disintermediation and certainty.[1] Deterministic, infallible, and unbiased code replaces unpredictable, corrupt, and biased humans. By eliminating humans from the process of performing contractual obligations, smart contracts eliminate the need to trust the other contracting party as well the need to rely on traditional intermediaries—including insurance companies. Once deployed, the code of the smart contract cannot be modified, and its execution cannot be stopped. This guarantees absolute adherence to the rules expressed thereby.[2] In the context of InsurTech, such rules are synonymous with the terms of an insurance policy. When the policy is set in stone (or *code*!), payouts are guaranteed when the relevant event occurs. Code cannot change its mind or decide to deviate from what was agreed. Ideally then, insurance policies could be made into smart contracts, revolutionizing the insurance industry by lowering transaction costs and delegating the compensation process to objective, trustless code. Ideally, this will result in a faster, fairer, less bureaucratic, and more cost-effective process of helping victims of natural disasters or, in more mundane scenarios, compensating insureds in developing nations, where insurance is unavailable or simply too expensive. There will be no investigation of the claim, no verification of the event and, most importantly, no human discretion. No pesky claim investigator will question the insured's

[1] Kalbantner (2021); Wood (2015).

[2] Szabo (1997).

E. Mik (✉)
Chinese University of Hong Kong, Shatin, New Territories, Hong Kong
e-mail: elizamik@cuhk.edu.hk

C. Poncibò, P. Tereszkiewicz (eds.), *European Insurance Law within the Digital Age*, AIDA Europe Research Series on Insurance Law and Regulation 14,
https://doi.org/10.1007/978-3-031-96496-1_12

entitlement or adopt a creative interpretation of the insurance policy to avoid or delay payout. A helpless flood victim *will* receive a payout when a specified area experiences heavy rainfall and a humble farmer whose crops suffered from a sudden drop in temperature *will* be compensated. We are told that:

> Novel insurance products like blockchain-based parametric insurance (BBPI) have the potential to amplify coverage among climate-vulnerable households. Parametric insurance (PI) does not require on-the-ground inspections, as settlements are based on pre-determined triggers that are linked to independent, objective measures that are correlated with damages. Integrating PI on the blockchain via 'smart contracts' benefits the insurers and policyholders by automating claims, enhancing trust, increasing transparency and ensuring immutability on securely distributed ledgers.[3]

Hidden behind such optimistic narratives is a technological reality that is far from promising. Given the preponderance of vulnerabilities in smart contracts, as well as their dependence on external data sources, it is necessary to re-examine the premises of technology-driven improvements to insurance practices that are—or could be—provided by blockchain-based smart contracts. The relevant technologies are complex, but the points made in this paper are simple. Neither blockchains nor smart contracts interface with the outside world. A smart contract devoid of access to information about real world events, such as weather data, is largely pointless. In the present context, insurance payouts are inextricably linked to occurrences relating to localised weather or seismic events, not to fluctuations in the prices of crypto currencies.[4] To gain relevance in InsurTech, smart contracts must be able to release funds (i.e., the agreed payout) in response to events extrinsic to the blockchain. For that to happen, they must be provided with information about what is happening in the real-world ("off-chain information"). Examples are the aforementioned weather data or the occurrence of natural disasters. Entities providing such information are called "oracles."

Throughout the discussion, it must be remembered that the fundamental idea underlying the use of smart contracts in InsurTech is that the verification of the fulfilment of the payment conditions *and* the payout occur automatically. The necessity to involve a human at any stage of the compensation process contradicts the very purpose of smart contracts.

[3] Sandland et al. (2019), pp. 89, 90; Cohn et al. (2017), p. 273.

[4] It is important to distinguish information about market events, which are relevant in the context of DeFi from information about weather and seismic events, which are more difficult to obtain, see: Chainlink blog, 'Market Manipulation vs. Oracle Exploits', 14 December 2022. Accessed 22 Oct 2024. https://blog.chain.link/market-manipulation-vs-oracle-exploits/.

1.1 Outline of the Argument

It is necessary to distinguish facts from fiction. The success of smart contracts is premised on the ability to solve multiple technical problems. To this end, this paper disentangles the interdependencies between blockchains, smart contracts and oracles. In principle, smart contracts operate on-chain and "codify the conditions" of releasing the payout. Oracles operate outside of the blockchain, or off-chain, and provide information regarding the fulfilment of such conditions. Smart contracts are supposed to guarantee that if X occurs, the funds will be released. The challenge lies in *describing* X (i.e., the triggering event, which is synonymous with the release conditions) in a programming language and in *determining* whether they have been met, that is, whether X has occurred. To this end, the discussion focuses on the technical challenges of creating secure, and robust smart contracts and oracles that could be entrusted with automating insurance payouts. For the sake of simplicity, it is assumed that the policyholder and the insured are the same person. It is also useful to limit the discussion to parametric insurance, as the necessity of involving a claims investigator contradicts the idea of eliminating human involvement. Traditional insurance would, by definition, require the interposition of an investigator, who would introduce human discretion and thus uncertainty into the compensation process. For both practical and ideological reasons, parametric insurance is the only viable candidate for blockchain-based smart contracts.

Two important qualifications are required. First, the only way to *guarantee* payout is for the relevant funds to be locked-in *ex ante*. If the funds are not available at the time the insurance policy is encoded in the smart contract, there can be no guarantee that they *will be available* when the triggering event occurs. The smart contract can only guarantee payout if it controls the funds to be paid out before the triggering event. The need to lock-in a certain amount of funds, however, constrains the financial feasibility of blockchain-based insurance. Second, as smart contracts *by definition* can only control and release cryptocurrencies, the insured must be willing to accept payouts in the form of cryptocurrencies. This may present a significant constraint given the limited uptake of cryptocurrencies in many economies and their extreme price volatility. Any reduction in transaction costs and the benefits of prompt payout may be annihilated in the event of a price decline of the cryptocurrency used for such payout. Moreover, it is questionable whether the proverbial farmer in a developing country will have the requisite technological literacy to accept and convert crypto-currencies.

2 The Role of Blockchains

It is useful to commence the discussion with a brief clarification of the role of blockchains and their main attributes. In principle, blockchains are supposed to be "trustless," that is: eliminate the need for trust.[5] Blockchain aficionados *believe* that something is "trustless" if it is decentralised.[6] If no single entity controls a system and if each node in the system is controlled by different entity,[7] then such a system eliminates the need to trust humans or traditional institutions, including courts, banks and insurance companies. In such a context, "trustlessness" denotes independence from such entities. From a technical perspective, however, the term "trustlessness" has different connotations and denotes the ability to determine the truth of certain information without recourse to a trusted third party in an adversarial environment where no-one can be trusted.[8] [T—no external confirmation] In simpler terms: trustlessness addresses the problem of how to achieve consensus among participants who cannot trust each other, but who must agree on some state of affairs without external confirmation. . Interestingly, in the context of blockchains, such "state of affairs" relates exclusively to the state of the blockchain or, more specifically, to the crypto-currencies recorded therein. The latter are generated by the consensus algorithm as an incentive provided to those who expand computational resources to append subsequent blocks and thus maintain the blockchain.[9] It follows that "trustlessness" only pertains to information about the state, or contents, of the blockchain. The term should not be used in relation to entities or organisations. This leads to the need to address the misunderstandings surrounding the concept of validation. Purportedly, blockchains "validate things" and can therefore serve as sources of truth.[10] In principle, "validation" denotes the process of establishing the accuracy, completeness, or authenticity of something.

In the blockchain context, however, validation has a narrower meaning and refers to the process of verifying the technical correctness of the computations leading to the addition of blocks and the inclusion of transactions in such blocks. In principle, blockchains are designed to provide a secure and decentralised way of storing and verifying information that is generated within the blockchain network. The key words in the preceding sentence are "information generated within the blockchain network." In the blockchain context, validation is limited to the verification whether

---

[5] Werbach (2018), pp. 17–25.

[6] Antonopoulos and Wood (2020), p. 10; Narayanan et al. (2016), pp. 278–283.

[7] Walch (2019), p. 39.

[8] "Trustlessness" is related to the Byzantine Generals' Problem, which is a classic problem in distributed computing and involves coordinating a group of actors who may be malicious or unreliable. It involves a group of generals, located in different places, trying to coordinate an attack. The generals can only communicate through messages, but some of the generals may be traitors who want to sabotage the attack; see Lampert et al. (1982), p. 382.

[9] For a description see: Antonopoulos (2017), p. 26.

[10] Casey and Vigna (2018).

the technical requirements of the relevant consensus algorithm have been met.[11] It does not—and cannot—encompass any information about events occurring off-chain, outside of the blockchain. Blockchains are distributed, cryptographically secured databases that are completely insulated from anything that happens "outside of them." The inscription of any information in a database does not render such information true or accurate, even if the database itself is technologically superior . This problem is commonly described as "garbage in/garbage out." As indicated, the only type of information contained in a blockchain that can be regarded as *always* true and accurate is the information pertaining to the addition of blocks (and the inclusion of transactions in such blocks) and, consequently, to the native cryptocurrencies generated as a reward for such addition. In sum, blockchains cannot validate anything outside of them and the inscription of information *in* them does not "magically" make such information true and correct—unless the information pertains to certain narrowly defined computations occurring "in" the blockchain itself. "Trustlessness" and "validation" are narrowly defined technical concepts that concern the operation of consensus algorithms. In InsurTech, blockchains can be used to store insurance policies and claim-related information but without assurances of their authenticity or correctness. They can also serve as execution platforms for smart contracts embodying the terms of individual policies and managing the release of native cryptocurrencies upon the occurrence of agreed events.

3 The Role of Smart Contracts

Smart contracts do not have a single, generally accepted definition. They have been described as "systems which automatically move digital assets according to arbitrary pre-specified rules,"[12] or the embedding of legal terms in hardware and software to prevent breach.[13] A technical paper defines a smart contract as a "collection of code and data (sometimes referred to as functions and state) that is deployed using cryptographically signed transactions on the blockchain network."[14] As has been described elsewhere,[15] there are no doctrinal obstacles for smart contracts to be contracts in the legal sense. The point here is not, however, to debate whether they are or can be legally enforceable agreements or whether it is legally admissible to "transform" insurance policies into smart contracts.[16] The point is that, in practice, most smart contracts are mechanisms of controlling and transferring cryptocurrencies. In the context of InsurTech, smart contracts can embody the conditions

[11] Antonopoulos (2017), pp. 24, 25.

[12] Buterin (2015).

[13] Szabo (1997); Lutz (2021).

[14] Yaga et al. (2018), p. 54.

[15] See, generally, Mik (2017), p. 1.

[16] Guadamuz (2019), pp. 1–2.

of releasing certain funds that are stored within a given blockchain. After all, each insurance policy can be regarded as a conditional payment obligation: if a certain event occurs, a specified amount will be released to the specified person. Unlike traditional insurance policies, which only document the agreement between the insurance company and the policy holder but do not perform any aspect of the compensation process, smart contracts not only embody the terms of the policy but constitute the performance mechanism. In other words, traditional insurance policies are passive documents whereas smart contracts are active computer programs that do not "just" document but actually "do something." Despite the unquestionable appeal of delegating the payout process to "blockchain-based code," the idea of representing an insurance policy by means of a smart contract must be approached with scepticism.

3.1 (Some) Problems with Smart Contracts

The ability of smart contracts to deliver on their promise is premised on the ability to write correct and predictable code. It is generally overlooked that "[a] smart contract will execute exactly what is written, which is not always what the programmer intended"[17] or "what the agreeing parties thought it would do."[18] Executing "as coded" is not synonymous with "achieving what was agreed" or "intended." The smart contract will execute *inclusive and irrespective of* any technical irregularities contained therein. It is thus necessary to criticise the blind belief in the superiority of this technology. It is also crucial to understand the technical underpinnings of smart contracts, which ultimately determine what they can or cannot do.

At the outset, it is necessary to distinguish between blockchains and smart contracts. As indicated, blockchains are distributed databases and are, first and foremost, designed to generate, store and transfer cryptocurrencies. It follows that the characteristics of blockchains, including their security and reliability assumptions, relate only to the existence of such cryptocurrencies and to the mechanisms of their generation and transfer. Consequently, although smart contracts execute *on* blockchains, they are not *like* blockchains. Smart contracts are written by human developers and are subsequently deployed (i.e., placed) on the blockchain.[19] When called, smart contracts are *executed* by the individual, distributed nodes in a blockchain system, which also run the consensus algorithm that generates individual blocks.

[17] Antonopoulos and Wood (2020), p. 171.

[18] The Ethereum website states: "A smart contract is code that lives on the Ethereum blockchain and runs exactly as programmed. Once smart contracts are deployed on the network you can't change them. (…) This also means you need to design your contracts very carefully and test them thoroughly." https://ethereum.org/en/developers/docs/dapps/.

[19] Technically, the code is not run "on the blockchain" but, in most instances, on the Ethereum Virtual Machine, see: Cohney and Hoffman (2020), pp. 340–344.

Smart contracts are not, however, *validated* by such an algorithm.[20] While consensus algorithms can determine whether the technical conditions for the generation of a new block have been fulfilled, they cannot determine whether a smart contract is technically correct and thus whether it will execute as planned. Consequently, smart contracts are neither "trustless" nor secure. The fact that they operate on blockchains affects the manner of their execution but not the quality of their code. Like all other computer programs, smart contracts often contain errors and vulnerabilities.[21] The former are mistakes in the implementation of a system design that result in programs not providing the intended functionality or producing unexpected results. The latter enables the malicious misuse of a system implementation to achieve effects contradicting its goals. Smart contracts are, in fact, notorious for such errors and vulnerabilities.[22] These problems are further aggravated by the fact that, once deployed on a blockchain, the code of the smart contract becomes immutable and hence impossible to correct. The broader technical shortcomings of smart contracts derive from three sets of interrelated problems.

The first set concerns the new execution environment, i.e., the type of location where the instructions contained in the code are implemented.[23] Given their decentralised and distributed nature, blockchains provide an execution environment that is robust in terms of availability and tamper-resistance. We are, after all, dealing with hundreds if not thousands of independent nodes blindly following the consensus algorithm. This means that, once deployed, smart contracts will continue operating and cannot be stopped or interfered with. This does not mean, however, that smart contracts will always operate as intended. Guaranteeing uninterrupted operation is not synonymous with ensuring predictable and consistent output. Blockchains do not protect smart contracts from unexpected interactions with other smart contracts or from the inadvertent execution of untrusted code.[24] Once deployed, a given smart contract may start interacting with other smart contracts, rendering it impossible to predict how that specific smart contract will execute. Consequently, even assuming that a particular smart contract did not contain programming errors or vulnerabilities, its correct execution cannot be guaranteed given the dangers posed by potential interactions with other smart contracts operating on the same blockchain. This problem is particularly pertinent in permissionless blockchains, such as

---

[20] Antonopoulos and Wood (2020), p. 320.

[21] A vulnerability can be caused by a coding error, but it is not the same as a coding error. A coding error is a mistake made by a programmer in the writing of the code that causes the code to behave in an unintended way. A vulnerability, on the other hand, is a weakness in the system or software that can be exploited by an attacker. A coding error can be the source of a vulnerability if it leads to a weakness in the system. However, vulnerabilities can also arise poor design practices, misconfigured systems, or lack of adequate input validation; see generally: McConnell (2004), p. 521.

[22] Aquilina et al. (2021); Zheng et al. (2020), p. 475.

[23] Schneidewind et al. (2021).

[24] Technically, permissionless blockchains constitute hostile computing environments, see generally: Kannengießer et al. (2020).

Ethereum, where anyone—including novice, malicious and plainly incompetent coders—is permitted to create and deploy smart contracts.

The second set of problems concerns the number and complexity of computational steps that can be executed in a distributed environment, that is, *on* the blockchain. This technical detail is particularly relevant because it circumscribes the practical capabilities of smart contracts, that is: what instructions they can execute. When extolling their great economic potential, it is often forgotten that on Ethereum, which remains the dominant blockchain for smart contracts, all "on-chain" computations[25] are extremely limited because they are constrained by the price of gas (a sub-unit of Ether) and by the amount of gas available in a block.[26] To prevent overloading the Ethereum network, computationally intensive (speak: complex) smart contracts are also more expensive.[27] Consequently, smart contracts must be kept simple and cannot express more elaborate instructions. In practice, it is infeasible to encode anything but the most basic terms of an insurance policy, possibly only the release conditions themselves, but not any elaborate legal terms.

Lastly, the third set of problems concerns the novel programming languages in which smart contracts are written. It is rarely appreciated that blockchains require specialised languages that are tailored to the characteristics of distributed execution environments. As indicated, the latter present multiple technical constraints in terms of computing resources, complexity, and security.[28] Traditionally, the focus is placed on the question whether a particular programming language is Turing complete, meaning that it can express any algorithm or solve any computable problem, given sufficient time and resources.[29] In simpler terms, Turing-completeness can be regarded as synonymous with being expressive and powerful. Theoretically then, Turing-complete languages would enable the encoding of more complex release conditions, which, in turn, might enable the creation of elaborate insurance policies. It is, for example, common to emphasise the Turing-completeness of Ethereum's programming language, Solidity, and praise its ability to create more sophisticated smart contracts.[30] It is overlooked, however, that Turing-complete programming

---

[25] Technically, most smart contracts are executed "in" a virtual machine, such as the Ethereum Virtual Machine (EVM), an abstract computing environment that emulates the functionality of a physical computer.

[26] Ether, Ethereum's native crypto-currency, is primarily used to constrain the use of computing resources. In contrast to Bitcoin, its use as a payment mechanism is secondary.

[27] Antonopoulos and Wood (2020).

[28] See generally: Zou et al. (2021), p. 2099.

[29] Turing completeness is a property of a programming language that is capable of performing the same computations as a Turing machine, the latter being a theoretical computing device that can simulate any algorithm or computation, as long as it is described in a finite number of steps. Turing-completeness means that any application that runs on a conventional computer can be executed on the blockchain, see: Turing (1937), p. 544.

[30] Ethereum has been originally described as "a blockchain with a built-in Turing-complete programming language, allowing anyone to write smart contracts and decentralized applications where they can create their own arbitrary rules for ownership, transaction formats and state transition functions" see: Buterin (2015), p. 13.

languages increase the likelihood of vulnerabilities and coding errors.[31] Turing-completeness comes at the expense of security.[32] An expressive but easily compromised smart contract seems, however, of limited value given that it controls cryptocurrencies.[33] Moreover, as smart contracts are supposed to ensure certainty, it seems crucial to be able to predict how they will execute. To this end, smart contracts should be written in declarative programming languages. Unfortunately, at present, the aforementioned, dominant programming language (Solidity) is imperative[34] and renders it difficult to create predictable smart contracts.

3.2 *Trusting the Code?*

Recalling the fundamental idea that smart contracts will eliminate the need for human involvement, it must be remembered that smart contracts are always written by humans.[35] If such humans are dishonest or incompetent, then it is impossible to trust the code they write. In practice, smart contracts are used by persons who have not created them and lack the rudimentary technical skills to evaluate their quality, not to mention predict the manner the smart contract will execute. Consequently, *those who use* smart contracts must trust *those who create* them. This creates a peculiar situation: instead of trusting the insurance company, which is portrayed as inherently opportunistic and unfair, it becomes necessary to trust another entity (or set of entities)—the coder who wrote the smart contract. What is the point of disintermediation if we are, effectively, replacing one type of intermediary with another? We must not be distracted (or misled!) by references to technology "replacing humans" if such technology is created by humans. Moreover, while it is possible to have legal recourse against the insurance company, it may be difficult—if not impossible—to seek legal recourse against those who write smart contracts. Coders are often anonymous and hence difficult to hold accountable. Needless to say, it is impossible to seek legal recourse against the smart contract itself.[36]

---

[31] Bartoletti et al. (2020).

[32] Rosu (2018).

[33] An expressive programming language is one that provides a rich set of features, syntax, and language constructs that enable developers to write concise, clear, and easy-to-understand code.

[34] Solidity is also an undecidable programming language. A language is decidable if it is possible to know from the code what the program will do.

[35] Werbach (2018), p. 69.

[36] Although this has been suggested in a recent enforcement action *against a smart contract* by the U.S. Department of the Treasury; see: https://home.treasury.gov/news/press-releases/jy0916.

3.3 Transparency Is Not the Solution

Anticipating the argument that the transparency of the smart contract permits the evaluation of its code, it must be remembered that the fact that the code is publicly visible on the blockchain is of limited practical significance. An inspection of the smart contract will only reveal the most blatant coding errors and will be insufficient to discover serious vulnerabilities.[37] The latter will only become apparent when the code is actually executed. Moreover, an inspection of the smart contract provides virtually no assurance as to its actual operation.[38] In simpler terms: the transparency of the code does not guarantee that the payout will be made on the occurrence of the relevant event. Readability does not translate into predictability or security. On a more practical level: can the average user be expected to investigate whether the smart contract controlling his or her insurance payout is free from programming errors and vulnerabilities? Assuming that the hapless farmer, the purported beneficiary of the technological revolution provided by smart contracts, cannot perform such inspection him or herself—who will? It is unrealistic to expect the farmer to hire a specialist to ensure the quality of the smart contract code. The only feasible solution to this conundrum is for smart contracts to be created by competent and known coders, who can be held legally accountable. In practice, this will require some form of centralization or, at least, reliance on an identifiable entity…

In sum, smart contracts are only as secure as their code. Moreover, since they are public and transparent, malicious actors may be able to find bugs and vulnerabilities with greater ease than in the case of closed, proprietary code. Paradoxically then, if a particular type of smart contract gains popularity and controls more funds, there will be a higher incentive to exploit it. Transparency enables both beneficial and detrimental behaviours. Combined with the fact that smart contracts become immutable once deployed on a blockchain, the discovery of such bugs or vulnerabilities is relevant only before the decision to use a particular smart contract—and only to a technically skilled person who knows the relevant programming language.

4 The Indispensability of Oracles

The above paragraphs focused on the challenges pertaining to smart contracts. The paragraphs below address the challenges pertaining to establishing the event triggering the release of the agreed payout. As indicated, neither blockchains nor smart contracts interface with the outside world. To remain "trustless and secure" blockchains have been designed to remain insulated from any external input—including information about real-world world events, commonly referred to as "off-chain

[37] Mik (2022), p. 106.

[38] To predict what a program will do, it must be tested and, ideally, formally verified; see generally: Kroll et al. (2017), p. 645; Liu et al. (2020).

information." It is worth re-emphasizing that the consensus algorithms underlying the creation of individual blocks are technically incapable of validating any off-chain information.[39] At the same time, it can be reasonably assumed that a smart contract devoid of access to off-chain information is pointless.[40] Especially in the context of insurance, where the payout is premised on the occurrence of events, which *by definition* occur off-chain, such as temperature fluctuations, rainfall or seismic activity. As observed in a recent policy paper, "the implementation of many potentially useful smart contract applications depends upon verifying that some real- world event has taken place (think insurance contracts). This is a problem. Given their fully decentralised nature, how does a smart contract select what the true state of the world is? More generally, how do fully decentralised systems function when their operation depends on the existence of a single, mutually accepted, record of the truth, but there is no single authority that can provide this record?"[41] For the smart contract to release the funds, it must be determined whether such events actually occurred. Entities providing such information are called "oracles."[42] Despite their name, oracles are not infallible. They do not constitute sources of truth and cannot guarantee the accuracy of any off-chain information. They are neither trustless nor inherently secure. Oracles must obtain the off-chain information from external data sources and, in principle, are incapable of verifying or establishing the correctness of such information.[43] Interposed between a data source (e.g., a weather report or sensor) and the smart contract, oracles can be seen as a new type of blockchain-specific intermediary: they provide smart contracts with off-chain information, which is obtained from various data sources.[44]

4.1 *The "Oracle Problem"*

Existing off-chain, oracles do not share the trust assumptions of blockchains. Just like smart contracts, they are created by human coders. There is also no single, reliable technical mechanism precluding them from providing incorrect information. Given that oracles effectively control the release of funds held by a smart contract, they must be trusted. A smart contract written in perfect code and embodying a perfect set of rules (assuming, for the sake of argument, that it is possible to create such) will be of little value if the off-chain information it obtains is incorrect. In

[39] Comuzzi et al. (2021), p. 75.

[40] Egberts (2017).

[41] Garratt and Monnet (2023).

[42] Caldarelli (2020a); Caldarelli (2021); see also: Caldarelli (2020b); Mammadzada et al. (2020).

[43] There are also computation oracles, such as Truebit or Provable, that perform user-defined computation-intensive tasks off-chain, and outbound oracles: once the payment is received, unlocks the lock in the physical world.

[44] For a technical description of how oracles interface with blockchains and smart contracts see: Ellul and Pace (2023).

such an event, the smart contract would release funds even if the release conditions were not met. The challenge of incorporating external information into the blockchain is known as "the oracle problem."[45] The latter can be summarised as follows:

> in an untrusted environment how does one bring information from outside the trusted blockchain environment onto the blockchain in a trusted manner? The problem particularly manifests itself when there is a single source of information: How does one trust that single source? If one trusted single sources, one might not bother with the computational costs of a blockchain solution in the first place.[46]

This quote provides not only a perfect description of the problem, but also the accompanying difficulties of trusting a single source. The off-chain information may be incorrect for multiple reasons, both technical and non-technical. Technical reasons may derive from programming errors, faulty design or external interference. They may concern the data source(s), the oracle itself or, in the case of oracle networks, the individual nodes, the entire network as well as relay mechanisms between the data sources and the oracles. It must be remembered that novel technology notwithstanding, we are talking about regular computer programs—and all the problems associated therewith. Each of the aforementioned programs can be badly designed or badly coded. The non-technical reasons for the incorrectness of off-chain information can be regarded as more interesting but also more difficult to address. They concern the fact that individual oracles as well as their data sources may be compromised. We must not forget that oracles do not self-create and self-operate but require that some *human* entity (or organisation) design and code them as well as manage their interactions with a given smart contract and with external data sources. Given sufficient commercial incentives, such entities may be inclined to alter the relevant information or even fail to provide it altogether. The likelihood of such compromise is directly related to the value of the crypto-currencies controlled by a smart contract. The higher the value of a given smart contract in terms of the amount (and market price) of the cryptocurrencies it controls, the greater the incentive to manipulate the source(s) of the off-chain information or the oracle itself. In such an instance, a potential attacker will not target the smart contract, which might be technically more challenging, but focus on compromising the oracle(s) and/or data sources. Unsurprisingly, exploits based on oracle manipulation are increasingly common.[47] As the non-technical problems are socio-economic in nature, they are more difficult to solve. Consequently, most efforts to address the oracle problem focus on its technical aspects.[48]

---

[45] Frankenreiter (2019); Damjan (2018).

[46] Bartholic et al. (2022).

[47] Caldarelli (2020a), p. 8.

[48] Egberts (2017).

4.2 Addressing the Oracle Problem

At present, the oracle problem remains unresolved. There are, however, multiple attempts to address or at least to alleviate it. Oracles can be regarded as the weakest point in the blockchain-smart contract model, especially in the context of InsurTech, where the provision of accurate and reliable information about off-chain events is paramount. For present purposes, oracles can be divided into two broad categories: centralised and consensus.[49] Centralised oracles, as the name implies, are controlled by a single entity. Examples are sensors operated by a company. Centralised oracles may be more suitable for the provision of information that is not publicly available, such as information concerning specific products moving through the supply chain or information concerning weather conditions in small areas that may deviate from the conditions prevailing in a broader region. As centralised oracles cannot be trustless because they rely on a single entity, they aim to be "probably" honest. In centralised oracles, such as Provable,[50] the objective is to determine that the relevant off-chain information has not been altered after being obtained.[51] Technically, centralised oracles can assist in ensuring the integrity and authenticity of the off-chain information—but only on the assumption that the entity operating them can be trusted. Consequently, it is questionable whether centralised oracles are capable of solving the oracle problem. Arguably, they only confirm the problem's existence and also contradict the ideology of *decentralisation* and disintermediation. There is little point, after all, to deploy blockchains and smart contracts if the feasibility of the entire ecosystem depends on the trustworthiness of a single entity. Centralised oracles would always remain the weakest element of such an ecosystem. In contrast, consensus oracles address the problem by creating networks of oracles, that is: larger groups of oracle nodes which collectively determine which (or whether) off-chain information should be provided to the smart contract.[52] Such "collective determination" can be based on voting or some form of consensus mechanism, both of which can be "enhanced" with economic incentives.[53]

[49] For an alternative approach that divides oracles into voting- and reputation-based see: Pasdar et al. (2022).

[50] Park et al. (2021), p. 12.

[51] See: https://provable.xyz.

[52] Al-Breiki et al. (2020); Wang et al. (2019), p. 258.

[53] The Band Protocol, for example, is a recent consensus oracle project which exploits multiple data sources and applies a mediatization of value to mitigate the effect of outliers.

4.2.1 Voting & Betting Strategies

An example of consensus oracles are so-called Schelling oracles,[54] which involve crowdsourcing knowledge about certain events. This type of oracle requires that the individual oracle nodes bet their reputation or assets in order to establish that information about such events is correct. In principle then, the information about the occurrence of a particular event is publicly evaluated by all participants in the system, the assumption being that if many participants confirm its accuracy, the information must be true. Unfortunately, Schelling oracles can only vote on information that is already publicly available, such as the prices of shares of publicly traded companies or exchange rates. It is questionable whether they can be useful in the context of natural disasters or provide reliable weather data in specific geographic regions, where the required information may simply be unavailable or derive from a single, centralised source, such as a governmental agency. On a theoretical level, it is also questionable whether "voting on the truth" is a feasible long-term strategy, especially when it comes to establishing the occurrence of localised or rare events. Voting on the truth is not necessarily related to establishing the truth. Furthermore, Schelling oracles are not Sybil-resistant, that is, the voting mechanism can be compromised by submitting a large number of votes from different accounts controlled by a single entity. While Schelling oracles can be seen as decentralised, they do not contain any mechanism guaranteeing—or even attempting to verify—the correctness of off-chain information. While betting some amount of crypto-currencies can be said to provide "skin in the game" as the funds may be forfeited in the event a voter provides incorrect information, there is no mechanism incentivizing participation in the vote or verification of the off-chain information. Why would anyone vote on the weather in a Schelling oracle? What happens if no-one wants to vote? Lastly, it is doubtful whether the term "verification" is suitable in the context of oracles relying on voting strategies. If the participants in the system are anonymous, then "betting their reputation" is of questionable value. If, on the other hand, the participants bet their cryptocurrencies to support their vote, the "value" of their vote is related to the value of the cryptocurrency. Logically, Schelling oracles would become less reliable when the staked cryptocurrencies decreased in value. When, for example, the aggregate amount of the payouts exceeded that of the staked amounts, it would become more profitable to provide incorrect information, forfeit the staked cryptocurrencies and abscond with the cryptocurrencies locked in the smart contracts controlling the payout. Oracles could collude with one another or become corrupted by third parties. As stated in the aforementioned policy paper, in the case of voting-based strategies, "agents report the truth that is most beneficial for them. Incentives to reward consensus do not necessarily make things better. Rather, they lead to a situation that is akin to a beauty contest where agents report what they think the majority of other agents will report. With or without reporting

[54] To grasp the multitude of problems concerning voting-based oracles, see: Al-Breiki et al. (2020); Xu et al. (2019).

incentives, the report of the true state that results from majority voting does not depend upon the true state."[55] Other voting strategies are exemplified by prediction markets, such as Augur, where users can bet on anything (e.g., outcomes of elections or sporting events) and be rewarded or penalised depending on the correctness of their predictions.[56] Prediction markets can be thought of as belonging to the more general concept of crowdsourcing which is designed to aggregate information on particular topics or events. Their main purpose is to elicit aggregate beliefs over an unknown future outcome. The risks of using prediction markets in the insurance context are immediately apparent: the majority prediction may turn out to be incorrect as there is no guarantee that those who vote or bet have access to the relevant information, not to mention the competence to evaluate such. Betting on the occurrence of a particular event is unrelated to establishing whether such an event occurred. Prediction is not confirmation—and it is the latter that seems more important in the context of InsurTech. After all, the payout should be unrelated to the correctness of an *ex ante* prediction of an event but depend on the actual, *post factum* determination thereof. In other words, we are not interested in the future but in the recent past.[57] Nonetheless, while it is questionable whether strategies based on voting or betting can provide a feasible solution to the oracle problem, they do create a semblance of objectivity and decentralisation. The "wisdom of the crowds" provides a perfect fit with the broader blockchain ideology, which promotes direct participation as well as disintermediation.

4.2.2 "DONs"

Another suggested solution to the oracle problem are decentralised oracle networks, ("DONs"). DONs comprise many nodes that reach consensus on the correctness of specific off-chain information, that is, determine which information should be "fed into" the smart contracts. For DONs to work in a manner that ensures such correctness, the number of nodes and data sources must increase in proportion to the value controlled by the smart contract. Smart contracts controlling more value should obtain information confirmed by a larger number of oracles, which obtained information from a larger number of data sources. Trust in a decentralized oracle network requires not only a larger number of oracle nodes but also a larger number of data sources. It would, after all, be illogical to multiply the number of oracles only to have them obtain information from a single or a small number of data sources. Similarly, it would be pointless to increase the number of data sources only to rely on a single or a small number of oracles that could become corrupted. Moreover, following the spirit of decentralisation, increasing the number of oracles *and* data

[55] Garratt and Monnet (2023), p. 2.

[56] Peterson et al. (2018); Wang et al. (2018).

[57] Additionally, prediction markets usually focus on events with short time horizons, rendering them unsuitable for insurance policies of longer duration, see: Antweiler (2013), p. 44.

sources renders it more difficult to attack the whole system and increases its reliability. At the same time, a larger number of nodes in the DON increases the risk of "disagreement" between them and introduces the need for mechanisms coordinating their "behaviour." Consequently, DONs require the creation of procedures addressing situations where different nodes report divergent information. In other words, in addition to finding the optimal balance between the number of oracles and data sources on one hand and the value of the locked funds on the other, mechanisms are needed to ensure that nodes "collectively exhibit correct behaviour," i.e., adhere to the DON protocols.[58] Examples of such mechanisms can be found in Chainlink. There, nodes are given economic incentives to report correct information while nodes providing incorrect reports are punished by forfeiting the tokens they have initially deposited—or staked—to participate in the DON.[59] Such a system "should render attacks such as bribery unprofitable for an adversary, even when the target is a smart contract with high monetary value."[60] Again, the staking approach only works if the market price of the staked crypto-currency exceeds the value of the funds controlled by a given smart contract. If, for example, the smart contract controls Ethereum but the staked cryptocurrency is, say, Link, then the entire DON is at risk of compromise whenever the market price of Link decreases and/or the market price of Ethereum increases. In principle, all mechanisms involving staking indirectly expose a given smart contract to the market risks of owning cryptocurrencies and introduce undesirable complexity into an already elaborate system. Moreover, to address conflicting reports concerning the occurrence of off-chain events, DONs must have two tiers of nodes: one tier with direct access to the data sources, which generates the reports; the second with the ability to respond to irregularities reported by the first tier. Some nodes act as "watchdogs"[61] and report incorrect behaviour of other nodes. Lastly, it must also be remembered that the consensus mechanism in a DON encounters different challenges than the traditional consensus mechanisms underlying blockchains. While the latter ensure compliance with a finite set of technical criteria concerning the addition of blocks and the verification of transactions in a closed, artificially constructed system, the former must confirm the veracity of information about real-world events—with all their uncertainties, complexities, and nuances. When reaching consensus on the correctness of off-chain information, the nodes rely on data sources that exist outside of the DON. Consequently, DONs can only establish how many nodes reported certain information as correct but are unable to verify whether such information is actually correct.

---

[58] Breidenbach et al. (2021), p. 78; Eskandari et al. (2021).

[59] See also: ASTRAEA, which is based on a voting game among stake-holders. Adler et al. (2018), p. 1145.

[60] Breidenbach et al. (2021), pp. 17, 18.

[61] Breidenbach et al. (2021), p. 88.

4.3 *Availability of Off-chain Information*

The above paragraphs focused on the difficulties of solving the oracle problem, that is: ensuring the correctness of off-chain information without the need to rely on a single, centralised entity. A separate problem concerns the very availability of such information or, to be more precise, the availability of adequate data sources. There is little point in debating various trust models for oracles and constructing elaborate oracle networks if there are no readily available sources providing off-chain information. It is useful to start with a basic division concerning the types (of sources) of off-chain information. The latter can be divided into those that are public and universally visible, such as stock prices or weather conditions, and those that do not possess those attributes. Some off-chain events generate public data that can be obtained from multiple authoritative sources. For example, it is easily established that at a particular time the NASDAQ reached a particular value. This value will be identical even if reported by different sources, e.g. Bloomberg and Reuters. The same principle applies to prices of publicly traded shares. *Prima facie*, the same could be said about weather information. After all, such information should be easily available from governmental sources, which control or have direct access to weather stations. The problem is that such sources are centralised and thus contradict the very assumptions of the smart contract model. As indicated, there is little point using decentralised oracles if all of them rely on a single source of information! Technically, it is easier to treat this source of information as an oracle without interposing a network of oracles. Even more importantly, when it comes to parametric insurance the required weather information may lack granularity, that is, it may be difficult to obtain accurate information about smaller geographic regions in which, for example, a given farm is located.[62] It is one thing to obtain information about the temperature or rainfall in a capital city; it is quite another to obtain reliable weather information regarding, say, the lower regions of the south slope located 125 km outside of a small provincial city. Farms are generally located further away from larger cities and may require "their own," localised weather information. It must also be recalled that the premise of decentralisation, not to mention the Oracle problem, necessitates the existence of multiple *and* independent data sources. The very idea of smart contracts falls apart once it becomes necessary to rely on—and to trust—a single source of off-chain information. Asking rhetorically: can it really be expected that a small agricultural region in Central America will be equipped with multiple, *independent* sensor networks that will report reliable information about conditions on the ground? Anticipating the argument that information about off-chain events will become easier to obtain automatically with advances in the adoption of the Internet-of-Things ("IoT"), which involves the installation of

[62] As observed by Sandland, "Adequate data is sometimes only available nationally, and occasionally not even at this level. It is well understood that data gaps are roadblocks to achieving optimal risk assessments and may detract from focusing provisions on the local level, especially in disaster-prone areas that are unaccounted for in the current system." [BBPI 100].

Internet-connected sensors providing real-time information about the weather conditions in various regions. Unfortunately, such claims underestimate the relative infancy of IoT technologies, particularly with regards to their lack of security and absence of standardisation.[63] More importantly, it is unrealistic to expect the existence or development of a reliable IoT infrastructure in less developed regions of the planet—the very regions that are supposed to benefit from blockchain-based parametric insurance. Particularly in the event of adverse weather conditions or a natural disaster, one must therefore be sceptical about the availability of reliable information from robust data sources. Who would be responsible to maintain the IoT infrastructure? Who will install and control the sensors? What would be the procedure of monitoring the sensors? How would one ensure that the sensors are not corrupted by, for example, someone placing them in a water container to mimic heavy rainfall? It is reasonable to assume that these examples are just the tip of the iceberg and that multiple paragraphs could be devoted to describing the technical problems surrounding the optimal sensitivity, density, and maintenance of sensors. As in the case of decentralised oracle networks, it may also become necessary to develop procedures to address discrepancies in the off-chain information provided by different data sources.

4.4 Adapting the Smart Contract to the Oracle

An additional challenge, one that is rarely acknowledged but which directly impacts on the feasibility of the entire idea of smart contracts in InsurTech, is the need to adapt the release conditions encoded in the smart contracts to the actual, technical capabilities of the given oracle model. It seems futile to encode complex conditions, such as a staged release of funds in the event of progressively deteriorating weather conditions, if an oracle (or its data source) is technically incapable of establishing whether such conditions have occurred. It must be remembered that, in practice, many oracles may be unable to deal with non-binary queries[64] or any type of query that involves gradations or evaluations of certain conditions. Instead of asking "what is the temperature at location A" it is more advisable to ask, "did the temperature at location A drop below [x] degrees Celsius?" This results in a situation where the payout conditions must be simple, and their fulfilment must be capable of objective and technologically straightforward verification. The practical limitations of oracles will therefore affect the substance of the smart contract and require that the parties state the release conditions in the most simple, if not simplistic, manner. Smart contracts must be tailored to the available sources of of-chain information. The complexity of the world must be adapted to the technical capabilities of a given oracle. The problem is less prominent in the case of parametric insurance, where the payout

[63] Reyna (2018); Uddin et al. (2021).

[64] Bartholic (2022), p. 2.

of the agreed sum is, by definition, dependent on the occurrence or *non*-occurrence of one specific event.

5 Concluding Observations

Readers who think that some of the technical details described above are irrelevant must be reminded that, as the saying goes, "the devil is in the detail" and that many claims concerning the potential role of smart contracts in InsurTech derive from a lack of appreciation—and *understanding*—of such details. It is necessary to abandon the common narrative that extolls the virtues of decentralisation and disintermediation and look at the actual, practical capabilities of blockchains and smart contracts. Ideology must be distinguished from technology.[65] In the context of InsurTech, we should be less concerned with fetishizing decentralisation and more focused on the practical problems we are trying to solve. If the problem is described as acceleration, facilitation, and elimination of human discretion from the compensation process, then it is necessary to inquire whether smart contracts can solve this problem. At all times, the accompanying trade-offs must be borne in mind. The fact that a particular technology is decentralised and eliminates, or reduces, the need for human involvement does not mean that such technology is automatically secure and more reliable. Decentralisation has many downsides, the main one being the lack of accountability and quality control. Ultimately, the entire idea of blockchain-based smart contracts can only bring practical benefits if multiple technical obstacles are overcome. The model is only as reliable, or trustworthy, as its weakest link—and the weakest link is the oracle. Instead of focusing on generalised (and shallow!) descriptions of the potential of blockchains, it is better to address the fact that consensus algorithms cannot determine the correctness of any off-chain information and that oracles obtain the off-chain information from external data sources. In principle, they are also incapable of establishing its correctness. In effect, a technically perfect smart contract (assuming, for the sake of argument, the possibility of its existence) is commercially pointless if the oracle—or one of the elements in an oracle network—can be attacked or corrupted. The risks are clear: if the off-chain information is incorrect, the smart contract is compromised, and the funds controlled thereby are released even if the conditions were not fulfilled.

It is becoming increasingly apparent that *in addition* to the challenges presented by smart contracts, an additional set of challenges concerns oracles. It is reasonable to assume that these technical challenges will remain unresolved in the foreseeable future. It is also reasonable to assume that "malfunctioning" or corrupted smart contracts and oracles may lead to losses. If, however, there are losses then it becomes necessary to allocate liability for their occurrence. Neither smart contracts, nor oracles can function as standalone applications but must be accompanied by

[65] See, for example, Bousquette (2022).

traditional agreements that will describe the consequences of programming errors and vulnerabilities in the case of smart contracts, and incorrect off-chain information in the case of oracles. A broader question arises: is it worthwhile to create an elaborate infrastructure of blockchain-based smart contracts, oracles, and data sources all of which carry their own problems, only to comply with a particular ideology?

It is useful to conclude with a quote from a technical paper:

> Given that oracle ecosystems operate in a different way with respect to blockchains, characteristics such as immutability, transparency, and trustless execution are not ensured. This discrepancy in attributes implies that when blockchain-based applications need data from the external world, the characteristics of oracles are to be taken into serious consideration. If the data source is unreliable, the node is not trusted (or private), and the smart contract is poorly audited, the fact that an application runs on the blockchain is practically irrelevant.[66]

References

Adler J et al (2018) Astraea: a decentralized blockchain oracle. In: 2018 IEEE International Conference on Internet of Things (iThings) and IEEE Green Computing and Communications (GreenCom) and IEEE Cyber, Physical and Social Computing (CPSCom) and IEEE Smart Data, Halifax, NS, Canada, pp 1145–1152

Al-Breiki H et al (2020) Trustworthy blockchain oracles: review, comparison, research challenges. IEEE Access 8:85675–85685

Antonopoulos A (2017) Mastering bitcoin, 2nd edn. Sevastopol, O'Reilly

Antonopoulos A, Wood G (2020) Mastering Ethereum, 2nd edn. O'Reilly

Antweiler W (2013) Long-term prediction markets. J Predict Mark 6(3):43–61

Aquilina SJ et al (2021) EtherClue: digital investigation of attacks on Ethereum smart contracts. Blockchain: Res Appl 2(4):1–18

Bartholic M et al (2022) A taxonomy of blockchain oracles: the truth depends on the question. In: 2022 IEEE International Conference on Blockchain and Cryptocurrency (ICBC)

Bartoletti M et al (2020) Verifying liquidity of recursive bitcoin contracts. Log Methods Comput Sci 18(1):22:1–22:33

Bousquette I (2022) Blockchain fails to gain traction in the enterprise. The Wall Street Journal. https://www.wsj.com/articles/blockchain-fails-to-gain-traction-in-the-enterprise-11671057528. Accessed 22 Oct 2024

Breidenbach L et al (2021) Chainlink 2.0: next steps in the evolution of decentralized oracle networks. https://research.chain.link/whitepaper-v2.pdf?_ga=2.138147696.1573418708.1621330901-1199595055.1621330901. Accessed 22 Oct 2024

Buterin V (2015) Ethereum white paper: a next generation smart contract and decentralized application platform. https://ethereum.org/en/whitepaper/ Accessed 22 Oct 2024

Caldarelli G (2020a) Understanding the blockchain oracle problem: a call for action (2020). Information 11:509

Caldarelli G (2020b) Real-world blockchain applications under the lens of the oracle problem. A systematic literature review. In: Proceedings of the 2020 IEEE International Conference on Technology Management, Operations and Decisions (ICTMOD), Marrakech, Morocco, pp 1–6

Caldarelli G (2021) Blockchain oracles and the oracle problem, 1st edn. Amazon Publishing

[66] Caldarelli (2022), p. 179.

Caldarelli G (2022) Overview of blockchain oracle research. Future Internet 14(6):175
Casey MJ, Vigna P (2018) The truth machine: the blockchain and the future of everything. St Martin's Press, New York
Cohn A, West T, Parker C (2017) Smart after all: blockchain, smart contracts, parametric insurance, and smart energy grids. Ga Law Tech Rev 273–303
Cohney S, Hoffman DA (2020) Transactional scripts in contract stacks. Minn Law Rev 105:340–344
Comuzzi M, Capiello C, Meroni G (2021) On the need for data quality assessment in blockchains. IEEE Internet Comput 71–78
Damjan M (2018) The interface between blockchain and the real world. Ragion Pratica 51:379–403
Egberts A (2017) The Oracle problem - an analysis of how blockchain oracles undermine the advantages of decentralized ledger systems. December 12, 2017. https://ssrn.com/abstract=3382343. Accessed 22 Oct 2024
Ellul J, Pace GJ (2023) Active external calls for blockchain and distributed ledger technologies: debunking cited inability of blockchain and DLT to make external calls. https://arxiv.org/pdf/2302.01764v1. Accessed 22 Oct 2024
Eskandari S et al (2021) SoK: oracles from the ground truth to market manipulation. In: Proceedings of the 3rd ACM Conference on Advances in Financial Technologies (AFT '21), pp 127–141
Frankenreiter J (2019) The limits of smart contracts. J Inst Theor Econ 149–162
Garratt R, Monnet C (2023) An impossibility theorem on truth-telling in fully decentralized systems. BIS Working Papers No 1117. https://www.bis.org/publ/work1117.pdf. Accessed 22 Oct 2024
Guadamuz A (2019) All watched over by machines of loving grace: a critical look at smart contracts. Comput Law Secur Rev 35(6):1–16
Kalbantner J (2021) A DLT-based smart contract architecture for atomic and scalable trading. https://arxiv.org/pdf/2105.02937. Accessed 22 Oct 2024
Kannengießer N et al (2020) Trade-offs between distributed ledger technology characteristics. ACM Comput Surv 53(2):1–37
Kroll JA et al (2017) Accountable algorithms. Univ Penn Law Rev 165:633–705
Lampert L, Shostak R, Pease M (1982) The Byzantine generals problem. ACM Trans Program Lang Syst 4(3)
Liu Y et al (2020) Towards automated verification of smart contract fairness. In: Proceedings of the 28th ACM Joint Meeting on European Software Engineering Conference and Symposium on the Foundations of Software Engineering, pp 666–677
Lutz O et al (2021) ESCORT: Ethereum smart contracts vulnerability detection using deep neural network and transfer learning. https://arxiv.org/abs/2103.12607. Accessed 22 Oct 2024
Mammadzada K et al (2020) Blockchain oracles: a framework for blockchain-based applications in business process management: blockchain and robotic process automation forum. BPM 2020. Lecture Notes in Business Information Processing, vol 393. Springer, pp 19–34
McConnell S (2004) Code complete, 2nd edn. Microsoft Press, Washington
Mik E (2017) Smart contracts: terminology, technical limitations and real world complexity. Law Innov Technol 8:269–300
Mik E (2022) Smart contracts: tales of trust and certainty. Technol Regul 100–112
Narayanan A et al (2016) Bitcoin and cryptocurrency technologies: a comprehensive introduction. Princeton University Press
Park J et al (2021) Smart contract data feed framework for privacy-preserving oracle system on blockchain. Computers 10(7):1–12
Pasdar A, Lee YC, Dong Z (2022) Connect API with blockchain: a survey on blockchain oracle implementation. ACM Comput Surv 55(19):1–39
Peterson J et al (2018) Augur: a decentralized oracle and prediction market platform. https://www.researchgate.net/publication/269705136_Augur_a_Decentralized_Oracle_and_Prediction_Market_Platform. Accessed 22 Oct 2024
Reyna A et al (2018) On blockchain and its integration with IoT. Challenges and opportunities. Future Gen Comput Syst 88:173–190

Rosu G (2018) Formal design, implementation and verification of blockchain languages. In: 3rd International Conference on Formal Structures for Computation and Deduction, FSCD 2018, Oxford, United Kingdom

Sandland C, Schilling D, Marke A (2019) A critical analysis on the capacity of blockchain-based parametric insurance in tackling the financial impact of climatic disasters' in In Commonwealth. https://policycommons.net/artifacts/1155044/a-critical-analysis-on-the-capacity-of-blockchain-based-parametric-insurance-in-tackling-the-financial-impact-of-climatic-disasters/. Accessed 22 Oct 2024

Schneidewind S, Scherer M, Maffei M (2021) The good, the bad and the ugly: pitfalls and best practices in automated sound static analysis of Ethereum smart contracts. In: Conference paper at the 9th International Symposium on Leveraging Applications of Formal Methods, ISoLA 2020, Rhodes, Greece, pp 212–231

Szabo N (1997) Formalizing and securing relationships on public networks. First Monday 2(9)

Turing AM (1937) On computable numbers, with an application to the Entscheidungsproblem. A correction. Proc Lond Math Soc 43:544–546

Uddin S et al (2021) A survey on the adoption of blockchain in IoT: challenges and solutions. Blockchain: Res Appl 2(2):173–190

Walch A (2019) In: Brummer C (ed) Deconstructing decentralization in cryptoassets: legal, regulatory, and monetary perspectives. Oxford University Press

Wang S et al (2018) A preliminary research of prediction markets based on blockchain powered smart contracts. In: 2018 IEEE International Conference on Internet of Things (iThings) and IEEE Green Computing and Communications (GreenCom) and IEEE Cyber, Physical and Social Computing (CPSCom) and IEEE Smart Data (SmartData), pp 1287–1293

Wang S et al (2019) A novel blockchain oracle implementation scheme based on application specific knowledge engines. In: 2019 IEEE International Conference on Service Operations and Logistics, and Informatics, pp 258–262

Werbach K (2018) The blockchain and the new architecture of trust. MIT Press, Cambridge

Wood G (2015) Ethereum: a secure decentralised generalised transaction ledger. https://ethereum.github.io/yellowpaper/paper.pdf. Accessed 22 Oct 2024

Xu X, Weber I, Staples M (2019) Blockchain patterns in architecture for blockchain applications. Springer, pp 113–148

Yaga D et al (2018) Blockchain technology overview. https://nvlpubs.nist.gov/nistpubs/ir/2018/NIST.IR.8202.pdf. Accessed 22 Oct 2024

Zheng Z et al (2020) An overview on smart contracts: challenges, advances and platforms. Future Gen Comput Syst 105:475–491

Zou W et al (2021) Smart contract development: challenges and opportunities. IEEE Trans Software Eng 47(10):2084–2106

Eliza Mik is an assistant professor at the Faculty of Law at the Chinese University of Hong Kong. Her PhD focused on the private law aspects of e-commerce and on general problems of transaction automation. From 2014, she has actively researched smart contracts and blockchains, with a special emphasis on the legal prerequisites of their successful implementation in mainstream commerce. Eliza has advised the World Bank and the Monetary Authority of Singapore. At present, she is a member of the UNCITRAL Expert Group for the Digital Economy, a member of the Inclusive Global Legal Innovation Platform on ODR (iGLIP, Hong Kong), a Research Associate at the Tilburg Institute for Law, Society and Technology (TILT, Netherlands) and an Affiliate Researcher with the Centre for AI and Digital Ethics at the University of Melbourne (CAIDE, Australia).

Insurance Contract Law and Smart Vehicles Under French Law

Victorine Tournaire

1 Introduction

Connected Vehicles and Self-driving Vehicles

From an insurance perspective, smart vehicles can be approached in two different ways: as new tools enabling insurers to develop new products, on the one hand, and as sources of new risks to be insured, on the other. The first approach in particular refers to the use of connected vehicles in the development of pay-as-you-drive and pay-how-you-drive policies; these raise legal issues related mainly to the protection of personal data.[1] Although several insurers have developed this type of product on the French market, their level of success has not been high.[2] It is for this reason that the second approach will be adopted here, which refers in particular to the question of insurance for self-driving vehicles; a subject that raises many legal questions, even though their introduction on the roads is only in its infancy.

[1] On this point, since 2017 a "Compliance package" has been drafted by the CNIL (French data protection authority), available at: https://www.cnil.fr/sites/default/files/atoms/files/cnil_pack_vehicules_connectes_gb.pdf.

[2] See Consigny (2022).

V. Tournaire (✉)
Claude Bernard Lyon 1 University, Laboratory of Actuarial and Financial Sciences (LSAF), Lyon, France

Jean Moulin Lyon 3 University, Liability and Insurance Law Center (Research Team Louis Josserand), Lyon, France
e-mail: victorine.tournaire@univ-lyon1.fr

C. Poncibò, P. Tereszkiewicz (eds.), *European Insurance Law within the Digital Age*, AIDA Europe Research Series on Insurance Law and Regulation 14,
https://doi.org/10.1007/978-3-031-96496-1_13

Authorisation of Self-driving Vehicles

After having allowed self-driving vehicles on an experimental basis since 2016,[3] on the 1 September 2022 France authorised the circulation of truly autonomous vehicles.[4] It should be noted at the outset that this authorisation remains theoretical for the moment since, on the one hand, the marketing of self-driving vehicles has not yet begun on French territory, especially as only one car manufacturer has received the approval necessary to sell these vehicles. On the other hand, and above all, the roads that can accommodate these vehicles have not yet been determined, which in fact prohibits the circulation of such vehicles on the French road network, including self-driving vehicles from abroad. The fact remains that the development of this technology has, therefore, begun to be apprehended by French law.

Definitions of Self-driving Vehicles

Independently of existing classifications at the international or European levels,[5] French law now distinguishes between three types of self-driving vehicles: partially self-driving vehicles, highly self-driving vehicles, and fully self-driving vehicles.[6] The first type refers to vehicles that require the user to take control in response to certain traffic hazards or system failures. The second are those that only require the user to take control of the vehicle for manoeuvres that have not been foreseen by the system. Finally, the third are those that, in principle, do not need the user to take control.[7]

In all three cases, the dynamic control of the vehicle can therefore be delegated for an extended period of time to an automated driving system, thanks to the sensors, radars and cameras that are present in these vehicles; these allow an algorithm to take control of them without human intervention. However, the first two categories of self-driving vehicles are distinguished from the third in that, concerning partially and highly automated vehicles, the user is obliged to be constantly ready to take control, without delay, when the system asks them to do so, as well as for certain manoeuvres (such as complying with the request of the police or facilitating the passage of a public interest vehicle).

[3] Act no 2016-1057 of 3 August 2016 on the experimentation of self-driving vehicles on public roads.

[4] Act no 2021-443 of 14 April 2021 relating to the criminal liability regime applicable in the event of the circulation of a vehicle with driver delegation and to its conditions of use; this has been in force since 1 September 2022.

[5] The best known is the classification of the Society of Automotive Engineers (SAE). At the European level, also available is the classification of the International Organisation of Motor Vehicle Manufacturers (OICA).

[6] See article R.311-1, 8° of Highway Code.

[7] NB: The latter must be further distinguished from "automated road transport systems", which are highly or fully automated vehicles intended for the transport of people on predefined routes, which do not have a driver physically present on board but for which a remote driver will have to supervise the driving at any time (see articles R.3151-1 et seq. of Transports Code).

Regulation of Self-driving Vehicles

Beyond these definitions, French law has, for the moment, only regulated the conditions for the circulation and approval of these vehicles, and established rules concerning the criminal liability that may result from a traffic accident involving this type of vehicle.[8] In contrast, to date no rules on civil liability and insurance have been specifically established concerning self-driving vehicles. This leads to the question of whether French liability and insurance law is already capable of addressing the new liability and insurance issues raised by these vehicles.

Although one of the promises of this technology is that it is able to reduce the number of road accidents (since the machine does not drink alcohol, take drugs, get tired, speed, etc.), the deployment of self-driving vehicles will never be able to reduce them to zero. Apart from the accidents that will continue to occur due to external factors and, initially, due to the surprise they could create, the automated driving system could experience technical failures (bugs, errors in reading road signs, hacking, etc.) since no technology, however sophisticated, is foolproof. Moreover, since the movement of such vehicles will no longer be the sole responsibility of the driver, but also of a machine equipped with artificial intelligence, a transfer of liability, and therefore of the burden of insurance, is likely to occur. The confrontation between insurance contract law and smart vehicles therefore prompts the literature to consider not only the question of the civil liability, that is to say the insurable risk, and the insurance of the "drivers" and "keepers" of self-driving vehicles (Sect. 2) but also those of the other participants involved in the "driving" of these vehicles (Sect. 3).

2 Insurable Risk and Insurance of the "Drivers" and "Keepers" of Self-driving Vehicles

Discussing the liability and insurance of the "drivers" of self-driving vehicles may seem surprising given that self-driving vehicles are sometimes seen as driverless vehicles, the idea is that the user of the vehicle would no longer be a driver as soon as they activate the vehicle's self-driving function. In fact, the development of self-driving vehicles does not necessarily lead to the removal of drivers. In addition, French law on traffic accidents refers to the concept of "keeper", who may be a separate person from the driver. In the case of self-driving vehicles, both the driver and the keeper could continue to be held liable (Sect. 2.1), and should therefore continue to be compulsorily insured (Sect. 2.2).

---

[8] See Act no 2021-443 of 14 April 2021 above-mentioned.

2.1 *Drivers' and Keepers' Liability Risk*

Identification of the Driver

Various texts recently adopted concerning self-driving vehicles do not undermine the existence of a driver.[9]

At the international level, the Vienna Convention on Road Traffic was amended in 2022 to include a new Article 34 bis, according to which: "*The requirement that every moving vehicle or combination of vehicles shall have a driver is deemed to be satisfied while the vehicle is using an automated driving system which complies with: [regulation and legislation].*"[10] The evolution of this convention has therefore not been to remove the requirement for a driver but, on the contrary, to *presume that it is satisfied*, regardless of the activation of the self-driving function. Such a provision makes it possible to identify a driver in any type of self-driving vehicle, regardless of its degree of automation.

This is not quite the case with the new French legislation. It is true that the newly adopted texts allow, in certain cases, a driver to be identified, which they expressly refer to. On analysing this text, it appears that they distinguish the user-driver of the self-driving vehicle from a simple user-passenger in that the former is *invested with the role of taking control when the system asks [them] to do so.*[11] The former is thus a driver invested with a new role, a "new generation driver", but a driver, nonetheless. While this conception of the driver allows the driver of partially and highly automated vehicles to be understood, it does not allow a driver to be identified within fully automated vehicles, since, by definition, no user is required to take back control. This tends to show that French legislation may be ready to regulate the first two types of vehicles but not yet the latter. However, the keeper must also be considered.

Identification of the Keeper

Under French law, the keeper of a thing is the person who has the power of *use*, *direction* and *control* of the thing.[12] Consequently, the keeping of a vehicle generally belongs to its driver. However, the owner of a thing is presumed to be its keeper. For this reason, if the owner of a vehicle does not demonstrate that he has transferred the powers of use, direction and control to its driver, he remains the keeper of the vehicle. For example, this situation often arises when the owner of a vehicle is a passenger while the vehicle is driven by another person. In this case, the driver and the keeper of the vehicle (the owner) are two different persons. The fact remains that the

---

[9] See Bonnardel (2023).

[10] Amendment to the Vienna International Convention on Road Traffic of 8 November 1968, adopted in Geneva on 14 January 2022 and in force since 14 July 2022.

[11] This is particularly clear from the new Article L.123-1 of the Highway Code, which requires the "driver" to "remain constantly in a state and position to respond to a request to take control of the automated driving system".

[12] Cass. 2 December 1941, Franck case.

keeper and the driver are subject to common rules concerning the victim compensation system.

Compensation Available to Victims

The French system of compensation for victims of traffic accidents, which has existed since 1985 and consists of a strict liability regime coupled with compulsory insurance,[13] can easily be implemented once a driver or a keeper has been identified. It is indeed sufficient that a motor vehicle that has been involved in a traffic accident for its driver or keeper to be held liable and for their compulsory insurer (or a guarantee fund) to be required to compensate the victim. Since a self-driving vehicle is undoubtedly a motor vehicle, its involvement in an accident will make it possible to engage the liability of its driver or keeper, on the grounds of the existing legislation, regardless of whether the automated driving system was activated when the accident occurred. Indeed, this risk of liability will be covered by the compulsory motor insurance contract that the owner is compelled to take out. It should be emphasised at this point that this does not mean that the motor insurer will necessarily have to bear the burden of the debt alone and definitively—as it has a subrogatory recourse against the real (or the other) person(s) liable[14]—but it will remain bound, in the first instance, by an obligation to compensate the victims.

Certain authors consider this implementation of the existing system of compensation to self-driving vehicles to be satisfactory, as it has already been widely proven to work well.[15] Others, however, point out its weaknesses. First of all, it is argued that the owner of the vehicle will pay overly high premiums even though they will only be a minor cause of the risk created by the self-driving car. Indeed, these premiums will need to take into account the cost of subrogatory recourse made by the car insurer and the possibility of non-recovery. Secondly, it seems that the cascade of actions brought by the motor insurer will unnecessarily clog up the courts. In response, it has been proposed that the human driver and the artificial intelligence be placed on an equal footing, with the human driver incurring liability and having to be insured when in control of the vehicle, and the vehicle manufacturer or artificial intelligence designer incurring liability when the accident occurs in self-driving mode.[16] But such a solution could be detrimental to victims, since it would then be their responsibility to identify the true liable party or parties, with the time and cost that this would take, and, if necessary, to assume the insolvency of a liable party who is not compulsorily insured.

However, in the case of fully autonomous vehicles, the conception of driver and keeper currently adopted by French law makes it impossible to conclusively determine against whom the victim could claim compensation. Moreover, the idea of placing the burden of liability for an accident, and the cost of compulsory insurance,

---

[13] Created by Act No.85-677 of 5 July 1985 on improving the situation of victims of traffic accidents and accelerating compensation procedures (also know as "Badinter Act").

[14] On this point, see below, II.

[15] See Bonnardel (2023).

[16] Barsan (2018).

on the user of such a vehicle—whether or not they are designated as the driver—is not unanimously supported. Indeed, it may be economically illogical to make them pay a compulsory insurance premium when they have no control over the risk created by the movement of the self-driving vehicle.[17] The attribution of the cost of this risk to the user could nevertheless be justified by the fact that it is up to them to bear the consequences of the risks generated by the vehicle thus placed at their service.[18] Not to mention taking into account the likely development of car-sharing, a political choice has not yet been made in this respect. As the technology is still far from this stage, we can, for the time being, focus on the insurance law applicable to partially and highly automated vehicles, that is to say, to the drivers' and keepers' liability insurance.

2.2 *Drivers' and Keepers' Liability Insurance*

Is current French insurance contract law already suited to self-driving vehicles or does it still need to be tailored to them? This question involves confronting self-driving vehicle insurance with issues that are not only relevant to motor insurance law (Sect. 2.2.1), but also to the general rules governing all insurance contracts (Sect. 2.2.2).

2.2.1 Implementation of Motor Insurance Contract Law

When compared to motor insurance contract law, self-driving vehicle insurance especially raises the question of the scope of compulsory cover and the application of the bonus-malus system.

Scope of Cover

On the one hand, as motor insurance is compulsory, the scope of cover is governed by various texts. The adequacy of this mandatory scope of cover for self-driving vehicles has been questioned, particularly with regard to the minimum amount of insurance cover. Foreign laws, such as the German and Italian laws, have indeed increased coverage limits in order to anticipate claims that might be more extensive. However, this does not seem necessary under French law.[19] Firstly, it is not certain that the development of self-driving vehicles can really lead to an increase in the number and scale of road accidents, as one of the arguments for marketing these vehicles is precisely their level of safety. Secondly, and more importantly, French law already requires insurers to provide unlimited liability coverage for personal

---

[17] Deffains and de Montcuit (2022).

[18] Touzain (2023).

[19] See Andreu (2018), no 02.281.

injury.[20] Thirdly, as for damage to property, although the law currently imposes a minimum limit of €1,300,000, in practice insurers generally provide for almost unlimited cover by stipulating limits of €100,000,000. No increase in the minimum amount of cover would therefore be needed.

Furthermore, with regard to the nature of the risks that must be covered, the technical specificities of self-driving vehicles could require an extension of the mandatory insurance cover to cyber risk.[21] However, the guarantee of this risk would perhaps be better placed in insurance that should be taken out by the manufacturers of self-driving vehicles or the designers of automated driving systems.

Bonus-Malus System

On the other hand, with regard to the setting of the compulsory motor insurance premium, French law requires the application of a bonus-malus system in all motor insurance contracts, which are designed to adjust the premium according to the insured's background and the number of claims for which they were liable.[22] By favouring good drivers and penalising bad ones, this system encourages careful driving while ensuring the insurer's economic equilibrium. As the law currently stands, self-driving vehicles are subject to this system.

Three reasons have nonetheless been put forward to suggest that the system is not suited to them.[23] Firstly, it would be unfair to apply a malus to the insured when the automated vehicle is entirely responsible for the accident. Secondly, it would be inconsistent to apply a malus to a single policyholder—the one affected by an accident—in order to readjust the premium to the level of risk, when this "aggravation" of risk concerns all vehicles operated by the same automated driving system. Thirdly, the fact that artificial intelligence can learn from its own experience could mean that the automated vehicle returning to the road after a loss is actually less of a risk than before the loss occurred.

However, these last two factors should be taken into consideration when pricing the risk independently of the application of the bonus-malus system, in the same way that the insurer already takes into consideration the brand and model of the vehicle when pricing car insurance. As for the first argument, coupled with the articulation presented here of the liability of the various participants in the driving of autonomous vehicles, the current functioning of the bonus-malus system should likely make it possible to avoid it. Indeed, French law tends to exclude the application of the bonus-malus when the claim is not caused by the insured driver. Thus, its application is excluded, in particular: (1) when the author of the accident drove the vehicle without the knowledge of its owner or of one of the designated drivers, except if they usually live in the home of one of them; (2) when the accident was caused by an event presenting the characteristics of force majeure; (3) when the accident was entirely attributable to the victim or to a third party; and (4) when the

---

[20] Article R.211-7 of Insurance Code.

[21] See Bensamoun and Loiseau (2019), no 241.

[22] Articles A.121-1 et seq of Insurance Code.

[23] See Rodriguez (2021).

accident was caused to a parked vehicle by an unidentified third party and the insured was not liable in any way.[24] In addition, the malus is reduced by half if the driver is only partially liable.[25] Admittedly, case law considers that the malus applies in all cases other than the aforementioned exceptions, even in the absence of fault on the part of the insured driver. However, it does not seem necessary to adapt this mechanism specifically to self-driving vehicles; for example, by adding "claims resulting from a failure of the automated driving system" as an exception. In the case of an accident resulting from the sole failure of the automated driving system, it should indeed be possible to consider the accident as entirely attributable to a third party (the vehicle manufacturer or artificial intelligence designer), in the sense of the third exception mentioned previously. Similarly, in the case of an accident resulting from a failure of the system *and* from the fault of the driver (who, for example, did not take control back when the system asked them to do so), the driver should only be considered partially liable, together with the manufacturer and/or designer, which should make it possible to reduce their malus.

In other words, in these two respects at least, current French motor insurance contract law already appears to be rather well suited to autonomous vehicles. It remains to be seen whether the same applies to French general insurance contract law.

2.2.2 Implementation of General Insurance Contract Law

A comparison of self-driving vehicle insurance with general insurance contract law raises, specifically, questions about the policyholder's duties to state risks and notify claims.[26]

Risk Statements

As mentioned in relation to the application of the bonus-malus system to self-driving vehicles, the fact that the vehicle is self-driving, as well as its level of autonomy and likely the model of the automated driving system, should be taken into account by the insurer when pricing car insurance, in the same way as the brand and model of the conventional vehicle is currently taken into account for this purpose. Consequently, insurers will have every interest in questioning the policyholder on these points when taking out insurance for this type of vehicle. Under French law, the policyholder's duty to disclosure is indeed limited to truthfully answering the questions asked by the insurer; there is no duty of spontaneous disclosure at the pre-contractual stage.[27] By contrast, during the execution of the contract, the policyholder is required "*to declare, during the course of the contract, new circumstances which either aggravate the risks or create new ones and thereby render inaccurate*

[24] Articles 6 and 7 of the Annex to Article A.121-1 of Insurance Code.

[25] Article 5 of the aforementioned Annex.

[26] See Andreu (2018), nos 02.283 and 02.284.

[27] Article L.113-2, 2° of Insurance Code.

or null and void the answers given to the insurer [at the time of the initial declaration of risks]."[28] Otherwise, the insurer may cancel the insurance contract if they can prove the policyholder's bad faith or, if not, a proportional reduction of the insurance indemnity[29]—it should be noted, however, that these penalties are not enforceable vis-à-vis the victim in the context of compulsory motor insurance, in which case the insurer must compensate the victim and then take recourse against the insurance holder to reimburse the compensation paid.[30] The enforcement of these sanctions in the case of the unreported conversion of a "traditional" vehicle into a self-driving vehicle is, however, uncertain. While such a transformation forms "new circumstances" contributing to the definition of the insured risk, it is not certain, however, that this constitutes an aggravation of the risk or the creation of a new risk within the meaning of the aforementioned article. Firstly, as already mentioned in relation to minimum insurance cover, one of the reasons for the deployment of self-driving vehicles is to limit the risk of accidents—not to aggravate it. Secondly, while it is true that the assessment of motor risk in relation to self-driving vehicles remains subject to many factors of uncertainty, it is difficult to see why this risk would be of a fundamentally new nature. In this sense, the United Nations Economic Commission for Europe's adoption of the notion of a "*competent and cautious human driver [who] could reduce the risks as much as possible*" as the standard behaviour of a Level 3 SAE (Society of Automotive Engineers) self-driving vehicle—corresponding to partially self-driving vehicles according to the French classification presented previously—is likely to contribute to the absence of any change in risk, since it requires a level of driving safety equivalent to that adopted by the human driver. Consequently, in the case of the unstated transformation of a traditional vehicle into a self-driving vehicle, the legal sanctions for failure to declare aggravation may not be enforceable. As a result, unless contractual provisions are sufficient to remedy the situation, it may be necessary to adjust the aforementioned text to the specific features of self-driving vehicles, as has been done with regard to the notification of claims.

Claims Notification

In order for the insurer to effectively claim recovery against the person actually liable, it is in their best interests to ascertain the precise circumstances of the accident and, in particular, to identify whether the automated driving system was activated at the time of the accident. In addition to the traditional role of presumptions and expertise, data recorders could greatly help them to collect useful information in this respect. As a result of a United Nations regulation that has been in force since 2021, all self-driving vehicles will have to be equipped with a "data storage system for automated driving" (DSSAD), which is intended to record data on the status of

[28] Article L. 113-2, 3° of Insurance Code.

[29] Articles L. 113-8 and L. 113-9 of Insurance Code.

[30] Articles L. 211-7-1 and R. 211-13 of Insurance Code.

driving delegation.[31] This "black box" will have to record, in particular, how many times the automated driving system was activated, how many times the driver was asked to take control back, whether this was followed up, and what manoeuvres were undertaken; this data will also have to be stored for six months.

However, the possibility of the insurer accessing this data was debated. Initially, it was conceivable that insurance policies might stipulate an obligation on the part of the insured to transmit all the data recorded by the computer system to the insurer, just as they generally combine the legal obligation to report claims with a contractual duty to transmit documents. Despite the consent thus given by the insured, such a stipulation could, however, seem to run up against the rules on the protection of personal data and fundamental rights and freedoms.[32] As a solution to this difficulty, some authors had imagined that the transmission of these data to the insurer would be made through the intermediary of the police services, which would have been responsible for sorting through the data recovered from the computer system.[33]

But, apparently yielding to the lobby of the French insurance federation,[34] the French legislature finally adopted a more drastic option in 2021.[35] Indeed, French law now provides that, in the event of a road accident, the insurers guaranteeing the vehicles involved in the accident (as well as the guarantee fund) have access to the DSSAD data relating to the conditions of the activation, deactivation and takeover of the automated driving system.[36] It is specified that this access is given "*for the purpose of determining the compensation necessary for the application of the [compulsory motor] insurance contract, exclusively when the processing of such data is necessary for the performance of the insurance contract concerned*" and that "*the consent of the data subject, driver or user of one of the vehicles involved, to the processing of such data is not required for these purposes*." Although a text is currently being prepared to complete the legal framework of this access,[37] this will undoubtedly facilitate the management of claims and make it easier for insurers to exercise their subrogatory recourse against other participants involved in the driving of self-driving vehicles.

To conclude, it should therefore be noted that, if not the specific motor insurance law, French general insurance law tends to require some adjustments to be able to adapt to self-driving vehicles.

---

[31] UN Regulation No 157, Uniform provisions concerning the approval of vehicles with regards to Automated Lane Keeping Systems [2021/389].

[32] See Noguéro (2019).

[33] Andreu (2018), no 02.284.

[34] See D. Noguéro, op. cit.

[35] Act no 2021-443 of 14 April 2021 above-mentioned.

[36] Article L. 1514-5 of Transports Code.

[37] See Namin (2023).

3 Insurable Risk and Insurance of Other Participants in the "Driving" of Self-driving Vehicles

Subrogatory Recourse of the Motor Insurer

After compensating the victims, the motor insurer of a self-driving vehicle involved in a traffic accident would not necessarily have to bear the burden of the debt definitively. Indeed, the law offers it a subrogatory recourse against the actual liable person(s) or against the co-liable person(s) and their insurer(s).[38] It is in this respect that the deployment of self-driving vehicles could be the cause of a shift in liability from the driver and keeper of the vehicle to other persons, of which there could be many.

Identification of the Other Participants

Among these, the manufacturers of self-driving vehicles and the designers of automated driving systems immediately come to mind. However, many other parties are likely to be involved here, such as the authority responsible for the proper functioning of the intelligent road infrastructure that communicates with the vehicle, the State that has issued an authorisation for the vehicle to be put on the road and, in the event of failure on their part, the service providers responsible for installing and monitoring the beacons. The latter should be able to be held liable for fault,[39] which would not raise many new questions. On the other hand, in the event of a failure in the automated driving system the liability of the autonomous vehicle manufacturer or designer raises more questions as to its grounds (Sect. 3.1) and could lead to a renewal of their insurance cover (Sect. 3.2).

3.1 Manufacturers' and Designers' Liability Risk

Regardless of the development of a liability regime for artificial intelligence itself, or pending the development of such a regime—and given that the transversal approach currently adopted by the European Union in this respect is somewhat frowned upon in France from an insurance perspective[40]—French doctrine has mainly considered two different grounds on which the liability of manufacturers or designers could be engaged:[41] liability based on the "keeping of the structure" of the self-driving vehicle (Sect. 3.1.1) and liability based on the defect of the self-driving vehicle (Sect. 3.1.2).

[38] Articles 1346 et seq. of Civil Code and L. 121-12 of Insurance Code.

[39] See Bensamoun and Loiseau (2019), no 150.

[40] See Touzain (2023) and Bessermann (2020).

[41] See Bonnardel (2023).

3.1.1 Liability Based on the "Keeping of the Structure" of the Self-driving Vehicle

Presentation

One of the most regularly invoked grounds for engaging the liability of manufacturers or designers is that of general liability for things, which makes it possible to engage the liability of the keeper of a thing that has played a causal role in causing damage.[42] Three conditions have to be fulfilled for a person to be held liable on this ground: there must be a thing (1) which caused damage (2), and that thing must be within the keeping of this person (3).

In the case we are interested in, this third condition is considered in a particular way. As above-mentioned, the keeper of a thing is the person who has the power of use, direction and control of it. In principle, the keeping is considered to be an alternative in the sense that it can be transferred to another person (from the owner to the driver, for instance) but cannot be held by several persons at the same time. However, there are some exceptions to this principle, and it is on the basis of one of them that the liability of manufacturers or designers is generally considered in the event of an accident involving a self-driving vehicle.

Indeed, for dangerous things with their own dynamism, the Court of Cassation has accepted that two persons could simultaneously exercise the powers of a keeper over different elements of these things, through a distinction between the keeping of the structure of the thing and the keeping of its "behaviour".[43] The keeping of the structure refers to the intrinsic defects of the thing. The producer is considered to be the keeper of the structure. The keeping of the behaviour deals with the use and handling of the thing. The user would be the keeper of the behaviour of the thing, and only liable for damages caused by improper use.

Although this distinction was originally made in relation to a gas cylinder, it is applicable to motor vehicles. Indeed, the Court of Cassation has recently applied this distinction to a traditional vehicle dropped off at a garage.[44] Accordingly, it is clear that the manufacturer or designer of a self-driving vehicle should therefore qualify as the keeper of its structure as soon as the automated driving system is activated. Meanwhile, the driver or even the owner, who would retain the choice of destination, would remain the keeper of the vehicle's "behaviour". Thus, the driver or even the owner would be liable for damage resulting from the use of an unimpaired self-driving vehicle. Furthermore, in the event of a failure of the automated driving system, the extra-contractual liability of the manufacturer or designer could be engaged.

---

[42] Based on the current Article 1242 of the Civil Code, this is a liability regime mainly constructed by case law.

[43] Cass. civ. 2^{e}, 5 January 1956, No.56-02.126 and 56-02.138 (concerning the explosion of a gas cylinder).

[44] Cass. civ. 2^{e}, 31 March 2022, No.20-22.594.

Limits

Enabling manufacturers or designers to be held liable on this basis could, however, raise a major drawback from the point of view of compulsory motor insurance.[45] Indeed, according to the French Insurance Code, this compulsory insurance not only covers the liability of the driver of the vehicle, but also that of any keeper of it, with the exception of professionals involved in the repair, sale and inspection of the vehicle.[46] While the driver and the keeper may be different persons, they are all insured. In this case, the insured would then be the driver of the autonomous vehicle, the keeper of its "behaviour" (the driver or the owner), and the manufacturer or designer (as the keeper of its "structure"). However, the insurer will not typically have a subrogatory recourse against its insured. This ground of liability would therefore not allow the motor insurer to make a subrogation claim against the manufacturer or designer (or their insurer), but would, on the contrary, force it to insure their liability.

This difficulty could be overcome in three different ways. The first option would be to consider manufacturers and designers as professional sellers of motor vehicles, since the liability of these professionals—who must underwrite another compulsory insurance policy—is already expressly excluded from the scope of compulsory motor insurance cover. Such an interpretation of the texts is, however, highly uncertain as they were not established for this purpose. The second option would then be to add to this existing exception the exclusion of manufacturers and designers of autonomous vehicles. However, such an amendment of the texts does not necessarily seem appropriate insofar as the third option seems possible and preferable: that of a claim based rather on the liability of the manufacturer and designer for defective products.

3.1.2 Liability Based on the Defect of the Self-driving Vehicle

Presentation

As a result of the transposition of the European Directive of 25 July 1985 concerning liability for defective products,[47] the French Civil Code contains such a liability regime.[48] Producers are thus liable for damage caused by defects in their product, regardless of whether they are bound by a contract with the victim; indeed, a product can be considered defective when it does not offer the safety that can legitimately be expected. Consequently, case law already allows the insurer of a conventional vehicle to bring a subrogatory recourse against the vehicle manufacturer on the ground of this regime, when the defect of a vehicle part (brakes, tyres,

---

[45] See Bonnardel (2023).

[46] Article L.211-1 of Insurance Code.

[47] Council Directive 85/374/EEC of 25 July 1985 on the approximation of the laws, regulations and administrative provisions of the Member States concerning liability for defective products.

[48] Articles 1245 et seq of Civil Code.

speed regulator, etc.) was the cause of a traffic accident.[49] In the same vein, the manufacturer of a self-driving vehicle or the designer of the driving delegation system, who would be the producers, should be liable towards the victims of an accident caused by the failure of the driving hardware or software, which would constitute a safety defect in a new part of the vehicle. Therefore, the insurer who compensated the victims should be able to exercise their subrogatory recourse against these manufacturers or designers on this ground.

Advantages and Limits

In addition to avoiding the aforementioned disadvantage of a recourse based on the keeping of the structure of the vehicle, the choice of this basis of liability would be relevant for at least two other reasons. On the one hand, as this is a liability regime resulting from a European directive, it would ensure that the motor insurer has a similar recourse regardless of the nationality of the vehicle manufacturer, as long as it is European. On the other hand, its implementation could be simplified from a probationary point of view thanks to the "black box" recording the self-driving data.

Here, the first difficulty encountered would be the existence of a cut-off period of ten years after the vehicle was put into circulation.[50] After this period, the insurer could be obliged to bear the burden of the debt, which is not entirely satisfactory. It might therefore be necessary to consider adapting the liability regime in this respect. Beyond that, the difficulty could arise from the absence of compulsory insurance guaranteeing this liability.

In short, although the ground of liability for defective products appears to be more appropriate than of the action of a thing, its complete adequacy with the new issues generated by self-driving vehicles may require a renewal of both manufacturers' and designers' liability insurance.

3.2 *Manufacturers' and Designers' Liability Insurance*

Current Limits

In France, the insurance of liability resulting from the defect of a product is fairly widespread but is not compulsory. As a result, neither the taking out nor the scope of cover is regulated and so is largely a matter of contractual freedom. Therefore, even when such insurance is taken out, the existence of exclusion clauses, aggregate limits or specific deductibles could leave the manufacturer of self-driving vehicles or the designer of artificial intelligence to bear a significant part of the cost of compensation, which may exceed their own financial capacities. Moreover, the marketing of self-driving vehicles manufactured abroad could also have the effect of confronting French motor insurers with foreign manufacturers or designers whose insurance coverage would be unrelated to the French insurance market. In any case,

[49] See e.g., Cass. com., 18 mai 2016, n° 14-16.234.

[50] Article 1245-15 of Civil Code.

there is thus a risk that the motor insurer may not be able to recover the compensation paid to the victim, which could increase the premiums of compulsory insurance for the drivers of autonomous vehicles.

A Potential Compulsory Insurance

In order to overcome these limits, the creation of compulsory insurance at the expense of the manufacturers of self-driving vehicles and designers of automated driving systems could be envisaged.

However, doubts have been raised as to whether the creation of compulsory insurance is justified.[51] On the one hand, they are based on the fact that such a measure would derogate from the general philosophy of compulsory insurance, which would be justified above all by the purpose of protecting the victims. On the other hand, there would be a question here of creating compulsory insurance for the benefit of an insurer, which would infringe upon contractual freedom in a way that the legislator would have difficulty finding a convincing justification for. On the other hand, and above all, the introduction of compulsory insurance would be difficult to reconcile with the free movement of goods as provided for in Articles 34 and 35 of the Treaty on the Functioning of the European Union. A foreign car manufacturer could argue that taking out such compulsory insurance would make it more difficult to market its products on the French market, especially since it could be in a less favourable position than a French competitor to take out cover in accordance with French rules. Moreover, the possibilities of derogation provided for in Article 36 of the Treaty would not be of much help in that it would be difficult to justify compulsory insurance on the grounds referred to in this text.

However, whereas the introduction of such compulsory insurance seems to be a good solution, these various arguments do not seem to be wholly decisive. Indeed, the purpose of compulsory insurance is not only to protect the victims; it also aims, in particular, to moralise those who are subject to it—in this case, the manufacturers and designers—if only by making all those who practise an activity bear the cost of compensation for the harmful consequences of that activity, since they benefit from it or are even in a position to prevent it from happening.[52] More precisely, the addition, to the existing compulsory motor insurance, of a compulsory products liability insurance would lead to an effective sharing of the cost of compensation for accidents caused by self-driving vehicles. Moreover, such a system would not be unprecedented, since it would be similar to the "double trigger" system of compulsory construction insurance that has existed in France since 1978, consisting of compulsory "decennial" liability insurance imposed on builders, and compulsory damage "to the works" insurance imposed on project owners; the latter intervening as prefunding.[53] It has been pointed out that this system of compulsory building

[51] See Andreu (2018) no 02.295.

[52] See V. Tournaire, L'assurance obligatoire. Proposition d'un droit commun, Dalloz, Nouv. bibl. de th., vol. 229, 2023, No.343 et seq.

[53] See Act No.78-12 of 4 January 1978 on liability and insurance in the field of construction, which gave rise to Articles L.241-1 et seq and L.242-1 et seq of Insurance Code.

insurance is not immune to invalidation by the European courts.[54] This difficulty could, however, be overcome by the introduction of such compulsory insurance at the European level or, from an even more protective point of view, at the international level. Nevertheless, it is true that such a hypothesis goes beyond insurance contract law and smart vehicles *under French law*.

4 Conclusion

Ultimately, French law appears to be relatively ready to properly compensate the victims of accidents involving partially or highly automated vehicles, thanks to the ability of the current special system of motor liability and compulsory insurance to deal with them. However, in order to adapt the framework of the relationship between the motor insurer and the insured to the specificities of these vehicles, it may be necessary to implement certain adjustments to the general insurance contract law. Furthermore, as regards the relationship between the motor insurer and self-driving vehicle manufacturers or automated driving system designers, both the basis of their liability and the framework for their insurance remain to be clarified, but the solution may not be in French law.

Legislation and Case Law

Act no 85-677 of 5 July 1985 on improving the situation of victims of traffic accidents and accelerating compensation procedures (also know as "Badinter Act")

Act no 2016-1057 of 3 August 2016 on the experimentation of self-driving vehicles on public roads

Act no 2021-443 of 14 April 2021 relating to the criminal liability regime applicable in the event of the circulation of a vehicle with driver delegation and to its conditions of use

Directive 85/374/EEC of the Council of 25 July 1985 on the approximation of the laws, regulations and administrative provisions of the Member States concerning liability for defective products

French Court of cassation, 2 December 1941, Franck case

French Court of cassation, second civil chamber, 5 January 1956, ref 56-02.126 and 56-02.138

French Court of cassation, second civil chamber, 31 March 2022, ref 20-22.594

French Court of cassation, commercial chamber, 18 may 2016, ref 14-16.234

French Civil Code (articles 1242, 1245 et seq. and 1346 et seq.)

French Highway Code (articles L.123-1 and R.311-1, 8°)

[54] See J. Roussel, Rép. civ. Dalloz, v° Assurance construction, 2016, No.42 et seq.

French Insurance Code (articles L.113-2, L. 113-8, L. 113-9, L. 121-12, L.211-1, L. 211-7-1, R. 211-7, R. 211-13, A.121-1 et seq., 6 and 7 to the Annex to Article A. 121-1)
French Transports Code (articles L. 1514-5 and R.3151-1 et seq.)
UN Regulation no 157, Uniform provisions concerning the approval of vehicles with regards to Automated Lane Keeping Systems [2021/389]
Vienna International Convention on Road Traffic of 8 November 1968, adopted in Geneva on 14 January 2022

References

Andreu L (ed) (2018) Des voitures autonomes. Une offre de loi, Dalloz
Barsan I (2018) La voiture autonome: aspects juridiques. Communication – Commerce électronique, étude 3
Bensamoun A, Loiseau G (eds) (2019) Droit de l'intelligence artificielle, LGDJ
Bessermann B (2020) Les enjeux du développement de la responsabilité numérique pour les assureurs. Dalloz IP.IT, p 170
Bonnardel N (2023) Les risques générés par les véhicules autonomes ». Responsabilité civile et assurances, dossier 4
Consigny C (2022) Assurance auto: pourquoi le *Pay as you drive* fait du surplace. Argusdelassurance.com
Deffains B, de Montcuit G (2022) Proposition d'un régime de responsabilité objective applicable au dommage causé par une machine auto-apprenante. Revue trimestrielle de droit civil, Dalloz, p 257
Namin L (2023) Assurance: esquisse en matière de gestion des sinistres automobiles impliquant des véhicules à délégation de conduite. Responsabilité civile et assurances, dossier 4
Noguéro D (2019) Assurance et véhicules connectés – Regard de l'universitaire français. Dalloz IP/IT, p 597
Rodriguez N (2021) Les premiers arbitrages du comportement d'un véhicule automatisé par le règlement ALKS. Revue générale de droit des assurances, p 6
Touzain A (2023) Les risques générés par l'intelligence artificielle. Responsabilité civile et assurances, dossier 3

Victorine Tournaire is an Associate Professor in Law at Claude Bernard Lyon 1 University, a member of the Laboratory of Actuarial and Financial Sciences and an associate member of the Liability and Insurance Law Center at Jean Moulin Lyon 3 University. She holds a PhD in Law from the University of Montpellier and a Master's Degree in Business Law from Paris Panthéon-Assas University. She specialises in Insurance Law.

Robo-Directors and D&O Insurance Markets: An Assessment

Adolfo Paolini

1 Introduction

Corporate bodies face one of the most significant challenges yet, only comparable with serious financial meltdowns. Strength and adaptability have played crucial roles in human evolution and companies, as 'persona ficta,' are no different. According to Siebel,[1] we are witnessing a mass extinction in the corporate world, with more than 52% of the Fortune 500 companies being liquidated, merged, or taken over since the year 2000.[2] Only companies with the ability to combine strength, adaptability and innovation will subsist. Strength within this context should not be necessarily associated with either financial or physical power; it is also the ability, tenacity, and determination to implement the necessary changes to survive the new technological era, fuelled by data.

Digital technology as precursor of digital transformation has disrupted the market to such an extent, that it is now clear that industries need to reshape, from every angle, the way they do business e.g., production, scalability, and work.[3] Therefore,

[1] Siebel (2019), p. 8.

[2] Ibidem.

[3] Ibidem.

The author is extremely thankful to Collegio Carlo Alberto Compagnia di San Paolo and the University of Turin, for the visiting research opportunity in the Autumn 2021. Time spent in Torino was of fundamental importance to develop these ideas.

A. Paolini (✉)
University of Buckingham, Buckingham, UK
e-mail: adolfo.paolini@buckingham.ac.uk

C. Poncibò, P. Tereszkiewicz (eds.), *European Insurance Law within the Digital Age*, AIDA Europe Research Series on Insurance Law and Regulation 14,
https://doi.org/10.1007/978-3-031-96496-1_14

the message for business organisations and incumbents is very clear 'you have reached the junction 'adapt or die.' Corporate Law and Corporate Governance are not immune to this novel trend consequently, we have seen dramatic changes in the way that companies are set up, new ventures, trade, raise capital with ICO's (Initial Coin Offerings) and of course how these modern structures are governed.[4]

Alongside, technological developments from the profit-making perspective, we find 'The New Customer' who is substantially different from 20 years back. These renewed market participants want more for less, expeditious effective transactions at the least possible cost. New customers' behaviour does not differ much from what business structures pursue namely profit maximisation (low manufacturing or service costs, increase output, sales growth) vs consumers' angle (inexpensive, good quality, easily available products, and services).

The question is how could both market players achieve what they want? This is where technology becomes handy.

Reconciling the aims of producers, manufacturers, and users (customers) results in several important common denominators, two of which deserve special attention time and size. Saving time in the manufacturing process and offering the final product to a significantly larger market arguably, increases profitability, or at least the likelihood of it. Additionally, finding the right product quicker in a well-supplied market leads to cheaper manufactured goods and/or services. What could reconcile both competing views? 'Data is the answer'!

Nowadays, data plays a significant role in designing the right product for a target audience and therefore, it has rightly gained its place as 'The New Commodity' and most importantly 'The Fuel of Artificial Intelligence'. Corporations, aware of this rapid development, have started to use AI not only in every stage of the manufacturing process or core business but also at a decision-making level. For a reason Siebel believes that "decision-making will change, with data-driven decision-making in particular taking on an entirely new meaning. Algorithms will become an integral part of most, if not all, decisions".[5]

Making accurate predictions by using AI in general or machine learning, is helping business organisations to design or identify the product that final users or consumers want. Consequently, storing, using, processing, and monetising the right data is, the new model or template that companies need to follow, of course with data protection regulation in mind.[6]

Of particular interest is the fact that AI is already sitting at the boardroom, helping with the decision-making process by analysing corporate data, along with other

[4] How is D&O insurance going to deal with Initial Coin Offerings (ICO's), would it offer the same sort of protection to either IPO prospectuses or ICO white papers? Alternatively, would Side C cover Decentralised Autonomous Organisations (DAOs) in the same way it protects companies?

[5] Siebel (2019), p. 118.

[6] REGULATION (EU) 2016/679 OF THE EUROPEAN PARLIAMENT AND OF THE COUNCIL of 27 April 2016 on the protection of natural persons with regard to the processing of personal data and on the free movement of such data, and repealing Directive 95/46/EC (General Data Protection Regulation).

variables, to make business predictions. Consequently, 'robo-directors' exposure to the misfortunes of the corporate body will soon reach a checking point.

In an environment where hard and soft corporate governance rules have significantly transformed the landscape by making directors more accountable and giving shareholders stewardship functions,[7] it becomes almost unavoidable to explore the effects of AI in reshaping regulation. However, what we did not foresee was how fast AI would disrupt the corporate world by even creating new business ventures, which sounded unfeasible in the past, in other words we expected changes but not so fast.

AI has been patiently waiting in the background! Therefore, these ideas aim at describing and theoretically explaining what artificial intelligence is by looking at its two main subsets: machine learning and deep learning. Secondly, it will try to reconcile and to some extent predict how existing rules underpinning directorship would adapt to robo-directors and what challenges lie ahead. Thirdly, it explores accountability and the reaction of directors' and officers' (D&O) liability insurance carriers to deal with this imminent robotic reality. Fourthly, perhaps somewhat prematurely, it will consider whether singularity is achievable so robots' personhood would put human brains to the test.[8]

Corporate Governance and D&O insurance must react to the digital transformation; hence, it is about time to speculate with some challenging thoughts.

2 Introduction to AI Basics: Machine and Deep Learning

According to Russell and Norvig,[9] there are four possible combinations that could be used to defining Artificial Intelligence: thinking humanly, acting humanly, thinking rationally and acting rationally. Reconciling acting or thinking humanly and rationally seems to be the neuralgic junction. The following two definitions underpin some examples.

Reconciling acting or thinking humanly and reasonably seems to be the neuralgic junction. The following two definitions underpin some examples.

Artificial Intelligence could be defined as "the art of creating machines that perform functions that require intelligence when performed by people"[10] (acting as human). Or "the ability of a non-natural entity to make choices by evaluative process" (thinking rationally).[11] In any event almost everybody's views converge in

---

[7] United Kingdom Stewardship Code 2020.

[8] Albeit some argue that existing regulation, "allows software systems to achieve a very close surrogate for legal personhood" See Bayern (2019), p. 24.

[9] Russell and Norvig (2021), pp. 20–21.

[10] Kurzweil (1992).

[11] Turner (2019), p. 16.

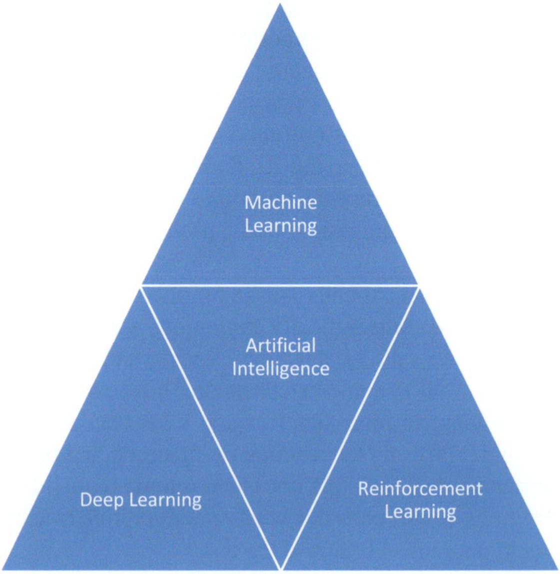

Fig. 1 Source: Adolfo Paolini

calling intelligent a machine that, after being fed with data, produces rational outcomes, without having been trained to do so.

Regardless of any philosophical choice, AI processes depend on 'algorithms' to predict outcomes thus data and computational speed are paramount. The equation is simple the larger the qualitative data[12] the better the result. However, algorithms need proper training to achieve acceptable ends. Outcomes improve by splitting the data (training/testing) thus giving more training as opposed to testing functions. Increasing the data for training and/or testing is proportional to the accuracy and granularity of the outputs,[13] so human 'check' remains necessary in most cases (Fig. 1).

AI uses two different methods to train algorithms and predict outcomes: machine learning and deep learning.

Machine learning (ML) learns insights from data and makes predictions from it.[14] Nowadays machines could learn and always improve their predictions by processing data, without having been trained or programmed for that purpose.[15]

ML uses three learning methods: 'supervised', 'unsupervised' and 'reinforcement learning'. In supervised learning, the algorithm employs labelled training data from which it will produce a desired outcome.[16] There are two subcategories of supervised learning: 'classification', classifies data points into certain categories to

[12] Yao et al. (2018), p. 131.

[13] Arslanian and Fischer (2019), p. 171.

[14] Ibidem.

[15] Taulli (2019), p. 41.

[16] Ashley (2018), p. 109.

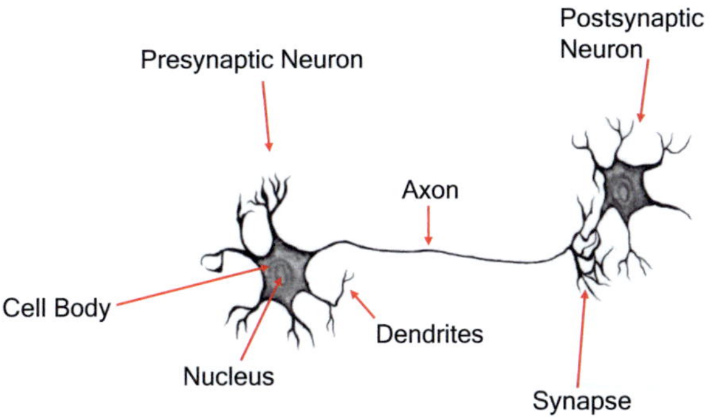

Fig. 2 Source: Adolfo Paolini and Maria Paolini

predict outcome class; whereas 'regression', on the other hand identifies how certain factors influence specific outcomes and predict value.

Unsupervised learning does not use pre-classified data;[17] this unstructured data aims at giving predictions by clustering information and providing an outcome, working on the premise 'if others like this you may also like it'. For example, it could identify, by finding hidden structures in the data,[18] which action movies have generated the largest income in the box office to attract one's interest.

In reinforcement learning, the algorithm does not receive labelled data nor the predetermined outcome; it reaches a conclusion or deals with decisions by interacting with the environment using a trial–and-error system, whereby every time it reaches a desirable outcome, it is rewarded with a 'good' response. This system is useful to improve the outcome for example by rewarding the algorithm when choosing only award-winning movies or best item of its class.

Deep learning relies on artificial neural networks, or machine learning 'using multiple layers of simple, adjustable computing elements'[19] which mimic the human brain (see Fig. 2 above); aiming at processing vast amounts of data to find and/or identify patterns and shapes that humans may find difficult to see.[20] From a basic structure of having a single input layer, a single hidden and a single output layer, deep learning works by adding more hidden layers to the process and allowing the system to feedback (backpropagation) unwanted results. Backpropagation, the bread, and butter of artificial neural networks,[21] allows the output layer to feedback to the hidden layer when the output contains unacceptable levels of error (cost of error). This function requests for the weight of the edges (computational biases) to adjust and reduce the error rate before feeding back to the output layer. Adjusting

[17] Wilkins (2019), p. 46.

[18] Raschka and Mirjalili (2017), p. 2.

[19] Russell and Norvig (2021), p. 44.

[20] Taulli (2019), p. 71.

[21] Wilkins (2019), p. 53.

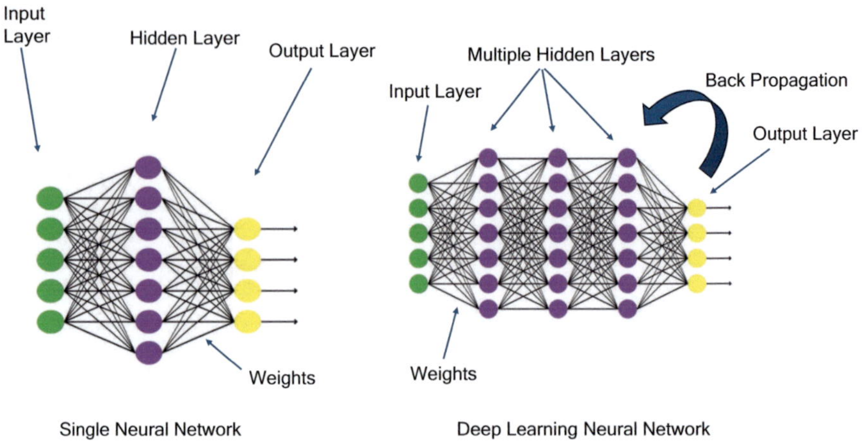

Fig. 3 Source: Adolfo Paolini and Maria Paolini

the errors allows the system to learn from itself[22] in an intuitive and sophisticated intelligent model.

Deep learning has proved very useful in specific tasks such as image recognition and perception, but it is vulnerable. For example, a 'tiny input perturbation'[23] or adversarial inputs may prevent a 'robust handwritten digit recognition'.[24] Lack of robustness is caused by 'obfuscated gradients' without which it is impossible to identify and correct the error.[25] These perturbations could be imperceptible to humans. One way to resolve the problem is designing a system, which minimises the impact of small variations by training the system with adversarial perturbations.[26] MNIST[27] has achieved certain success (88.79%) by allowing a pre-defined attacker to perturb the brightness of each pixel, in image recognition, yet this process has not been able to influence the majority of samples so the classification of mini-images proved insufficient. The solution appears to be developing a stronger attack which 'leverages the generative structure to the classification model' thus making the output more accurate.[28] The following illustration may assist in visualising what deep learning neural networks look like (Fig. 3):

[22] Ibidem, p. 55.

[23] Schott et al. (2018).

[24] Brendel (2018).

[25] Athalye et al. (2019).

[26] Madry et al. (2018).

[27] MNIST: Modified National Institute of Standards and Technology Database.

[28] Schott et al. (2018).

2.1 *Data as the New Oil:*[29] *What Would We Do Without It?*

Business is facing fundamental changes especially in the way decisions are made, the way business processes execute them and how products are distinguished.[30] One of the main market changes experienced today is the way we perceive 'data', and soon it became obvious that data represents a very good source of income. Monetising data, for example, helps corporate structures to subsidise some of their services and even offer them free[31] maximising services and therefore, attracting customers.

Nowadays, data is the 'new oil' and is therefore treated as 'a commodity'.[32] Whoever has access to it, significantly improves revenue incomes. AI, for example, heavily, if not exclusively, relies on either structured or unstructured data to make predictions and assess customer and market fluctuations. The downside is, nevertheless, that in the wrong hands, data could lead to damaging results when used for unintended purposes; therefore, "the entity that we really have to trust ... is not the robot... it is the company behind the robot...that collects the data from the robot... that company... should be an information fiduciary"[33]

Arguably, financial, and corporate markets face several challenges regarding the gathering, processing, and use of data without even mentioning cyber risk management. For example:

- Assessing the nature of the data held by the corporate body.
- Assembling mechanisms to protect such data.
- Adapting to current and future legislation.
- Monitoring and supervising the data protection system.
- Identifying weak or exposing areas.
- Accountability for failing to apply, use or improve the monitoring system.

Market players are at the centre of this turbulence therefore, there is a need to develop the framework for the safety of 'data as the new oil'. The D&O insurance market is consequently facing high risks in this area; the latest Directors' and Officers' Liability survey 2023 jointly produced by Clyde & Co and Willis Tower Watson[34] shows that for the last three years running, cyber-attacks have been the number one risks faced by directors and officers.

AI is experiencing an even larger thrust, so attempts to deploy machine and deep learning to help boardrooms have not escaped innovation. This is the result of the dramatic change experienced by the financial and corporate world. According to

[29] Balkin (2016), p. 6.

[30] Siebel (2019), p. 118.

[31] Balkin (2016), p. 23.

[32] Ibidem, p. 6.

[33] Ibidem, p. 25.

[34] Directors' and Officers' Liability Survey 2023 - WTW (wtwco.com).

Susskind[35] the legal market (and the author adds the business market), is suffering serious transformations propelled by three drivers: whoever fails to adapt will face failure.

- More for less: customers want better, quicker, more reliable, and cheaper services
- Liberalisation: would financial licensing be required to provide worldwide banking services? Would companies be able to raise capital worldwide without having to enlist in stock markets or centralised clearinghouses?
- Information Technology: the answer is to use AI.

Two examples of how AI is reshaping the system in the short and mid-term are 'robo-trading' and robo-advice'.[36] The first example is algorithmic trading which resolves speed and latency; The Depository Trust and Clearing Corporation for example, deals with 10,000 transactions per second,[37] so it is physically impossible to keep up with the updating and reconciling of transactions. Robo-advice on the other hand gives customers, (to some extent), full control of their accounts; all they need is advisory tools to make informed-decisions about financial products.

Nevertheless, in the 'data as the new oil' era, AI faces the challenge of financial predators who, by predicting variables, could build unscrupulous profit-driven markets full of sharks.[38] Companies therefore face the double-edged sword scenario of being either the agent or the victim of such wrongdoings, and using automated boardrooms could exacerbate the risk.

Against this background, what challenges do robo directors face?

3 Today's Reality v Fiction

Isaac Asimov[39] is credited with the famous Three Laws of Robotics widely used by scientists as inspiring tools to develop AI.

These rules are:

1. A robot may not injure a human being or, through inaction, allow a human being to come to harm.
2. A robot must obey the orders given to it by human beings, except where such orders would conflict the First Law.
3. A robot must protect its own existence as long as such protection does not conflict with the First or Second Law.[40]

[35] Susskind (2016), p. 3.
[36] Buyers (2018), p. 101.
[37] Casey and Vigna (2018), p. 162.
[38] Yao et al. (2018), p. 31.
[39] Asimov (1942).
[40] Ibidem.

Without attempting to receive any credit from the above rules and with due respect for the brilliance of Dr Asimov, corporate boards could adapt the above rules as follows:

- A robo director may not injure the company or through inaction, allow the company to come to harm. Therefore, matching the fiduciary position and the resulting duties that directors owe to the corporate body.
- A robo director must obey the orders given to it by the majority of members of the board of directors, except where such orders would conflict with the First Law. Consequently, acting in line with corporate decisions yet exercising independent judgement.
- A robo director must protect its own directorship if such protection does not conflict with the First or Second Law, thus in line with the principle of separation between company ownership and management control.

Whether these principles would work is a matter of time!

However, reality shows that robots are already acting as members of the board in providing almost instantaneous predictions and services, which would probably take humans more than a lifetime to do. In 2016, Tieto Corporation appointed Alicia T (AT) to its leadership team to provide assistance and innovation in data driven opportunities.[41] The company Deep Knowledge is using 'Vital' (Validating Investment Tool for Advancing Life Sciences) for internal corporate prediction.[42] The Fintech Start-up 'Bettermen' is another example of 'robo advice', which promotes the idea that human financial advice has been outperformed by the new technology.[43] Hence, robots have already reached the boardroom.

3.1 *Should We Worry?*

It is not too difficult to imagine why companies were created in the first place, with the idea of separate legal personality developing thereafter. There are several reasons, which force us to seek assistance, and these ultimately depend on what the aims of the business or charitable work are. Arguably, time, skills and capital have heavily influenced our desire or, indeed, need to associate yet fear of failing to achieve our objectives has either deterred us or triggered innovation.

Separate legal personality was the innovative idea, developed as an effective way to manage financial risk and exposure.[44] Such an innovative idea created a 'fiction' a—quasi-person—to whom legal systems recognise rights, impose obligations, and

[41] https://www.tieto.com/en/newsroom/all-news-and-releases/corporate-news/2016/10/tieto-the-first-nordic-company-to-appoint-artificial-intelligence-to-the-leadership-team-of-the-new-data-driven-business/. (Accessed 5 August 2024).

[42] Zolfagharifard (2014).

[43] King (2018).

[44] Albeit History proves that tax avoidance could have been the main reason.

even protect their reputation. Companies as persona ficta are human creations incorporated to manage risk and alleviate the fear of unlimited liability to, in principle, an unlimited number of people.

Furthermore, is there any problem in accepting and regulating self-driven companies and robo-directors? Are we not yet prepared to pass on the business and decision making to machines, which could prove more skillful, at least in certain aspects, than their inventors and developers? Are we not sufficiently financially and technologically savvy to reinvent 'persona ficta', and give to IT something more than protecting capital and generating revenue for capital providers?

Not long ago, the possibility of appointing corporate bodies as company directors was debated. In fact, it was not uncommon to find companies being directed by other companies up to three or four tiers in corporate structures. The system therefore trusted corporate bodies to carry out directorship and the only requirement was that at least one natural person was appointed to the board. The enactment of the Small Business, Enterprises and Employment Act 2015 removed such a possibility and now all directors must be natural persons.[45] Company Law soon realised that board composition could lead to tangled structures, difficult to penalise or rectify, when things went wrong. Most importantly, having only natural persons appointed to directorship acts as a deterrence principle because company directors can incur personal liability and respond to the corporate body without the veil of incorporation protection. Consequently, fear of personal ruin motivates positive behaviours. However, these concerns may be slightly different where the reins of the company pass on to a fully skilful predicting machine, which or who, with the right algorithm training could, in principle, be incorruptible and, in theory, always diligent.

The same level of protection afforded to corporate creditors, when the business organisation is used as an 'unlawful device', may operate with its AI counterparts. As a general ethical principle, robo directors should not be corporate shields to mitigate or avoid responsibility.[46] In the same way, that companies should not be shams or façades to evade legal responsibilities, ethically speaking AI should not be either. It is true that creating and appointing robo directors without financial means to respond to their own liabilities would render victims claims futile. This probably explains why the company Deep Knowledge is using 'Vital' for internal corporate prediction purposes only avoiding any interaction with parties outside the corporate body. Bias in the algorithm could result in the company innocently hiding financial assets or overexposing its capital to the detriment of company creditors. Therefore, it is paramount that the trained data is sufficiently accurate and clean so the output would reflect it.

[45] The Small Business, Enterprise, and Employment Act 2015.

[46] Turner (2019), p. 191.

3.2 *Dichotomy: Robots Acting as the Company or for the Company?*

Behaviour, or rather intelligent behaviour, is what may distinguish directors from their robotic counterparts, making it very difficult to reconcile the three robo-directors' laws with existing legislation.

We are not yet ready to attribute personhood to robots; AI is still in its infancy albeit progress is made at astonishing pace.[47] All this means that the day will come when robots will be able to perform human-like activities in a way that it will be difficult to notice the difference against human performance. In fact, machines already outperform humans in certain tasks where strength and time, including speed, are required; calculations and predictions using big data[48] seems to be the obvious example nevertheless, the process does not involve understanding. In other words, a programme can simulate understanding yet it does not understand it at all. This was seen in the Chinese Room experiment,[49] where Professor John Seale cleverly proved that it is possible to communicate in perfect Chinese language, without understanding the language; all that the Non-Chinese speaker requires is access to the right structured data.[50]

Therefore, we find valid arguments objecting to AI personhood, Gunkel emphasises, quoting experts, that "robots are tools and cannot and should not be considered persons-entities who have moral and legal standing and possess rights and/or responsibilities."[51]

Solum also emphasises that objections to robot personhood belong to one of two different sorts, responsibility objections and judgement objections.[52]

Regarding responsibility objections, it is difficult to argue against the possibility of AI being trained in a way that guarantees acceptable levels of competence and care. In fact, the test to ascertain the duty of care, according to section 174 of the Companies Act 2006 in the UK,[53] is objective (albeit the duty of skill is subjective), consequently transferable, with the right data set and algorithm training, to AI or

---

[47] See for example ChatGPT at https://openai.com/blog/chatgpt.

[48] https://www.oracle.com/uk/big-data/what-is-big-data/ "The definition of big data is data that contains greater variety, arriving in increasing volumes and with more velocity. This is also known as the three Vs. Put simply, big data is larger, more complex data sets, especially from new data sources. These data sets are so voluminous that traditional data processing software just can't manage them. But these massive volumes of data can be used to address business problems you wouldn't have been able to tackle before." (accessed 10 August 2024).

[49] Searle (1980).

[50] Ibidem.

[51] Gunkel (2018), p. 64.

[52] Solum (1992), p. 1244.

[53] The Companies Act 2006 s 174: "Duty to exercise reasonable care, skill and diligence (1) A director of a company must exercise reasonable care, skill and diligence. (2) This means the care, skill and diligence that would be exercised by a reasonably diligent person with—(a) the general knowledge, skill and experience that may reasonably be expected of a person carrying out the func-

robo-directors. Assuming that such training is possible, how would robo-directors meet their liabilities, and be punished and deterred from future wrongdoings?

The answer to the first problem may be found in allowing only robo-directors who have been set up in a quasi-company form, (with its own capital) or by using insurance products[54] like D&O insurance cover. Albeit criminal liability and the deterrence principle are more challenging,[55] robo-directors, with separate legal personality, could be punished 'in the same way companies, as persona ficta, are punished'. For example, by winding them up.

The judgment objection, on the other hand, is substantially more complex and is closely connected with the black box problem in AI.[56] Professor Solum wisely identifies three circumstances, which lead to serious concerns about AI personhood both in general and in robotics in particular: change of circumstances, moral choices, and legal choices.

Now, if it is assumed that robots could not make judgements and exercise discretion how would they react when faced with situations that escape their training? Corporate groups could provide some guidance to explain the issue.

Appointing a robo director (where possible)[57] looks straightforward, yet the implementation of AI in corporate groups may pose significant problems about decision-making. The principle of separate legal personality implies that each company retains its own personality regardless of being part of a group. Most jurisdictions recognise that directors owe duties to the appointing company and not to the group; nevertheless, it is inevitable that some decisions will take into consideration the interests of the group, even though this would mean a relaxation of the duty.

A robo-director, as any other director, must exercise independent judgement but its algorithm may lack sufficient training to exercise discretion, leading to decisions made in the exclusive interest of the appointing company. Consequently, biased decisions may happen, which, albeit legal, go against the interest of the corporate group (presenting an undesirable end). AI prediction or judgement could be too narrow,[58] that impedes the robo-director from adapting to change of circumstances thus leading to unwanted outcomes. Such lack of discretion, affecting the efficient functioning of the corporate body has been eloquently highlighted by Professor Solum as follows: "The law provides that a trustee may be required or permitted to deviate from a term of the trust if following the terms would defeat the purpose of the trust due to unanticipated change in circumstances" (Fig. 4).[59]

tions carried out by the director in relation to the company, and (b) the general knowledge, skill and experience that the director has."

[54] Solum (1992), p. 1245.

[55] Ibidem.

[56] The Black Box problem still unanswered in AI, it basically means that even though the data fed to train the algorithm and the corresponding outputs are known, it still is impossible to know how the algorithm reaches that result.

[57] The UK Companies Act 2006 does not contemplate such a possibility.

[58] Buyers (2018), p. 122.

[59] Solum (1992), p. 1249.

Fig. 4 Source Adolfo Paolini

Focusing on moral and legal choices, the UK Companies Act 2006 contains an array of duties that directors should observe,[60] three of which deserve special attention for the purpose of AI implementation; the duty to act in good faith, the duty to exercise independent judgement and the duty of care and skill.

The first two depend on the state of mind of the individual director; therefore, judgement is required to assess breaches. Regarding the duty of care and skill, the test is what a reasonable person with those skills would have done. Consequently, how would the duties work if robo-directors lack consciousness?[61]

The duty to act in good faith and promote the success of the company having regard of the interest of suppliers, employees, customers, and so forth,[62] deserves some comments. Good faith is a state of mind (subjective), consequently how are we to measure whether a robo-director has acted in good faith if we do not know why it has reached the decision, (black box/opaque decision).

What would happen if the trained robot promoted the success of the company yet disregarded the interest of suppliers or employees? This arguably will lead to biased decisions, favouring the company at the expense of other constituencies or promoting inequality in the workplace.[63] The potential solution requires significant training

[60] See Fig. 4 above.

[61] Solum (1992), p. 1265: "If consciousness is a property of the mind, and if all such properties are the result of brain processes, and if brain processes can be modelled on a computer, then perhaps consciousness itself can be reproduced by AI. If consciousness is a computation property of the brain, then in principle we ought to be able to reproduce it with the right sort of computer. Putting in another way, we can get consciousness out of neurons. Why not transistors?"

[62] The Companies Act 2006 s 172.

[63] Rouhiainen (2019), p. 165.

and analysis; in the meantime, robo directors need supervision until conscious intelligent machines are fully developed.[64] Consequently, robo-directors' decisions may help in corporate decision-making, yet they should not be final deciders.

This argument opens the door for some speculation: should robots only act as company agents? Could directors delegate to robots? Would the same principles apply to robo-directors and robo-employees? Alternatively, robo-directors to human employees and/or vice versa?

The duty of care, skill, and diligence[65] on the other hand, requires further analysis. The modern UK approach used in construing the duty distinguishes between the duty of care and the duty of skill. The duty of care is assessed objectively,[66] what a reasonable person would have done in that specific circumstance. The duty of skill, on the other hand is assessed subjectively,[67] what a reasonable person, with that specific knowledge, experience and position would have done in the circumstances. AI robo directorship poses the challenge of identifying whether the robot has acted reasonably! Now, according to the Cambridge dictionary, the word 'reason' is 'the ability of a healthy mind to think and make judgments, especially based on practical facts.[68]

A question then may follow: is it feasible that a robot director could be careless?

Nowadays the answer is 'not', AI still in its infancy and even though the author's view is that singularity is achievable, it will be only then when the reasonable person test applies to robo-directors.

This last argument may help Directors' and Officers' Liability insurance (D&O) carriers, whose primary service is to insure directors' and officers' liability for negligently discharging their duties, to come up with innovative products.

4 D&O Response to Robotic Negligence: Some Ethical and Legal Implications

There are several aspects of insurance suitable for automation for example small claims procedure (motor insurance) actuarial services, insurance reserves, reinsurance treaties and retrocession, brokerage, and compliance. The Lloyd's market is already using AI to comply with the London Premium Advice Note in which a

---

[64] Wooldridge (2018), p. 50.

[65] Companies Act 2006 s 174. "Duty to exercise reasonable care, skill, and diligence.

(1) A director of a company must exercise reasonable care, skill, and diligence.

(2) This means the care, skill and diligence that would be exercised by a reasonably diligent person with—(a) the general knowledge, skill and experience that may reasonably be expected of a person carrying out the functions carried out by the director in relation to the company, and

(b) the general knowledge, skill, and experience that the director has."

[66] *Dorchester Finance Co Ltd v Stebbing* [1989] BCLC 498.

[67] *Brazilian Rubber Plantations& Estates Ltd* [1911] 1 Ch 425.

[68] https://dictionary.cambridge.org/dictionary/english/reason (accessed 10 August 2024).

registry of policies is centralised, because depositories are easier to automate yet insurance claims are not. A simple motor insurance claim may just need to send a picture of the damaged car to the insurer to activate cover. However, distinction needs to be drawn between insurance claims where factual elements are used to ascertain the loss and those where the state of mind of the insured (subjective elements) are required to trigger liability insurance cover. As several directorial duties are subjectively assessed, applying them to robo-directors may be complicated.

D&O insurance has its origin in third party insurance and more specifically professional indemnity insurance. Consequently, incurring liability to third parties is the risk that D&O insurance is meant to cover. Being a contract of indemnity insurance means that the insured may recover only where he has suffered a loss caused by the occurrence of a peril insured against under the policy and this loss is caused when the insured's liability is ascertained[69] by court's decisions, arbitration, or settlements out of court.

Consequently, in the absence of personhood, robo directors cannot be insured under D&O insurance, because they would not owe duties to the corporate body, would not be exposed to liabilities and basically even if they did, would not face any financial risk. For the time being,[70] all that is left open for D&O cover is the negligent use of AI robot director super tools by non-robotic members of the board.

D&O policies provide three types of cover A, B and C. Side A covers the liability of directors arising out of any breach of their duties. Side B covers what we know as Company Reimbursement when the Company has lawfully indemnified its directors and Side C, or Corporate Entity covers the company itself. Side C cover has proven to be problematic in terms of policy limits and aggregation. In fact, the company's claims may exhaust the total aggregate limit of the policy leaving directors without protection.[71]

As mentioned above, side A protects directors' and officers' liabilities and developing AI/EI (emotional intelligence) is of fundamental importance in assisting the insurance market where subjective elements find liability on corporate directors. For example, breaching the duty of good faith connects with emotions/ judgement or perception/reasoning e.g., intrapersonal, and interpersonal intelligence. Most directors' tasks are not routine jobs therefore automation is challenging.

[69] *Post Office v Norwich Union Fire Insurance Society Ltd* [1967] 2 QB 363; *Omega Proteins Ltd v Aspen Insurance Ltd* [2010] EWHC 2280 (Comm); *Astrazeneca Insurance Company Ltd v XL Insurance (Bermuda) Ltd & Anor* [2013] EWCA Civ 1660.*Teal v Assurance Co v WR Berkeley Insurance (Europe)* Ltd [2013] UKSC.

[70] Albeit the author is convinced that this will change soon because robotic personhood is achievable.

[71] This is for example the reason why the market has developed new products like POFI cover (Public Offer of Securities Insurance), which alongside D&O ring-fences the amount to indemnify to directors for breach of securities regulation.

Focusing on potential robo directors' negligence and its insurability, in addition to the wording of section 174 of the Companies Act 2006,[72] *Re Barings Plc* (No 5)[73] is authority for construing the nature and extent of directors' duty of care:

- The duty is continuous and requires directors to constantly update their knowledge and understanding of corporate operations and financials.
- Articles of association (bylaws) permitting directors are entitled to delegate particular function however, delegation triggers two ancillary duties, the duty to supervise and monitor those in whom authority is delegated.
- Questions of whether the duty has been discharged depend on the particular facts of the case and the directors' role in the company.

The author agrees with Montagnani,[74] that having a robotic board or robo members may provide additional advantages. First, it could simplify the board composition (reduced membership), setting up a board more oriented to operational matters, and secondly, it could allow directors to focus more on strategic matters, without having to constantly monitor and supervise their robotic counterparts. This makes sense since robo members, in principle, with adequate data training, will almost always efficiently perform and discharge their duties. Nevertheless, using this computational supper tool,[75] also triggers risks, especially those involving conscious decisions where AI does not yet outperform humans. Corporate directors and D&O insurers need to be aware therefore, of these risks and the challenges that they pose. If knowing what someone is thinking is crucial for understanding their behaviour, then not knowing how robots draw conclusions (black boxes)[76] results in new unexplored areas of law undermining the possibility of applying current corporate directorial principles, rules, and guidelines.

D&O insurers may need to re-examine the insurable risk of companies using robo directors and include within the 'bubble of negligent acts' the new delegation of directorial powers to automated machines and the effects of unwanted results. There is a great potential for AI in the insurance market yet in D&O insurance there is still a long way to go. For as long as robot 'Reason or Consciousness' remains a challenge for scientists, AI may assist but not replace the human director.

With the use of robo-directors, corporate risk and its insurability poses some challenges. For example, where Companies robots provide advice on strategic or operational corporate matters.[77] Any conscious or unconscious bias in the algorithm could lead to negligent misstatements, discriminatory statements, or unequal pricing. The question is therefore, should robots have rights and incur liabilities in the

[72] See note 68 above.

[73] *Re Barings Plc (No 5)* [2000] 1 BCLC 523.

[74] Montagnani (2021), p. 94.

[75] Ibidem, p. 95.

[76] Christianini and Norvig (2017), p. 47.

[77] King (2018), p. 236.

same way legal persons do?[78] Would a company have a claim against the robo director in breach? Could companies have a solely automated board?

The answers are unclear; robots could be the company itself therefore liability will be on the company. Robots could be employees or agents in which case companies could incur vicarious liability or robots could have legal personality and incur liability as any other legal person.

5 D&O Response to Robots and the Rules of Attribution: Who Is Liable?

One of the most controversial areas of corporate law, in the UK, is the never-ending argument of whether directors act as or for the company. Are directors company agents? Alternatively, a company's organ without which it cannot function.

The point is of utmost importance and closely connected with the rationale behind the principle of separate legal personality: 'companies are personally liable for their own wrongdoings or for the wrongdoing of those acting on companies' behalf and/or within the scope of companies' authority'. Company's liability is therefore a reality; however, the nature of that liability poses some challenges for the robotic board. At this junction, it is necessary to distinguish whether the company faces primary or vicarious liability. Briefly, primary liability means that it is the company itself, which has committed the wrongful act, which triggers the victim's claim; being primarily liable precludes the company, after having indemnified the third-party victim, for seeking any redress against directors, officers, or any other employee (who acted on company's behalf).

Conversely, should the company incur vicarious liability and having indemnified the third-party victim of the wrongful act, the company will still have a claim against its directors, officers or employees, whose actions led to the third-party claim. In other words, being vicariously liable does not preclude the company from claiming against the actual agents of the wrongful act.

The whole point is to identify whether the company is the victim (a wrong done to the company) or the agent of the wrongful act (a wrong perpetrated by the company itself). The rules of attribution aim at ascertaining if the controlling directors' misconduct could be attributed to the company as to make the corporate body primarily liable (as if the company itself committed the wrongful act).

It has been suggested,[79] that assessing a company's size and structure is crucial in arguing attribution of knowledge between the company and its directors. Directors typically exert that control in small and medium-size companies, in other words the larger the company the less likely that the wrongdoer director controls it.

[78] Calverley (2011), p. 213.

[79] Paolini (2015).

Of course, there are exceptions to the rule, all contained in the pivotal decision in *Re Hampshire Land*:[80]

a) The rules of attribution cannot be used to defeat a claim for breach of duties or fraud committed by the agent against his/her principal.
b) The defence of illegality, as decided in *Bilta v Nazir*,[81] cannot be invoked by the company directors for breaching the duties they owe to the claimant company. Otherwise, the entire set of duties and liabilities that directors may incur to the corporate body will be undermined or circumvented by alleging attribution.
c) When in the company's structure there are shareholders and/or directors who have not committed any wrongdoing or are not privy to certain knowledge, the rules of attribution do not proceed because the company will be the victim, as opposed to the agent, of the wrongdoing. In other words, the wrongdoing or knowledge of one or a group of directors or officers cannot affect the right of the company to vindicate such wrong.
d) The rules of attribution cannot be invoked when they offend public policy namely trying to circumvent, for example, the effects of breaching securities regulation (*Meridian Global Funds*)[82] or free trade/competition rules (*Safeway v Twigger*).[83]

One may think that these ideas are trivial and bear no effect on robo directors, yet the following comments may prove otherwise. Banteka rightly argues that…. "[I]n order for legislators and courts to resolve how the law can address the challenge of legal responsibility for AI entities, they need to first answer a more fundamental question with both ontological and epistemological angles: the question of legal personhood for AI entities."[84]

These fundamental questions surround the issue of whether the wrongful acts of robo-directors could be attributed to the company in the same way that the acts of their counterparts (human directors) are. In fact, cognitive science supporters assumed that the nature of human intelligence is computational consequently "the human mind can be modelled as a program that runs on a computer[85]

Would the reasoning of Lord Chancellor Viscount Haldane in *Lennard's Carrying Co. v. Asiatic Petroleum Co.*[86] be relevant in today's robotic world?

He said:

> My Lords, a corporation is an abstraction. It has no mind of its own any more than it has a body of its own; its active and directing will must consequently be sought in the person of somebody who for some purposes may be called an agent, but who is really the directing

---

[80] *Re Hampshire Land Company* [1896] 2 Ch 743.

[81] *Bilta v Nazir* [2015] UKSC 23; See also *Stone Rolls in Liquidation v Moore Stephens* [2009] UKHL 39.

[82] *Meridian Global Funds Management Asia Ltd v Securities Commission* [1995] UKPC 5.

[83] *Safeway Stores Ltd & Ors v Twigger & Ors* [2010] EWCA Civ 1472.

[84] Banteka (2020), p. 1.

[85] Solum (1992), p. 1231.

[86] *Lennard's Carrying Co. v. Asiatic Petroleum Co* [1915] A.C. 705.

mind and will of the corporation, the very ego and centre of the personality of the corporation[87]

A self-driven corporation[88] will certainly have a mind of its own! Therefore, the need to distinguish between AI and non-AI directors. The above principles apply to the latter so let us focus on the former.

This paper suggests that regardless of primary or vicarious liability a company with AI directors will always have a claim, which is not the case where the board is composed of human beings. Would it be sensible to suggest that in case of the company incurring primary liability, the corporate body would still have a claim against the robot manufacturer, data trainer, software developer, algorithm coding etc., all in product liability?

A legal rather than ethical question is the issue of identifying who would own the software and the hardware should AI be a legal person. One could suggest that general principles of separate legal personality apply, in the same way that companies own assets, AI could have ownership rights. However, robo-directors would be manufactured products, requiring trained data sets and algorithms to perform either narrow or general activities, in other words their competence is dependent on the quality of data and algorithm training used by robot manufacturers. Arguably, companies who incur liability for the malfunctioning of a robo director may have a claim against its manufacturer and this claim exclusively falls within the remit of contract law in general or product liability.

The following illustrations may graphically help (Fig. 5):

But the issue goes beyond the company as primarily or vicariously liable, and concerns Insurance fraud. Some fraudulent insurance claims have challenged the well-established principle of the company's separate legal personality. The decision in *Standard Chartered Bank v Pakistan National Shipping Corporation*[89] is authority for attributing fraud to a company director, who has personally committed the tort, in his closed held company. Consequently, the director at issue could not hide behind the corporate veil to escape his tortious liability. Nevertheless, fraud in the insurance context seems to follow a different pathway. The decisions in *Joseph Fielding Properties (Blackpool) Ltd v Aviva*,[90] and *Sharon's Bakery (Europe) Ltd v Axa Insurance UK and Aviva*,[91] provide the legal forum with uncertainty as to when and how insurance carriers could attribute the directors' fraud to the insured company to avoid cover. The question is in what circumstances insurance carriers could successfully, on fraud grounds, deny cover to the insured company who is controlled by the fraudster, (or at least the alleged one).

---

[87] Ibidem, pp. 712–713.

[88] Bayern et al. (2017).

[89] *Standard Chartered Bank v Pakistan National Shipping Corporation* [2002] UKHL 43.

[90] *Joseph Fielding Properties (Blackpool) Ltd v Aviva* [2010]. EWHC 2192 (QB).

[91] *Sharon's Bakery (Europe) Ltd v Axa Insurance UK and Aviva* [2011] EWHC 210 (Comm).

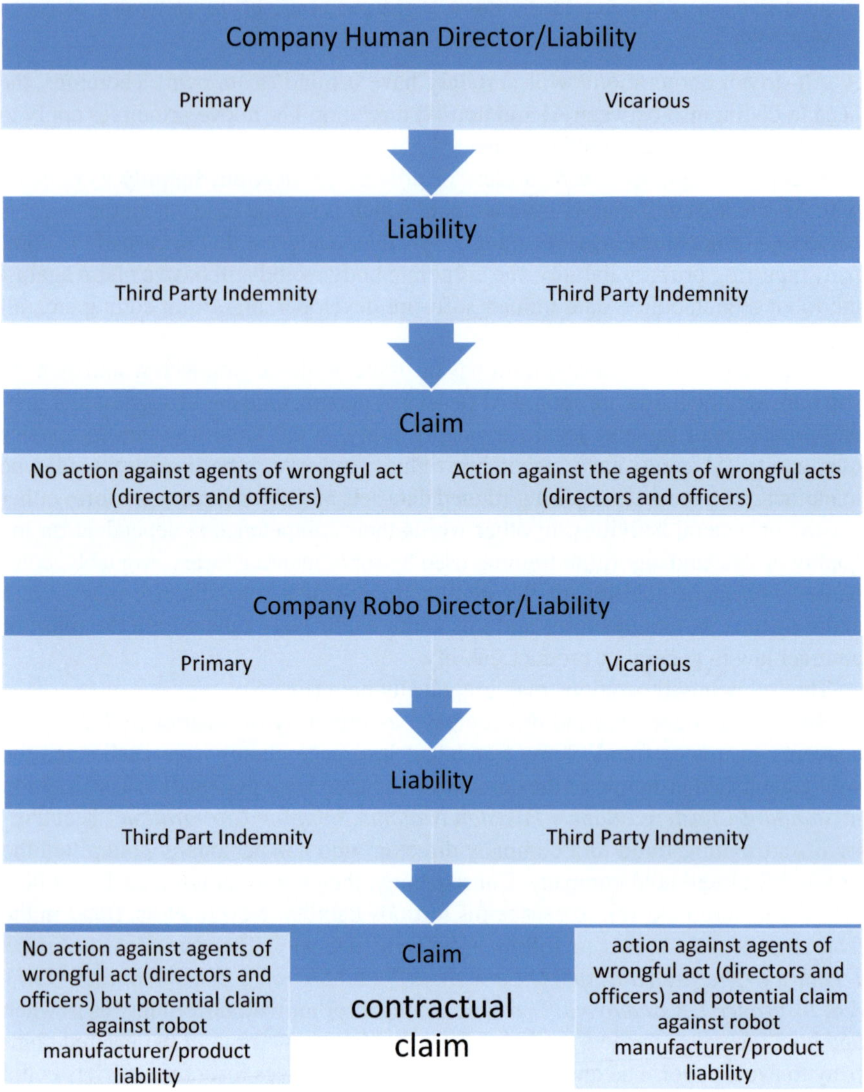

Fig. 5 Source: Adolfo Paolini

In Joseph Fielding Properties (Blackpool) Ltd v Aviva,[92] the High Court was satisfied that the insurer was entitled to avoid the policy, from its inception, if a fraudulent claim was made or intentionally exaggerated and or a false declaration was given by the insured. The majority shareholder and director of the claimant company did not disclose to the insurer that under a prior insurance contract, he and

[92] *Joseph Fielding Properties (Blackpool) Ltd v Aviva* [2010]. EWHC 2192 (QB).

his wife were found to have made fraudulently and intentionally exaggerated payments to a contractor for property repairs. The High court concluded that the non-disclosure was material, so the insurer avoided the policy from inception. The knowledge of the majority shareholder and director was attributed to the insured company for the purpose of triggering the material non-disclosure condition.

Equally in *Sharon's Bakery (Europe) Ltd v Axa Insurance UK and Aviva,*[93] the insured company sustained losses caused by fire in its premises. Some of the destroyed equipment was obtained from another company (Wholesale) where the majority shareholder and director of Sharon's Bakery, was also the majority controller.

In order to obtain finance for the acquisition of the equipment, Sharon's Bakery approached a finance provider (Lombard) who requested an invoice from whomever had originally sold the equipment to Wholesale. Such an invoice was fraudulently made to prove title to the damaged equipment.

The insurer successfully rejected the claim on the grounds of substantial fraud, the insured presenting a fraudulent invoice defeated what otherwise would have been a valid claim. Sharon's case represents another example where the fraudulent act of the majority shareholder and controller was attributed to the insured company to trigger fraud, forfeiting the insurance claim.[94]

In the AI context, could D&O fraudulent claims be efficiently controlled? Alternatively, in civil wrongdoings could the rules of attribution apply in a company/AI relationship? These two questions in the absence of AI consciousness and reason may prove unsurmountable for insurers.[95]

Without sounding too pessimistic there is another area which D&O insurance carriers need to explore, that is deferred prosecution agreements and AI implications. Public Companies are subject to stringent financial regulation thus it is inevitable that at some point regulatory investigations happen. Companies may end the investigation by entering into a deferred prosecution agreement (DPA) with the prosecutor who may decide to defer prosecution of the company, pending some conditions: paying a fine, assuming responsibility and/or refraining from contesting liability. Company's own admission of liability does not, in principle, affect former directors' individual rights to clear their names.[96] The questions of how DPA could

---

[93] *Sharon's Bakery (Europe) Ltd v Axa Insurance UK and Aviva* [2011] EWHC 210 (Comm).

[94] One could suggest that the reasoning in *Standard Chartered Bank v Pakistan National Shipping Corporation* [2002] UKHL 43 was not followed in *Joseph Fielding Properties (Blackpool) Ltd v Aviva* [2010]. EWHC 2192 (QB) or *Sharon's Bakery (Europe) Ltd v Axa Insurance UK and Aviva* [2011] EWHC 210 (Comm).

[95] See *Agapitos v Agnew* [2002] EWCA Civ 247 at para 30, Lord Justice Mance, as he then was, put it very eloquently: "A fraudulent claim exists where the insured claims, **knowing** that he has suffered no loss, or only a lesser loss than that which he claims (or is **reckless** as to whether this is the case). A fraudulent device is used if the insured believes that he has suffered the loss claimed but seeks to improve or embellish the facts surrounding the claim, by some lie." (Emphasis added).

[96] Albeit in reality if a director decides to challenge the DPA to clear his/her, the DPA itself may be breached with the unwanted consequence of making the company vulnerable to prosecution.

be reconciled with robo directors, and whether robo directors would follow suit and abide by the DPA deserve some comments.

DPAs are agreements, equivalent to contractual undertakings whereby the company and its directors promise to abide by the DPA terms, in exchange of regulatory immunity. As any other agreement it requires the meeting of minds and an unequivocal willingness to be bound by its terms. AI lack of consciousness may represent several obstacles to the DPA formation, operation, and enforceability. Algorithms may require extraordinary training and any biased decision against the company or fellow directors could breach the DPA, suspend the immunity and reinstate legal proceedings against it.

A robot director may not have been trained to be silent and/or avoid contesting liability especially if the third rule of corporate robotics is challenged ‘a robo director must protect its own directorship if such protection does not conflict with the First or Second Law’. A DPA could widely open the door for companies blaming their directors for securities regulation breaches and directors do have the right to defend, so the risk is latent. Consequently, as an ethical principle, algorithm training should guarantee that robo directors do not admit or challenge liability, to the detriment of the corporate body or fellow directors.

6 Conclusions

Robotic decision-making systems without or minimal human input may trigger ethical questions,[97] especially in the robo director era where AI may lead to undesirable ends and result in loss of accountability.[98] Exploring some of the practical and ethical challenges[99] faced by the corporate world in general and D&O market, may have helped in understanding the problem. Should this be possible then a robo-director framework is needed for IT being able to “assume both duties and the corresponding liabilities”.[100]

Arguably the implementation of robo directors leads to more questions than answers, in fact difficult questions to unknown answers. Therefore, let us speculate with some thoughts.

Ethically speaking the algorithm must be trained in a way that in full compliance with the main principles of robotics (as adapted to companies), robo directors must not harm the company or its stakeholders.

Despite AI developers’ extraordinary efforts, singularity is still some time ahead, so the issue of matching humans/robots still causing some concerns. AI uses structured and unstructured data to produce outcomes without being trained to do so yet the ‘black box’ or the inability to understand why the AI machine has produced such

[97] Finlay (2018), p. 111.

[98] Russell and Norvig (2021), p. 1032.

[99] Several others can surely be identified.

[100] Solum (1992), p. 1245.

outcome is unknown. This inability, combined with lack of consciousness and cognition pose important challenges to robo directorship and potential liabilities. Some directorial duties are subjectively assessed for example 'acting in good faith' or promoting the success of the company, some criminal liability requires an intentional element (mens rea) and change of circumstances may disrupt robo directors' behaviour and we do not yet understand why AI has acted in such a way. Consequently, for the time being liability still needs to fall on AI users (the company) until AI becomes fully autonomous, conscious and rational.

In the absence of robotic personhood there is no scope for third party liability insurance (D&O) cover. The robot insured under these policies can not incur or sustain financial losses thus there would not be any insurable interest in securing cover. Side C cover on the other hand leaves the door open for D&O carriers who may decide whether they want to take on the corporate risk of using these super tools.

Artificial Intelligence is developing at a pace with results difficult to imagine. Research funding in this area is vast, so more innovative findings are yet to come. It is safe to say that despite its intricacies and algorithmic complexities, Artificial Intelligence still is in its infancy. Just imagine what would happen when singularity is achieved! The message is therefore clear D&O insurers please think ahead and get ready; it is better to be proactive than trying to keep up with AI speed.

"The fact that human neural systems operate on the basis of a combination of electrical transmissions and biochemical processes does not make them any less subject to the laws of physics than are computers".[101]

Legislation

REGULATION (EU) 2016/679 OF THE EUROPEAN PARLIAMENT AND OF THE COUNCIL
The Companies Act 2006
The Small Business, Enterprise, and Employment Act 2015
The United Kingdom Stewardship Code 2020

Table of UK Case Law

Astrazeneca Insurance Company Ltd v XL Insurance (Bermuda) Ltd & Anor [2013] EWCA Civ 1660
Aviva Insurance Ltd v Roger George Brown [2011] EWHC 362 (QB)
Bilta v Nazir [2015] UKSC 23
Brazilian Rubber Plantations& Estates Ltd [1911] 1 Ch 425
Dorchester Finance Co Ltd v Stebbing [1989] BCLC 498
Joseph Fielding Properties (Blackpool) Ltd v Aviva [2010]. EWHC 2192 (QB)

[101] Solum (1992), p. 1273.

Lennard's Carrying Co. v. Asiatic Petroleum Co [1915] A.C. 705
Meridian Global Funds Management Asia Ltd v Securities Commission [1995] UKPC 5
Omega Proteins Ltd v Aspen Insurance Ltd [2010] EWHC 2280 (Comm)
Post Office v Norwich Union Fire Insurance Society Ltd [1967] 2 QB 363
Re Barings Plc (No 5) [2000] 1 BCLC 523
Re Hampshire Land Company [1896] 2 Ch 743
Safeway Stores Ltd & Ors v Twigger & Ors [2010] EWCA Civ 1472
Sharon's Bakery (Europe) Ltd v Axa Insurance UK and Aviva [2011] EWHC 210 (Comm)
Standard Chartered Bank v Pakistan National Shipping Corporation [2002] UKHL 43
Stone Rolls in Liquidation v Moore Stephens [2009] UKHL 39
Teal v Assurance Co v WR Berkeley Insurance (Europe) Ltd [2013] UKSC

Other Online Sources

https://dictionary.cambridge.org/dictionary/english/reason
Directors' and Officers' Liability Survey 2023 - WTW (wtwco.com)
https://openai.com/blog/chatgpt
https://www.oracle.com/uk/big-data/what-is-big-data/
https://www.youtube.com/watch?v=18SXA-G2peY
https://www.youtube.com/watch?v=AWJJnQybZlk
https://www.tieto.com/en/newsroom/all-news-and-releases/corporate-news/2016/10/tieto-the-first-nordic-company-to-appoint-artificial-intelligence-to-the-leadership-team-of-the-new-data-driven-business/

References

Arslanian H, Fischer F (2019) The future of finance. Hong Kong. Palgrave Macmillan
Ashley K (2018) Artificial intelligence and legal analytics. Cambridge, Massachusetts
Asimov I (1942) Runaround. Astounding Fiction Magazine
Athalye A, Carlini N, Wagner D (2019) Obfuscated gradients give a false sense of security: circumventing defenses to adversarial examples. 2018. https://arxiv.org/pdf/1802.00420.pdf. Accessed 19 Aug 2019
Balkin J (2016) The three laws of robotics in the age of big data. Sidley Austin Distinguished Lecture on Big Data Law and Policy at the Ohio State University Moritz College of Law on October 27, 2016
Banteka N (2020) Artificially intelligent persons. Houston Law Rev 58. https://ssrn.com/abstract=3552269 or https://doi.org/10.2139/ssrn.3552269. Accessed 19 Aug 2019
Bayern S (2019) Are autonomous entities possible? Northwest Univ Law Rev Online 114:23
Bayern S, Burri T, Grant T, Häusermann D, Möslein F, Williams R (2017) Company law and autonomous systems: a blueprint for lawyers, entrepreneurs, and regulators. Hastings Int Comp

Law Rev 9:135. http://repository.uchastings.edu/hastings_science_technology_law_journal/vol9/iss2/1
Buyers J (2018) Artificial intelligence the practical issues. Law Brief Publishing, Minehead, Somerset
Brendel W (2018) AI still fails on robust handwritten digit recognition (and how to fix it). https://medium.com/bethgelab/ai-still-fails-on-robust-handwritten-digit-recognition-and-how-to-fix-it-a432d84ede18. Accessed 19 Aug 2019
Calverley D (2011) Legal rights for machines some fundamental principles. In: Anderson M, Leigh Anderson S (eds) Machine ethics. Cambridge University Press
Casey MJ, Vigna P (2018) The truth machine the blockchain and the future of everything. Harper Collins Publishers, London
Christianini N, Norvig P (2017) Machines that think. New Scientist
Finlay S (2018) Artificial intelligence and machine learning for business: a no-nonsense guide to data driven technologies. Relativistic
Gunkel D (2018) Robot rights. MIT Press
King B (2018) Bank 4.0. Singapore. Marshall Cavendish Business
Kurzweil R (1992) The age of intelligent machines. MIT Press
Madry A, Makelov A, Schmidt L, Tsipras D, Vladu A (2018) Towards deep learning models resistant to adversarial attacks. https://openreview.net/forum?id=rJzIBfZAb. Accessed 19 Aug 2019
Montagnani ML (2021) Il Ruolo Dell'Intelligenza Artificiale Nel funcionamiento del Consiglio de Amministrazione Delle Societa Per Azioni, Egea, 2021
Paolini A (2015) Auditors' liability and corporate fraud in the UK: does corporate size and structure matter? J Bus Technol Law 10:245
Raschka S, Mirjalili V (2017) Python machine learning. Birmingham UK. Packt.
Rouhiainen L (2019) Artificial intelligence. Lasse Rouhiainen
Russell S, Norvig P (2021) Artificial intelligence a modern approach, 4th edn. Pearson, New Jersey
Schott L, Rauber J, Bethge M, Brendel W (2018) Towards the first adversarially robust neural network model on MNIST. 2018. file:///F:/Oxford%20Artificial%20Intelligence/Schott%20Patern%20recognition%20article. pdf. Accessed 19 Aug 2019
Searle JR (1980) Minds, brains, and programs. Behav Brain Sci 3(3):417–457
Siebel TM (2019) Digital transformation, survive and thrive in an era of mass extinction. Rosetta Books, Canada
Solum LB (1992) Legal personhood for artificial intelligences. North Carolina Law Rev 70:1231
Susskind R (2016) Tomorrows' lawyers, 2nd edn. Oxford University Press, Oxford
Taulli T (2019) Artificial intelligence basis. Apress
Turner J (2019) Robot rules, regulating artificial intelligence. Palgrave Macmillan
Wilkins N (2019) Artificial intelligence. Neil Wilkins
Wooldridge M (2018) Artificial intelligence. Ladybird Books Ltd., London
Yao M, Jia M, Zhou A (2018) Applied artificial intelligence a handbook for Business Leaders. Topbots Inc.
Zolfagharifard E (2014) Would you take orders from a ROBOT? An artificial intelligence becomes the world's first company director. https://www.dailymail.co.uk/sciencetech/article-2632920/Would-orders-ROBOT-Artificial-intelligence-world-s-company-director-Japan.html. Accessed 26 Aug 2019

Adolfo Paolini is a professor in Corporate and Insurance Law and Dean of Law University of Buckingham in the United Kingdom. His area of research and interest also includes Fintech and Artificial Intelligence. He is the co-author of Directors' and Officers' Liability Insurance the winner of the British Insurance Law Association Insurance Book Prize in 2009. He is also the vice chairman of the civil liability insurance working party in the International Insurance Law Association (AIDA).

MIX
Papier aus verantwortungsvollen Quellen
Paper from responsible sources
FSC® C105338
FSC
www.fsc.org

If you have any concerns about our products,
you can contact us on
ProductSafety@springernature.com

In case Publisher is established outside the EU,
the EU authorized representative is:
Springer Nature Customer Service Center GmbH
Europaplatz 3, 69115 Heidelberg, Germany

Printed by Libri Plureos GmbH
in Hamburg, Germany